Mexico City, 1808

Diálogos Series

KRIS LANE, SERIES EDITOR

Understanding Latin America demands dialogue, deep exploration, and frank discussion of key topics. Founded by Lyman L. Johnson in 1992 and edited since 2013 by Kris Lane, the Diálogos Series focuses on innovative scholarship in Latin American history and related fields. The series, the most successful of its type, includes specialist works accessible to a wide readership and a variety of thematic titles, all ideally suited for classroom adoption by university and college teachers.

Also available in the Diálogos Series:

Tides of Revolution: Information, Insurgencies, and the Crisis of Colonial Rule in Venezuela by Cristina Soriano
Murder in Mérida, 1792: Violence, Factions, and the Law by Mark W. Lentz
Nuns Navigating the Spanish Empire by Sarah E. Owens
Sons of the Mexican Revolution: Miguel Alemán and His Generation by Ryan M. Alexander
The Pursuit of Ruins: Archaeology, History, and the Making of Modern Mexico by Christina Bueno
Creating Charismatic Bonds in Argentina: Letters to Juan and Eva Perón by Donna J. Guy
Gendered Crossings: Women and Migration in the Spanish Empire by Allyson M. Poska
From Shipmates to Soldiers: Emerging Black Identities in the Río de la Plata by Alex Borucki
Women Drug Traffickers: Mules, Bosses, and Organized Crime by Elaine Carey
Searching for Madre Matiana: Prophecy and Popular Culture in Modern Mexico by Edward Wright-Rios

For additional titles in the Diálogos Series, please visit unmpress.com.

Mexico City, 1808

POWER, SOVEREIGNTY, AND SILVER IN AN AGE OF WAR AND REVOLUTION

JOHN TUTINO

University of New Mexico Press ❧ Albuquerque

Library of Congress Cataloging-in-Publication Data

Names: Tutino, John, 1947– author.
Title: Mexico City, 1808: power, sovereignty, and silver in an age of war and
revolution / John Tutino.
Description: First edition. | Albuquerque: University of New Mexico Press, 2018. |
Series: Dialogos series | Includes bibliographical references and index. |
Identifiers: LCCN 2018006294 (print) | LCCN 2018028082 (e-book) |
ISBN 9780826360021 (e-book) | ISBN 9780826360007 (printed case: alk. paper) |
ISBN 9780826360014 (pbk.: alk. paper)
Subjects: LCSH: Mexico City (Mexico)—Politics and government—19th century. |
Mexico City (Mexico)—Politics and government—18th century. | Silver industry—
Mexico—Mexico City—History—19th century. | Silver industry—Mexico—Mexico
City—History—18th century. | Power (Social sciences)—Mexico—Mexico City—
History—19th century. | Power (Social sciences)—Mexico—Mexico City—History—
18th century. | Government, Resistance to—Mexico—Mexico City—History—
19th century. | Government, Resistance to—Mexico—Mexico City—History—
18th century.
Classification: LCC F1386.3 (e-book) | LCC F1386.3 T88 2018 (print) |
DDC 972/.53—dc23
LC record available at https://lccn.loc.gov/2018006294

Cover illustration courtesy of the Benson Latin American Collection,
University of Texas at Austin
Cover by Felicia Cedillos
Composed in Minion Pro 10.25/13.5

For

Luis Fernando Granados,

who taught me about Mexico City,

and

Alfredo Ávila,

who taught me about the politics of popular sovereignty as

New Spain became Mexico

Contents

~ℓ

Illustrations

Preface

Pivotal Years and Historical Dialogues

Decades of war, political conflicts, and popular uprisings begun in the 1750s transformed the Atlantic world—better, the world—in a history marked by pivotal years: 1776 announced North American colonials' intent to exit Britain's empire, leading to the first American nation; 1789 marked the opening of the French Revolution, leading to new participations and proclamations of rights in Paris. It set off reverberations that opened the way for conflicts in Saint-Domingue that became a Haitian revolution as former slaves founded the second American nation in 1804. Other key years followed: 1815 marked Napoleon's fall and the unchallenged rise of Britain; 1848 brought revolutionary risings in Europe that briefly challenged the new order—and confirmed its consolidation.[1]

Less recognized yet arguably as transforming, the events of 1808 in Madrid and Mexico City made another year of pivotal change, mixing endings and beginnings that reverberated across the Atlantic, the Americas, and the world. By May, Napoleon's armies had invaded Spain, captured the reigning Spanish monarchs, tried to impose a French puppet king—and faced the crowds in the streets made famous by Goya's stunning portrayal of defiance in the face of violent power. That sequence broke legitimate sovereignty in Spain's empire and set off a summer of unprecedented politics in Mexico City, the capital of New Spain, where people debated loyalty to an empire suddenly without a sovereign—and with a very uncertain future.

For more than a century the people of Mexico City had played pivotal, and for a few, profitable roles in sending the rising flows of silver that kept

Spain alive in global affairs and fueled trade across Europe and the Americas, China, India, and Africa, too. As the nineteenth century began, the city and its silver remained essential to the world economy and to all the belligerents in the Euro-Atlantic wars set off by the French and Haitian revolutions. Then in 1808, Napoleon—his military power another legacy of the conflicts begun in revolutionary Paris in 1789—invaded Spain dreaming of gaining New Spain's silver. Instead, he broke the monarchy that kept Spain's empire together, setting off conflicts that soon broke New Spain's silver capitalism, cutting the flows of specie that had long sustained Spain's power and global trades. Unimagined debates, disruptions, and dissolutions followed.

The clearest legacy of 1808 was the fall of Spain's American empire and its fragmentation into diverse nations (and a still-loyal Cuba). Equally important, 1808 began a pivotal transformation in the ways regime powers operated in New Spain and across Spain's empire. After centuries of rule by council consultations and judicial mediations under a monarchy claiming divine sanction, 1808 brought new assertions of popular sovereignty tied to and soon contained by unprecedented impositions of military power. A decade of political conflict and popular insurgencies followed beginning in 1810. Diverse claims of popular rights fueled conflicts ever more militarized. New Spain's silver economy and the trades it fueled dissolved. Then, in 1821, military forces based in Mexico City, mobilized since 1808 to defend Spain, silver capitalism, and the regime that sustained them, turned to proclaim a Mexican monarchy (that became a republic in 1824).

The fall of silver capitalism in a decade of social and political violence guaranteed that Mexico would struggle to find prosperity and stability in a new North America dominated by the United States. The year 1808 thus proved a pivot of change, leading to Spain's imperial collapse, the foundation of Mexico, a struggling new nation, and continental transformations with global ramifications.

The years 1776 and 1789 are celebrated because they mark historical changes seen by many as powerfully creative: national independence and the rise of representative rule in the United States; the fall (for a time) of monarchy and the proclamation of new rights and participations in France. In contrast, 1808 may seem to open a sequence of collapse: of Spain's power in the world; of New Spain's time at the center of silver capitalism. Yet historical trajectories are rarely so simple. For all their political creativity, slaveholders committed to the persistence of slavery led the foundation of the United States. Production by enslaved people expanded massively and tragically in the new republic after 1800, profiting planters who provided cotton to new industrial powers in Britain and the northern United States. The expansion of slavery led to the wars that took Mexico's north from Texas to California in the 1830s and the 1840s, then to the devastating (yet finally liberating) Civil War of the 1860s.[2]

With parallel complexities and contradictions, the proffered liberations of the French Revolution led to deadly political violence at home, to war and to mass mobilizations to preserve "the revolution," and to Napoleon's wars of expansion. The contradictions of revolutionary France helped stimulate conflicts in Saint-Domingue in which armed ex-slaves claimed freedom, made Haiti an independent black nation, and ended plantation production— the latter demanded by armed former slaves who took land to provide for families, a turn lamented by nation makers desperate for resources to build a state. And the loss of the resources and revenues of Saint-Domingue drove Napoleon to invade Spain in 1808—a search for power that would destroy both Napoleon's dreams and Spain's empire.[3]

The outcomes of 1808 were equally mixed for the people of Spain, New Spain, and the world. People in Madrid and across Spain quickly rose to defend cities, towns, communities, and their rights to restore a Spanish sovereignty—setting off debates about rights and sovereignty while defending a shared Catholic culture. After 1810, amid wars against French armies in Spain and insurgents, political and popular, in New Spain, political men from across the empire met at Cádiz, on an Atlantic peninsula at the edge of Spain, to write the world's first liberal constitution in 1812. It imagined a monarchy grounded in popular sovereignty and electoral participations that would hold Spain's empire together to defeat French invasion. With British allies, Spanish liberals and local guerrillas expelled French armies from Spain in 1814. Napoleon's dream of ruling Europe ended—leaving Spain the impossible task of restoring its empire as the restored king, Fernando VII, abrogated the Constitution and its liberal promises while deepening his reliance on military power to rule.[4]

In Mexico City, 1808 brought an explosion of popular participations, dreams of local autonomies, and then closure in the Americas' first military coup. But closure proved difficult. Conflicts and uncertainties spread to the countryside and key provinces—to explode in 1810 in uprisings simultaneously political and popular. A decade of corrosive, often stalemated violence broke silver capitalism and Spain's power in the world. When Mexico began in 1821, the imagined nation faced militarized powers, a broken economy, and endless political instability—providing openings to communities on the land (where the majority of Mexicans lived) to claim new autonomies of sustenance and culture. Mixed and contradictory dreams, actions, and outcomes generated amid unimagined and unplanned intersections of power and production, politics and social demands, utopian visions and crass legitimations make history.

Throughout such uncertain and contested times of conflict and change, people and communities found ways to press their own visions and goals in politics and production, aiming to claim what gains they could to improve everyday lives. The people rarely ruled—despite or because of ideologies of popular sovereignty. The events of 1808 and after in Mexico City, New Spain, and Mexico show that they would not be ignored.

This book focuses on 1808 in Mexico City. It opens with an inquiry into the power, prosperity, and social disparities concentrated there after 1760. It goes on to explore the city's role in the power, politics, and financing of Spain's empire during decades of conflict, to culminate in a close analysis of the debates, closures, and consequences of the summer of 1808—months that turned the history of the Americas and the world far more than we have recognized.

As I developed this analysis, I saw New Mexico's Diálogos Series, founded by Lyman Johnson and sustained by Kris Lane, as an ideal venue for presentation. This is a book of many and diverse dialogues. First, I aim to open a dialogue between the many who study the age of revolution, focusing on events set off in 1776 and 1789, and the few who know the importance of 1808 and the transformations that followed in Spain, New Spain, and the world. I also seek an integrating dialogue with the many who study the politics that led to New Spain's becoming Mexico and the few who have focused on the questions of production and social relations that underlay an otherwise incomprehensible conflictive process. That is part of my larger search for dialogues seeking an integrated history. Power and production, politics and social relations, gender and culture are never lived separately (however facilitating it may be to study them separately). People cannot think and imagine if they do not eat—and we always eat in culturally shaped ways. Production is gendered in pursuit of profit—and gender relations shape production, social ties, and political processes. Racial and ethnic differences and amalgamations, too, are inseparable from power, production, gender, and culture.

In seeking dialogues to link too-often fragmented fields of history and ways of analysis, this study also honors and aims to continue another hallmark of the Diálogos Series: integrating primary research and synthetic engagement with the best existing scholarship to seek a more comprehensive understanding. Readers will find chapters and sections of chapters based on previously unpublished archival research mixed with new readings of historic political texts (all translations from the original Spanish are mine), set in contexts enabled by key studies of imperial power and politics, the financial operations of Mexico City merchant financiers, life in the popular barrios, and the insurrectionary conflicts that began in 1810. My integration of fields and themes, approaches and sources surely remains limited. That recognized, the goal must remain. Others, I expect, can and will do better.

Direct acknowledgment must begin with series editor Kris Lane and Clark Whitehorn, executive editor at University of New Mexico Press; together they provided encouragement and the flexibility to bring this project to fruition. Press readers, including Kris Lane, Michael Ducey, and one who remains anonymous, offered suggestions that made this a stronger book. Along the way, three Mexican scholar-colleagues provided stimulation, ideas, and materials of key importance: Alfredo Ávila, who knows the politics of New Spain's becoming Mexico better than anyone; Luis Fernando Granados, who understands life in Mexico City with unique depth and perspective; and Guillermina del Valle Pavón, who knows Mexico City merchants in unmatched depth and complexity—and at the last possible moment sent me an advance copy of a new book that made chapter 7 and the larger analysis more comprehensive in pivotal ways.

In the DC region, Alejandro Cañeque and Brian Owensby not only wrote books that shaped my understanding, they joined in a seminar with Georgetown colleagues (led as always by John McNeill and including the diverse visions of Tommaso Astarita, Kate de Luna, Alison Games, and Gabor Agoston) that improved the analysis, the integration, and hopefully my ability to engage a wider audience. If I have not succeeded, they tried. An illuminating result of that afternoon of engagement among three scholars deep in studies of New Spain (Alejandro, Brian, and me) and five who know the era across a wider world (John, Tommaso, Alison, Kate, and Gabor) was a recognition that scholars of Spanish America see a history and a language of empire and politics that is little known beyond specialists. Those who view this era of conflict and change from "outside" (including most analysts of Latin America who look back from later centuries) have kept concepts and terminologies that are often deflecting inventions—too often misleading, sometimes just wrong. The group encouraged me to write the critical explo- ration of prevailing "terms of analysis" that follows this preface—to limit "language shock" and hopefully make New Spain, Spain's empire, and the conflicts that made nations there less alien places and processes. They were societies shaped by historical processes that were part of and pivotal to larger global transformations.

Others have powerfully shaped this work in less personal ways: Juan Ortiz Escamilla has shown the many scholars focused on politics and those like me focused on production, social relations, and popular resistance that military power quickly became pivotal to the conflicts that broke New Spain and made Mexico. Esteban Sánchez de Tagle and Annick Lempérière pro- duced studies of imperial politics in Mexico City that made my analysis pos- sible. Felipe Castro Gutiérrez's studies of resistance and regime response outside the city in the 1760s and of the city mint that made money for the world are essential. Most of all, this study builds upon, depends upon, and honors the massive four-volume work of Barbara and Stanley Stein focused on rethinking political and economic relations between Spain and New Spain from 1760 to 1810. My analysis could not have been attempted without their massive research and evolving interpretations. My innovation is to link the economic power and social relations of Mexico City to new visions of regime operations and challenges in the context of the wars and revolutions intensifying across the Americas and the world. Without the Steins, those mentioned above, and many more cited in the bibliography, this work would not have been possible.

On a more personal level, the understanding that led to this volume emerged in large part while I joined in seemingly endless gatherings to celebrate and better understand the turn toward independence that Mexicans see as focused on the year 1810. I often joked that I was invited so that scholars focused on politics would remember that popular insurgency mattered too. Along the way, they taught me how much politics mattered. Here I aim to integrate the political, the popular, and the economic, too. Jane Tutino joined me at most of those gatherings, reveled in the conversations and the community of scholars, and engaged many of the diverse people who came in search of new understandings of their complex and at times confounding nation. I hope those encounters were enough to compensate the time I have taken to write the book.

I dedicate the book to Luis Fernando Granados and Alfredo Ávila—young (to me) Mexican scholars who introduced me to the worlds that came together in Mexico City in 1808. I met Luis Fernando first. He approached me at a seminar in Mexico City in the late 1990s and asked if I would read his *licenciatura* thesis, still in draft, on the popular uprisings in Mexico City against the US Marines' occupation in 1847. He became my doctoral student, my colleague, and my friend—and he taught me the importance of the city and its diverse peoples in a society I had long viewed as mostly rural. Luis Fernando helped make me an urbanist, while showing that serious scholarship can ground a life committed to political participation and social justice in the face of concentrations of power and too-often deadly coercions.

He also told me I should meet and read Alfredo Ávila, a scholar of politics and sovereignty in the era that New Spain became Mexico. We all came together in a seminar at Georgetown in 2008—joining others (including the great and now departed Richard Stites) to contemplate the importance of 1808 in the Hispanic world—better, in the world. I did not imagine then that a decade later I would—or could—complete this book.

After that gathering, Alfredo began to invite me into dialogues with those who study the politics of Mexican independence. His understanding of the attempts to create a politics of popular sovereignty in Mexico and Spanish America is without equal. We jointly authored an essay attempting an integrated understanding of "Becoming Mexico" in the *New Countries* volume. Alfredo made me at least minimally competent to attempt a study of politics in Mexico City. And while he continues to study and promote the politics of popular sovereignty and participation, he too laments deeply the violence that plagues too many lives in Mexico, the Americas, and the world in our most difficult and challenging times.

This study of a search for popular participations blocked by militarized coercions on the eve of Mexico's foundation—part of a larger process that forged and defined modern national states—aims to honor the lives and dreams of Luis Fernando, Alfredo, and the many Mexicans and others across the Americas (including in the United States) who dream of futures that enable popular needs and goals and limit impositions by coercion.

Terms of Analysis

New Spain in Spanish America

The understanding of New Spain, the Spanish empire, and the conflicts that led to the foundation of Mexico and other nations after 1808 has been inhibited by persistent use of terminology that is too often misleading and sometimes just false, yet continues to mark too many studies, often by Anglophone scholars presuming that certain labels—for example, calling New Spain "colonial Mexico"—will help engage readers. Too often we communicate wrong understandings. This critical exploration of terms engages that language, its limits and fictions, and offers a more accurate terminology, aiming to clarify New Spain's history and to limit readers' surprise as they read this book. The critiques and meanings offered here derive from my work on three recent volumes, *Making a New World*, *The Mexican Heartland*, and *New Countries* (plus the analysis here). Together, they provide the context for this study—which aims to clarify a political pivot essential to understanding the larger challenges they explore.

castas. Should never be translated as "castes." The castas of New Spain were people of mixture and constant flux—never closed endogamous groups. Nearly all shared Spanish language, Hispanic culture, and work in the commercial economy; thus, they concentrated in the cities (including Mexico City) and regions from the Bajío north. Those favoring indigenous ancestry were often labeled mestizos, those accepting African roots were commonly called mulattos or *pardos* (see entries below). The "casta paintings" that have claimed so much interest recently were idealized portrayals by "enlightened" artists who aimed to define precise categories that were all but irrelevant to everyday life in New Spain and Mexico City. People were overwhelmingly Spanish or indio, mestizo or mulatto (see below)—with the plural castas (precisely by its insistent plurality) designating the universe of mixing that shaped so much between the heights of power and the indigenous republics (see below).

colony, colonial. The regions of the Americas under Spanish rule are too often referred to as colonies, the era from 1492 to 1824 as colonial. In historical organization, the regions were kingdoms (see *kingdom* and *New Spain,* below) divided into varied subjurisdictions. The invented and imposed use of the labels *colony* and *colonial* created and continues visions of a Spanish America subject to powers parallel to those of the later European empires that ruled with more modern, industrial means of military assertion and communication, thus with more efficient, pervasive, and powerful ways of imposition and extraction. There was no such society as "colonial Mexico" (see *Mexico,* below).

conquest. Studies of Spanish America continue to assert that its societies were formed in conquest, implying a sudden, thorough, and complete European domination of the region and its native peoples—by means of arms, cultural imposition, political dominance, and economic extractions. Yet studies of the "conquest era" reveal uncertain encounters as Europeans constantly negotiated with and depended upon indigenous allies, were slow and uncertain in claiming rule, repeatedly negotiated cultural adaptations in which native peoples rejected impositions and found their own visions—and in the end, European power was primarily enabled not by military might, but by the devastating impact of disease-driven depopulation on indigenous peoples as silver capitalism (see below) created new economic opportunities for European entrepreneurs and revenues for the Spanish imperial regime.

cortes. Traditional Spanish parliaments, gatherings of representatives of the pueblos (organized towns, see below) who met to recognize sovereigns and address questions of rights and revenues. The towns, as first recipients of the divine gift of sovereignty, met to delegate (and limit) the same to those who would rule as kings. Cortes met regularly in the several Iberian Christian kingdoms through the medieval era, less often in the sixteenth century and into the seventeenth. Never called in the eighteenth century, cortes remained strong in political memory. In the face of

Napoleon's invasion and the crisis begun in 1808, a transatlantic cortes met at Cádiz in 1810, to write the liberal constitution issued in 1812.

creole, creoles. The mislabel—or misleading label—that will not disappear. Scholars of Spanish American independence have long used the label creole (criollo) for the Hispanic peoples of the Americas who presumably forged national identities as they resented Spanish rule—and then led their people to independence. The term was rare in Spanish America before 1800. And as this study shows for Mexico City, there was little hint of an emerging national identity or any move toward independence before Napoleon invaded Spain in 1808. The people so often labeled creoles saw themselves as Spaniards (see below) before 1808—and for some, long after.

empire, imperial. From the sixteenth into the nineteenth centuries, Hapsburg and the Bourbon power in the Americas and beyond was imperial—a regime of one monarch overseeing many kingdoms (Castile, Aragon, and Naples in Europe; New Spain [see below], Peru, and later more in the Americas). The multiplicity of kingdoms required and enabled an evolving multiplicity of institutions and legislation, allowing regional and local negotiations of autonomy within a larger whole—the empire.

indigenous republics, repúblicas de indios. Jurisdictions built on the remnants of pre-Hispanic city-states, granted rights to self-rule by local councils and dominion over lands for community use and family cultivation. Within the kingdom of New Spain, there were over four thousand such republics; they included the great majority of the indigenous population in regions around Mexico City and extending south into the Kingdom of Guatemala. They were scarce in the Bajío and regions north. The republics ruled local affairs, including religious life; they dealt with Spanish magistrates and clergy via special legislation; they had (and used) rights to appeal to special indigenous courts. While most indigenous republics were rural, the Mexico City parcialidades (jurisdictions) of San Juan Tenochtitlan and Santiago Tlatelolco were urban—and the largest native republics in New Spain.

indio. There were no Indians in the Americas before Europeans arrived. Insisting he had arrived in the Indies (Asia), Columbus labeled the diverse peoples of the Americas as indios. The misnomer became a category of the European mind (later claimed as a category of unity among peoples who knew expropriations, exploitations, and exclusions at the hands of diverse Europeans). In Spanish America, *indio* became most broadly a label for subordinate peoples subject to the tribute (a head tax on male heads of households). An important subset of indios gained rights to land and self-rule in indigenous republics (see below). I avoid the label *Indian* for the diverse indios of New Spain: it creates images of homogeneity in exploitation that do not apply. I use *indio* where appropriate, and with distinctions as necessary.

kingdom, reino. New Spain (see below) was a kingdom within the Spanish empire, ruled by a viceroy based in Mexico City who represented the king. Guatemala was also a kingdom—but without a resident viceroy. Thus Mexico City exercised broad oversight in a vast jurisdiction that ranged from California through regions now in Costa Rica. In theory, the many kingdoms of the Spanish empire were equal, subject to diverse laws and including diverse republics within—all ruled by the king in Madrid, advised by his diverse councils (notably for the Americas, his Council of the Indies).

mestizo. People of mixed indigenous and European ancestry, usually speaking Spanish, participating in Hispanic culture, and working in Hispanic commercial enterprises. A small minority across New Spain, more numerous in Mexico City (see *castas*).

Mexico, México. The only place or jurisdiction named Mexico before 1821 was the city that focuses this study. It was the capital of the kingdom of New Spain (see below), a large domain that was never conterminous with the Mexican nation created after 1821. Textual references to Mexico and *mexicanos* (Mexicans) before that date refer to the city and its residents—yet too often are misread to imply an early Mexican national identity. That confusion has served those who have sought (or imagined) an early Mexican nationalism, inhibiting attempts to understand the unplanned and conflictive origins of the Mexican nation.

mulatto (or pardo). People almost always of mixed African and indigenous ancestry—despite regime rules and scholarly presumptions of a mix of Spanish and African peoples. Few Spanish women married (or otherwise reproduced with) Africans—mostly men who arrived enslaved. Many indigenous women did—ensuring that many enslaved men's offspring would be free (as status followed the mother) and usually identified as mulatto. Like mestizos, mulattos generally spoke Spanish, joined in the Hispanic cultural world, and worked in commercial enterprises. Rising numbers lived in Mexico City, the silver-driven commercial zone of the Bajío, and regions north.

New Spain, Nueva España. The kingdom overseen from Mexico City, its most extensive jurisdiction reached from San José (now Costa Rica) to San Francisco (then and now California), from Cuba and the surrounding Spanish Caribbean to Manila and the Spanish Philippines. Its domains included the subordinate kingdoms of Guatemala with its own high court (audiencia), Nueva Galicia and Nueva Vizcaya (both linked to a high court at Guadalajara), and the Philippines (with a high court in Manila). Like the empire of which it was a pivotal part, the kingdom of New Spain was marked by diversity adapted to local realities—not an imposed uniformity.

pueblo, town. Key term of dual meaning—too often misunderstood. A pueblo was an organized town, in Spanish political tradition a community led by a council. Indigenous republics (see above) were pueblos. Mexico City was a very large and complex pueblo. In Spanish political tradition, sovereignty came first from God as a gift to the pueblos—who then delegated it to monarchs, often in gatherings called cortes (see above). When Anglo-American political innovations began to call for a sovereignty of "the people," the notion was often translated as the sovereignty of el pueblo—a generic notion encompassing an abstract whole distinct from the organized pueblos. The political debates of 1808 in Mexico City often pitted calls for the sovereignty of los pueblos against the sovereignty of el pueblo—a debate of pivotal importance, too often missed or misunderstood.

silver capitalism. A label I have created to describe the economy focused on mining and the commercial, agricultural, and textile sectors that sustained it in the Andes and New Spain. In the latter, it developed two distinct variants: one grounded in Mesoamerican communities rebuilt as indigenous republics (see above) around Mexico City; the other built in the Bajío and regions north, where states and landed communities were scarce before 1520, sparse natives died of diseased and faced wars of displacement, and Europeans built a thoroughly commercial society populated by immigrants, mixing a minority of enslaved Africans (who often became free) and a majority who came north from Mesoamerican regions around Mexico City. The regime and the financial and commercial powers set in that capital integrated the two silver societies of New Spain into one complex silver capitalism that was pivotal to global trades and European empires through the eighteenth century and into the nineteenth.

Spaniard, American—español americano. When Spaniards rooted in the New World aimed to distinguish themselves from those newly arrived from Iberia, they called themselves *americanos*, Americans. They almost never saw themselves as creoles (criollos)—until that label became a badge of difference during the conflicts that led to independence. *Spaniard* linked identity to the empire; *American* to its New World societies. Neither hinted at a nationalism rarely imagined before 1808.

Spaniard, español. From the late sixteenth into the early nineteenth centuries, the vast majority of people of European ancestry in New Spain and Spanish America called themselves Spaniards—including those arriving from Iberia and the growing majorities born in the Americas (while people in Iberia still claimed identities as Castilians, Catalans, Andalusians, etc.). "Spaniard" became an identity shared by people of European origins, language, and culture in the Americas (including some of mixed ancestry)—in contrast to the diverse peoples they labeled as indios and castas (see above).

Spaniard, European or peninsular—gachupín. Immigrant Spaniards in New Spain most often called themselves europeos (Europeans), *peninsulares* (from the Iberian peninsula), and sometimes *paisanos* (from the homeland), distinctions also used by American Spaniards to identify newcomers. The latter might be insulted as *gachupines* (no translation useful) as they gained reputations for grasping dealings in local trade backed by a cultural arrogance that seemed to rise as "enlightened" visions promoted notions of European superiority. *Gachupín* was rarely used in text or polite correspondence until the crisis of 1808 inflamed conflicts between Americans and resented immigrants—increasingly cursed as gachupines.

Imperial Crisis and Regime Transformation in the Silver Metropolis

⭐ IN THE SUMMER OF 1808, THE PEOPLE OF MEXICO CITY FACED A political crisis without precedent. In June and July they learned through a haze of rumors and official reports that Napoleon had invaded Spain, captured the royal family, and set his brother Joseph on the throne in Madrid. They learned, too, that people across Spain had taken to plazas, streets, and hills to resist, leaving Spain's imperial monarchy without a recognized legitimate sovereign. Viceroy don José de Iturrigaray, the king's representative in New Spain, consulted men of power in Spain's North American capital: the Mexico City Council, Archbishop don Francisco Javier de Lizana y Beaumont, leading landlords such as the Conde de Santiago, mining magnates led by the Conde de Regla, and pivotal merchant financiers like don Antonio de Basoco.

The viceroy engaged key officials of the Spanish regime and pivotal players in the silver capitalism that made New Spain the richest kingdom of the Americas, its capital the largest and most powerful city in the hemisphere as the nineteenth century began. All had much to lose as war toppled the Madrid monarchy that had long integrated Spain's empire and regulated trades essential to their wealth and power. And men of power in Mexico City were not alone worrying about Napoleon's decapitation of the Spanish regime. New Spain's silver fueled global trade and generated revenues for all the belligerents in European and Atlantic wars that seemed without end. Napoleon invaded Spain and took the throne in Madrid dreaming of New Spain's silver.

In Mexico City, everyone knew that silver must continue to flow to sustain New Spain's wealth and its role in the global economy. While the powerful debated the way forward, news of the monarchs' capture could not be contained. People middling and poor met in taverns and plazas to share rumors and debate the future. Political, ideological, and popular voices talked about popular sovereignty—an old tradition in Spain's domains given new life in time of crisis. Spain's kings had long accepted that while sovereignty ultimately belonged to God, he first delegated it to the *pueblos*—towns with councils—who passed it on to monarchs. The pueblos retained rights to be consulted on local affairs, regime revenues—and on succession in times of crisis. The summer of 1808 was such a time.

The sovereignty of the pueblos was limited—open to the men who sat on councils. Still, any attempt to mobilize that sovereignty raised hard questions in New Spain. The Mexico City Council and those in the dozen or so Spanish cities and towns across the kingdom should be consulted, of course. But, what of the thousands of *repúblicas de indios*—indigenous towns with councils and rights to self-rule? The two native republics within Mexico City held jurisdiction over nearly a third of the city's diverse people. There were hundreds more pueblos nearby, home to 90 percent of the native majority that surrounded the capital. Would they be consulted?

And while Spanish tradition required a turn to the pueblos—the councils—if the throne became vacant, recent decades had generated other popular sovereignties in the Atlantic world: British North American rebels claimed the sovereignty of the people to take independence as the United States; French revolutionaries asserted the sovereignty of the nation while toppling Bourbon kings. People in Mexico City, powerful, middling, and poor, had heard these new claims. In the summer of 1808, they debated diverse ways of popular sovereignty even as most proclaimed loyalty to the captive prince they imagined king—Fernando VII. In Spanish tradition, popular sovereignty was part of monarchical legitimacy. The two could be— and would be—debated together.[1]

The privileged men who presumed to rule worried as people debated. They did not aim to share power with the populace, yet there was no clear way forward. They began to split between those first committed to sustaining Spain and the fight against Napoleon and others ready to step back, rule locally in the name of the captured Fernando VII, and await the uncertain outcome of European wars. Viceroy Iturrigaray and many powerful mining and landed entrepreneurs leaned toward the latter course—a route of de facto autonomy through times of conflict and uncertainty. They aimed to keep silver capitalism thriving, perhaps trade beyond the bounds of an empire falling apart, and adapt to what might come.

But many high officials of the decapitated regime insisted on committing to Spain—even while not knowing who ruled there. Without that link, their roles and powers might dissolve quickly. Merchants newly arrived from Spain and tied to its trade kept parallel loyalties for similar reasons. Weeks of debate followed, drawing the people of the city into streets and plazas to press their views of sovereignty onto to men who presumed to rule. Then, in September military officers, regime officials, and frustrated merchants (nearly all immigrants from Spain) mobilized armed force to oust Viceroy Iturrigaray, commit New Spain's silver to the fight against Napoleon, and close debates about popular sovereignty. Or did they? The troops that toppled the viceroy proclaimed that they, too, acted as the people. The 1808 coup asserted military force to change a government while claiming to serve popular sovereignty. Debate, conflict, and uncertainty had only begun.[2]

The summer of crisis that ended in the September coup broke proven ways of rule that had sustained Spanish power, silver capitalism, and social stability in New Spain for centuries. A regime of multiple rights and privileges had long included the powerful and the producing majority, including urban and rural indigenous communities, in a regime focused on consultation by diverse councils and judicial mediation when conflicts were not resolved there. The turn to militarized rule backed by claims of popular sovereignty kept silver flowing at peak levels to the Spanish forces fighting Napoleon for two more years. But while new officials of uncertain legitimacy extracted rising revenues, drought stalked the land. In the core regions of silver capitalism, recent decades had seen landlords press hard on producing families, cutting wages and food rations, raising rents, and evicting many who could not pay. Now they took the profits of hunger from people desperate to feed families. Frustrations spread. Outrage soared where working families locked in insecurities faced deepening famine—and a regime stripped of legitimacy and incapable of mediating.[3]

The coup asserting military power and claiming popular sovereignty contained the political conflicts of 1808. Two years later, in September of 1810,

Father Miguel Hidalgo led a group of provincial notables in the Bajío, the heart of silver capitalism northwest of the capital, in a call for political participations—rights debated and then denied in the summer of 1808 in the capital. Hidalgo and his allies, including regional militia leaders, took arms to defend the rights of the captured Fernando VII and to insist on their own rights as leaders of provincial pueblos to participate in deciding who should rule, and how, in his absence. Don Ignacio Allende and other militia commanders brought troops to the movement for provincial rights. Knowing the limits of those forces, Hidalgo and Allende called the people of the region to join them.

People in arms quickly revealed their own visions of popular sovereignty: first, they emptied granaries to claim sustenance; then after Hidalgo and the political movement were crushed early in 1811, popular insurgents across the Bajío turned to taking the land to control the production of sustenance. Their grievances focused on the inequities of silver capitalism—grievances contained under the old regime. When the regime turned from mediation to military force, rebels in the Bajío and other regions saw armed power as the only way to press their goals and needs. A summer of crisis, a military coup, and two years of political debate in times of famine transformed the relationship between regime and society in New Spain—setting off a decade of violent conflict. In the face of insurgents assaulting power, property, and silver capitalism, the privileged and powerful in Mexico City reunited to defend shared interests. Through a decade of violent conflicts, they held the heights of power, yet they could not restore the silver capitalism that sustained their wealth and their role in the world.[4]

When independence came in 1821, only one outcome was clear: politics and power were affairs of armed men proclaiming variants of popular sovereignty. New ways of rule prevailed. Mexico was born with militarized politics asserting popular sovereignty—and without the silver wealth that had made New Spain pivotal to global trade. The summer of 1808 in Mexico City proved a key turning point, breaking the regime of consultation and mediations, leading to the insurgencies of 1810, setting the stage for national struggles.

The events of 1808 in Mexico City and New Spain were part of a wider political turn. The years from 1765 to 1825 have long been seen as the era of New World independence, breaking the rule of the European empires and creating diverse American nations. We now recognize that these were also years that broke a centuries-old global commercial system and saw the rise of a new industrial order led by Britain.[5] In an Atlantic crucible forged at the violent intersection of political and economic transformations, regimes long sustained by consultations and mediations gave way to states of violent assertion backed by claims of popular sovereignty: in England and British America from the 1650s to the 1780s;[6] in France and Saint-Domingue from 1789 to 1804;[7] in Spain, New Spain, and across Spanish America from 1808 to 1824.

By diverse routes in different places within different European empires, conflictive processes broke regimes of mediation and led to states grounded in new accumulations of coercive force backed by claims of popular sovereignty. The transformation came amid escalating Atlantic wars that created unprecedented pressures on regimes and the global commercial system they tried to promote. Revenue demands rose, established empires aligned and realigned in wars and coalitions. Popular groups found new openings—often pressing interests opposed to those of the powerful. The process was sequential in moving from British, to French, then Iberian empires. It was little planned—and rarely imitative.

Established imperial powers used military force to press commercial and strategic goals that were often inseparable. Imperial subjects and popular communities repeatedly objected to revenue demands backed by coercive power. Popular demands and claims to serve popular interests, rarely identical, mixed everywhere with military assertions—with diverse goals in different empires and the diverse societies within them. Still, ever more militarized polities proclaimed diverse popular sovereignties as empires broke into nations—very different nations working to forge new states in changing economic times.

This study delves deeply into a pivotal case within a globally transforming sequence. Mexico City was the political capital and economic center of New Spain, the most powerful place in the richest region of the Americas in 1808. That year of crisis brought a shift from a mediating monarchy backed by claims of divine sanction first granted to the pueblos, the towns, to a state of coercion claiming a popular sovereignty increasingly lodged in *el pueblo*, an abstract totality open to uncertainty and debate. Years of conflict followed, leading to economic collapse, the end of Spanish rule, and a Mexican nation defined by militarized politics, economic uncertainties, and social instabilities—all marked by repeated popular risings.

It is often asserted that the people of Spain's Americas came late to the liberations brought by regimes of popular sovereignty.[8] This analysis suggests that they came late to the fusion of militarized powers and legitimations by popular sovereignty because the few had prospered and diverse majorities had negotiated viable lives for centuries. Spain's mediating monarchy, grounded in the sovereignty of the pueblos, had sustained and stabilized a dynamic silver capitalism. Mexico City and New Spain remained the most prosperous places in the Americas in 1808, while others faced disruptive and often destructive conflicts, notably in a young United States and even younger Haiti, both facing legacies of slavery—the former preserving and expanding bondage, the latter ending it. Mexico City led a late turn to debates about popular sovereignty because its silver capitalism held strong, essential to global trade and imperial conflicts after 1800—still stabilized by a mediating regime that enabled viable lives for a diverse populace that included many with rights of participation and few held in slavery.

Napoleon's invasion of Spain and decapitation of its monarchy came as a destabilizing assault on New Spain's power, prosperity, and role in the world. We must understand the former before we explore the unimagined and unscripted course and consequences of the popular mobilizations and military assertions that rocked Mexico City in the summer of 1808.

Mexico City: American Capital in a Regime of Mediation

Mexico City included over 120,000 people around 1800; some thought it neared 150,000 in 1808. By either count it was by far the largest city in the Americas as the nineteenth century began. From 1790 to 1810 New Spain mined over 20 million silver pesos yearly, all minted in Mexico City—a pivotal contribution to the money supply that stimulated trades from Europe to China. (The peso was then equivalent to the US dollar, which was built on the peso when Spain and New Spain funded the war against Britain that led to US independence.)

Mexico City merchant-capitalists financed New Spain's mines and global trade. The regime historically took 10–15 percent of the silver as taxes on mining, an equal amount from taxes on the commercial economy it stimulated. The rest enabled Mexico City entrepreneurs to finance mines, profit in global trades, and secure their wealth in landed estates that profited by feeding people in mining centers and the capital—especially in years of scarcity. During the wars that escalated after 1793, the Spanish Crown claimed a growing share of New Spain's silver. By diverse means (some sanctioned, others not), rising flows also went to US, British, and French merchants—and to the treasuries of Britain and France as they faced off in war. Throughout, New Spain's silver flows held high, peaking at more than 26 million pesos in 1809, the year after the coup. Few cities were as rich, as polarized, as stable, and as pivotal to the world as the capital of silver capitalism in 1808.

We have begun to recognize the importance of the silver capitalism that made New Spain and Mexico City essential to the world economy in the eighteenth century.[9] It is time to reconsider the regime that sustained it: an imperial construct with the flexibility to extend across the globe; to engage diverse peoples, ways of production, and cultural visions; and to endure through three centuries that shaped the origins of the modern world.[10] It is especially important to recognize the regime's role in sustaining the economic dynamism and stabilizing the social inequities at the heart of silver capitalism. Capitalism has never been egalitarian. It combines profit-seeking production, the integration of markets, the mobilization of workers, and the provocation of inequities essential to profitability—in differing ways in distinct regions, changing over time. Inequity is essential to profitability; so is stability if profits are to be more than fleeting. Yet inequities driven to extremes may destabilize society, inhibiting production and corroding profit, capitalism's driving object.[11] The stabilization of inequities is essential to capitalist dynamism.[12]

Understanding diverse ways and means of stabilizing inequities and exploitations is a key to the history of capitalism. The history of New Spain as it became Mexico offers a revealing case study. A dynamic engine of global capitalism in the eighteenth century, its inequities and exploitations were stabilized by the Spanish regime centered in Mexico City. It was a regime focused on consultation and mediation, with little power to coerce. The crisis and coup of 1808 broke its capacity to mediate disputes and stabilize inequities. Violent political and social conflicts followed, in the process corroding and then destroying silver capitalism.

Spain's imperial regime effectively integrated and stabilized a key sector of early capitalism—precisely because it was nothing like the violent,

autocratic, closed, imposing behemoth it is imagined to be in too many
scholarly works and political claims. The prevailing vision has a long history—first promoted by Spain's imperial rivals, then by Latin American liberals who struggled to rule in its wake. They forged and maintained a vision
of an empire built in violent conquest, a regime that imposed a closed
Catholic culture, a force that dominated economic life, entrenched a stratified ethnic/racial order, and ruled by coercion. That vision first served (or at
least legitimated) British imperial interests and then furthered (or at least
legitimated) liberal national goals in the Americas. What is astonishing is
that the vision lives—strong among modern Anglophone scholars and
among liberal (and neoliberal) Mexican and Latin American analysts.[13]

   The contrasting evidence is longstanding and overwhelming. Iberians
did not conquer by force of arms; they took power, sooner or later, by taking
advantage of the devastating impact of smallpox and other Old World diseases while depending militarily on indigenous allies.[14] Native peoples were
not—could not be—forcibly converted. Facing epidemic death and social
disruption, they weighed old understandings against new visions to form an
array of local Christianities that the clergy often lamented, yet had no choice
but to include within a diverse American "Church."[15] The economy that
became silver capitalism was not designed, legislated, or imagined by the
regime. Entrepreneurs pursuing the profits of silver pressed their interests in
a changing world—and made officials adapt, repeatedly.[16] Nor did the regime
design or enforce the complex ethnic stratifications that differed in differing
regions and changed over time. Again, diverse people and communities
negotiated, and authorities had to adapt.[17] And finally, the regime rarely
coerced because it had minimal military forces on land (mostly unreliable
militias) until the 1760s. When it then tried to increase its military power,
success proved limited—and the attempt provoked destabilizing conflict.[18]

   Given the overwhelming countervailing evidence, why does the vision
of a closed coercive Spanish regime persist? Perhaps because it complements
the presumption of a "colonial economy" that was only destructive and coercive.[19] Likely more important, the combined vision of an autocratic coercive
state and a destructive coercive economy serve those who see (or seek) an
inevitable Anglo-American rise to eminence—and others who need to set
the difficulties of modern Latin American nations in a Spanish-imposed
past. Presumptions of an inevitable Anglo-American rise and an inevitably

destructive Spanish American past, ultimately the same presumption, cannot survive a close encounter with the Spanish regime in the Americas and the silver capitalism it sustained.

A radically different understanding of the Spanish regime in New Spain has been developing for decades (ignored by those who would not see). It emphasizes a monarchy that asserted sovereignty based on divine right—rights first delegated to the pueblos, towns with councils, and then shared with the monarchs. The regime sanctioned rights for diverse corporations and councils, religious institutions, merchants' chambers, mining guilds, and universities too—and for diverse cities and towns, including thousands of indigenous pueblos. The regime coordinated, negotiated, and mediated—at the heights of power by means of petition and response; among fragmented majorities by judicial mediation of disputes. Absent effective military force on land, it was a regime of negotiated compromises—not treating people, institutions, and communities as identical, but dealing with them according to their means and interests, favoring the powerful while knowing the populace could not be alienated or marginalized in the extreme. Profit persisted and people survived. The regime mediated and collected ample revenues while silver capitalism fueled global trades for centuries.

Our understanding of the mediating regime began in a series of deeply researched studies of how courts and judicial decisions became the primary way officials engaged indigenous communities—all written by leading North American historians: first William Taylor and Woodrow Borah, then Brian Owensby.[20] Their works were honored—and generally ignored in synthetic studies. More recently, scholars have reexamined the heights of power to find similar mediations. Alejandro Cañeque documented that viceregal power was never autocratic, but from the start focused on negotiation.[21] He too was mostly ignored. Regina Grafe and Alejandra Irigoin, economic historians, looked closely at the late imperial regime and its role in economic life. They saw a "stakeholder regime," enabling the institutional organization of diverse sectors, allowing them to mediate their own conflicts whenever possible, with the regime a final arbiter. No autocratic imposition, no state-ruled economy of closed monopolies.[22] Esteban Sánchez de Tagle recently explored the Mexico City Council's response to Bourbon reformers who pressed changes that appeared autocratic; he found a regime drawn to negotiate with the powers that led Mexico City.[23] And Annick Lempérière has offered an integrated analysis of the Spanish regime and its power in Mexico City, detailing its decentralized conciliar and judicial structures and mediating ways through to the eve of the 1808 crisis.[24]

All these studies link Spain and New Spain to a new understanding of early modern European regimes and empires, emphasizing that, for all the claims of absolutism, the means of communication, integration, and coercion were limited. Unable to impose, they negotiated and mediated among estates and institutions, cities, and communities with unequal powers and diverse rights. Working to maximize regime revenues and stabilize changing ways of power, production, and inequity, before 1800 few regimes were strong enough to rule internally by force. (The forces essential to interregime conflicts might be mobilized against rebellious subjects when mediations failed, a possibility more real in European homelands.)[25]

This study builds on the understanding of the Spanish regime as a mediating set of conciliar and judicial institutions, to show how it was essential to the dynamism and stability of silver capitalism before 1808, and then to detail how that year of crisis transformed the regime, corroding its ability to mediate and stabilize. The breakdown of consultations and mediations just as silver capitalism peaked, faced wartime challenges, and pressed new insecurities on the people who produced everything led to the insurgencies that began in 1810. Silver capitalism fell soon after, undermined by violent, destabilizing conflicts. Spanish rule ended in New Spain in 1821. The Mexican nation that followed lived a long commercial crisis while militarized politics tied to claims of popular sovereignty crippled the search for a new stabilizing regime.

Urban Power, Mediating Rule, Imperial Crisis, and the Rise of a Coercive State

Regime power and silver capitalism fused in eighteenth-century Mexico City. The capital's economic powers integrated production across New Spain; its regime offices mediated to stabilize power and social inequities; together they tied the kingdom and its diverse peoples to Spain and global trades. To understand the transforming importance of the summer of 1808, it is essential to know first the economic power, social relations, ethnic complexity, and enduring stability of the city during the decades before the crisis. That is the focus of part 1, exploring the city's life as the capital of silver capitalism.

Chapter 1 reviews the origins of the city in the indigenous past and its rise as a pivot of regime power and silver capitalism in Spain's empire. Chapter 2 explores the heights of oligarchic power, probing the coalition of merchant financiers, mining entrepreneurs, and agrarian capitalists that ruled silver capitalism—and forged ties to insert their interests at the heights of a regime that depended on silver revenues. The family of the inordinately powerful Conde de Regla, the silver magnate and landed entrepreneur who was likely the richest man in the Americas, if not the world, in the 1770s, focuses the analysis. The clan's integration of mining and commercial cultivation, its merger with the commercial and landed family led by the Conde de Jala, and their multiple links to the heights of regime power show the ways of silver capitalism in personal detail.

Chapter 3 explores the world of the less-powerful provincial elites who led the Mexico City Council and the city's ecclesiastical establishment. Its leading men were often modest landed entrepreneurs who doubled as legal or clerical professionals. They might speak for the city or the Church—yet most lived as dependents of the oligarchs who ruled the heights of silver capitalism. The relations linking oligarchs, imperial officials, provincial elites, and learned professionals were pivotal to negotiating city politics, sustaining the stability essential to power and prosperity before 1808. The summer of crisis began to fracture their coalitions, contributing to the instability that led to the coup—and soon enough to the dissolution of silver capitalism.

Chapter 4 turns to a diverse urban majority: middling and poor American Spaniards, mestizos and mulattos, and tens of thousands of indigenous people who held separate rights in the city's indigenous republics. The analysis explores their economic activities as guild-organized crafts became less important while commercial labor and insecure marginality marked an increasingly capitalist city. A mix of prosperity, dependence, and fragmentation kept the majority at work and at peace. Chapter 5 focuses on active attempts to promote order and stabilize inequities, exploring how oligarchs, provincial elites, and city authorities worked to maintain social peace: bringing new judges to the neighborhoods to refine the regime of mediation; increasing surveillance in hopes of limiting cultural independence (with little success); delivering relief in times of scarcity and disease.

Part 2 turns to political life in the city before, during, and after the crisis of 1808. Chapter 6 begins with a deeper exploration of the regime of diverse

rights, petition, and mediation and its operation in the city in the middle of
the eighteenth century. Then analysis turns to how the Bourbon regime
pressed new demands for direct power and increased revenues in the 1760s—
and the city council asserted its right to petition and gain revisions and concessions. While they debated, pressures for new revenues and militarized
powers in the mining center of Guanajuato and nearby regions provoked
riots that threatened the mining at the core of silver capitalism. Militias from
surrounding regions eventually contained the risings, authorities imposed
exemplary punishments—and then backed off the most disruptive demands
to restore the politics of mediation. The Mexico City Council took advantage
of that regime learning to press its historic rights, negotiating to draw to its
chamber new men on the rise who would serve limited terms overseeing
justice in the city (often as they rose to oligarchic eminence and married into
the capital's leading clans). It then reminded chastened reformers in Spain
that the empire depended on New Spain's silver and the American Spaniards
who kept it flowing.

Chapter 7 traces how that negotiated restoration held through decades
of rising silver prosperity and enduring Spanish power in the Americas.
When powers in Madrid joined the war against Britain in 1779, supporting
the independence of rebellious North American colonies, New Spain sent
millions of pesos in support of the effort. When in 1780, while the North
American conflict carried on, native peoples across the Andean highlands of
South America took arms to challenge Spanish rule, New Spain's dynamic
silver capitalism stimulated a Pacific economy that funded the successful
effort to suppress the native challenge. Having helped fund the triumph of
British rebels in North America and the defeat of indigenous insurgents in
the Andes, the powerful in New Spain easily absorbed and deflected Bourbon
reformers' attempts to assert new control by naming intendants in the late
1780s. When renewed wars and others' revolutions led the regime to call for
new militias in the early 1790s, oligarchs and provincial elites took command. Rising flows of silver again fueled Atlantic trade and filled regime
coffers as wars stressed the empire through the 1790s. An attempt by a few
city artisans and petty traders to replicate the French Revolution in 1799
proved notable for its failure to thrive.

Chapter 8 turns to the escalating revenue challenges and political divisions that struck the empire and Mexico City after 1800. While Napoleon lost

the revenues of Saint-Domingue as it became revolutionary Haiti, he pressed his Spanish ally for funds. Madrid's attempt in 1805 to tap the loan capital of the convents that doubled as banks in New Spain led to rising voices of protest in the capital and beyond. The regime of petition and mediation adapted to limit collections, maintain power and silver production, generate new revenues, and keep social order. The new revenues, however, did not suffice to save the monarchy in Spain from soaring debts, internal divisions, and Napoleon's 1808 invasion. He dreamed of gaining the lion's share of New Spain's silver revenues.

Three chapters then focus on the political summer of 1808, the coup that closed it, and the reverberations that led to the explosion of insurgencies north of the capital in 1810. Chapter 9 explores how news of the fall of the Bourbons and Napoleon's attempt to impose a Bonaparte king came slowly in rumors and delayed reports. A new public politics gripped the city: the viceroy, High Court judges and other ministers, and the oligarchs who ruled finance and trade, mining, and commercial cultivation all joined in; so did provincial elites and the city council they led, and many—including clergy—who saw openings to new possibilities. Popular groups including artisans, workers, and people of the indigenous republics also discussed, debated, and demanded participation. There were meetings and street demonstrations proclaiming loyalty to deposed Bourbon kings. Many claimed the traditional sovereignty of the pueblos; others sought the sovereignty of the people or the nation. Who the people might be, what the nation could be, remained unclear.

There were diverse and shifting alliances: the viceroy, the city council, and key mining and landed oligarchs held strong in seeking rights to assemble and determine New Spain's sovereign interests—interests focused on the city and New Spain's silver economy. Most High Court judges, regime ministers, and military commanders opposed such claims and gatherings. Most were immigrants from Spain; their roles in New Spain depended on ties to their homeland. That left swing power to the financiers of silver capitalism—insistently loyal to Spain, yet committed first to the profits of silver. When they turned to join those seeking an assembly of New Spain and de facto autonomy, a coalition of military officers, judges, and lesser merchants tied to Spain raised armed forces to oust the viceroy, block any assembly, and mandate loyalty, service, and shipments of silver to a junta rising in Seville to fight Napoleon.

Chapter 10 shows how the coup fused military power and claims of popular sovereignty while tying New Spain to uncertain authorities in Seville. The oligarchs and councilmen who had backed the viceroy in seeking an assembly and de facto autonomy acquiesced. None among the powerful were ready (or able?) to turn to countervailing force to undo the coup that broke the regime of mediation. Still, a few young oligarchs did join in conversations with a few artisans the day after the coup. They dreamed of raising outlying pueblos to blockade the city—and of calling one of the governors of the city's indigenous republics to take power as an indigenous king of New Spain. Others talked of similar dreams, revealing a subcurrent of opposition to the military coup and the regime it imposed. But the dreams proved fanciful—or impossible; no one, not the outlying pueblos, not the indigenous governors, came to the imagined revolutions. The summer of politics may have called the pueblos sovereign; the leaders of the coup insisted they served a sovereign people; but few pueblos or people were ready to rise against the coup and the new regime it imposed in September of 1808.

Still, the men who imagined a revolution the day after the coup offered a perceptive analysis of its meaning. As narrated by the young Conde de Peñasco, son of a powerful landed oligarch, men who monopolized the forces of coercion had made the coup; the only way to counter their rule was for nearby pueblos to rise and deprive the city of sustenance. As military force remade the regime, ending mediation and turning to coercion in the name of the people, the only recourse was for the people, the indigenous pueblos, to assert their power to produce and deliver sustenance. No rising came in 1808, yet young Peñasco saw the future of Mexico. After 1810, endless risings saw landed communities assert control over sustenance to challenge armed men who presumed to rule in the name of the people.

Chapter 11 explores the complex links leading from the urban coup of September 1808 to the rural insurgencies of September 1810. For a year the city and silver capitalism carried on while popular opposition simmered. New anger focused on resented *gachupines*, the immigrant Spaniards who had implemented the coup, blocked customary mediations, and prevented emerging participations. Rumors and anonymous broadsheets revealed simmering discontent, worrying rulers who knew their own illegitimacy.

Still, silver flows peaked in 1809 in support of Spain's fight for independence. In the same year, drought drove scarcities that made life from Mexico

City to the Bajío, the core of silver capitalism, impossible for many and too costly for many more. Landed oligarchs profited while people faced desperations layered onto exploitations that had deepened in recent decades. When 1810 brought news of the imminent collapse of resistance in Spain, provincial elites in the Bajío began to discuss regional juntas, aiming to assert rights to join in remaking sovereignty. When military authorities broke planning at Querétaro, a key commercial center linking the capital and the Guanajuato mines, provincials at nearby San Miguel and Dolores led by Father Miguel Hidalgo called a rising in defense of Fernando VI and Catholicism, against Napoleon—and in opposition to illegitimate powers in Mexico City. Long struggling and recently starving people quickly took arms—pursuing their own goals focused on land, justice, and local autonomy, an agenda pursued in violence that would transform New Spain and the world.

Popular insurgents broke silver capitalism while political insurgents rattled Spanish rule. Mediation proved impossible in a decade of deadly political wars and social challenges. Armed forces, loyalist and insurgent, shaped a decade of conflict. They endured to dominate politics in the Mexican nation that began in 1821—always backed by claims to serve the people, the nation, or the pueblos. Militarized politics, claims of popular sovereignty, and popular insurgencies forged a nation of recurring conflicts and uncertain prospects. The conclusion suggests how the history linking the regime transformation of 1808, the fall of silver capitalism after 1810, the end of Spanish rule, and the emergence of Mexico in 1821 was a culminating piece of a broader rise of armed, more coercive states backed by claims of popular sovereignty—a shift that came within a larger transformation from a global commercial capitalism, in which Mexico City and New Spain held pivotal roles, to a new industrial capitalism in which Mexico would struggle.

The fall of silver capitalism shocked the world economy. China, its production and trade long tied to New Spain's silver, fell from hegemony to dependency on British power and trade.[26] The economic trials and political instability of the emerging Mexican nation opened the way for the United States, independent since the 1780s and by the 1840s a more stable, prosperous, and militarized nation built on a combination of industry and plantation slavery, to go to war in 1846 and take the lands from Texas to California.[27] Power in North America shifted decisively. The New World hegemon of silver capitalism had fallen; the American engine of industrial capitalism was rising.[28]

The summer of 1808 was a key moment in an era of transforming change. In the face of imperial crisis, a political opening raised possibilities of popular sovereignty that were quickly closed by military powers—that also claimed popular sovereignty. Armed power broke the regime of mediation that had stabilized silver capitalism and Spain's empire just as drought deepened exploitations in key regions. Insurgencies followed, breaking the silver economy that fueled global trades, disintegrating Spain's empire, opening the way for the rise of Britain and industrial capitalism. Mexicans faced a difficult national birth. The United States expanded, favored by British industrial demand for slave-made cotton. And everywhere, a new industrial capitalism promoted states seeking monopolies of coercion while proclaiming the sovereignty of their peoples.[29] The crisis of 1808 in Mexico City was a pivotal episode in the rise of coercive state powers said to serve the people— yet built to serve those who pursued power and profit.

PART I

City of Silver

Power and Social Order, 1760–1810

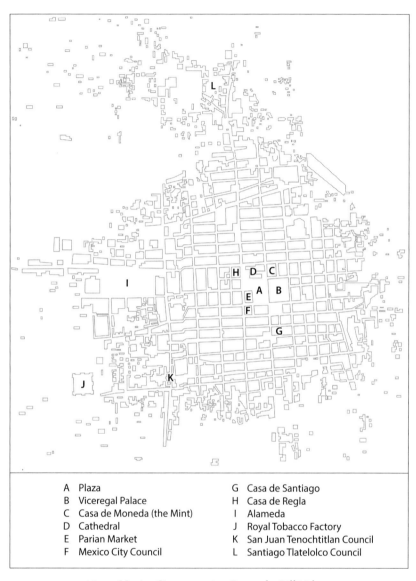

A	Plaza	G	Casa de Santiago
B	Viceregal Palace	H	Casa de Regla
C	Casa de Moneda (the Mint)	I	Alameda
D	Cathedral	J	Royal Tobacco Factory
E	Parian Market	K	San Juan Tenochtitlan Council
F	Mexico City Council	L	Santiago Tlatelolco Council

Map 1. Mexico City, 1790–1810. Drawn by Bill Nelson.

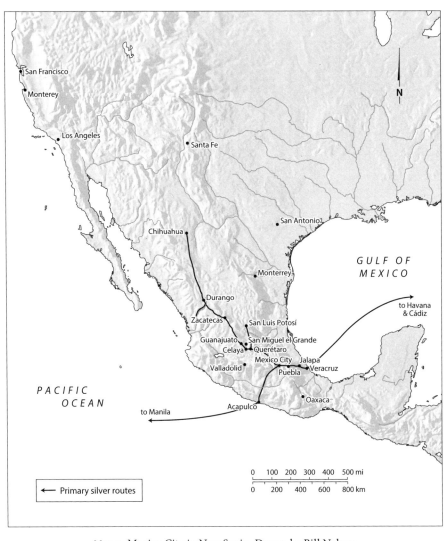

Map 2. Mexico City in New Spain. Drawn by Bill Nelson.

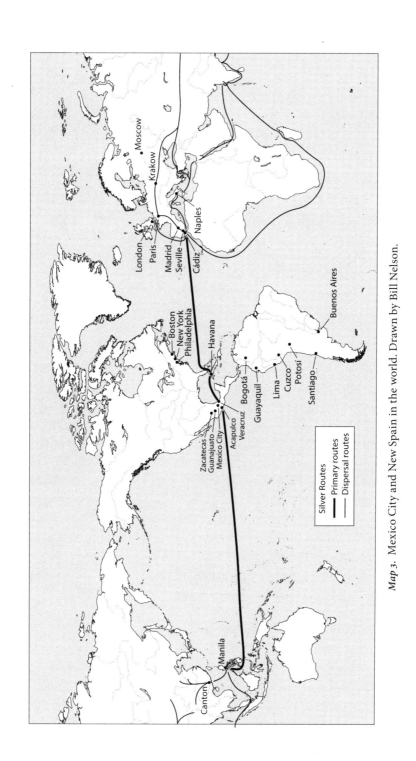

Map 3. Mexico City and New Spain in the world. Drawn by Bill Nelson.

Silver Routes
—— Primary routes
—— Dispersal routes

Moscow
Krakow
London
Paris
Madrid
Seville
Cádiz
Naples
Boston
New York
Philadelphia
Havana
Bogotá
Guayaquil
Lima
Cuzco
Potosí
Santiago
Buenos Aires
Zacatecas
Guanajuato
Mexico City
Acapulco
Veracruz
Canton
Manila

CHAPTER 1

From Mexica Capital to Silver Metropolis, 1350–1770

~ IN 1808, THE CITY NAMED MEXICO WAS DEEP INTO ITS FIFTH CEN-
tury as a center of power and population—far older than the Spanish empire
it served as North American capital, older too than the global capitalism it
stimulated with unprecedented flows of silver. To understand the New World
metropolis and the crisis that began to unravel its power in 1808, we must
trace the city's indigenous origins and the history that made it pivotal to
Spain's empire and early capitalism. Around 1800, the metropolis was a place
of regime power, high finance, and cultural engagement sustained by an
economy mixing diverse crafts and emerging industries. A pivot of Spanish
rule and world trade, it included the largest concentration of native peoples
in the Americas while surrounded and sustained by a hinterland simultaneously Hispanic and capitalist, Amerindian and republican. Without seeing
all that, we cannot understand the crisis of 1808.

A Military-Hydraulic City: Mexico-Tenochtitlan, 1350–1520
Founded in the 1340s as a refuge for the Mexica, nomadic people who came
from the north seeking a place in the world of warring Mesoamerican states,
Mexico-Tenochtitlan became the largest city in the hemisphere and the dom-
inant center of power north of Inca Cuzco during the fifteenth century. The
Mexica arrived as warrior-nomads ready to fight in the violent conflicts of

Mesoamerica. They settled on an island in the shallow lakes in the center of the high basin since known as the Valley of Mexico. They joined in political wars, protected by shallow waters that allowed a struggling new community to live by gathering aquatic life. The Mexica rise mixed military assertion, urban expansion, hydraulic construction, and religious legitimation. The result was the parallel construction of an armed polity and a burgeoning city built on hydraulic works that concentrated power and sustenance in the capital—all proclaimed as service to demanding gods.[1]

While the Mexica fought to rule, the city grew. To sustain a rising population, they remade the lakes to expand *chinampa* cultivation. Raised fields built in shallow waters, chinampas had helped feed the pyramid city of Teotihuacan a millennium earlier. To supply Tenochtitlan, the Mexica mobilized labor to build an expanding land and waterscape of dikes, causeways, canals, and fertile chinampas that were planted year-round in maize and other crops. As Mexica power expanded and Tenochtitlan's population grew past one hundred thousand in the fifteenth century, the urban sustenance grounded in adjacent hydraulic works and chinampa harvests fell short of city needs. Increasingly, crops, cloth, and other goods taken as tribute from conquered peoples became essential to the city's survival and prosperity.

The city, the Mexica regime, their allies, and their conquered subjects all lived by enabling family production of foodstuffs and craft goods. Commoner (*macehual*) families organized in communities (*calpultín*) worked chinampas or dry land milpa plots while pursuing diverse crafts. They paid tributes in produce and labor to lords who ruled city-states in conflict. The powerful Mexica and their allies in Texcoco and Tlacopan expanded outward from bases around the lakes; people in outlying regions from Chalco to Cholula, Tlaxcala, and beyond faced wars pressing them to subordination. Everywhere men fought in military campaigns framed with religious legitimations that increasingly demanded the blood of captive warriors to sustain the Mesoamerican cosmos—and the victors' powers.[2] But ultimately war aimed to take tributes in goods and labor service to sustain the victors, their cities, and armies—and deprive the defeated of the same. Markets were everywhere, but everywhere subordinated to a central dynamic of family production, military power, and tribute exaction. Local markets enabled exchange among producers; great markets in Tenochtitlan, nearby Tlatelolco, and other cities of power enabled warlords and their merchant allies to trade wares taken in tribute from subjects near and far.

The Mexica's foundational advantage in this Mesoamerican world of conflict was the hydraulic construction and chinampa cultivation that early on sustained the city and its military power independent of its neighbors. Yet after 1450, the city's growth drove a rising reliance on imperial expansion that threatened those autonomies. The Mexica capital and its militarized regime faced a tipping point around 1500, its population estimated as at least 150,000 to over 200,000. Hydraulic works and chinampas only partly sustained them. Distant campaigns required long marches that stretched supply lines; conquests provoked rising resistance among people who saw little gain in Mexica rule—and real losses in tribute demands.[3] And Mexica expansion was legitimated by a religion demanding the blood of sacrificial victims for the war-god Huitzilopochtli—the blood of captured enemy soldiers. Their defeat and death, followed by rising demands for tribute goods, drained outlying states and communities of people and produce in order to sustain the Mexica city and war regime.[4]

As long as the Mexica triumphed in battle, delivering sacrificial victims to fuel the cosmos and tribute goods to feed the metropolis and fuel trade, the regime, its rulers, and religion held legitimate in the eyes of city dwellers and nearby cultivators who benefited from regime power, hydraulic works, and the tributes of expansion. But when flood, plague, or failure in war made city life—and the pleasure of the gods—uncertain, regime power and city life faced challenges. As conquests drove outward to bring rising costs and diminishing returns, city sustenance was less effective and outlying peoples became more resentful and resistant to Mexica demands. Until the Spanish incursion, the city survived. The beneficiaries of Mexica power lived in part by their own production—and in growing part by taking tributes from conquered peoples. A mix of military power, tribute taking, labor mobilization, and trade built the first city of Mexico deep in interior highlands, at the center of shallow lakes, near geologic fault lines that brought periodic earthquakes.

Imperial Capital and Silver Metropolis: Mexico City, 1520–1700
Don Fernando Cortés and his band of freebooters first saw Tenochtitlan in 1519, welcomed by Moctezuma II, who believed he had little to fear—and

soon paid with his life. The newcomers saw a city they imagined equal to
Naples. The metropolitan complex of cities around the lakes included more
people than then crowded around Paris. Urban concentrations ruled
Mesoamerica.[5] The coming of Europeans carrying smallpox and other diseases, searching for profit and insisting on Christian truth, provoked radical
change: depopulation, incorporation in a European empire—and after 1550
a leading role in a new and growing global commercial capitalism. After the
siege of 1521 that broke the Mexica regime, the city of Mexico survived to
become Spain's capital in North America. After 1550, it became the financial
and commercial pivot of a silver economy of global reach.

   The smallpox and other diseases that struck beginning in 1520—after the
death of Moctezuma, before the siege in which Cortés and his Tlaxcalan
allies broke Mexica power—rapidly destroyed the population of the city and
surrounding regions, enabling Spanish rule far more than did European
weapons.[6] The city survived, its population in 1550 but a quarter of its pre-
contact number; it would regrow to about eighty thousand by 1600, perhaps
half its indigenous peak—while outlying regions faced a 90 percent
depopulation.

   Mexico-Tenochtitlan became a Euro-Mesoamerican center, a Mexico
City reborn to serve Spanish power in Mesoamerica.[7] A high court (audiencia) to oversee justice came in 1530, followed in 1535 by the first viceroy, don
Antonio de Mendoza.[8] Bishops settled in to lead the Roman Church.
Franciscans, Dominicans, Augustinians, and others built convents to promote efforts to bring native survivors of devastating epidemics to Christian
salvation. Meanwhile, Mexica commoners continued to plant chinampas
and pursue crafts to sustain themselves. Mexica labor drafts were revived to
draw men to build halls for Spanish power where Moctezuma once ruled and
Christian churches to replace temples dedicated to Huitzilopochtli and other
fallen deities.[9]

   New diseases came in waves and population continued to plummet.
Power and truth remained uncertain in Mesoamerica and its leading city.
The silver boom that accelerated after 1550 gave the capital new life. China,
the largest polity with the largest population and most dynamic economy
in the world, decreed in 1551 that silver would be the primary currency for
paying taxes and balancing major trades. From the 1400s Europeans had
taken to the seas seeking the elegant products of Asia: notably Chinese silks

and porcelains. From the 1550s, they could only be bought for silver (Europeans made little of interest to the Chinese).[10] Taxco, a few days' ride southwest of Mexico City, saw silver mining begin in the 1530s. The founding of a mint in Mexico City in 1535 showed the early importance of mining and trade in Europeans' vision for New Spain. With rising Chinese demand Pachuca, northeast of the capital, took off in the 1550s. There in 1555, Bartolomé de Medina perfected the *patio* process using mercury to separate silver from midgrade ores. Production soared across Spain's Americas.[11]

The first great silver boom of 1570 to 1640 was led by production at Potosí, high in the Andes. That center surpassed Mexico City as the largest city in the America for decades after 1600; its 150,000 people mined and refined over 60 percent of the America's silver. Into the 1590s, Taxco, Pachuca, and other mines around Mexico City flourished as the second region sending silver into rising global trades—to be surpassed by production at Zacatecas, Guanajuato, and other sites to the north after 1600, when resistant Chichimecas were defeated by war and disease.[12] As silver stimulated new commercial ways first in nearby Mesoamerica and then in the Bajío and regions north, Mexico City grew to about 75,000 people after 1570 as New Spain's center of government and justice, minting and taxation.

It was the site of Church administration and of education to prepare professionals to serve the regime and religion in a new world. The coming of Jesuits in the 1570s confirmed that role. The merchant financiers who funded mining and sent silver into global trade concentrated in the city. So did artisans who served the new economy and the European culture it promoted: silversmiths, tailors, and dressmakers supplying Spaniards' visions of luxury; carpenters, bricklayers, and others building their homes. Growing numbers of spinners and weavers made cloth for the many without the wealth to buy the Chinese silks, South Asian cottons, and other fabrics bought with the Americas' silver.

Once the leading city of a Mesoamerican world of states at war, the city still named Mexico became a cosmopolitan center of European governance and commercial dynamism in a new and larger world of commercial capitalism. An expedition sent from New Spain by authorities in Mexico City established direct trade with Manila in the 1570s; a rich and growing Chinese merchant community settled there to trade American silver for wares from across Asia. During the union of the Iberian crowns under Hapsburg sovereignty from 1580 to 1640, Portuguese New Christian (recently Jewish) merchants came to Mexico City, tying its silver to ever more global trades. Diverse others came too: Africans arrived enslaved to work in crafts, construction, and transport services; many found freedom for their children by reproducing with indigenous women who by law were always free after 1550, as were their mulatto children.[13] Indigenous migrants came too, working in reconstruction, taking up crafts, planting chinampas, and more. They reinforced the surviving urban indigenous communities of San Juan Tenochtitlan and Santiago Tlatelolco, then being reorganized as republics led by governors and councils that oversaw native neighborhoods, their adaptations of Christian worship, and their crafts, cultivations, and markets.

While the city reconsolidated around 1600 as the center of the silver economy in New Spain with about eighty thousand residents, it faced new problems. Waves of epidemics had driven the population of the surrounding countryside to only 10 percent of precontact levels, leaving few native producers to feed the city—and few workers to maintain its hydraulic system of canals, chinampas, and causeways. To sustain mining and feed the city that organized its dynamism, the regime oversaw a rural reconstruction after 1570. Scarce surviving villagers were congregated into indigenous republics granted self-rule and lands for sustenance; vacated lands were awarded to Spaniards who built commercial estates to supply mines and cities. Villagers retained land enough to feed families and sell surplus maize and other native sustenance in the city; estate builders mostly raised wheat, sugar, livestock, and other European staples. Villagers provided essential seasonal labor for commercial harvests, by draft mandates to the 1630s, then in response to wage incentives. Native notables ruled landed republics, sold maize in city markets, and organized work gangs to labor in estate fields.[14]

After 1600, landed indigenous republics mixed with commercial estates to sustain the mines and Mexico City markets. Indigenous survivors rebuilt communities and adapted Christian cultures. Their produce and labor supported silver production and fed urban consumers. But they could not provide the greater labor needed to maintain the hydraulic works essential to Mexico-Tenochtitlan before 1520. Flooding became a recurrent problem from the 1550s, culminating in a devastating inundation in 1629. Unable to maintain the dikes, causeways, and canals that made chinampas essential to

Figure 1. Mexico City, 1628. Courtesy of the Benson Latin American Collection, University of Texas at Austin.

city sustenance, Spanish authorities decided to drain water from the basin in a great public work known as the *desague*—the drainage. Through decades of trial, error, and limited success, the project diverted much of the water of the Cuautitlán River north of the capital into a cut in the mountains and then on to the dry Mezquital basin. Native chinampas and commercial irrigation were prejudiced north of the city; the desague's limited success left chinampas to thrive across the southern basin from the capital to Xochimilco and Chalco, along with the canals that linked them to city markets. A combination of landed republics—some cultivating on dry land, others working chinampas—and emerging commercial estates would sustain the city and the silver economy for centuries.[15]

Meanwhile, as the rural reconstruction consolidated and depopulation slowed after 1600, an oligarchy of officials, merchant financiers, high churchmen, and landed clans struggled to consolidate power in the capital. Viceroys often of noble Castilian lineage oversaw everything but generally stayed for terms of only three to five years; High Court judges and bishops served longer and often forged ties of family and interest with powerful mining, commercial, and landed clans. The Condes de Santiago Calimaya became the city's leading family: they descended from the viceroys don Luis de Velasco, father and son, who built family and financial alliances with the Altamiranos, leading miners who invested in vast estates centered at Atengo just west of the capital in the Valley of Toluca. As mining soared from 1600 to 1635, newcomers from Spain and Portugal profited in mining and trade; the most successful invested in landed estates—often by marrying into established families. And every family of power sought allies in the regime and the Church, along with seats for themselves or their kin on the Mexico City Council. A high politics of power and influence became a constant of city life.[16]

Families and factions jockeyed for advantage. The profits gained by commercial newcomers aided by official allies might provoke resentments among sons of old families. Meanwhile, their sisters married immigrant entrepreneurs to merge commercial and landed wealth. Viceroys and bishops also jostled for precedence—even as bishops often served as interim viceroys. Diverse religious orders sought precedence too, especially as missionary zeal waned and the Jesuits became New Spain's leading educators, sustained by rich landed estates. When the Portuguese broke with Spain in 1640, some in New Spain's capital turned on merchants suddenly "discovered" as "crypto-Jews"—pressing Inquisition inquiries mostly aimed at ousting rivals from silver trades then facing a downturn.

In 1624 the city lived its greatest political crisis between the siege of 1521 and the summer of 1808. Factional struggles set the viceroy against the archbishop in time of silver boom, commercial dynamism, and a drought that made food scarce and costly. City people saw powerful men caught in political spats while profiteering in scarce sustenance. Viceroy Gelves ousted Archbishop de la Serna; people rioted, accusing the powerful of taking profit while they faced starvation. The viceroy fled. The Conde de Santiago Calimaya, leader of the city's landed establishment, mobilized local militias to calm the crowds and press his peers to deliver food to city markets at less than starvation prices. Calm had barely returned when the great floods of 1629 brought a different threat to urban survival.[17]

In the 1640s a new stability began to set in. Portuguese traders were pressed aside, leaving merchants and landed entrepreneurs self-defined as Spaniards, *españoles*, to jockey for eminence. In the same decade, a global crisis brought war and regime change to Europe and China as silver production plummeted at Potosí. Silver had declined earlier at Taxco and Pachuca near Mexico City; to the north production at Guanajuato and Zacatecas held strong into in the 1630s, and then fell there too. But mining rose at far northern Parral, keeping the stimulus of silver solid in New Spain and its capital.

In that context, a Hispanic-Mexican culture consolidated in the city as clergy and others turned to adopt Our Lady of Guadalupe. Indigenous villagers outside the capital had discovered her powerful protections a century earlier; for decades Hispanic churchmen resisted her as too indigenous. Now she became protector of the capital and New Spain: a Christian mother shared by city Spaniards and indigenous Mexicas. Seeking to root their claims to eminence in a native past, American Spaniards began to imagine themselves heirs to deposed Mexica lords—rulers their ancestors had ousted (while a few married their daughters). Hispanic residents of Mexico City adopted Guadalupe, seeking precedence grounded in the city's indigenous past—while finding little of value (beyond produce and labor) in the indigenous communities living all around and sending sustenance to the city.[18] The city produced intellectual lights from the revered poet Sor Juana Inés de la Cruz, honored by viceroys and oligarchs, to don Carlos Sigüenza y Góngora, a savant who promoted Hispanic devotion to Guadalupe and rose to find welcome as cosmographer in the court of France's Louis XIV.[19]

The end of the seventeenth century brought new challenges to the city. The 1680s saw another downturn in the silver economy accompanied by popular resistance across New Spain. Rebellious Pueblo communities rose to evict Spaniards from far northern New Mexico in 1680. In the city of Mexico, 1692 riots mobilized women and men, indigenous and mixed, to protest another round of profiteering from drought and famine—this time involving high officials, perhaps even the viceroy. Indigenous women began the protest, indigenous and mixed men carried it forward; they burned part of the viceroy's palace and sacked the Parián market (named for the Chinese merchant quarter in Spanish Manila) where luxury goods from across the world were sold in the great plaza facing the palace and the metropolitan cathedral. Again, militias restored order once the city granary sold food. Again, city folk made it clear that acquiescence in lives of productive subordination depended on fair access to essential sustenance—and fair mediation by authorities.[20]

Pivot of Silver Capitalism: Mexico City, 1700–1770

As riots ended and the city calmed, silver production dipped below four million pesos yearly in the last years of the seventeenth century. Dark economic prospects faced imperial uncertainty in 1700 when Carlos II, the last Spanish Hapsburg, died without a successor. England and France mobilized opposing alliances within Spain and across Europe to press favored candidates: England backed an Austrian Hapsburg; Louis XIV and France promoted a Bourbon claimant. They fought a War of Spanish Succession on Iberian soil and across Europe—with access to Spanish American silver and the markets it stimulated the prize. Authorities and entrepreneurs in Mexico City mostly stood back, jostling over revenues and local economic advantages as the Bourbon Felipe V asserted power and New Spain's silver output rose to pass six million pesos yearly after 1710.[21]

New Spain's silver funded Spanish Bourbon power through the eighteenth century. Production rose to over 12 million pesos in the 1750s, held steady through the 1760s, and then soared to approach 24 million pesos annually in the 1790s and early 1800s. Too often, Bourbon reform policies gain credit for the eighteenth-century silver boom. Yet the boom predated Bourbon policies—which aimed to raise revenues by strengthening regime power. Across much of Spain's Americas where economies struggled, Bourbon reforms became resented intrusions—as in the Andes where silver regained dynamism but slowly and Bourbon demands helped provoke the risings around Tupac Amaru in the 1780s.[22] In New Spain, reformers would learn to negotiate with powerful entrepreneurs to keep silver flowing.

As New Spain's silver rose to stimulate trade from Europe to China, Mexico City grew. With perhaps 80,000 people around 1700, it passed 120,000 around 1800. After three centuries, the city approached its precontact, predisease population. Across the surrounding basins, the numbers in native republics nearly tripled during the eighteenth century—yet in 1800 most held fewer than half the people they sustained before the depopulation. Still, many faced struggles for sustenance as lands allocated to Spaniards' commercial estates in the reconstruction around 1600 could not be reclaimed to increase family and community production as numbers grew after 1700. People facing the pressures of a growing population on limited lands consumed most of their own produce, limiting sales of indigenous surpluses of maize and other native staples in mining centers and expanding city markets.

Hispanic estate operators responded by adding native maize and pulque (a popular fermented drink made from the maguey cactus) to their long-standing production of Old World wheat, sugar, and livestock. They found new profit meeting urban demand. And they drew growing numbers of village men and boys to work as seasonal hands paid wages to plant and harvest maize and wheat crops and to transplant maguey in commercial fields to expand pulque production. The capital's landed entrepreneurs took rising profits planting native staples to supply the city; rural villagers facing land shortages took wages at expanding estate harvests to sustain families and communities. Ties of symbiotic exploitation stabilized rural life and production, supplied city markets, and profited those who invested profits taken in mining and trade in commercial estates around the capital.[23]

Mexico City authorities worked to stabilize the supply of maize to urban consumers, regulating to cushion the extremes of a capitalist food system. They concentrated sales at the city granary, the *alhóndiga*, helping them to know and respond to trends in supply and price in an environment in which periodic drought (about once a decade) cut harvests and sent prices rising. In years of good rains and ample harvests, innumerable small growers in nearby chinampa communities and native republics farther out still sent small surpluses to city markets at low prices. Meanwhile, landed entrepreneurs paid villagers to raise maize, held stocks until harvests failed and prices peaked, and sold when drought came to drive up prices. Capitalists profited. City people ate at prices that were periodically painful, but never set off destabilizing, regime-threatening food riots after 1700—even during the great drought, frost, and famine of 1785–1786, or in the post-crisis scarcity of 1808–1810.[24]

Midcentury decades brought new challenges—mostly outside the capital. A great matlazahuatl (typhus) epidemic struck the highlands in the late

1730s, halting population growth. Urban demand and rural production both declined.[25] Renewed demographic rise in the 1750s came with a downturn in Chinese demand for silver, followed quickly by a round of wars from 1757 to 1763 that aimed to reset European power in the world. The British took Canada from France and forced it to deliver Louisiana and its claims to land west of the Mississippi to Spain. Britain's primary goals were revealed in naval expeditions that occupied Havana and Manila in 1762 and 1763. The former was the port where silver accumulated for shipment to Europe; the latter the entrepot where Chinese merchants traded Asian wares for New Spain's silver. British occupation showed naval power; the abandonment of both after a year revealed that holding ports did not bring access to silver— which found other routes to global trade. In the end, the global war left France without Canada and Louisiana, Britain in command of the seas—and Spain still entrenched in New Spain, its coveted silver essential to growing trades and the treasuries of regimes at war and in peace.[26]

A war that cost much yet settled little left the belligerents with burdensome debts. They saw solutions in new taxes on American subjects backed by stronger administrative powers and new military forces—threats to regimes of mediation everywhere. In British colonies from Massachusetts to the Carolinas, imperial demands for new revenues set off opposition among merchants and planters who voiced protests in 1765 that led to violence by 1774, a declaration of independence in 1776, and independence as the United States in 1783—followed by difficult years founding a regime and rebuilding an economy.

Spain's Bourbons pressed parallel revenue demands backed by attempts to build new administrative and military powers in New Spain. They provoked riots among workers in key mining centers from Guanajuato to San Luis Potosí in 1766 and 1767. American entrepreneurs led by the first Conde de Peñasco, a rich mine operator becoming a leading landed capitalist in San Luis Potosí, mobilized regional militias to contain the risings. That done, Spain's Visitor General don José de Gálvez announced repressions while working to return the mines that sustained New Spain, Spain, and its empire to production. Spain's Bourbons and their reforming agents learned the costs of disrupting silver capitalism.[27]

Capitalism with Limited Coercion:
Mediating Power, Production, and Prosperity

In the long history of Mexico City from 1350 to the 1760s, key transformations marked the sixteenth century. Europeans came and linked Mesoamericans to an empire based in Spain and to a Christian world centered on to Rome. The imperial project was enabled by depopulation and the rise of silver.[28] Less recognized yet equally important was the shift from a Mexica polity grounded in military power to a Spanish regime focused on mediation and weak in coercive force.[29] It is time to recognize the demise of military rule in sixteenth-century New Spain—and the transforming importance of its return in 1808.

Power in pre-Hispanic Mesoamerica was ultimately military: states rose and fell by military conflicts; they extracted surpluses from producing families and communities by coercive force. Markets mattered: families traded small surpluses in communities everywhere; warlords worked with merchant allies to profit trading the large surpluses taken in wars of conquest and sanctioned as tribute rights. Communities and families ruled production on the land. To take surpluses and solidify power, military force prevailed.

With the arrival of Europeans, their diseases, and new ties to global trades, coercion receded from the center of regime power—in the city and across Mesoamerica. Early Spaniards claimed rights to rule as proud *conquistadores*, made powerful by astonishing military victories. Every careful analyst knows that smallpox and other diseases destroyed the Mexica state and most of its people—enabling Europeans to use what little military force they had and alliances with native lords to build a new regime. Struggling to consolidate rule, they denied native peoples the right to carry arms, indigenous or European. The same "conquerors" quickly learned that to fend off the resistant Chichimecas who held the Bajío and regions north, they had to rely on indigenous forces. That second "conquest" done in the 1590s, Spaniards moved again to demilitarize New Spain.

Why had much to do with the very small numbers of Europeans who had come; a military contest would be no contest at all. *How* had everything to do with the stimulus of silver in times of radical depopulation: Silver offered unprecedented opportunities for wealth and regime revenue; depopulation left resources ample for scarce survivors. Families had ample lands to sustain themselves in the sixteenth and seventeenth centuries; entrepreneurs faced opportunities to profit in an environment of reluctant and expensive workers. Parallel conditions along Atlantic coasts would lead to "war capitalism"—social relations of production grounded in war and slavery.[30] In the Mesoamerican heartland, the stimulus of silver brought a turn from coercion and rule by mediation.

Why the difference? In New Spain's Mesoamerican core, a million people remained after depopulation—skilled cultivators and craftsmen, open to trade, and accustomed to providing surpluses and labor service to their betters. Mining required few workers for often dangerous labors. In that context, drawing enslaved Africans to the Mesoamerican highlands proved both costly and risky; meaningful numbers came, but they remained a small minority, often serving as managers and skilled craftsmen. Instead, New Spain's entrepreneurs tapped the wealth of silver to build a commercial economy relying primarily on paid labor, permanent in mining, often seasonal in agriculture, while regime builders used the revenues of silver to found a regime of mediation. Councils and consultations ruled at the heights of power; special courts served native republics when they faced conflicts among themselves and with Spaniards.[31]

Military power thus recedes from the main narratives of the histories of Mexico City and New Spain in the sixteenth century. In times of crisis and popular challenge, in 1624 and again in 1692 in Mexico City, militias mobilized to restore peace—followed by negotiations addressing the demands of the populace. When in the 1760s Spain's Bourbon reformers tried to create new forces of coercion to take new revenues, they provoked disruptions in key mining centers, threatening the silver economy that was the sovereign's first interest. The mediating regime returned to sustain silver capitalism to the end of the eighteenth century.[32] Then in 1808, Napoleon's invasion of Spain set off Mexico City's summer of politics. It led to the coup that brought a hard turn to militarized power. The fall of silver capitalism and Spain's American empire followed quickly.

Before returning to focus on the last decades of mediating rule and the turn to coercion in 1808, it is essential to explore power and production, social relations and mediated stabilizations in Mexico City—the capital of silver capitalism.

CHAPTER 2

Oligarchy

Power in the Capital of Silver Capitalism

⤫ DURING THE DECADES AFTER 1760, WHILE THE BRITISH COLONIES
of coastal North America struggled to become the United States, France and
Haiti lived revolutionary violence, and so much of Europe and the Atlantic
world faced wars that would not end, Mexico City carried on as the richest
and largest city in the Americas. It flourished as the center of power and production that integrated a silver economy pivotal to a commercial world in
which the powerful worked to take profits while states drove to find revenues
to pay for wars that approached a crescendo in the late eighteenth and early
nineteenth centuries.[1] The capital of New Spain oversaw domains from Costa
Rica to California, Cuba to Manila. Revenues taken in Mexico City funded
Spanish rule across those vast regions—and sent ample surpluses to Madrid.
City financiers and merchants funded silver production and profited in
global trades; landed entrepreneurs profited selling sustenance to a city
growing past 120,000 people. Mexico City was a place of power and profit for
a fortunate few. Many more lived in service and support of their rule.

There were politics in the city, too. They focused on petitioning for favorable rulings before administrators and courts and on negotiating favorable
policies. The field of power was first and foremost ruled by the few who held
economic sway in a silver economy that integrated mining, commerce, and

commercial cultivation as they engaged another few who ruled the heights of government. An oligarchy ruling a world of profit dealt with men holding the reins of government—and dependent on the silver economy for essential revenues. The heights of politics were open almost exclusively to men already powerful at the intersection of silver capitalism and the Spanish regime. They formed a small, yet never closed, oligarchy, dominant in Mexico City and New Spain, pivotal to Spain's empire and global capitalism as the eighteenth century drew to an end.

Just beneath them lived a larger elite I characterize as provincials. Mixing modest landowners and learned professionals, they led the Mexico City Council and oversaw urban affairs. They, too, joined in the politics of petition and mediation, gaining avenues of expression and redress pivotal to integrating and stabilizing city life. The provincial elites of the capital were wealthy and powerful by any standard—but those of the oligarchs above. The provincials' roles, powers, and social relations, often as dependents serving oligarchs, are detailed in chapter 3. Power belonged to the oligarchy—before the summer of 1808 called the people to politics and the September coup saw military men impose a new closure that began to marginalize oligarchs, provincial elites, and the people suddenly proclaimed sovereign.

Power defined Mexico City from its foundation; the intersection of entrepreneurial and regime power forged after 1570 continued to shape the metropolis after 1770. The viceroys exercised oversight across New Spain— and from Central America to California, Cuba to Manila. The Mexico City Mint, the Casa de Moneda so visibly adjacent to the viceroy's palace, turned nearly all New Spain's silver into pesos of eight reales—the pieces of eight historically coveted by Chinese emperors and traders, European kings and merchants, and Atlantic pirates, too. Millions went to fund the US war for independence in the 1770s and 1780s—leading the young republic to adopt New Spain's peso as its dollar. Treasury officials in Mexico City controlled the imports of mercury essential to refine silver, enabling them to gauge production and collect taxes to fund Spain's struggle to retain power in the world. The High Court (Audiencia) there had less extensive jurisdiction—but it counseled on administrative issues and decided pivotal judicial questions across the core of New Spain and its silver centers (Zacatecas and regions northwest dealt with an audiencia at Guadalajara). Mexico City was the leading center of Spanish power in the Americas into the nineteenth century.[2]

Figure 2. The confluence of powers in Mexico City: monarchy, mint, and cathedral. Photograph by the author.

That regime focused on promoting silver production, controlling the minting of the pesos that were the world's primary money, collecting revenues, and overseeing a complex system of consultation and justice that kept social peace and sustained the silver economy in the Americas' richest domain. Military power was notably limited. New Spain's revenues funded naval forces to protect the flow of silver to Spain and Manila. There were garrisons in key ports at Veracruz and Acapulco—and in the north to keep independent native peoples, struggling Apache and rising Comanche, away from centers of silver production.

In the capital and the nearby heartland basins, and in mining regions extending from the Bajío north, the regime had few forces of coercion, troops or police. Militias were everywhere, sanctioned by the authorities but dependent on funding and command by entrepreneurs—miners, merchants, and estate operators. Training was uncertain at best. Many militiamen, urban

and rural, were mulattos—men of mixed ancestry and middling fortune who
found honor and advantage by enrolling in militias. Regime officials did not
command the militias. They could be mobilized when the interests of the
regime and key entrepreneurs coincided in the face of threats, as in the risings of 1766–1767 in the mining zones—and when militiamen remained loyal
to their commanders. Outside militias had to be brought in to pacify
Guanajuato in 1767.[3]

With broad administrative and judicial powers, yet limited coercive
capacities, the regime in Mexico City concentrated on regulating property,
money, and trade, on promoting the silver economy, global trades, and revenue collection, and on judicial mediation of disputes among the powerful
and between the powerful and the populace. Power in the city reflected that
enduring structure. Silver, finance, and trade were inseparable from viceregal power. In a context of soaring silver production, a regime weak in coercive power constantly negotiated relations among regime officials and
leading entrepreneurs, the latter organized in powerful clans that integrated
financial, commercial, mining, and landed interests—and high officials too.
Oligarchic power shaped regime interests, policies, and possibilities more
than the regime shaped silver capitalism.

The Pivot of Silver

Silver was the dynamic center of New Spain's economy. The Mexico City Mint,
the Casa de Moneda, was the pivot that turned the product of entrepreneurs'
investments and mine workers' labor into the commodity-money that Mexico
City merchants sent into global trades. That nexus made relationships among
financiers, miners, merchants, and the regime critical to silver production and
to profit and power in the capital. During the first silver boom of 1570 to 1640
and the decades that followed, the mint was leased to private financiers who
gained a percentage of all minted silver. They operated as bankers funding
production at diverse mines. Minting held around three million pesos yearly
in the early seventeenth century. It fell in the 1630s, to rise and hold near four
million pesos annually from the 1660s to the 1680s. The late seventeenth-
century decline turned quickly to recovery after 1700. During early Bourbon
decades, key mint offices were let to the Sánchez de Tagle and Fagoaga families,
who flourished as silver bankers. Reported coinage held below two million
pesos yearly into the early 1720s, while production rose to eight million pesos.

Figure 3. The Mexico City Mint. Photograph by the author.

Either silver escaped the mint or minted coin escaped reporting to the Crown, surely profiting the silver bankers. In the mid-1720s, minting suddenly caught up with mining output—followed in the 1730s by a regime decision to take control of the mint.[4]

The silver bankers' access to unreported silver gave them the capital to stimulate and profit from the early Bourbon silver boom. When the regime took back control of the mint as the boom persisted to midcentury, the shift did not hurt the Sánchez de Tagle or the Fagoagas, who remained key financiers and merchants as mining and minting rose together from the 1730s to 1810.[5] It did enable the regime to ensure the coin quality that made New Spain's pesos global money and collect the taxes that sustained Spain's empire.

The world economy needed steady flows of silver. Yet mine operations were defined by potential for great profit limited by enormous costs as tunneling drove deep underground and by constant uncertainties of dealing with water and workers. A shaft could collapse; a promising vein of ore could suddenly end. Global trades linking New Spain, Europe, and Asia brought the risks inherent in slow and dangerous ocean shipping and in delayed communications about production, prices, and markets—risks made extreme by recurrent wars. To flourish in that world of profit and risk, Mexico City financiers, merchants, and officials negotiated complex relationships that kept capital available to finance mining and trade and left mine operators to face the endemic risks of mining—while they kept the incentive of potential bonanzas.

Financiers ranged from silver bankers (still led after 1770 by the Fagoagas) to merchants who advanced supplies to mine operators in exchange for silver. Most bankers and merchants worked with multiple mine operators at diverse centers, spreading the risks of any one collapse or bankruptcy while drawing silver from numerous operations. The steadiest profits of mining flowed to financiers—who used the silver to join in oceanic trades. Still, a few mining entrepreneurs found unparalleled gains: the Obregóns and the Sardanetas gained enough from the Valenciana and Rayas mines in Guanajuato to become Condes de Valenciana and Marqueses de San Juan de Rayas. Don Pedro Romero de Terreros took profits from trade at Querétaro, invested in drainage to revive the mines at Real de Monte, and emerged the richest man in New Spain, likely the Americas, and perhaps the world, in the 1770s—ennobled as Conde de Regla. Such stunning successes and many lesser bonanzas kept the promise of mining alive—and silver flowing to financiers, merchants, and world trade.

Among the few who lived in this complex world of power and profit, no one held a singular role defined by a dominant institution. The Fagoagas and the Sánchez de Tagle were merchants aiming to finance mines and won contracts to rule key functions in the mint. They simultaneously joined the consulado—the court and chamber that served the leading merchants of Mexico City, lobbying for their interests and mediating their disputes. After they separated from the mint, the bankers remained powerful in the consulado that coordinated trade between New Spain and Spain and Manila— and lobbied the regime to keep trade, profit, and silver flowing. When the regime founded the Mining Tribunal in the 1780s, merchant financiers and mine operators all found representation there. And when authorities promoting a limited "free trade" within Spain's domains enabled the founding of consulados in the port of Veracruz and Guadalajara in the 1790s, Mexico City merchants still financed mines, sent silver into global trades, and profited nicely. There were spats, negotiations, and adaptations with every change, but the links among Treasury officials and the mint, silver financiers, mine operators, and international traders held strong to 1808.

An Oligarchy of Power

An oligarchy long in formation and reinforced in the boom of the eighteenth century sustained and profited from the silver capitalism that made New Spain pivotal to the world after 1770. It was a small group, depending on definitions and ongoing fusions: perhaps two to three dozen extended families—nearly always linked to viceroys and High Court judges, Treasury officials, and Church leaders. And while small, the oligarchy of power was not closed. Every generation new men gained entrance: rising merchants, successful miners, and new officials out from Spain. Patterns of ascent and incorporation defined the oligarchy and sustained its enduring power—patterns that began to break in 1808.

In the formation and ongoing renewal of the silver oligarchy, there were well-known paths of migration, mobility, and integration. Most viceroys and archbishops came from Spain, expected to serve the interests of the monarchy in New Spain. Many High Court judges, Treasury officials, and leaders of religious orders also came from Europe, joined by colleagues of American birth—often but not always rotated across the empire's vast jurisdictions to limit loyalty to home communities. From the 1760s the Bourbons increased the preference for officials from Spain in New Spain and across the Americas, creating resentments among American aspirants to office.[6] In a parallel preference for immigrants, most new merchants came from Spain, often from small towns in the mountainous north, to seek fortunes in trade. Those who found wealth repeatedly recruited nephews (or other kin) from home to join them, inherit the business—and with another generation of profit recruit another nephew or two to carry on. Accumulation in trade was an immigrant domain.[7] The preferences gained by newcomers from Spain in high office and profitable trade fueled lurking prejudices against presumably domineering and greedy gachupines.

Still, the preference for immigrants from Spain in office and commerce was but one part of the social trajectory of power in Mexico City and New

Spain. Bourbons aimed to favor newcomers in office to counter long traditions of American influence in affairs where economic interest and regime
powers intersected. Yet in Mexico City and New Spain, new Bourbon appointees were as likely to join the oligarchy as to counter its interests. And while
immigrants found preference in the risky world of commerce, the most successful repeatedly married American women and invested in landed properties that they left to American-born sons and daughters. Successful mine
operators might be of old American mining families like the Bustos and
Sardanetas in Guanajuato, or immigrants like don Pedro Romero de
Terreros—who wed an American heiress and invested in land around his
Real del Monte mines. Constant fusions of commercial, mining, and landed
wealth, of immigrant and American Spaniards, built, sustained, and integrated Mexico City's oligarchy of power.

The regime favored men trained in Spain in appointments to high office;
the risks and profits of commerce were open mostly to newcomers from
Spain; the greater risks of mining drew both Americans and immigrants.
Nearly all married American women and invested their fortunes in the land.
Capital flowed constantly from the risks of mining and trade to more secure
grounding in the land—and from immigrant to American control. Mexico
City oligarchs kept strong ties to regime officials and constantly renewed
their own wealth while sending rising flows of silver to the world economy.
It was an economy of capital accumulation, elite integration, family mainte-
nance, and risk management.

Immigrants from Spain found preference in the risky world of commerce that led to capital accumulation; American Spaniards with vast
holdings on the land ruled the domain of risk management and elite maintenance. In New Spain, especially in the heartland basins around the capital and in the deeply commercial Bajío, landed estates operated as
profit-seeking agribusinesses raising crops to sell for profit in urban markets and mining centers. Unlike landlords in most of Europe, they were not
proprietors drawing rents from peasant villagers or dependent tenants.
They were agrarian capitalists taking profit by selling essential staples and
favored beverages to people in mining centers and the capital.

In the basins around the capital, where the city's landed entrepreneurs
concentrated their holdings, estates that historically raised sugar, wheat, and
livestock added maize and pulque to their production in the eighteenth

century—and generated profits ranging from 6 to 8 percent of the capital value of their properties. Those harvesting wheat and maize on often-irrigated fields stored the bounty of years of good rains, using their capital to hold stocks until the droughts that came every decade drove prices, desperation, and profits to peaks. Others took more regular profit by monopolizing the supply of pulque to the taverns that catered to workingmen in the capital and mining towns like Real del Monte. As urban population grew and the silver economy soared, the commercialization of everyday life made landed estates a profit center far more secure than mining or ocean trades. For men fortunate enough to take wealth from risky mines and trades, estate operation proved a secure haven for capital seeking long-term profits.[8] The regular investment of the profits of mining and trade in landed estates was not a turn from profit seeking to status seeking. It was a way to balance the exceptional risks of mining and trade with the secure profitability of selling essential sustenance to growing urban populations.

With the constant flow of capital from mining and trade to landed investment and estate operation, most leading families joined in both simultaneously. There was never a commercial elite, a mining elite, or a landed elite. An integrated capitalist oligarchy built wealth and power taking risks in mining and trade and then investing in land to gain the more secure profits of selling sustenance.

Oligarchs and Regime Powers

Inevitably, an oligarchy integrating entrepreneurship in finance, mining, trade, and agriculture faced constant negotiations with diverse regime officials, along with conflicts among themselves and those who worked in their mines and fields. To deal with such challenges, the great families of Mexico City built strong ties with key regime leaders. The Condes de Santiago Calimaya were the oldest and most established of Mexico City's great clans—pivotal to stabilizing the city and the silver economy in the crisis of the 1620s. With wealth generated in the late sixteenth century at the intersection of regime power and mining entrepreneurship, they remained a dominant landed clan for centuries. After 1770 they produced pulque in the Mezquital basin near the mines of Real del Monte, cereals at Molino de Flores near Texcoco in the eastern basin of Mexico; they dominated commercial cultivation in the southern Valley of Toluca with their vast Atengo holdings. And

Figure 4. The home of the Condes de Santiago. Photograph by the author.

they made powerful regime officials members of the family throughout the eighteenth century.

Don Domingo Balcarcel came from Spain to take a seat on the Mexico City High Court in 1721. He soon married a daughter of the Conde de Santiago and lived in the clan's inner circle until his death in 1783. At the end of a long career he sat as dean of the court. His official role was to lead the court. His political role was to enable the Santiagos' power, which he did by offering legal advice, inside information, and help with land conflicts and other disputes. Yet when his family in Spain tried to claim one of the Santiago family titles and landed patrimonies in the 1790s, they were blocked at every turn.[9] They failed in good part because the Condes de Santiago brought another High Court judge into the family immediately on Balcarcel's death.

Don Cosme de Mier y Trespalacios came out from Spain as one of the appointees presumed to confirm Bourbon control in Mexico City. In 1785 he married doña Juana María de Velasco y Ovando, heir apparent to the Santiago title and landed power. Mier had his sights on heading New Spain's leading landed clan—but doña Juana María died soon after the wedding, leaving the title and inheritance to a younger sister who never married. The judge, however, never stepped back from the powerful family that embraced him. As the senior male in a generation of women, he often led in public events—even as his sisters-in-law ruled the family economy. In private letters, they always addressed him as "mi hermano"—my brother. He used his legal knowledge and seat on the High Court to back the family's interests in repeated interventions—from spats with villagers in the Valley of Toluca to blocking the claims of Balcarcel's kin in Spain.

Mier too rose to a senior post on the court. He followed Balcarcel in overseeing the great drainage project still aiming to keep the capital free of floods. He led in managing the provision of foodstuffs to the capital in years of drought and profiteering—profit taking that was the base of the Santiagos' continuing prosperity. On his death in 1805, the *Gazeta de México* honored his service in an obituary of powerful praise. Throughout, he served the regime and the interests of the Condes de Santiago Calimaya.[10]

Every major entrepreneurial clan found men to serve them in the halls of power. The Fagoagas gained legal advice from High Court judge don Ciriaco González Carbajal and employed a former viceroy, the Conde de Revillagigedo, as their agent in Spain from 1789 to 1804.[11] In a direct route to the integration of commercial, landed, and regime power, don José Tomás González Calderón arrived from Spain before 1735, joined the business of an uncle already in Mexico City, married his cousin, and amassed a fortune he promptly invested in commercial estates. His eldest son, don Tomás, was born in 1740, educated in the capital, and joined the Bourbon administration. By 1790 he held a seat on the High Court of Lima, sent as an outsider to serve Bourbon aims—perhaps also to bring lessons in New Spain's economic dynamism and social stability to the Andes in the aftermath of the Tupac Amaru risings of the 1780s. By 1801, don Tomás was back home and sitting on the Mexico City Audiencia—a post he would hold into the years of conflict that began in 1808.

Meanwhile, his brother don Miguel González Calderón followed their father into trade, financed mines in the boom years, and bought additional estates. The American-born brothers mixed global commerce, mining finance, estate entrepreneurship, and high office to live near the pinnacle of Mexico City's oligarchy of power. Marriage, business, and interest tied them to the Condes de Santiago Calimaya, the city's most established landed clan, and the Condes de Regla—the most successful of the eighteenth-century newcomers who used trade and mining to become the greatest of landed entrepreneurs in the 1770s.[12]

Capitalist Oligarchs: A Family Biography of Power

The broad pattern of entrepreneurial rise in mining and trade, investment in land to limit risk and sustain wealth and power, and alliance with high officials to ensure regime favor is clear. Perhaps it is too clear. The historical trajectories of the clans that rose to rule Mexico City in the late eighteenth century were never simple, never without twists of uncertainty, never free of conflict, never without unforeseen challenges. An understanding of the oligarchy of silver capitalism, its power and its politics, emerges best from an exploration of complex family histories. The families founded by the men eventually honored as the Conde de San Bartolomé de Jala and the Conde de Santa María de Regla, families of independent power that fused to become one pillar of oligarchic dominance, illuminate the complex, often twisting, and sometimes conflictive paths that led to the heights of power in Mexico City before 1808.

The rise of don Pedro Romero de Terreros to become Conde de Regla is well known.[13] His life was also atypical, thanks to a stunning bonanza at Real de Monte and the fortunate timing that allowed him to buy his choice of the Jesuit estates expropriated in the expulsion of 1767. The life of don Manuel Rodríguez de Pedroso that led to great wealth, title as Conde de Jala, and eventual fusion with the Regla clan is more illustrative of the never-certain paths that led to oligarchic power in Mexico City.

Don Manuel was born in 1697 in the Villa de Viguera, in the La Rioja region of Old Castile. Like many others, he came to New Spain in the early decades of Bourbon rule and silver boom to trade under the auspices of an uncle already in Mexico City. It was there in 1722 that don Manuel married his cousin, doña Juana García de Arellano, who brought a dowry worth 8,000 pesos. Soon after, the young immigrant called himself a *mercader*, a modest merchant, worth a total of 20,000 pesos—including his wife's dowry. When she died less than a decade later, he declared total wealth of 63,583 pesos— including the estates she left to their still-minor children (thus controlled by don Manuel). In 1732 he married doña Josefa de Soria Villaroel, gaining a dowry valued at 12,000 pesos and estates worth over 100,000 pesos. She too died young, leaving don Manuel with another pair of minor children and control of the properties they inherited from their mother.[14]

From his second marriage in 1732 to 1750, his wealth rose from 150,000 pesos to nearly 1,140,000, a gain of a million pesos during decades when silver output in New Spain grew from 9 to 13 million pesos yearly. He built that accumulation by joining diversified trades that spanned the globe to concentrate wealth in Mexico City. He learned to trade from his uncle— who also provided his first wife, her dowry, and modest estates. After gaining a larger dowry and more estates by his second marriage, don Manuel mobilized the advantages of family to profit spectacularly in a boom economy. Keeping his base in Mexico City, the pivot of the silver economy, he stationed brothers in Seville and Manila. Through them he sent silver east and west to buy the luxuries of Europe and Asia to sell in cities, towns, and mining centers across New Spain. He traded in cacao harvested at expanding plantations worked by enslaved Africans around Caracas; he earned a Crown reprimand in the 1740s for cornering the market on the tasty stimulant so in demand in Spain and New Spain when sweetened with slave-grown sugar. Don Manuel also traded in cochineal, the red dye made of insects carefully attended by women in the Mixtec highlands of Oaxaca, purchased there by district magistrates, funded as monopoly merchants by Rodríguez de Pedroso and others, and sold to cloth makers in New Spain and Europe. Like every strong capitalist, don Manuel tapped goods produced in diverse ways— laborers paid high wages to face the risks of silver mining, Africans bound to make cacao, indigenous women producing a valued dye in household economies—to profit in markets wherever he found them.[15]

Along the way he rose to leading positions in the Mexico City Consulado. By 1736 he served as the deputy overseeing the Xalapa commercial fair where goods arriving in the great annual fleet from Seville were traded. By then he earned recognition as a *comerciante almacenero*—a merchant warehouseman participating in the highest levels of trade. In 1739 he was one of two consuls overseeing commercial questions in the capital. In 1759—a time of war that made trade difficult—he won election as prior, the consulado's highest post. He gained the honor of commanding the chamber's militia regiment—part of the forces that in times of crisis might help keep the peace in and around the capital.[16]

While rising to become a leader in global trade, don Manuel pioneered commercial production of pulque, taking profit from growing markets for the fermented brew (the social equivalent of beer) so popular in mining towns and the capital's taverns. By marriage and purchase he acquired grazing properties in the dry northeast of the Valley of Mexico around Otumba. He turned pastures to vast fields of transplanted maguey to sustain commercial production of pulque. He bought city taverns, and from 1742 to 1753 he paid 128,000 pesos for a contract to provide the drink across the city. Estates worth less than 200,000 pesos in the early 1730s rose to nearly 700,000 pesos in value by the late 1760s. Pulque proved profitable; don Manuel's success drew the Jesuit owners of the nearby Santa Lucía estates to the business; together they ruled provision of the capital's taverns in the 1760s.[17]

Commercial capitalism and agrarian capitalism were not separate or sequential businesses for the future Conde de Jala; they were inseparable components of his participation in the silver capitalism focused on Mexico City. In the 1750s, don Manuel briefly tried his hand financing mines, with limited success, likely because reduced Chinese demand had lowered silver prices.[18] That did not inhibit his continued success in silver-funded trade and silver-stimulated pulque.

Inevitably, he drew several immigrant kin to join him in business. Don Francisco Saenz de Sicilia and don Diego Adalid Saenz de Tejada, both from Viguera, were trading under don Manuel by 1752. Not every nephew found wealth equal to his sponsor. Don Francisco's limited success enabled him to buy the single Tomacoco estate at Chalco, a cereal property, and leave it to his son who became a priest.[19] Don Diego Adalid found greater profit in trade, set up his own commercial house in the capital, and left five pulque properties around Otumba and Cempoala to his son don José Adalid, who remained prominent in city affairs through the 1780s and 1790s. His heirs were leaders in Mexico City society and pulque production into the 1840s.[20]

Don Manuel Rodríguez de Pinillos came from Spain to work in his uncle's business in 1757, directing commercial affairs until the conde's death in 1772. The founder supplied capital, contacts, and knowledge; the younger don Manuel oversaw to day-to-day trading in return for a quarter of the profits. He married one of Jala's granddaughters, invested in pulque properties, and in 1778 won title as Marqués de Selva Nevada.[21] The original immigrant don Manuel Rodríguez de Pedroso sponsored three young immigrants.

All took capital in trade and invested in landed estates, the most successful in pulque.

The founder's American children were born to Mexico City's oligarchy of power. Don José Julián Rodríguez de Arellano was the only child of Jala's first marriage to live to adulthood. First son, he was fated for family leadership—when the founder died. In 1751 don José Julián married doña María Francisca Pablo Fernández, daughter of another rising merchant investing in pulque. The goal was the union of two powerful entrepreneurial clans. On marriage, don José Julián gained control (but not ownership) of a share of his future inheritance; he entered the pulque business and joined his father in trade. He became a member of the consulado, appointed a captain in the militia regiment. He formed a trading company with his powerful father, gaining a third of the profits—more than the fourth allowed the immigrant nephews who ran day-to-day business. Yet don José Julián never held an independent role, as his dominating father wrote in a later will.[22]

The patriarch ruled family affairs as long as he lived. Having seen his first son and future patriarch married in a union of entrepreneurial clans in 1751, a year later the founder arranged the marriage of his only daughter, doña Josefa Bernadina, to don Yldefonso Ygnacio Gómez—holder of the pivotal post of secretary of the viceroyalty, ensconced at the heights of regime power. Gómez also operated a small pulque property. As a dowry, doña Josefa Bernadina brought additional pulque estates worth 150,000—and the couple soon profited enough to buy more while producing ten children.[23] Through his daughter's marriage, Jala gained an ear (and likely a voice) in the halls of power, while Gómez became a prosperous purveyor of pulque.

Jala's youngest son don Antonio Julián Rodríguez de Soria was, like doña Josefa Bernadina, a child of the founder's second marriage. In 1761 he married doña Gertrudis de la Cotera y Rivascacho, daughter of another rising merchant also investing in land, more focused on cereals than pulque. The goal was another alliance of powerful clans and a bit of diversification on the land. As don Antonio Julián would not inherit the primary Jala title and properties, the union would not lead to a merger of entrepreneurial-landed power. Still, the younger son gained status and prosperity: on his marriage he received rich pulque estates, a place in the consulado, and a militia command, too. During the 1760s, his pulque sales were second only to his father's within the family.[24] Both don José Julián, presumed to be the future patriarch, and don Antonio Julián prospered under their father's iron rule.

The founder turned seventy in 1767, as riots contested Bourbon impositions in key silver centers not far north in the Bajío. Amid challenges to the regime and economy that had enabled his rise, he found satisfaction in all he had achieved. He had built a vast fortune in global trades, pioneered the pulque business, and set his children and several nephews at the heights of power in Mexico City. He had forged ties with two other rising merchant clans—and found an ally at the heart of the regime. He surely had attained all he imagined when he arrived as an immigrant from Viguera in the 1720s—likely more.

Yet as long as family organized entrepreneurship, power, and succession, nothing was certain. The vagaries of life and death could undermine the best of plans. In 1769, Viceregal Secretary Gómez died, leaving doña Josefa Bernadina a widow with ten children and the family without a place in the halls of power. Then don José Julián Rodríguez de Arellano, heir to family rule and title, died in 1770, while his aging father lived. Amid grief and uncertainty, the founder decided to alter the succession. He granted his widowed daughter additional estates plus a 3,000-peso stipend for life to ensure that she and his many grandchildren would live comfortably. He aimed to alter the succession to the Jala title and the rich pulque estates tied to it by locking them together in an inalienable entail—a regime-sanctioned corporate unit. Without the change, they would go to the late don José Julián's daughter, doña María Josefa Rodríguez Pablo Fernández. The aging patriarch insisted she would gain ample property from her mother's family (the Pablo Fernández). He decided to remove her from the primary succession in favor of his younger son, don Antonio Julián Rodríguez de Soria. The attempt set off conflicts within the heights of power worthy of a soap opera—yet ultimately revealing of the ways that sustained power in Mexico City's ruling oligarchy.[25]

As soon as the aging conde filed the new will removing his granddaughter from the primary inheritance, the Pablo Fernández family went to court demanding reinstatement of the original succession. An enraged Jala responded by cutting doña María Josefa fully out of his legacy, stating that he would rather support his widowed daughter and her many children than a granddaughter who brought him nothing but bother and insolence. In a strong countermove, the Pablo Fernández family arranged the marriage of

the disinherited granddaughter, a minor of only sixteen, to don Francisco
Leandro de Viana in 1771.

Viana was a European Spaniard, educated and drawn into the service of
the Bourbon regime. He had risen to become a senior judge on the High
Court of Manila, where he negotiated relations between Mexico City merchants and the resident Chinese traders who exchanged the wares of Asia for
New Spain's silver. Viana had dealt with the British occupation of 1763, the
return to Spanish rule, and the revival of Pacific trade that followed.[26] Few
knew the heights of regime power and the ways of global silver trades better
than Viana. On appointment to the court in Mexico City, he quickly learned
the pivotal importance of capital's oligarchy, its power over commerce and
landed investment, and the opportunities they might bring to an official with
power and vision. A man of mature years, he accepted the hand of the disinherited young woman and led the challenge to Jala's new will—a challenge
destined to go before the court on which Viana sat. Nothing was resolved
before the elder Conde de Jala died in early 1772, as he neared seventy-five
years. His adamant power had stymied any compromise or resolution.

In February, as they faced unknowable sentiments of grief and perhaps
relief at the iron-handed patriarch's passing, the claimants called a council
to resolve the disputed inheritance without recourse to the court. To arbi-
trate, they invited the Conde de Santiago Calimaya, the city's leading landed
patriarch, the Conde de San Mateo Valparaíso, a great landed entrepreneur
in northern mining regions, and the Conde de San Pedro de Alamo and the
Marqués de San Miguel de Aguayo, both heirs to fortunes built by silver
bankers, now consolidating on the land. Also present were a leading cleric,
Doctor don Luis de Hoyos y Mier, dean of the Mexico City Cathedral, and
judge don Vicente de Herrera, an immigrant Spaniard recently appointed to
serve Bourbon interests alongside Viana on the High Court.

Powerful men represented each of the three claimants—though two
were women. Viana pressed the interests of his young wife. Don Manuel
Rodríguez de Pinillos, the founders' last *cajero* who had married a granddaughter, looked after the claims of his mother-in-law, the widowed doña
Josefa Bernadina. Don Antonio Julián, designated in his father's last will to
become principal heir and Conde de Jala, represented himself. They reached
an agreement that kept close to the founder's final goals—and made meaningful concessions to Viana and his young wife.

Don Antonio Julián would receive the title and entailed properties, con-firming his role as patriarch and leading pulque producer. Doña Josefa Bernadina would receive most of her father's unentailed properties, plus the promised 3,000-peso stipend to help her support her many children. She too would remain a leading pulque grower—surely aided by Rodríguez de Pinillos, who was a rising producer, too. And the young doña María Josefa Rodríguez Pablo Fernández was paid 150,000 pesos—120,000 from the now-confirmed second Conde de Jala and 30,000 from the widow doña Josefa Bernadina—in exchange for an agreement, signed by Viana, to cease all claims to the title and entailed estates. Would that concession have come without Viana's power and the presence of his colleague Herrera among the arbitrators? To pay, don Antonio Julián had to sell his only property free of entail, the rich pulque estate named Ojo de Agua just north of Texcoco. Viana and his young bride invested their windfall in other pulque properties, tying regime power to prosperity in the pulque economy. For decades to come, capital built in silver trades and invested in the Mexico City pulque economy would generate profits to sustain the many branches of the family empire built by don Manuel Rodríguez de Pedroso, first Conde de Jala. They competed with each other while prospering together in a rich agrarian capi-talism that supplied drink to the capital's growing population.[27]

Firmly in power as patriarch of one of the capital's dominant entrepre-neurial clans, the second Conde de Jala still had obligations. First, he had to keep the profits of pulque flowing—which he did with good success. Second, he had to see to patriarchal succession. His only heir was his daughter, doña María Josefa Rodríguez de la Cotera, who would one day inherit the title and entail. In 1780, she wed don Pedro Joseph Ramón Romero de Terreros, eldest son and heir apparent to the fortune built in silver and invested in once-Jesuit pulque estates by his father, the Conde de Regla. The union arranged by powerful fathers was a merger of immense impact, consolidating a near-monopoly in the pulque economy and defining power at the peak of the Mexico City oligarchy for decades to come.

A year after the marriage, the founding Conde de Regla died and the merger was set. Don Pedro Joseph became second Conde, leader of the rich-est and most landed family in the capital, exceeding the great holdings of the long dominant Condes de Santiago Calimaya and, by alliance with the Jala clan, ruling the pulque market. His dynastic work done and long widowed,

Figure 5. The palace of the Condes de Regla. Photograph by the author.

Figure 6. Façade of the palace of the Condes de Regla. Photograph by the author.

the second Conde de Jala took Holy Orders to become a priest in 1784. Did that mean he retired to a life of contemplation, leaving business to his powerful new son-in-law? Perhaps, but we know that don José Sánchez Espinosa, another landed patriarch, widowed around 1780, became a priest, yet for decades kept adamant and profitable control of landed operations from the outskirts of Mexico City, through the pulque zone and the Bajío, to northern San Luis Potosí.[28] However active or retired, the second Conde de Jala kept his title and properties until his death in 1817—when the merger with the Reglas was completed (in very different times of conflict).[29]

The founding Conde de Regla's rise to the pinnacle of wealth in New Spain's silver economy is famous.[30] His ties to the regime are less known, yet essential to understand his unprecedented accumulations and the enduring importance of Regla family power during the decades after his death. Following a long line of uncles to New Spain, Romero arrived from a town in Extremadura to trade in Querétaro in the early 1730s. After his uncle's death, he took over the business, operated an *obraje* (textile workshop), and in 1741 began to fund mining at Real del Monte, draining once-rich mines in search of new bonanzas. From 1741 to 1762, he invested nearly 2.5 million pesos, part from profits of trade, part from reinvested silver. Then, during Spain's involvement in the wars of 1757–1763, silver began to flow beyond imagining. During forty years of mining at Real de Monte, Romero paid the Crown over 2.5 million pesos in mining taxes—indicating output of over 20 million pesos.[31]

His entrepreneurial drive and success cannot be doubted. Yet at key moments in his rise to wealth and landed investment, relations with regime officials mattered. He faced riotous workers protesting his profit-seeking attempts to cut ore shares and wages in 1766. He tried to negotiate a solution personally, proposing that the skilled keep ore shares, but that laborers' wages still fall 25 percent; worker solidarity turned to violent anger that cost the life of one of Romero's managers; the entrepreneur barely escaped. The authorities mobilized three hundred militiamen to restore order and sent High Court judge don Francisco Javier de Gamboa to mediate a solution accepted by Regla and his workers. Silver kept flowing.[32]

Knowing the importance of the regime to mining and economic success, Romero found a key ally during the late 1760s and through the 1770s as his mines yielded peak flows and he invested in expropriated Jesuit estates. Don Fernando José Mangino was another Iberian sent to represent Bourbon interests, serving as director of the mint and administrator of ex-Jesuit properties. Any assistance Mangino provided to Romero in favorable dealings at the mint or in access to and the pricing of Jesuit estates remains undocumented. But the well-placed official did assist in founding three entails based on those properties, in negotiating the union of the Regla and Jala clans, and in the complex distribution of the Regla properties among six heirs in 1782. Such assistance was not an obstacle to advance in the regime. In 1787, Mangino was appointed superintendant in Mexico City, a new position that rivaled the viceroy in the capital and nearby regions. When bureaucratic conflict questioned the change and viceregal power prevailed, Mangino won a seat on the Council of the Indies, which oversaw all of Spain's imperial affairs.[33]

As Mangino moved from serving as a powerful ally in Mexico City to become a more powerful ally in Spain, the second conde drew another senior official into the Regla family. Don Vicente Herrera was an audiencia judge

sent from Spain to ensure Bourbon rule. He had joined in the arbitration that
settled the Jala family inheritance in 1772—guaranteeing the wealth of the
woman who became second Condesa de Regla by marriage in 1782. Herrera
also helped his colleague Viana gain a rich settlement for his young bride.
Herrera clearly knew how to negotiate at the heights of power where great
entrepreneurial clans engaged high regime officials. What better husband for
the second Conde de Regla's young sister, doña María Dolores. She married
Herrera with reluctance in the 1780s; having fled a first wedding to the aging
judge, she bowed to patriarchal pressure in a second ceremony. Herrera
gained control of a landed patrimony valued over 600,000 pesos, richer than
Viana's. Both Herrera and Viana gained titles, the former as Marqués de
Herrera, the latter as Conde de Tepa. Both won seats on the Council of the
Indies; together they authored a famous *memorial* advising the king not to
challenge the power of the Mexico City oligarchs who ruled the economy
that sustained Spain in the world economy and European power politics.[34]
That respect became policy in the 1780s and 1790s, when in the face of the
war for independence in British North America and then the French and
Haitian revolutions and the wars they stimulated, Madrid recognized that
the silver economy ruled by Mexico City oligarchs was essential to its survival in the competition for Atlantic power.

When the second Conde de Regla inherited the Real del Monte mines
in 1781, they had flooded again and barely operated. Aiming to emulate his
father's legendary success and responding to a soaring demand for silver in
the world economy, from 1781 to 1801 he invested 3,450,000 pesos in draining and operating mines and 400,000 in updating refineries, while paying
822,000 to the Crown for mercury essential to refining. In the same decades he produced 6,400,000 pesos of silver—paying another 833,000 in
taxes. From the second Regla's efforts and investments, the Crown gained
1,650,000 pesos, minus the cost of making and shipping mercury. Regla
profited just over 900,000 pesos—a handsome sum, but far less than his
father gained for less investment.[35] Such were the vagaries of mining; such
uncertainties were the reason men who built capital in mining and trade
repeatedly sought safer investments in commercial estates.

In landed entrepreneurship, few approached the power of the second
Conde de Regla after 1782. His personal landed inheritance exceeded
640,000 pesos of prime former Jesuit estates; he ran the properties of his

younger brother, don José Terreros, Marqués de San Cristóbal, famed in youth as a playboy, later in life as a Paris physician, whose estates were worth nearly 450,000 pesos. The second conde also operated the estates of his three younger sisters, each holding properties valued over 600,000 pesos. Only doña María Dolores married, and when she joined Herrera on his appointment in Madrid, they lived on income generated by her brother's managers. The second conde ruled properties mixing pulque, cereal, and livestock production, many clustered between Mexico City and Real de Monte, and valued at 3 million pesos. Presuming low yields of 5 percent yearly, the estates provided at least 150,000 pesos yearly to sustain the conde, his kin, and dependents.[36]

Through the 1780s, the Regla family empire of silver and pulque prospered nicely. In the 1790s, as mining costs rose and yields fell while war made finance and trade risky, the second conde began to borrow to keep his mines working—just over 80,000 pesos, a minor sum in the context of his huge wealth and valuable estates. In 1801 he shut down the mines again. Wartime made mercury and iron scarce, uncertain, and expensive—and profit margins at Real del Monte were already low. He kept borrowing. By 1808, he owed 130,000 pesos, most to silver bankers of the Valdivieso, Fagoaga, and Aldaca families, some to diverse Church lenders.[37] Carrying those debts cost 6,500 pesos yearly, a small sum in Regla's annual earnings. Meanwhile, he drew close to don José de Iturrigaray, viceroy from 1803 to 1808. Again, entrepreneurial and regime powers worked together, seeking mutual benefit in difficult years—until Napoleon's invasion provoke the unimagined crisis that toppled the viceroy in 1808. The second Conde de Regla died in 1809; his wife, Condesa de Regla and future Condesa de Jala, took family leadership and held it through trying times.[38]

The Power of Silver Capitalism

At the heights of power in Mexico City, powerful entrepreneurial clans mixed finance, mining, global trade, and agrarian capitalism with strong ties to leading officials of a Bourbon regime that aimed to strengthen its powers—and recognized its dependence on the silver economy ruled by New Spain's oligarchs. Within Mexico City's oligarchy of power, there were competitions and conflicts—within and between entrepreneurial clans, between financiers and mine operators, among competitors in the capital's pulque market, and between landlords competing over favored properties. From the 1760s to the 1780s, many resented and resisted the officials led by the arrogant Visitor General don José de Gálvez who pressed to strengthen regime power while entrepreneurs struggled to instruct him in their—and his—essential interest: the preservation of silver capitalism. By the 1790s, the oligarchs had prevailed. Throughout, the common interests of the silver oligarchy kept conflicts contained. The silver flowing from New Spain's mines and through Mexico City's mint rose from 12 million pesos yearly around 1770 to average nearly 24 million from 1790 to 1809. The wealth generated by that prosperity was both cause and consequence of the oligarchs' dominating powers and enduring negotiations with each other and regime officials.

Among the conflicts that did not divide the oligarchy that ruled Mexico City, New Spain, and silver capitalism after 1770 was an opposition between American and European Spaniards. All considered themselves Spaniards first. Americans among them were simply españoles; only immigrant new-comers gained a modifier—as europeos or peninsulares. (No one in the oli-garchy called her or himself a criollo; no one insulted immigrants as gachupines.) While immigrants found favored roles in commerce and office, they so regularly married their American-born cousins and left their wealth to American-born children that a fundamental rift was somewhere between impossible and dysfunctional at the heights of power. Oligarchy ruled.

That does not mean there were no prejudices against the immigrants from Spain who rose so visibly to join the oligarchy of power. But the resent-ments that generated the pejorative gachupín lived outside the oligarchy, among the less powerful and working peoples of the city and elsewhere. As long as oligarchic power and silver capitalism flourished, those resentments were contained—as we shall see. Those powers began to crack in 1808 when armed gachupines led the September coup that ended the mediating regime. When the silver economy collapsed after 1810, anti-immigrant resentments soared to focus new political debates and conflicts. Before the crisis, oligar-chy ruled, silver soared, most city people found livable lives, and resentments against gachupines were limited. To understand both the resentments and their limits, we must look into lives negotiated in the shadow of oligarchic power.

CHAPTER 3

In the Shadows of Power

Oligarchs, Provincials, and Professionals

THE VAST MAJORITY OF THE MORE THAN 120,000 PEOPLE IN MEXICO City around 1800 lived far from the heights of power. While perhaps two dozen exceptionally powerful clans mixed entrepreneurship in finance and trade, mining and agriculture, and engaged top regime officials, a larger community of estate operators, professionals, and modest traders lived in their shadows. A few hundred families in the latter group found lives of prosperous comfort beyond the possibilities of most in the city and across New Spain. Yet they were more likely to serve powerful oligarchs and high officials than to engage them as equals. While oligarchs jockeyed for power in a politics of empire and global trade, the landed professionals locked in a second tier of prosperity and service in Mexico City saw their politics limited to the city and its council—and petitions to regime magistrates. They were provincial elites subject to and dependent on the oligarchy that ruled silver capitalism.

Did lesser powers, limited wealth, and dependence lead to resentments? Probably. But as long as silver capitalism held strong they were muted by shared, if unequal, participations in the powers that ruled the city and silver capitalism. While oligarchs with towering power engaged men who led the empire, provincial elites dealt primarily with the Mexico City Council and

Church institutions based in the capital. The council worked to regulate life in a city dependent on an economy ruled by the oligarchs. The archbishop and other leading clerics aimed to speak for Christianity as they faced a regime that aimed to limit Church funds and independence, leaving church-men and women dependent on an economy ruled by the oligarchy.[1] The landed professionals—legal, clerical, and others—who formed the core of Mexico City's provincial elite ruled the metropolis and staffed the Church in the shadows of the oligarchy of power.

The immigrants who came from Spain to serve uncles or other kin in trade lived parallel lives of dependence. They too prospered in service to powerful oligarchs. Yet in the capital's second tier of wealth and power, only immigrant traders had prospects of ascent into the oligarchy—as seen in the biographies of oligarchical power.[2] So young men on the make stayed close to their merchant-uncles, kept distant from the landed professionals who lived in parallel yet less promising dependence on landed oligarchs. Immigrant traders perhaps did develop a bit of the arrogance of advantage that marked them as resented gachupines. Still, their goal was to rise to the oligarchy, marry an American landed heiress, and father American children. As long as silver boomed and the regime held, the fissures inherent in lives of stratified power remained limited—contained until the crisis of 1808 turned them into fractures that helped break imperial legitimacy and shook silver capitalism.

Provincial Elites: Subordinate and Separate

Families with modest landed properties, some built on mining and trade in the distant past, others acquired more recently, formed the core of the city's provincial elite. They mixed estate operation with professional roles, at times complemented by food processing and distribution. A large sample of 113 Mexico City-based families holding 314 estates between 1770 and 1810 dif-ferentiates landed oligarchs from provincial elites: 17 rich clans held 161 prop-erties, nearly 10 estates each, spread around the capital, clustered in the pulque zone, and extending across the Bajío and regions north. Fifteen per-cent of proprietors, oligarchs all, held over half the estates tied to the city. The 96 remaining families held 153 estates, one or two each, most in basins near the city. While the landed wealth of the great families often exceeded a mil-lion pesos each, and in the case of the Condes de Regla passed three million, most provincials held properties in the range of 100,000 to 200,000 pesos. Such holdings would yield 5,000 to 10,000 pesos yearly—great wealth when rural families nearby lived on less than 50 pesos, and urban producers got by on less than 100. The provincials were landed elites by any standard—except that of the Mexico City oligarchy.[3]

With fewer and less valuable properties, provincials were less able to diversify production, less likely to have capital from merchant kin, less able to fund production and hold crops for years to await peak prices. As a result, while oligarchs took profits ranging from 6 to 8 percent yearly, provincials often gained 4 or 5 percent—and they often had to share those gains with mortgage lenders, usually Church bankers. Provincial elites' estates helped feed the city; they sustained their families and the Church in prosperous comfort. In the effort, always short on capital, they struggled in ways most oligarchs did not.

To diversify their social roles and sources of income, many joined the professions, legal and ecclesiastical. Others operated bakeries or other city food businesses. In a sample of thirty-six provincial landed families in Mexico City, 60 percent included professionals: eight lawyers, seven clerics, three bureaucrats, and three physicians. In their learned endeavors, many served the Church; more depended on oligarchs. Nearly half joined in food processing, including six operating bakeries, four running pork butcheries, and three keeping pulque taverns (a business ruled by oligarchs). Four found income leasing out urban real estate. Yet even with that diversification and the income it brought, they depended on Church mortgages for financing, thus sharing their profits. Provincials could not compete with the oligarchs.[4]

With lesser landholdings, lesser profits, and lesser political powers, provincial elites lived lives marked by dependence—on credit and the Church, on service to oligarchs and the regime. Don Luis Gonzaga González Maldonado and don Antonio Rodríguez de Velasco, both lawyers, held proprietary seats on the Mexico City Council. González Maldonado operated modest estates in the southern Mezquital; Rodríguez de Velasco held small but productive properties in the chinampa zone south of the capital between Coyoacán and Xochimilco. To stay afloat and profit modestly, the pursuit of mortgages and extensions was a constant focus.[5] Similar reliance on modest estates and credit marked the efforts of don Pedro Alcántara del Valle, judge of weights at the Mexico City Mint in the 1780s and 1790s.[6] Don José Mariano Beristáin de Sousa, dean of the Mexico City Cathedral and a leading intellectual in the years leading to 1808, held properties worth but 15,000 pesos and kept them to his death.[7] More prosperous was don José Patricio Uribe, who in the 1780s and 1790s rose to serve as canon at the Cathedral and hold the Chair in Sacred Scripture at the Royal and Pontifical University. His three estates near Acolman were worth 147,000 pesos, and he prospered enough to lease and operate a neighboring property.[8]

Confirmation that men of the capital's provincial elite led an integrated community of secondary power, distinct from the oligarchy that dominated the viceroyalty, comes from a revealing source. When prominent residents of Mexico City died—and both oligarchs and provincial elites were prominent—printed funeral notices shared the news. The deceased's principal kin and social allies signed (in print) as mourners. Among landed oligarchs such as the Condes de Santiago Calimaya and merchant banking Fagoagas, signatories were few and included only close kin, top officials, and members of other leading clans.[9] In contrast, notices of the death of provincial elites included few truly powerful men—and large circles of modest estate owners, bureaucrats, clerics, professionals, and produce dealers.[10]

When don Miguel Mota Sanz, holder of an old but small landed entail, passed away in 1801, thirty signatories mourned. Included were his son and heir, four members of similarly old but enduring landed families, and one newcomer to landed status. The latter, don Bartolomé Guardamino, belonged to a family that had begun in trade, never scaled the heights of commercial success, and invested in modest estates in the Tlalpujahua valley—next to the Mota properties. In addition, at least five professionals (lawyers and clergy), one bureaucrat, and a pulquero mourned don Miguel's passing. An array of academic degrees announced the education and professional participation of many more. The circle that mourned don Manuel Mota Sanz was the Mexico City provincial elite in microcosm.[11]

The career of don Vicente Gudiel Roldán illuminates the struggles and endurance of such elites. Trained as a physician and pharmacist, he practiced both professions in the capital. From an uncle he inherited the Gudiel entail, founded in 1598 and including two estates near Acolman, plus a bakery and retail space in the city. Don Vicente operated the estates on his own account while leasing out the urban holdings. After gaining the entail, he used credit to buy additional city income properties and a pulque rancho near Acolman. Mortgage liens encumbered just under half the value of the new acquisitions.[12] The medical practice and estate operation allowed Gudiel to buy 200 pesos' worth of books, pharmaceutical and medical treatises as well as volumes on government, commerce, and religion. Professional knowledge and political awareness defined his life. He bought luxuries to announce his status in the city: 758 pesos on wardrobe; 678 pesos on gold, silver, and jewelry.[13] A working family in the city would need to devote a decade of income to buy such fine clothes and ornaments of elite life. Still, Gudiel's wealth in property and luxuries paled before the holdings of the great families.

After his death in 1790, inventories and accounts showed his medical and pharmacy practices were economically sound, as were his estate operations around Acolman—though the latter yielded less profit than the larger diversified holdings of the Regla and Jala families who ruled the countryside just north. Yet his testamentary estate faced difficulty. He had kept up payments on the mortgages he took to buy and operate his own properties. But he had signed as guarantor for a friend's loan of 13,000 pesos from the Cathedral's Juzgado de Capellañías (a mortgage bank). The debtor defaulted, the obligation fell to Gudiel, and in 1785 the Juzgado embargoed his city properties.[14] He kept them until his death—when creditors forced the operation of all Gudiel's holdings by an executor while the heirs remained minors. The executor paid the Church creditor and the 240 pesos in annual tuition for Gudiel's two sons at a city seminary. Destined to be landed priests in the provincial elite, both succumbed to early deaths (likely to smallpox). The small entail passed to their sister, who married don José Robles, a lawyer. Combining her estates and his profession, they lived comfortably into the nineteenth century as landed provincials.[15]

Provincials and Politics: The City Council

Provincials had long ruled the Mexico City Council, until a reform negotiated in the early 1770s (detailed in chapter 6) brought in a minority of oligarchs. In the late eighteenth century, the council consisted of fifteen *regidores propietarios*, permanent councilmen whose families had purchased seats that passed on by inheritance on each generation's payment of a confirmation fee. That core of proprietors elected six *regidores honorarios* to two-year terms and two *alcaldes* (magistrates) serving one-year each. The great majority of proprietors were members of older landed clans settled in the provincial elite. The nineteenth-century historian Lucas Alamán called them "ruined."[16] A sample of twenty-four families with thirty-four offices on the council shows only older and usually lesser clans holding proprietary seats; rising newcomers did not see the roles as worth the investment. Yet a council ruled by provincials chose rising newcomers to hold the pivotal yet rotating offices of alcalde, the magistrates overseeing city justice, by a two-to-one margin over their provincial peers. And when selecting honorary councilmen after 1770, they nearly always chose rising oligarchs to sit for limited terms.[17] The council was a bastion of provincial elites who, as proprietary regidores, regularly chose men on the rise to join them for a time.

The primary role of the council was to regulate urban affairs—streets, canals, markets, and food supplies—and to promote the social peace (called *policía*) that kept the city's diverse peoples in order. As the primary business of landed oligarchs and provincials was seeking profit supplying the city with food and drink, they shared key interests. Yet their common goals came laden with contradictions. Landed entrepreneurs great and small aimed to sell wheat and maize, meat and pulque to city consumers at the highest price possible. City consumers demanded ample supplies at low prices. The contradiction came to the fore when drought drove maize prices to peaks. Commercial growers storing accumulated stocks held them off the market awaiting prices three to four times the norm; consumers faced deepening poverty as they paid all they had to buy staples. A council of men seeking profit from scarce staples was charged with delivering regular supplies at bearable prices to the city granary—the alhóndiga.[18] The contradiction was clear—and favored landed entrepreneurs with or without council seats.

Still, all knew of the riots of 1692 and lesser protests since. All knew that neither the council nor viceregal authorities had forces able to control a population passing one hundred thousand in the 1770s. Ultimately, all understood that for the city to prosper in the long run, the short-term goal of profit from scarcity had to be balanced by a long-term interest in sustaining social peace and silver capitalism. In the search for that balance, older proprietors holding permanent seats drew rising newcomers with great capital and greater estates to join them on the council—if briefly. Their collaboration fed the metropolis and kept the peace—allowing landed entrepreneurs, great and small, to profit without threatening stability.

Why did rising oligarchs with ample capital and vast and profitable estates seek and accept brief roles on a council where they would be outvoted by lesser provincials? Such terms brought learning about council ways, roles overseeing city life, and relationships with men who would continue in such roles. For capitalists shifting from accumulation in trade to estate operations, a year or two as councilmen brought knowledge of urban markets while announcing a new place in the oligarchy.

Most coveted were terms as magistrates: in the sample of city power, twelve rising oligarchs and seven established provincials took on the obligation of overseeing justice in the city for a year. Everyday governance in New Spain was primarily judicial. The regime and the council set regulations; judges negotiated implementation. Every year, two elected magistrates oversaw judicial implementation of the most important questions of the day. Men on the rise, whether inheriting estates or turning commercial gain into landed wealth, regularly sat as magistrates. These were active, demanding roles giving the holder pivotal influence for a year—and announcing his power across the city. It was effort worth the time of men on the rise. Then they left, leaving council affairs to provincials and judicial oversight to another newcomer who would serve for a year and move on. Sequentially, men on the rise helped regulate and stabilize city life and then turned to the politics of power that linked oligarchical families and regime leaders at the heights of silver capitalism.

Who ruled the Mexico City Council? Whose interests did it serve? Day-to-day and in the long run, landed provincials held the majority of proprietary seats and selected the newcomers who joined briefly yet regularly as magistrates and honorary councilmen. In times of crisis, the magistrates might lead. Perhaps the provincials who dominated the council needed the influence and respect brought by newcomers who passed through on their way to higher power. Rising oligarchs found council service a useful step in their climb. In the long run, oligarchs dominated New Spain; a council of provincials, most dependent on oligarchs, regulated and mediated everyday life in the city.

Provincials and the Church: Ties of Interdependence

Provincial elites and the Church also linked in complex ways, creating a strong interdependence. Many provincials relied on Church credit to join in the estate economy that fed the capital. While the Augustinian and Dominican orders still held a few estates operated to support their activities, after the expulsion and expropriation of the Jesuits in 1767, clergy and Church institutions in New Spain gained most of their income by taxing commercial agriculture, lending to estate operators, and taking fees for services from parishioners. Mexico City provincial landlords paid tithes that sustained the bishops and held mortgages that supported many clerics, often their kin.

The bishops received tithes (10 percent of harvests and livestock reproduction—levied on the Hispanic sector of the economy). Private contractors ruled collection for a fee into the 1760s; the Church took over direct collection from 1770. Given their dominance of estate agriculture and commercial grazing, oligarchic landlords might have paid most to the Church in and around Mexico City. But like tax-avoiding entrepreneurs everywhere, many oligarchs found ways to escape the tithe. Membership in the Spanish noble orders of Santiago, Calatrava, and Alcántara—too often seen as mere emblems of honor—brought exemption from the tithe. Most oligarchic cultivators belonged.[19] Others found different ways to escape: the estates that made don José Sánchez Espinosa a leading entrepreneur were incorporated as an *obra pía*—a pious foundation exempt from the tithe, an exemption he defended adamantly despite taking Holy Orders as a priest.[20] Such exemptions left the tithe to be paid primarily by less-powerful estate operators, tenant growers, and smallholders. (Indigenous growers of native produce were exempt.) Provincial landlords in New Spain's capital and outlying provinces were the primary contributors to the tithes that funded the bishops and cathedral chapters.

Priests serving parishes, urban and rural, did not gain income from the tithes. They relied on combinations of fees paid by parishioners—and chaplaincies. The latter were endowments ranging from 1,000 to 5,000 pesos and paying 5 percent interest, providing 50 to 250 pesos yearly. Many merchants and mine operators founded chaplaincies as they invested in landed properties; established landowners, men and women, did the same when they wrote wills. A preferred elder son (or a daughter in his absence) normally inherited most lands and any title; younger sons and daughters gained lesser estates. Chaplaincies offered support to nephews and more distant kin. The founder named the first recipient and the rules of succession; the endowment remained a charge against annual estate earnings—the cleric receiving payment from family managers. Lesser endowments, often left by women who inherited wealth but did not manage estates, were let out as mortgages by the Juzgado de Capellañías, the Cathedral office that lent mortgages, oversaw collections, and pressed foreclosures if stipends were not paid. The best-paid clergy outside cathedral chapters, and some within them, gained stipends from oligarchs or the juzgado. The latter became a leading mortgage lender, enabling provincial elites and other proprietors to gain capital to expand, repair, or otherwise finance estates.

Relations among the juzgado, provincial entrepreneurs, and clergy were negotiated among relative equals. Provincials invested in chaplaincies, their clerical kin lived on them, and the juzgado negotiated between them. Similar ties linked nunneries and provincial elites. Landed testators regularly left dowries to fund young women's entrance to convents. Over the centuries, convents accumulated endowments that made them leading mortgage lenders, best called convent banks, advancing funds to provincial elites to buy, expand, and develop estates while funding convent life with the 5 percent annual returns.

The juzgado and the convent banks sustained—and were sustained by— provincial elites (in the capital and the provinces). As the goal of Church lenders was to fund clerics, they left capital invested as long as income flowed. Church bankers and provincial elites became partners in the agricultural economy. Only if interest was not paid did problems develop that might lead to foreclosure. In late eighteenth-century Mexico City, foreclosures were rare, usually postponed until the debtor-landholder died. At Chalco, the capital's historic granary and a bastion of provincial elite landholding, only four estates faced bankruptcy auction in the 1780s, another four in the 1790s; in the face of new pressures from 1800 to 1809 only six properties faced auction.[21] Mexico City provincials depended on Church mortgages to sustain estates, families, and clerical kin. They juggled credit and profit; their prosperity was not automatic—but it was real and often enduring. When in 1805 the regime in Madrid pressed the Consolidation of Royal Bonds, a revenue program that called in Church mortgages, provincial elites faced new uncertainties. They protested, backed by key oligarchs—and carried on for a few more years.

Oligarchs and Provincials: Ties of Dependence
While Church mortgages financed provincial estate operators and sustained clergy, many clerics depended on endowments maintained and paid directly by oligarchs. Responsible for bequests by generations of pious ancestors, the

Condes de Santiago had perhaps the largest such obligations. A 1785 account listed chaplaincies due twenty-three clerics and two institutions; endowments totaling 64,880 pesos delivered 2,600 pesos, about 100 pesos each if they gained equal sums (unlikely). Another list of obligations from 1794 accounted for an additional 161,900 pesos in endowments, with stipends due sixteen clerics and religious houses. These richer endowments averaged 10,000 pesos, paying 500 annually to each recipient. In 1799, a member of the Santiago family described the family estates as "heavily burdened" with chaplaincies due priests "who need them in order to eat."[22]

For a provincial elite family, obligations on capital of 200,000 pesos would direct its entire income to the clergy; for the Santiagos with holdings exceeding 2 million pesos in value, such obligations directed about 10 percent of annual earnings to clerics and Church institutions—ensuring their dependence. Don José Sánchez Espinosa owed over 6,000 pesos yearly to pay dowries for young women entering convents, equivalent to an endowment of 120,000 pesos. He also named holders of several chaplaincies for priests. And he named and paid resident chaplains at several northern estates that were far from town centers. His correspondence includes endless letters from clerical aspirants politely begging for favors he might bestow.[23] In those solicitations, relations of dependence became clear and at times abject. When in 1800 don Francisco Calzado won a chaplaincy, he sent a note to thank Sánchez Espinosa. The news had come via Sánchez Espinosa's friend, don Antonio Rubín de Celis, prior of the Collegiate Church of Guadalupe—called by Calzado "mi protector."[24] Clergy dependent on education, piety, and chaplaincies lived at the base of the provincial elite, serving oligarchs while engaging the populace.

Economic power and religious life could mesh among the powerful in Mexico City. The second Conde de Jala and don José Sánchez Espinosa both took Holy Orders after consolidating vast properties. They lived for decades as priest-oligarchs. Don Francisco Ignacio Gómez Rodríguez de Pedroso, priest and nephew of the priest-Conde de Jala, was one of ten children of a widowed mother with limited lands. He served as Treasurer of the Mexico City Cathedral in 1801, supported by his kin's landed wealth while bringing deep knowledge of the business of the land to the Cathedral.[25]

More often, priest-managers served powerful oligarchs. Don José Fernández Mora was a distant cousin of the priest-patriarch don José Sánchez

Espinosa—linked by the latter's short-lived marriage to the daughter of the Conde de Peñasco. For more than two decades Fernández Mora lived in Sánchez Espinosa's Mexico City household, helping manage the landed patriarch's businesses.[26] Yet when the dependent cleric-manager died in 1802, the funeral announcement did not list his powerful sponsor. Instead, the mourning signatories were bureaucrats, professionals, and clergy. Fernández Mora lived and served in the household of a landed oligarch, a priest-patriarch who was his kinsman. Still, the priest-manager lived as a dependent, socially anchored in the capital's provincial elite.[27]

Other managers were not clerics. Don José and don Luis Marrugat called themselves merchants, but they served the first Conde de Regla as general managers in the capital while he oversaw his bonanza at Real del Monte and invested in ex-Jesuit estates. Both aided in the division and distribution of Regla's vast estates in the early 1780s. As reward, don Luis gained a lease to operate one property through the last decades of the eighteenth century—a role his widow retained in 1821.[28] Such leasing, of course, was administration with the incentive of profit sharing. When Marrugat shifted to leasing in 1785, don Antonio Salinas lived on a clerical stipend from the Condes de Santiago.[29] He soon became confessor and business counselor to the second Conde de Regla, a tie that lasted three decades. For his service, the priest gained several chaplaincies administered by Regla family.[30]

Don José Sánchez Espinosa kept numerous dependents to facilitate his estate operations. Don José Torijo trained in the 1780s as a notary, a specialist in recording property transactions—a profession useful to any landed entrepreneur. He borrowed funds to pay for the royal patent he needed to work but struggled to extract it from the bureaucracy. Appealing to Sánchez Espinosa, for whom bureaucratic dealings were a way of life, Torijo got the license. He prospered as a notary and assisted the priest-patriarch whenever he could.[31] In the 1790s Torijo's brother won an important clerical post in San Luis Potosí—with Sánchez Espinosa's help. The professional brothers' dependence gained the oligarch an ally in a region where he held important estates.[32]

Don Fernando Roldán was legal adviser to Sánchez Espinosa during the decade after 1800, handling the merger of the oligarch's holdings with the properties of the Condes de Peñasco, formally inherited by the priest-patriarch's son don Mariano Sánchez y Mora. The Peñascos, led by the widowed ex-Condesa (an ally of San Luis Potosí military commander don Félix Calleja), opposed a succession that cost them regional eminence. Roldán arranged the legal transaction and joined the young Conde on a journey to San Luis Potosí to take over the Peñasco title and entail—and face angry opposition.[33] A Mexico City provincial lawyer helped a Mexico City oligarch assert power over a northern provincial elite.

In addition to clerical and legal professionals, Sánchez Espinosa employed a series of business managers. At times he called them cajeros, suggesting commercial ambitions. Most often, he called them *dependientes*—dependents serving him by dealing with Mexico City produce buyers, tradesmen, and others. Don Manuel Posadas served from at least 1779 through 1800, assisted from 1782 to 1789 by don Juan Pérez Gómez, an immigrant from Spain. After the latter's early death, don Ángel María Merelo oversaw the priest-patriarch's affairs from 1789 until at least 1811.[34] Two of the three served more than two decades.

After Pérez Gómez's death, Sánchez Espinosa received a letter from the young cajero's father. Writing from a village in the mountains of Santander in northern Spain, the grieving parent sought confirmation of his son's death and perhaps compensation for his work in the priest-patriarch's service. In a tone of humility that contrasts sharply with the polished self-abnegations that filled letters from Mexico City professionals seeking favors, the father wrote of his family's loss—and his son's loss of hoped-for opportunity in New Spain's capital.[35] The letter reminds us that not all immigrants seeking fortunes in Mexico City found it, that a decade serving a powerful oligarch and living among provincial elites did not always bring social ascent.

The Condes de Santiago Calimaya, the oldest and most established great landed clan in Mexico City, also employed an array of lawyers and managers. In the 1780s the family relied on legal advice and business direction from don José Lebrón. Trained as a lawyer, Lebrón was legal counselor to the chief royal magistrate in the capital, the *corregidor*, then to Superintendant don Fernando José Mangino (himself tied to the Conde de Regla). All the while Lebrón served don Juan Lorenzo Gutiérrez Altamirano y Velasco, Conde de Santiago, until his death in 1793. Lebrón was first called *abogado de la casa* (house lawyer). As his role broadened, he was named *director general de la casa* (general director of the house). In 1793 he gained 500 pesos for his service. Like so many provincial elites, Lebrón also owned and operated modest estates—in the Valley of Toluca, near the Santiago's Atengo holdings. His properties were worth 130,000 pesos, mortgaged to half their value. Mixing legal training, bureaucratic office, managerial service, and estate operation, Lebrón typified a successful provincial elite.[36]

In the 1790s, don José Mombiela joined Lebrón in providing legal services to the great clan as it faced two difficult inheritance transitions. Mombiela had also trained as a lawyer and served as *oficial mayor* (senior manager) in the office of accounting at the Gunpowder Monopoly—a key supplier of mining operations. He helped the Santiagos deal with the passing of don Juan Lorenzo and the shift of the title and properties to his nephew, don José Manuel de Velasco. When the latter died in 1797 and the title and entails went to don Juan Lorenzo's daughter, don Manuel Lucio Basail rose to serve as abogado de la casa. Through the first decade of the nineteenth century, he arranged the legal details of every important family question. When the powerful clan faced another disputed inheritance after the condesa died in 1802, Basail mediated among factions and remained legal adviser to the entire clan.[37] Through all that, the lawyer was a subordinate—a member of the provincial elite. Never a signatory to the funeral notices of the great family he served, he signed at least twice to mourn provincial elites—including don Miguel Mota Sanz.[38]

The Santiagos operated their vast properties through a mix of oligarchic control and managerial implementation. While the long-ruling don Juan Lorenzo was conde, his brother don Mariano de Velasco was general administrator. Their letters indicate that the conde made key decisions about production, labor relations, and court challenges while they worked together on implementation.[39] When don Mariano's son don José Manuel inherited the title and entails in 1793, he turned to a general manager, don Manuel de la Bastida to oversee business affairs. When don José Manuel died in 1797, ending his brief time as conde, the family no longer needed Bastida's services. After he helped with the transition, the new condesa gave him a lease to operate Olivar del Conde, an estate and flour mill in the hills above Mixcoac, just southwest of the capital, while his mother lived rent-free in one of the Santiagos' city properties.[40] Even after it ended, service to the Santiagos could ensure a place in the provincial elite.

The new condesa did not need Bastida's services; she relied on her younger sister, doña María Josefa de Velasco y Ovando, to run the family's landed businesses. Doña María Josefa's letter books (drafts of business correspondence from 1797 to 1802) reveal that her titled sister took no role in economic questions—the rare case in which a titled oligarch did not join in at least major decisions. They make it equally clear that doña María Josefa ruled estate operations and city marketing with a sharp eye and an iron hand.[41] A woman could rule a powerful family as the nineteenth century began, but she could not do so publicly. She could not appear before the city council; she could not go to the alhóndiga to check on grain prices and sales. So she employed an aging manager to serve as her public face.

Don Bernardo de Palacio gained an education that enabled him to rise through the administrative ranks at the Mexico City Cathedral, attaining the position of chief notary—recording the mortgages that linked so many provincial elites to the Church. He used his salary and learning to build modest wealth; by 1794 he had invested 50,000 pesos in the Santiagos' estates—earning 2,500 pesos annual income.[42] By education and experience, investment and dependence, don Bernardo was perfectly prepared to become doña María Josefa's adviser and representative. She valued his opinions—as she made decisions. He dealt with produce dealers and local officials.[43] Like many managers, he lived in the Santiago mansion that served as business headquarters. He was the only person not among close oligarchic kin to sign the 1802 notice mourning the condesa he served.[44] Yet however much that inclusion honored don Bernardo, he knew he lived in dependence. In 1800 he wrote a professional friend referring to "mi Señora doña María Josefa de Velasco y Ovando," adding "I serve without pay and faithfully she who appreciates me."[45]

With the death of the condesa, her sister's administration ended. Don Ygnacio Leonel Gómez de Cervantes, head of another great landed clan and married to a younger sister, claimed Santiago family leadership based on his wife's inheritance. Don Bernardo facilitated the transition, including the leasing of a pulque estate, Tulancalco in the Mezquital, to doña María Josefa. Palacio carried on as an adviser while the new conde ruled. Don Bernardo also advised doña María Josefa as she proved that a woman could profit in the pulque business.[46] Don Bernardo de Palacio exemplified provincial elite life in Mexico City—with a few twists. Educated, he rose through the Church bureaucracy, gained modest wealth, invested in landed property (by mortgage, not purchase), and served as a faithful managerial dependent of a powerful entrepreneur (in his case a woman).

Doña María Josefa de Velasco y Ovando, daughter of a Conde de Santiago, sister of a titled condesa, exercised power rare among women in Mexico City around 1800. She understood oligarchic power and provincial elite dependence. In 1799 she wrote a letter in which she casually divided society into "persons of respect, dependents, and servants." [47] Her kin and allies in the oligarchy of power—financiers, merchants, mine operators, great landed entrepreneurs, high regime judges, and officers—gained respect. Provincial elites—lesser landowners, professionals, managers, and bureaucrats—were dependents. They served oligarchs. Everyone else was a servant. In eighteenth-century New Spain, a *sirviente* was an employee; household help was a *criado*, living in more abject dependence. One way or another, nearly all served the oligarchs who ruled the silver capitalism that made New Spain rich and important in the world.

A Power Elite: Integration, Dependence, and Fissures

A powerful clique of Mexico City oligarchs ruled a stratified elite integrated by ties of dependence. Oligarchs concentrated exceptional financial and landed power, towering wealth, and ties to the highest levels of the viceregal regime. Provincials were less landed, limited financially, well educated, linked to the Mexico City Council, and dependent in diverse ways—often by direct service to oligarchs. Inequity integrated by dependence kept the Mexico City elite united in pursuit of wealth in the silver economy, and of power in the city and across New Spain—as long as the regime held and silver flowed.

There were potential lines of fissure and resentment. Immigrants from Spain enjoyed favored access to profit in global trade and to high imperial office. They alone could regularly and visibly rise from modest beginnings to join the oligarchy of power by taking wealth in trade or prerogatives of rule—to then marry landed heiresses and gain entrance to powerful oligarchic clans. At the heights of the oligarchy, relations between European and American Spaniards were shaped by the continuing integration of the former as they joined the latter—to generate more American Spaniards.

Among provincial elites, the great majority of landed professionals and of legal, clerical, and managerial dependents were Americans. They knew that only immigrant Spaniards scaled the heights of power. Provincials surely held resentments. Yet they lived as dependents of oligarchs ruling families that regularly integrated commercial newcomers and landed Americans. Provincial elites knew themselves as españoles, Spaniards, rarely as criollos. They surely also knew the anti-immigrant stereotype that saw immigrants as gachupines—grasping, haughty, men on the make. Did provincials whisper such insults among themselves when far from the oligarchs who ruled so much? Perhaps. Yet if such resentments percolated among provincials, they remained muted for decades. Oligarchic power and provincial elite dependence sustained cohesion among the powerful as long as silver capitalism prospered all. It took the crisis of 1808 to turn fissures into fractures threatening to divide Mexico City's stratified community of power.

Before turning to that crisis, we must explore life in the city's barrios—popular neighborhoods. There too, ties of dependence integrated and complicated sharp inequities, stabilizing urban life while silver capitalism flourished. Stability held in the barrios during the crisis of 1808, in the face of the provincial insurgencies that began in 1810, and long after. Understanding why the barrios—sites of popular work and survival, inequality and exploitation—held stable during the decades of silver boom after 1770 helps understand why the urban populace stood back as the powerful divided in 1808. The city's barrios would remain at work when popular insurgencies exploded in 1810 in the outlying Bajío and then in the nearby Mezquital, assaulting the economic foundations of silver capitalism. The city was a place where power consolidated—and could fracture. It was also orchestrated by deep dependencies that inhibited overt resistance. Insurgency found its home in the countryside—where autonomies on the land, however limited, could sustain popular risings. That is another history.[48]

CHAPTER 4

Getting By

Life and Work in the Barrios

IF POWER BELONGED TO THE OLIGARCHS AND INFLUENCE FILTERED
through provincial elites who were often professionals, most city people
worked to get by as producers—as artisans and workers, as shopkeepers and
street vendors, as builders and haulers, and in so many other roles held by
men and women struggling to survive and sustain families. They made a
diverse majority. Like oligarchs and landed professionals, many claimed status as españoles. Others were labeled mestizos or mulattos, showing mixed
ancestry and lesser prosperity. And a large group retained status as *indios*, at
least a quarter, perhaps a third of the city's people. They worked in most of
the same activities as their neighbors, while belonging to the city's two indigenous republics: San Juan Tenochtitlan and Santiago Tlatelolco.

After 1770, Mexico City was defined by commercial dynamism, stratified
in ways marked by concentrated powers, deep inequities, and widespread
insecurities while fragmented by ethnic divisions. This chapter explores the
diverse ways the city's diverse peoples worked to survive and sustain families
in the capital of silver capitalism. The one that follows engages popular cultural expressions, social disconformities, and periodic difficulties in the face
of death and disease—and how oligarchs and provincial elites worked

together to mediate and sustain the productive stability essential to the capital's pivotal roles in New Spain and the world.

The city bustled with challenges and uncertainties. Ultimately, diverse and changing ways of dependence defined life in the barrios. Social fragmentation in the face of changing ways of work tied to deepening insecurities kept city people at work, at home, in taverns, and at festivals in the public squares. A focus on getting by, finding relief from the challenges of work, and joining neighbors in festivals celebrating community and honoring saints kept an urban peace that sustained silver capitalism.

Diversity, Fragmentation, and Power

The city was a place of great ethnic diversity—including the largest concentrations of people classed as españoles, mestizos and mulattos, and indios, too, anywhere in the Americas. It is important to remember that being español, Spanish, did not mean being born in Spain. Very few came from the peninsula—though as we have seen, the few were sometimes favored and often resented. *Español* labeled a status that presumed Iberian ancestry, Hispanic culture, and solid prosperity—and prosperity and Hispanic culture could bring Spanish status to people of mixed ancestry.[1] The oligarchs who ruled were always españoles, rising immigrants from Spain constantly joining and reinforcing Americans established on the land. The provincial elites who prospered and exercised influence were normally españoles—and overwhelmingly American. Españoles also worked as artisans, shopkeepers, and laborers, sharing roles with mestizos, mulattos, and indios in production and service—while they lived with different rights and obligations. Notably, indios and mulattos paid tributes that marked a presumed subordination; Spaniards and mestizos did not. Spaniards had rights to seek justice before the city council; indios had rights to house lots and justice provided by city's two indigenous republics.

City politics were fragmented: the oligarchy that integrated the most powerful American and immigrant Spaniards enjoyed privileged yet informal access to the heights of regime power; the landed professionals of the city's provincial elite pursued formal politics through the city council; the mestizo and mulatto shopkeepers, artisans, and workers who did so much to keep the city alive had little access to regime officials except before the courts. Meanwhile, the city's indigenous thousands found rights, representations, and justice through the two urban republics. Economic stratification shaped by ethnic and political fragmentations reinforced power and helped keep a divisive urban peace.

Meanwhile, important changes were underway in the city's workshops and barrios. Artisans remembered the days when guilds had powers to represent them before the council and mediate disputes among members. As the city grew and its economy accelerated and diversified in the late eighteenth century, the power and reach of the guilds diminished. Growing numbers pursued trades without organization and representation, striving to find work or offer services as individuals with limited skills and few rights. Still, as long as silver capitalism boomed, most city people found work and ways to survive and sustain families—some in new factories that hinted at an industrial future.

Amid all the division and fragmentation, politics were everywhere. Surviving guilds still sought rights and appealed grievances before the city council. Shopkeepers ruled along many streets, vendors dominated market plazas—and passed the news that kept everyone informed and involved in debates. The indigenous republics of San Juan Tenochtitlan and Santiago Tlatelolco included nearly thirty thousand people. Led by indigenous governors, councilmen, and other native officials, they oversaw housing, regulated markets, and offered justice in dozens of barrios surrounding the center. The larger and more powerful San Juan Tenochtitlan collected tributes in its barrios and among the large number of indios living and working in the center. Both republics represented indigenous interests before city and viceregal authorities.[2] Participations were constrained among the less powerful, but most in the city had a vision and a voice—if not a say. After 1770 and until 1808, the city majority never rose to challenge established powers. That did not mean people were calm, quiet, or inattentive to their interests in a city of bustling inequity.

In a city growing past 120,000 people around 1800, the oligarchy that included leading entrepreneurial families, high regime officials, and their close dependents surely included fewer than 500 people. Provincial elites, professionals, their kin, and allies likely included no more than another 2,000 who lived favored lives of solid comfort. Viceregal and clerical bureaucrats and the commercial dependents of merchant financiers perhaps added another 2,000, bringing the community of the favored close to 5,000. By any calculation the

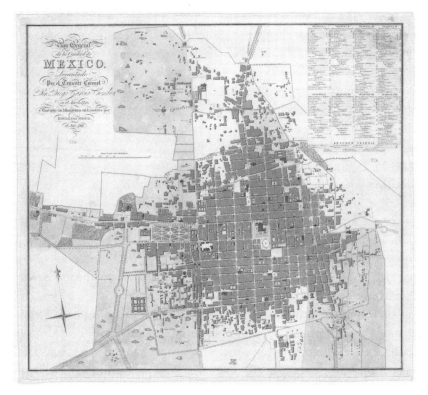

Figure 7. Mexico City, 1793. Courtesy of the Benson Latin American Collection,
University of Texas at Austin.

diverse population of urban producers passed 100,000 around 1770 and
approached 120,000 by 1800—the majority in barrios where diverse people
grappling with uncertain lives sustained the city and silver capitalism.

Artisans Losing Independence

Historically, large numbers of Mexico City's producers lived as artisans organized in guilds, with men presumed to progress from training as apprentices
through years of work as *oficiales* (badly translated as journeymen; better as
craftsmen), to eventual examination and independence as shop-owning
masters. Led by masters and officers they elected, guilds were linked to the
city council, which oversaw and sanctioned guild elections and resolved

disputes within and between guilds, their competitors, and customers. The guild-organized sectors of the urban economy found representation and rights to petition and mediation via the city council, which in turn had parallel rights to address the viceregal regime.

No sharp line separated provincial elites and prosperous operators of city craft shops. Among the landed professionals at the core of the provincial elite, a few owned and operated important shops—notably bakeries and hog butcheries. These were wholesale operations that might be valued at from 4,000 to 40,000 pesos, as much as a small landed estate. Carriage makers' and silversmiths' shops were less valuable as properties, but they enabled pursuit of profitable trades that served the wealthiest city consumers. Such prosperous artisans were nearly all classed as Spaniards, maintained solid guild organizations, and lived at the intersection of the provincial elite and the producing majority. All but silversmiths led large operations that employed several dozen workers. Silversmiths might employ about five skilled craftsmen—and the best took ample profits.[3]

When such prosperous guild-organized entrepreneurial craftsmen faced challenges, they turned to the council for assistance and mediation. In 1791, a baker saw opportunity in setting up a hog butchery, diversifying his participation in the city's food economy. The butchers' guild protested, and the council sent don José Lebrón—the legal adviser to high regime officials and house lawyer for the Condes de Santiago—to investigate. He looked into the hog butchers' complaint, recognized that the baker's intrusion did break guild regulations—yet concluded that the city would benefit from the new butchery and allowed the project to proceed. In accepting Lebrón's decision, the council supported the accelerating commercialization of life in the capital—while recognizing remnant guild rights and its own role in mediating craft disputes.

Another sign of changing times: in 1800 there were six carriage works run by guild masters, while sixteen flourished "without license." The carriage masters protested to the council; it recognized their concerns but did nothing to stop production that profited middling entrepreneurs and employed large numbers of workers who had little prospect of becoming masters with guild rights.[4] The provincials who ruled the city sustained the interests of the oligarchs who profited from widening commercial ways—and bought carriages. Their council mediated the dispute to enable commercial expansion.

The most successful masters with larger enterprises, bakers and hog butchers, carriage makers and silversmiths, retained guild rights and used them to prosper even as their dominance waned. But they led only a small segment of the city's economy: the fifty bakeries of 1793 employed a total of about 600 workers; in 1794, thirty-six silversmiths employed 44 aspiring apprentices and 190 craftsmen; the same year, twenty carriage makers utilized 39 apprentices and 105 skilled workers.[5] We lack parallel counts for hog butchers, and there were a few other prosperous, large-scale, guild-organized enterprises. A generous estimate is that such operations employed a total of 1,500 producers, with perhaps three dependents each (apprentices were teenagers); we may suspect that no more than 6,000 of Mexico City's more than 100,000 producing people lived with the limited benefits—declining for masters; vanishing for workers—of enduring guild organizations.

In metalworking and carpentry, trades essential to so much of city life, large numbers of independent shops carried on with limited guild protections as urban dynamism created opportunities for entrants outside the guild structure. A 1788 survey reported eighty-six metal shops with 63 apprentices and 267 workers. Most masters in the sector also worked, so over 400 men engaged in essential metalwork. Many more pursued carpentry: 170 masters, 157 apprentices, 498 craftsmen—totaling 825.[6] Again presuming three dependents each, another 5,000 city residents lived by this less prosperous, yet vitally essential, sector of metal- and woodworkers.

Many more of the city's producers, men and women, worked in household shops ruled by merchant financiers—what scholars of European development call protoindustrialization. Especially in textile and clothing trades, yet also in leatherwork and perhaps in other trades we see less clearly, rising entrepreneurs drew small producers into integrated enterprises. In many, women began to find new—or more visible—paid roles. Let us begin with textiles, the oldest of industries and the most essential sector of the economy after sustenance and the silver that drove everything in New Spain.

Mesoamericans had made cotton cloth for millennia before Europeans came; production remained women's work in indigenous households from Mexica times through the eighteenth century.[7] With the disease-driven depopulation of the sixteenth century, sheep replaced people across the dry countryside north of the capital, and woolen cloth production became an expanding industry, mostly among Hispanic peoples.[8] The urban textile industry evolved through two sectors, one of household workshops under guild oversight, the other of large workshops called obrajes working a dozen on more looms and concentrating many dozens of workers. They used parallel technologies: large handlooms wove cloth. As each loom required yarn produced by multiple spinners, plus ancillary cleaning, washing, dying, and finishing tasks, every weaver gave work to four to ten others. In household workshops, that meant family members: women and daughters spun yarn; sons and others helped clean and prepare wool and finish the cloth. And in household production, finished cloth brought income to sustain the family; the work of women and children was essential, but rarely paid in wages.

The obrajes were large workshops concentrating men weaving and finishing cloth. Some spinning might be done in the manufactory—but most was put out to urban and rural households, where women gained a share of the yarn or cash payments. The household and obraje sectors evolved side by side for centuries. To a degree they competed in the market for everyday woolen cloth that served so many purposes in New Spain. They were also complementary; in times of peak demand, obrajes contracted out weaving to household craftsmen. The obrajes had the advantage of economies of scale. Early on they had the disadvantage of needing large numbers of permanent workers, many with skills, in an economy of scarce population and diverse opportunities. Obrajes at times used enslaved Africans, notably in the seventeenth century. But slaves were expensive, so obrajes took in convict workers when available—and increasingly adopted the practice of obligated labor: that is, they paid large advances—perhaps a year's income, sometimes more—to help fund a young man's wedding or a child's baptism and then tried to hold him in to work off the debt. The result of the sequential mixing of enslaved, convict, and obligated labor was a mix of uncertain skills among workers rarely content with obraje life. Pressed by growing European imports in the late eighteenth century, many obrajes closed.[9]

The demise of the obrajes revealed their inability to compete in the face of cheaper imports, and the ability—and necessity—of household weavers to keep making woolens as merchants pressed down remuneration in the face of competition. Families had to make do with less to keep home shops working and income flowing, if at reduced levels. In 1788, as European imports rose, ten obrajes operated in Mexico City. They employed 697 oficiales, adult workers, and 298 young men classed as apprentices—paid little and forming nearly a third of the workforce. The same year, there were seventy-five small woolen workshops, with 370 adult workers and only 39 young apprentices— but 10 percent. The city's struggling woolen industry then employed nearly 1,500 men and youths—and uncounted women as household spinners.[10] The turn to youth in the obrajes was a way to cut costs; the adults who still predominated in household shops saw earnings fall in the face of market pressures ruled by merchant financiers.

The guild of cotton weavers was an eighteenth-century foundation. Hispanic weavers made cotton a business after 1700, competing with and displacing indigenous women who made cloth for family use and local markets (a shift parallel to estate operators' taking up commercial production of maize and pulque in the same era, in pulque also displacing women).[11] The 1788 survey listed fifty-seven master cotton weavers in the city, employing 300 workers and 30 apprentices—the same 10 percent of youth as in household woolen shops. A 1796 survey (after the outbreak of war disrupted shipping and cotton imports) reported thirty-seven masters with shops operating 150 looms, while seven masters without independent shops worked 20 looms, and five widows kept 21 looms operating in their late husbands' shops. Thus forty-nine "masters" kept guild ways alive while working 191 looms. Meanwhile, nine men listed as *intrusos*—intruders, masters without license—worked 36 looms, bringing the total of "masters" to fifty-eight, essentially the same number reported in 1788.

More revealing, in 1796 136 oficiales without masters worked 126 looms— over half the shops in the city with well over a third of the looms weaving cotton.[12] The masters without independent shops, the intrusos, and the oficiales operating looms without guild license all surely worked under merchant-clothiers: 93 men operating 182 looms, over half of those making cotton cloth in the city, lived in a growing protoindustrial sector. While woolen producers struggled and obrajes closed, cotton production expanded in the 1790s—under merchant-financier control.

The city textile sector lived difficult times after 1770: competition from imports, the decline of large obrajes, new reliance on young workers in woolens, a rising cotton sector ruled by merchant financiers, and shrinking guild coordination—all pressed on producers earnings. Still, cloth making combining woolens and cotton goods remained a major sector in the city. If we take the fifteen hundred men estimated as employed making woolens, add an equal number producing cotton goods, and presume three dependents each, then twelve thousand people depended on that sector—not including uncounted numbers of women spinning wool and cotton. In household shops, women spinners were among those listed as "dependents"—in fact they were key producers. Obrajes and merchant-clothiers also contracted women in the city and nearby villages to spin—bringing income to diverse households. Adding women spinners to the estimate of working cloth producers suggests that fifteen to twenty thousand people depended fully or in important part on textile production to live in the city.

Including tailors and dressmakers who turned cloth into clothing for the city's more prosperous consumers (in poor households, women made clothing from cloth they made or bought) adds to the apparel sector. The 1788 survey reported ninety-four master tailors employing 698 adults and 423 apprentices—a nearly 40 percent reliance on youth.[13] Tailors too took advantage of the low costs of holding youths in long terms of apprenticeship. A few tailors were famous and successful; they kept shops southwest of the plaza near the oligarchs' palatial homes—where silversmiths also concentrated. Most tailors worked dispersed across the city's rich, comfortable, and poor neighborhoods. Presuming few apprentices had dependents, the 1,215 men working in tailor shops likely sustained about 3,500 people—another ample sector of the city.

The 1788 survey excluded women. An 1811 census suggests that large numbers of dressmakers worked at home—and never in shops open to the public. The most prestigious and prosperous lived and made dresses in the wealthy neighborhoods southwest of the plaza; there was another concentration north of the plaza—and more scattered all around.[14] Presuming an equal number of dressmakers as tailors, one thousand women surely sustained one to three dependents each, mostly children, adding another three thousand to the total estimate of the population grounded in the cloth and clothing sector of the city economy. With fifteen to twenty thousand making cloth or dependent on those that did, and another six to seven thousand making clothing (or depending on tailors and dressmakers), from twenty-two to twenty-seven thousand people, nearly 20 percent of the city population, lived by making cloth and clothing.

Parallel developments marked the leather-working sector. There too, the first stages of production, the washing and salting of hides obtained at the capital's slaughterhouses, were done by women—most in indigenous households on the city's edges. The hides then moved on to shops that tanned and dressed them, male-dominated work that prepared leather for sale to shoemakers, saddlers, and others. Merchant financiers ruled the first stages linking female washers and male tanners and dressers; they sold finished leather to more independent craftsmen who made shoes, boots, saddles, and other goods for sale to the public. Again, the women who labored in the first stages remain uncounted. The 1788 survey reports thirty tanning shops employing 90 adults and 47 apprentices—joining the move to relying on younger workers paid little. The twenty-five dressing operations did not join that shift; perhaps requiring greater skills, they included 92 adults and only 7 apprentices. Shoe and saddle making remained traditional trades. In the former, thirty-seven shops included 168 adults and 32 apprentices (likely an undercount); in the latter, twenty shops employed 82 adult craftsmen and only 18 apprentices.[15] The leather trades thus included 648 male producers, likely half that number of women preparing hides, and a dependent population that brought the sector to sustain another 2,500 of the city's people.

Diverse other crafts—from coopers to kettle makers to hat makers and more—added another 1,000 producers to the craft sector, some still operating independent shops open to public trade, others ruled by merchant financiers. They added another 4,000 to the population sustained by crafts around 1800—bringing the estimated total to 42,500 for the urban population sustained by crafts as they shifted from guild-sanctioned workshops to lives of protoindustrial dependence and reliance on younger workers facing low wages and uncertain prospects for advance. After 1770, a craft sector once shaped by guilds moved toward commercialization, pressures on earnings, and widening insecurities.

Heavy Insecurities: The Building and Carrying Trades

Low earnings and pervasive insecurities plagued other large sectors of the city's population: those who lived by day labor, most in construction and carrying trades, some in service to the prosperous (numbers that would be clearer if officials had counted women in household service). Again, the 1788 count is revealing. In the building trades, there were 2,015 bricklayers—including no masters, 810 adult workers, and 1,210 youths listed as apprentices. The turn to reliance on the young and minimally paid is again striking. Among 555 stonemasons, the balance of 405 adults and 150 apprentices seems more traditional. Among pavers, there were 35 masters employing 428 adult men—surely recruited from among the many apprentice bricklayers and stonemasons. Pipe layers also kept a traditional hierarchy among 8 masters and 87 adult laborers.[16] Still, the construction sector that included over 3,000 workers employed more than 1,350 youths paid very little while struggling to begin households and sustain dependents. We may estimate that the sector supported another 6,000 of the city's people very poorly.

The city's over 1,200 carriers and over 600 water haulers in 1788 also worked hard for little pay—all reported as adults in the 1788 survey.[17] While construction workers mostly labored under commercial contractors who turned to youths to keep wages down, carriers were mostly independent haulers offering their services to whoever might need them—perhaps using sons as helpers in household economies. They were insecure and poorly paid, struggling to sustain families. Today we might call them an informal sector. Their efforts supported another 5,000 of the city's poorest people. Less independent and perhaps better paid were the 967 men listed as coachmen and the 513 reported as grooms, all adults.[18] Most worked in service of the few prosperous enough to own a coach or maintain stables in the city—or those who rented carriages or kept horses for those without stables. Another 5,000 people depended on their efforts. Adding the population sustained by construction workers, carriers, coachmen, and liverymen brings the total to nearly 60,000. Presuming a minimum of 10,000 for the uncounted numbers of women laboring in household service and suspecting that at least half supported a child adds another 15,000—bringing the accounting of the city's economy to 75,000 of a population estimated near 120,000 around 1790.

Remembering the 5,000 counted as among the powerful, the prosperous, and their comfortable dependents, how did the other 40,000 live? Some survived as famed *léperos*, seemingly everywhere on the streets, lamented by the powerful and prosperous as thieves, honored by many for their lives of independent informality. But before we presume that street-corner entrepreneurs, informal survivors, and the desperate were nearly 40 percent of Mexico City's population around 1790, we must recognize a rising sector of factory labor.

Factories and Workers

Three key factories developed in eighteenth-century Mexico City, reshaping the city economy and city lives in important ways. In the 1730s the new Royal

Mint incorporated complex technologies and divisions of labor to ensure the precise production of the rising flows of pesos that kept New Spain at the center of the world economy. After 1770 it regularly employed four to five hundred workers. The Royal Tobacco Factory opened in 1769 and expanded to employ of over seven thousand by the 1790s, increasingly wage-earning women, by far the largest concentration of workers in the Americas at the time. In the same decade, a private entrepreneur built the *indianillas* factory, bringing together five hundred workers to stamp-dye and finish cotton cloth—imitating the products of India so valuable in global trade. New factories created new employment and new ways of life in the silver metropolis.

The mint was the pivot of the silver economy—built adjacent to the Viceregal Palace (see map 1, figure 1, and figure 3). It drew all of New Spain's silver to be taxed (claiming 12 to 15 percent for the regime), made into coin, and then returned as pesos, the leading global currency of the eighteenth century, to the merchants who financed mining and sent it into world trade. For the economy to prosper, the mint had to deal with weekly fluctuations and long-term rising production. Its efficiency was pivotal to oligarchs' wealth, regime power, and the economic dynamism of New Spain. It served its function well while providing employment to hundreds of men who gained solid incomes facing hard, often health-threatening labor—in that, parallel to the dangers faced by the larger numbers who worked at outlying silver mines and refineries.[19]

The new mint divided coinage into multiple steps—smelting, cutting, stamping, and finishing—each done by specialized skilled workers, assisted by general helpers, and backed by replacements ready to step in to keep production flowing should a primary worker be hurt, ill, or otherwise unavailable for a day, a week, or longer. Production was mechanized: there were machines to cut, press, stamp, and finish coins—and to reprocess cuttings to maximize coinage. Power came from men and mules, but machines organized the mint.[20]

In 1779, a core of nine administrators earned 3,000 to 6,000 pesos yearly to oversee minting and guarantee security, placing them among the most prosperous residents of the capital. A larger group of thirty managers and skilled supervising producers gained salaries of 1,000 to 2,000 pesos, providing solid prosperity. In the larger working community of over three hundred in the 1770s (rising to over four hundred as mining and minting rose to hold at peaks in the 1790s and after), the most skilled gained salaries that ranged from an ample 900 pesos yearly to a comfortable 400. Others earned daily wages of 4 to 10 reales, creating incomes of 150 to 375 pesos for those who worked steadily year-round. Still others faced piece rates that pushed productivity and provided similar incomes. The highest wages and piece rates went to permanent workers, about two-thirds of the total. The replacements who stepped in to keep production steady gained lesser wages and rates— and only when they worked.[21]

Mint workers, even replacements, seem favored among the throngs struggling to survive in the city. But injuries on the job led many among the skilled to work and thus gain income during only part of each year. The replacements faced similarly insecure employment and earnings. And all faced the high cost of life in the city—costs that rose when a worker or family member was injured or became ill, when a worker aimed to marry and start a household, or when a couple had a child. The mint paid high wages—and offered no advances, a practice common elsewhere in New Spain, used to draw men to employment, help them fund marriage, and pay for children, baptismal celebrations, and more. Mint workers facing such costs at times gave into the temptation to sweep up a few scraps of the silver expected to return to the smelters for minting. To managers, that was theft and had to be contained. Mint workers were not remunerated in ways that kept such temptations away—as many saw chances to supplement earnings.[22]

With greater or lesser incomes and security, with uncertain supplements from their own "silver economy," the five hundred employees of the mint around 1800 likely supported nearly twenty-five hundred of the city's people. As befitted such remunerative if dangerous and insecure work, over 60 percent were classed as Spaniards, including a few immigrants from Spain. Indios formed the next largest group—nearly 20 percent, followed by 13 percent classed as mestizos and 6 percent as mulattos. Among managers, Spaniards (by category, not birth) ruled; among workers, skills counted more than category in this most important of factories. Men of all categories mixed in every stage of minting—keeping silver flowing.[23]

The regime founded the Royal Tobacco Factory in 1769 to generate revenue by controlling production of a key commodity of popular consumption—addictive, but not basic to sustenance.[24] Set at the southwest edge of the city (see map 1), early on the Mexico City factory recruited a mostly male workforce. In 1774 it employed about six thousand men and one thousand women.[25] Drawing women into a factory was unprecedented in New Spain. At first, many came from among those who had rolled cigars and cigarettes at home and in small shops before the monopoly; displaced by the monopoly, they found work and the factory gained skilled hands. The larger number of men surely came from the large urban underclass and nearby villages. Few had experience making tobacco products; none had experienced labor in a factory drawing so many together. Throngs came to a new factory offering steady work at low wages as the economy came out of the midcentury slowdown.

There was no mechanization and minimal division of labor in the tobacco factory. The primary tasks were cutting tobacco, preparing paper to roll cigarettes and leaf to make cigars, and then the constant rolling of product. Demanding lesser skills, inflicting lesser wounds (the long-term effects of tobacco then unknown), and less pivotal to the global economy, the tobacco factory paid less than the mint. Two to three administrators earned 1,500 to 2,000 pesos yearly. Most workers earned 3 to 7 reales per day, promising annual incomes of 100 to 250 pesos—if they worked full time and year-round, always uncertain. To cushion the uncertainties of life without paying for them, managers founded a mutual aid program called the Concordia. It required workers to pay half a real weekly to gain the right to claim limited earnings if ill or injured, to pay for a funeral, and to borrow small amounts to pay for key events of family and religious life. In the tobacco factory neither advances nor sick pay would come at the cost of profits that were regime revenues.[26]

Once the factory was operating and fully staffed, managers pressed wages and piece rates down to maximize revenues. They quickly learned that six thousand men drawn together to work in close quarters while struggling to sustain families with low wages that were declining would not acquiesce without resistance. A series of protests led managers to a dual solution: they dispersed expanding production to new factories in cities across New Spain and cut the numbers of men in the factories, turning to women who were paid less, less accustomed to wage labor, and often had fewer dependents. In 1795, the Mexico City factory still had over seven thousand workers, over 40 percent women; by 1809 total employment had fallen to nearly fifty-five hundred—now over 70 percent women. Stated differently, men's employment, which peaked at six thousand in 1774, fell to four thousand by 1795 and fifteen hundred by 1809. Women working in the tobacco factory increased from one thousand in 1774, to three thousand in 1795, to almost four thousand by 1809. Men protesting insecurities saw employment disappear, along with Concordia benefits they found insufficient. Women, often single and mothers needing to support children, found work at wages less than had been paid men, kept limited Concordia benefits, and saw the factory begin to provide child care.[27]

In the calculation of total support for urban people, the six thousand men and one thousand women of 1774 likely sustained twenty thousand—almost 20 percent of the city's working population. The four thousand men and three thousand women of 1795 probably supported a total of eighteen thousand. The fifteen hundred men and four thousand women of 1809 surely sustained no more than fifteen thousand—about 10 percent of an increased population. Still, the tobacco factory remained the city largest employer and, through its increasingly female workers, the largest support of urban people.

From 1774 to 1809, factory women gained rising access to wage work, modest benefits, and wages lower than men's—all to sustain cigar production, profits that were regime revenues, and their own children. The frustrations and adaptations of the forty-five hundred men pressed out of the factory can only be imagined. Did they move to labor in new provincial factories? Perhaps, but those factories, too, turned increasingly to women. Did displaced men fall back into the capital's underclass, a reminder to them and others of the costs of challenging power in an economy of limited employment? Could anything be more modern, more capitalist?

The indianillas factory also brought the cutting edge of capitalism to the silver metropolis. We know very little about its origins; what we do know suggests we need to know much more. Francisco Iglesias y Capdevila arrived from Catalonia in 1789 and joined in a company with Josep Delgado (likely also Catalan). They established a factory to print cotton cloth by industrial stamping of dyed patterns in imitation of the products of India—long a staple of the world economy. They brought Mexico City into a wider process in which Atlantic producers aimed to replace Indian cottons in growing markets.

For centuries South Asian producers had ruled production of fine printed cotton cloth. Using locally grown cotton, household workshops produced cloth purchased by merchants—who sold it to European, Arabic, Chinese, and other traders in vibrant ports. For Europeans, the price of

Indian cloth was paid in silver; in the eighteenth century that meant silver from New Spain. Silver sent across the Pacific also paid for cotton cloth made in India, brought by Chinese merchants to Manila, and shipped to New Spain on galleons that crossed the Pacific. Much of the cotton cloth of India bought with silver and taken west by Europeans paid African kings and merchants for people sold into slavery—then shipped to the Americas, most to Atlantic plantation regions to labor in sugar and other commodities.

The 1780s brought diverse attempts to make cloth in the Indian style outside of India, without the need to pay in silver that had to be gained in trade with New Spain. It was then that British inventors turned to machines to spin cotton yarn with minimal labor, drawing hand-loom weavers to shift from woolens to cotton wares. In the same era, in the regions where Catalonia met Pyrenean France, new mills began to stamp dyed prints—in the style of India—onto locally made cotton cloth. It was such a mill that Iglesias y Capdevila brought to Mexico City in 1789. Why the 1780s brought a turn to replace Indian cottons is not entirely clear. Europeans had many and growing needs for silver, notably the rising costs of war, beyond paying for South Asian cloth. Early British mechanization and the turn to stamping in Catalonia and Mexico City all aimed to meet consumer demand without paying in silver.[28]

The indianillas factory in Mexico City aimed to displace Indian cotton cloth in New Spain's markets, imports that had historically arrived via Manila in exchange for silver that now might be turned to other trades—and toward Europe. Beginning with about 350 workers, after 1800 it employed nearly 500: women to prepare dyes; men in dying and stamping. An 1804 inventory (not including the building) showed dyestuffs worth 9,000 pesos in a total value of 14,000. Cochineal from Oaxaca was valued at 6,500 pesos; indigo from San Salvador another 2,500. The Mexico City factory's cost advantage was in locally produced dyes. The workforce divided among apprentices paid 3–4 reales daily; adult men paid more (perhaps 4–6 reales daily); and women who prepared dyes—surely for less than the men. The division of labor among adults and youths, men and women, saved on costs. Mint workers gained more, tobacco workers less. The owner claimed that with dependents, the indianillas factory sustained 2,000 people.[29]

Equally revealing, it showed an emerging "globalization of production." The factory dyed finished cotton cloth. The sources suggest that some arrived unfinished from Asia and went directly to the factory for printing. There were also imports of cotton yarn from Asia, put out to household weavers to make into cloth prior to printing. And when wars inhibited imports, the factory relied fully on locally made cotton cloth. To the extent that the factory used local cloth, it stimulated household production including women spinners and men weavers—uncountable, but at times surely larger than the numbers working in the factory.

The indianillas factory shows Mexico City joining a new industrial order. Adding the 2,500 people it supported after 1800 indicates an industrial sector combining the mint, the tobacco factory, and the indianillas factory sustaining nearly 20,000 of the city's people in stratified, gendered, and often insecure labors. Having accounted for the work that sustained perhaps 100,000 of a city population passing 130,000 after 1800, how did the rest survive? Most of the counts that report on artisans, workers, and factories focused on the Hispanic city. It is time to turn to the indigenous barrios.

Metropolitan Indios

The demise of artisan life and guild organization, the spread of protoindustry that dispersed producers while concentrating power and profit in the hands of merchant financiers, and the rise of factories and the growing numbers of workers within them were developments shared across a broad, multiethnic producing population that included people classed as Spaniards, mestizos, mulattos, and indios. The city's indios, about thirty thousand around 1800, nearly a quarter of the urban population, retained separate political rights and access to justice via two indigenous republics: the larger San Juan Tenochtitlan that surrounded and penetrated the center, and the smaller Santiago Tlatelolco with a jurisdiction on northern edge of the metropolis.[30]

The indigenous people of San Juan Tenochtitlan divided into three broad groups. Nearly half lived inside the *traza*, the "Spanish" center, where they did all variety of work—including many women in household service; a third remained in the barrios, indigenous neighborhoods that surrounded the traza; and 15 percent were in outlying pueblos just beyond the barrios, where urban lives and rural ways mixed.[31] All owed tribute to the indigenous republic, and through it to the Spanish regime. Together, the republics and the regime provided a separate system of justice for indigenous peoples—the republics in the first instance, the General Indigenous Court in cases of appeal. For the half in the barrios and pueblos, indigenous justice was primary—along with rights to house lots (and in the pueblos, plots to cultivate) free of rents. There were advantages to being indio there. For the half in the traza, indio status and tribute payment did not bring access to lots, yet did offer access to separate justice. The *tecpan* (council hall) of San Juan Tenochtitlan was southwest of the center, near where the ancient aqueduct delivered water from Chapultepec, not far from the new tobacco factory (see map 1).

A tribute census completed in 1807 reveals much about how the thousands identified as indios were essential to the urban economy while socially incorporated in distinct ways. General city censuses showed indigenous men engaged in nearly every activity—from artisan crafts, to protoindustrial labor, to factory work, to the construction and carrying trades. The tribute census of 9,500 people in the indigenous barrios reveals that few entered the most prosperous activities: there was one native silversmith, one merchant, two weapons makers, two printers, and a religion teacher.[32] While the tribute census listed women (whether a man was married or not determined whether he paid full or half tribute), it never recorded their economic activities— whether at home or out in the city. There may have been few indigenous male merchants, but many women sold goods in formal and informal markets. And the listing of only one male teacher reminds us that women provided most education, religious and otherwise, in native households.

The indigenous men in the barrios did hard, burdensome work. The largest number, 676, were listed as *albañiles*, stone- or brickmasons who did the hard work building the city's buildings, homes, and streets. Another 303 lived by hauling heavy loads through the city, while 113 more, most in the southeastern barrio of Santo Tomás de la Palma, gathered hay and hauled it to stables across the city. Still, there were skilled craftsmen in the barrios: 401 made shoes while 121 did tanning and leather work; 168 made cloth, including 82 weavers, 32 spinners, and 34 who worked in the indianillas factory (the exclusion of women surely led to a serious undercount of cloth producers). The census did not report how many of those who worked in leather and shoemaking, spinning, and cloth making lived under merchant-financier control; surely many, perhaps most. Likely more independent were the 139 native carpenters in the barrios, building homes and furniture, often for their neighbors. The 89 button makers, 82 candle makers, 81 butchers, and 74 potters sustained everyday needs in the barrios and the larger city.[33]

Indigenous men living in the traza, the Spanish center, also did a lot of heavy work: 781 masons and 164 helpers—the latter likely boys or newcomers from the country—while 347 water carriers provided essential service to those who could pay for their efforts. More skilled, another 491 made or repaired shoes, 249 tailors clothed men (with women dressmakers again not reported), and 235 spun or wove cotton goods (with many more women surely involved, especially in spinning). Including uncounted women, the apparel sector surely employed more people than the heavy trades dominated by men and boys. Commercial food supply mattered in the center: 474 indigenous men worked in bakeries; 136 in pork dispensaries. (In the barrios, food and meal preparation mostly remained women's work—often unpaid within households and unreported even if it led to sales in local markets.) Also among the more skilled in the center, 251 worked as carpenters and 151 as blacksmiths—the latter showing native men moving into traditionally "European" trades. Finally, the largest number of indigenous men reported doing work in the traza, 838, labored in the tobacco factory in 1807.[34] They were the great majority of the 1,000 men, more or less, still employed there after the turn to women. What clearer sign of capitalist modernity: mixing struggling, often single women with ethnically other men to create a dependent workforce paid as little as possible to maximize profit?

Native women often lived and served in rich or at least prosperous households in the traza—lives of often difficult, very personal dependence. In the barrios, less-prosperous native families found greater independence and community cohesion. Many worked subject to merchant financiers—but the homes of the rich were many blocks away. Indigenous families led by men enrolled as citizens (*vecinos*) of the republics and living in the barrios had rights to house lots. And the nearly fifty barrios, most with from two to three hundred residents each, maintained community chapels that focused worship and social life among kin and neighbors.

The barrios were also places where indigenous people arriving from outlying communities settled in the city. Men concentrated there—as rural indigenous women often went directly to household service in the center. The barrios were simultaneously places of urban community cohesion and accommodation of newcomers. Most barrio residents spoke Spanish—essential to working in the city. Most newcomers spoke Nahuatl or Otomí, making the barrios places of social and linguistic adaptation. Rural migrants kept the population growing in a city that saw more deaths than births. The mix of indios in the center, the barrios, and the pueblos—old residents and new migrants—added to the fragmented complexity of the great American metropolis as the nineteenth century began.

Facing Change and Carrying On

The overlapping populations of artisans losing independence and struggling to keep influence and income while subject to merchant financiers, of workers gaining wages in exchange for dependent labor in the factories, and of indigenous peoples in the barrios keeping communities and doing diverse work from artisan crafts to wage labor, while holding rights in their separate republics, combined to make the city a place of enormous complexity and diversity. There were inequities and ethnic divisions. Workers linked to declining guilds had one set of limited rights; families in the indigenous republics used others to forge neighborhood communities. And despite—or perhaps because of—the uncertainties and inequities of life in the silver metropolis, social stability held through the decades before 1808, in the face of the crisis and coup that year, and during the times of conflict and insurgency that followed. Why?

Explaining what did not happen is always uncertain. Still, three factors seem important to the enduring social stability of the silver metropolis. First, it was the capital of a globally important silver capitalism to 1810, a place of persistent economic dynamism. For all the insecurities that plagued the city's diverse people, work was generally available, if not in old trades, then in new factories, in lives of hard hauling and in service to the powerful and the prosperous. Second, the economic, ethnic, and political-judicial fragmentation that shaped the city made organized resistance difficult. When thousands of men in the tobacco factory did resist, they were dispersed to find new ways to survive. And third, dependence defined city lives; people depended on labor, trades, and markets to survive. They might protest locally and briefly, but unlike rural people, they could not turn to the land, feed families, and resist for months or years. Power, fragmentation, and dependence defined the working city.

CHAPTER 5

Keys to the City

Stabilizing Power and Inequity

~ BY FAR THE LARGEST CITY IN THE AMERICAS AND THE PIVOT OF THE
New World's most dynamic economy, in 1800 Mexico City was at once a
center of power, an economic engine, and an unfathomable social and cultural maze shaped by deep inequities—all undergoing complex and uncertain changes in times of expanding trades and disruptive wars. An economy
shaped by entrenched oligarchic power, the decline of guilds and independent artisans, the spread of protoindustrialization led by merchant financiers
ruling household producers, and the rise of factories with segmented labor
forces sustained a growing urban population as the majority hustled to adapt
to new dependencies and insecurities.

The silver metropolis might appear a city precariously balancing profitable prosperity for a powerful few against polarizing divisions plaguing a
populace ready to erupt at any time. Yet social stability sufficient to sustain
power and prosperity held to 1808, through the summer of politics that year,
and after the coup that closed them. Calls for popular risings gained little
response in the city. Such stability in the face of exploitation and inequity
requires explanation.

Fragmentations: Ethnic Complexity and Gender Inequity

Ethnic complexity marked the social fragmentations that inhibited resistance in the city. Yet after 1790, those fragmentations lessened, giving way to
a more polarized, dual division. The number and proportion of Spaniards
and indios rose; those recognized as mixed decreased. The 1790 census
reported a population 50 percent classed as Spaniards (only 2 percent from
Europe); 23 percent designated indigenous; 12 percent mestizo, 7 percent
mulatto, and 9 percent as *castas* (uncertain mixes), bringing the mixed total
to 28 percent.[1] The 1811 census indicated that Spaniards had increased to
57 percent (a number reinforced by those who fled to the city in the face of
the uprisings then threatening the powerful and prosperous in the nearby
Mezquital and more distant Bajío); tribute-paying indios rose to 26 percent,
while the mixed population fell to 17 percent—a notable decrease of those
presumably in the middle.[2] By 1808, Mexico City was the most Spanish city
in the Americas—with a growing population of urban indios. Mixed people
had either declined in numbers or gained recognition as "Spaniards." Might
clear polarization between Spaniards and Indians have led to resistance
among the latter?

The growing population classed as Spaniards did not result from immi-
gration from Spain. Among the twenty-five hundred newcomers from Spain
reported in 1790, fewer than two hundred were women—unlikely to contribute to a large increase in the "Spanish" population. The increase came by
reproduction among American-born Spaniards—and by people of mixed
ancestry claiming Spanish status. In the mining center of Guanajuato, the
only other city in New Spain with a majority of Spaniards in the 1790s and
the only place in the Americas of equal importance to the global silver economy, a majority of mixed origins—mostly mulattos merging African and
Mesoamerican ancestries—faced danger, deep insecurities, and downward
pressures on incomes while they mined and refined the silver that filled
regime coffers and drove global trades. The one concession they gained—or
claimed—was status as Spaniards.[3] It appears that many long identified as
mixed in Mexico City also claimed Spanish status as the eighteenth century
became the nineteenth.

Their gains were limited. While Spaniards ruled the heights of power
and populated the provincial elite and the professions, most españoles
worked as artisans, household producers, and in factories—notably in the

mint, where they formed a majority. If Spaniards seemed a bit more prosperous, they shared nearly every economic role, skilled and unskilled, with people of mixed and indigenous status. Was the spread of Spanish status a concession to mixed peoples, a status ascent compensating material decline and widening insecurities—perhaps aimed at separating them further from indios living parallel lives?

The city's indigenous population did grow due to migration, a powerfully female migration from the countryside. The metropolis included more women than any other place in the hemisphere—56 percent of 120,000 counted around 1790, the same percent of over 160,000 reported in 1811. While native barrios at the city's edge reported nearly balanced sex ratios, migrant indigenous women concentrated among the Spanish and mixed populations near the city center. Census samples from 1790 and 1811 show that 60 percent of newcomers came from nearby heartland basins: the Valleys of Mexico, Toluca, Cuernavaca, and the Mezquital. Another 10 percent came from the Puebla basin, just east, with nearly as many from the Bajío to the northwest. The rest came in small numbers from across New Spain.[4] The few internal migrants classed as Spaniards came in gender-balanced numbers. Among migrant castas and the larger flow of indios, women outnumbered men two to one.[5]

Why? Pressures of population on limited lands in indigenous republics around the capital curtailed the ability of young men to gain a plot and start a family. They adapted by laboring seasonally at the nearby commercial estates that supplied the capital's markets. Meanwhile many young women left the villages for the capital.[6] They and young castas from nearby towns served in city households, prosperous and middling; others found work in the tobacco factory. Many had children: thus the need for day care there in the factory; many, perhaps most, young women who came to the city remained, sustaining the gender imbalance and helping the population grow. Migrants to the city approached 40 percent of its population in 1790; they were over 40 percent in 1811. The pull of the city economy held strong and heavily female migration fueled urban growth.[7] The large number of indigenous migrants and the large portion of single women among them layered another fissure into the city's diverse population, inhibiting resistance among a growing urban majority as the economy boomed, insecurities spread, and divisions deepened.

Declining Traditional Powers

As social fragmentations turned toward polarities, city powers looked to new ways of governance. The original structure in which a Spanish council ruled the Hispanic center, led by established elites and linked to guilds that organized and regulated an artisan economy and provided judicial mediation when needed, corroded in the eighteenth century. Commercial acceleration left the council ever less able to oversee a center populated by people outside the guild structure yet claiming Spanish status.

After 1770 the heights of power soared above the council. Financial, commercial, and landed oligarchs worked directly with the highest officers of the viceregal regime to negotiate questions of silver and imperial power. Men on the rise might spend a year as a magistrate, perhaps two as an honorary councilman, then move on. The council chamber remained mostly a domain of provincial elites mixing modest estate operators and learned professionals, dependent on the oligarchs and high officials who ruled above them. Meanwhile, the corrosion of guild power in all but a few trades left most economic activities and most producers and their families without sanctioned access to the council and without access to mediation in their own craft activities—except when conflict brought them to court. Accelerating protoindustrialization and expanding factories reinforced the power of oligarchs and the viceregal regime. Provincials and their council retained little oversight as guilds that regulated crafts, sanctioned access to the council, and organized artisans' social and religious lives lost power in a commercializing city.

The indigenous republics—San Juan Tenochtitlan and Santiago Tlatelolco—had their own councils to regulate life and oversee justice in the barrios where artisan and laboring families mixed, and in the pueblos at the city's edges, where chinampa cultivation mixed with crafts and labor. The native governments continued to serve key functions in the barrios and pueblos—providing house lots, overseeing markets, seeing to justice, and collecting the tributes that marked adult native men as indios and funded the operations of the native republics in the city. But after 1800 half the city's native people lived in the Spanish center; their links to the indigenous republics were unclear but for the expectation that they pay tributes. Old institutions of urban governance, Spanish and indigenous, carried on while they faced new challenges grounded in commercial expansion and changing ethnic participations.

Reforming Urban Justice

New ways of city governance developed. In the aftermath of the riots that threatened silver production at nearby Real del Monte and in more distant Guanajuato and San Luis Potosí in the 1760s and amid rising laments of an urban populace out of control as guild organizations waned, viceregal authorities looked to respond. They did not seek to bolster fading guilds or create new ways of participation to replace them. Instead, after a study led by audiencia judge don Baltásar Ladrón de Guevara, locally rooted and close to powerful oligarchs, a new system of surveillance and judicial oversight began in 1782—perhaps stimulated by knowledge of the uprisings then threatening Spanish power from Cuzco to Potosí high in the Andes (surely known yet never mentioned in Mexico City discussions). The city was divided into eight sectors, each overseen by a regime magistrate: five judges of the Audiencia's Criminal Court, the corregidor who represented the monarchy in the city, and the two city council magistrates. These were men of power with other duties; the reform left daily oversight to thirty-two barrio magistrates—four in each sector. New judges, each aided by one constable, were charged to know their barrios; make lists of residents, shops, and markets; prevent disturbances; and find justice when crimes or conflicts came.[8] The reform was an extension of governance by judicial mediation with a bit of new surveillance. It was not a turn to policing: thirty-two constables could not coerce a population passing one hundred thousand. A 1784 Audiencia report, honoring the plan and the judges' new oversight, saw good pacification under the barrio magistrates.[9]

Still, in 1790 a reforming viceroy, the Conde de Revillagigedo, added a new layer to city surveillance. With the revenues of a soaring silver economy, he added street lamps to most of the city center and hired *guarda-faroles*—light guards. Responsible for twelve lamps each, they carried arms while patrolling newly illuminated barrios at night. The city moved toward policing. Still, with thirty-two magistrates and an equal number of constables on duty during the day, and another sixty guards patrolling at night, police power remained limited.

How effective was the new system of magistrates, constables, street-lights, and night patrols? Crime and court data are irregular and uncertain for the decades from 1790 to 1810. Available evidence suggests that in a city shaped by accelerating commercialization, deep inequities, and enduring insecurities, the new system succeeded by containing crime within the bar-rios and among the poor. Many persisted in profiting from petty crime, keeping it close to home, rarely impacting the powerful, and never threaten-ing the larger urban economy. Frustrated and insecure men (and a few women) might take a bit of profit on the streets and settle scores with neigh-bors in new barrio courts without destabilizing the social order.[10] Crime and disorder were kept in the barrios—enabling the powerful and their profit-seeking allies to carry on.

A contested public culture operated in parallel ways. Complaints of too much lasciviousness, too much inebriation, too much popular control of reli-gious festivals and of the streets in the general, even too much popular expression in the theater, led the powerful to try diverse reforms. In the the-ater, attempts to stop plays that portrayed lives challenging sanctioned moral ways and to limit boisterous responses from commoners in the cheap seats had little success. The need to fill seats to pay for performances kept edgy presentations on—and the people kept approving with outbursts that showed the powerful and the prosperous, sitting separately and high above in the balconies, that popular voices would not be silenced.

Reformers also worried about the public festivals that gave vibrant expression to popular religious visions, often fueled by ample food and drink. They ordered them into the churches, where the clergy might control them. People responded by staging their own fiestas in the courtyards of the *vecindades* (tenements) where they lived—and where they could express themselves without oversight. Laments about pulque and drunkenness led to declining shipments to city taverns—if tax accounts are to be believed. Knowing that leading oligarchs profited by producing pulque, delivering it to the city, and selling it in taverns—and never lamented declining sales or profits—suggests they found ways to bypass tax collectors and keep pulque consumption strong.[11]

In all this, as in the domains of crime, the populace faced new con-straints yet found space to carry on—in ways that did not challenge power or disrupt the city economy. The result was a city of power and inequity sustained by constraining the working poor and allowing them to continue in often informal or illegal avenues of petty entrepreneurship while keeping their own ways of personal and local cultural and religious expression. Ultimately, the city kept social stability in times of deepening inequities and widening insecurities by a mix of economic dynamism, limited surveillance, social and cultural fragmentation, enduring spaces for popular expression—and capitalist charity mobilized in times of crises. The importance of the continuing dynamism of the silver economy to sustaining the city economy and its social peace cannot be overstated. For all the insecurities and inequities that came with the shift from guild-organized craft production to protoindustrialization and new ways of labor, all profiting merchant financiers and leaving growing numbers to scrape by in insecure dependence, the dynamic core economy of silver capitalism kept production and employment strong from 1770 to 1810—with the exception of years of crisis. Immigrants from outlying pueblos still came to the city; for all their struggles, they found ways to get by and sustain vibrant lives in popular and indigenous barrios. For all the challenges of the era, the urban majority found the flexible ingenuity to carry on; some even prospered.

Dependence, Insecurity, and the Power of Fragmentation

Cities are defined by dependence. Mexico City depended on the production of silver in regions near and far, and on trade links to the wider world, to prosper—even as powers concentrated in the city were pivotal to that prosperity. The city depended on rural regions all around for food, regions where great landed oligarchs and provincial elites who lived in the city ruled commercial production, yet relied—depended—for labor on hands recruited in landed native republics. Nearly everyone else in the city depended on the economy ruled by the oligarchs of silver capitalism. And dependence can be a strong stabilizer—if it provides access to viable lives for subordinate peoples.

The dynamism of silver capitalism kept the city economy strong through the eighteenth century and into the nineteenth. Its population grew by drawing migrants from rural regions facing pressures of population growth on limited community lands. Opportunity seemed to expand in the city. Still, the organization and mediations once provided by guilds were receding memories. Permanent secure ways of skilled work and craft production were

giving way to day labor and household production subject to merchant financiers whose drive for flexibility and low costs kept security scarce and wages
down. As the city grew, its resources and opportunities became increasingly
scarce and insecure for a majority struggling to adapt. Mediations continued
in remnant guilds and new barrio magistrates' courts—but easy solutions
also became scarce.[12]

Two cases highlight the persistence and the fragility of mediation in the
capital. In 1796, city leaders decided to close an alley—el Callejón de los
Muertos (the Way of the Dead), part of its public domain—delivering it to
men aiming to open a fireworks shop. The indigenous citizens of the barrio
of Tepito (they described themselves as such) sued in court to stop the closure. The alley gave them access to a source of clean water, to canals that
brought food and firewood to the city, and to the church where many went
to confess. Closing the alley would limit full access to the city. After long
considerations, the court reopened the alley.

In 1805, a city council facing heightened revenue pressures received a
petition from don Martín José Muguieros, *vecino del comercio* (merchant
citizen), asking to use an area of land he characterized as open, unused, and
not generating revenues for the city. He would pay a continuing annual fee
for the right to enclose the property and set a border of trees. He would beau-
tify the city with a park-like development—for his own unstated purposes.
The *parcialidad* of San Juan Tenochtitlan sued to block the transfer. It insisted
that the land Muguieros saw as vacant had long served the people of nearby
barrios as a place to graze a few animals, collect a bit of firewood, and make
adobes for their homes. It was a public resource of the indigenous republic,
serving its people. Muguieros would make it private and provide revenues to
the Spanish council. The republic pressed rights to *bien común*—the common good. The merchant saw entrepreneurship generating revenues. The
council that would gain the revenue decided the case—and favored the merchant promising to feed its treasury. Mediation continued—but the Spanish
council favored itself over the indigenous republic.[13] Could legitimacy last?

What is clear is that social stability held in the city before, during, and
after the summer of 1808. Despite spreading insecurities and uncertain
mediations, dependence reinforced by fragmentations infused with diverse
and crosscutting economic, ethnic, and gender divisions, made mobilized
resistance difficult, if not impossible, in the city. Provincial elites and

professionals might resent the power of the oligarchs, but they so depended on them for their prosperity that opposition was unlikely and likely unwise. Declining artisan sectors still found some prosperity in the city and still gained some mediation from the city council. The vast numbers laboring under protoindustrialization worked isolated at home while dealing with merchant financiers—powerful men who ruled the ability of families to produce and survive. The many who struggled as day laborers still found work in the booming city, scrambling alone or in small crews to get by in construction and the carrying trades. The men and women in new factories might gain better earnings and access to mutual aid—while divided in the mint between permanent workers and insecure replacements, in the tobacco factory between diverse, often single women and mostly indigenous men, and in the indianillas factory among, men, women, and boys. When men challenged the tobacco factory, most lost their jobs—a powerful lesson to those who might resist. And across the city, migrants from the country, most women, but many men too, kept coming in search of work—a constant reminder that producers, especially the less skilled, were replaceable.

Dependence, fragmentation, and competition for work mixed as powerful pacifying forces among urban producers. At the heights of power, oligarchs shared Spanish status with less-prosperous and dependent provincials, reinforcing elite unity. Among the producing majority, status as Spaniard, mestizo, mulatto, and indio brought status divisions that cut across diverse economic roles—creating double fragmentations among the always-dependent majority. If the flow of rural women to take up service in prosperous households reinforced traditional gender roles, the opening of the tobacco factory to thousands of women laborers challenged them— as did the smaller number of men who took up work spinning cotton. The distinct rights of the indigenous republics kept another line of separation. Any search for common cause or coalition against the powerful faced real obstacles. Among the populace, in the best of times many prospered a bit; most of the time the majority adapted, juggled, negotiated, and got by. Uncertain numbers scraped by at the bottom.

Capitalist Charity

At the heights of the city, dependence cemented reciprocities that consolidated the power of oligarchs and allowed provincials and professionals to join in implementing that power and share in the prosperity it concentrated. For the producing majority, lives of dependence implied access to work and the basics of survival. When survival came into question, as it did in periodic droughts and epidemics, insecurities and exploitations became blatant and ties of dependence might open to debate. The powerful had to respond—to preserve their power, the social relations of dependence that implemented it, and the urban economy that sustained everything.

In earlier times, the people of the city had risen in disruptive riots during crises that threatened urban sustenance and family survival—notably in 1624 and 1692. During the eighteenth century, the city council effectively regulated maize supplies—keeping availability good and prices modest into the 1770s.[14] In the decades of boom and challenge after 1780, the oligarchs and provincial elites of Mexico City developed ways of capitalist charity to keep the peace—and the potential for profit alive—in times of rising prices and threatening catastrophes.

In 1785 and 1786, a rare combination of extreme drought and early frost spread famine across the highlands from the capital and the nearby heartland to the Bajío. Crops were lost and staple prices soared to four times the norm of years of good harvests. As always, the great oligarchic growers held supplies accumulated in previous years, awaiting the peak prices of scarcity.[15] They were poised to profit, but the scarcity was so extreme that unmitigated profiteering could become destabilizing: maize supplies were so limited, prices so high, that death began to stalk the land.

The city council stepped in to organized profit-sustaining ways of relief. It collected 80,000 pesos in loans, mostly from merchants, to buy beef—often from the same merchants—to sell to mostly prosperous Hispanic consumers. Leading landed grazers and merchants of beef profited selling meat from livestock that would have perished in the drought. The council repaid the loans over time—subsidizing oligarchs' profits and urban sustenance. The council collected another 100,000 pesos in loans, mostly from landed oligarchs, to buy maize—most from the same oligarchs—to stock the city granary. The granary sold the maize at high (yet stabilized) prices to desperate city consumers—and later repaid the oligarchs. Merchants and oligarchs announced both loans and sales as acts of Christian charity.[16] They profited, if a bit less, in months of desperation while sustaining city people who were essential producers in the complex economy of silver capitalism—and the

primary market for the oligarchs' estate produce. The city council demonstrated that it still had a role mediating between powerful oligarchs and the
city populace it was charged to serve with justice in search of bien común,
the common good.

A decade later, when smallpox struck the capital in 1797, the archbishop
led a parallel system of funding to sustain the city through another deadly
crisis. He led a *junta de caridad* (charity council) that included don Cosme
de Mier y Trespalacios, the audiencia judge linked to the Condes de Santiago;
don Antonio de Basoco, the leading merchant financier in the city and a
leading meat supplier; a few landed professionals; and several high church-
men.[17] The junta assigned sectors of the city to oligarchs ready to fund the
provision of assistance. The second Conde de Regla, the landed Marqués de
Vivanco, the landed merchant don Miguel González Calderón, and the rising merchant don Ysidro Antonio de Ycaza shared the costs of care in one
sector. Each paid 1,575 pesos toward expenses of 2,635 pesos for food, 2,489
for blankets, 765 for medicines, 110 pesos each for three physicians, and 100
each for two phlebotomists.[18] They offered palliative care to families facing a
disease that had become a recurrent killer of children (no longer the devastating, depopulating plague of the sixteenth century). The goal was to help as
many as possible survive the epidemic—to keep the city growing in population and production while sustaining the archbishop's, the oligarchs', and
many provincials' reputations for charitable concern.

Contributions of less than 1600 pesos each were minimal for oligarchs.
They could do more when it served their primary interests. The second
Conde de Regla was then working to revive the mines at Real del Monte,
aiming to replicate the earlier bonanza that had made his father and the family inordinately rich and landed. There and at nearby Pachuca he spent
11,787 pesos on smallpox relief, with uncounted additional funds spent at the
family estates.[19] Did he pay to provide inoculations, a new, experimental, and
generally successful preventative, among those who produced his wealth? We
know that in Guanajuato, people in the mining center got inoculations while
others, urban and rural, did not.[20] Particulars might differ, but in the capital
and other regions pivotal to silver capitalism, oligarchs delivered charitable
relief in service of capitalist interests while proclaiming Christian commitments. When economic dynamism, social fragmentations, neighborhood
justice, and limited patrols might prove insufficient to keep the peace and

sustain the population essential to profit, capitalist charity came to save the people.

Capitalist Power, Regime Mediation, and Urban Stability

Social stability held in the capital of silver capitalism through the late eighteenth century and into the nineteenth, before, during, and after the crisis of 1808. Calls to popular revolution in 1799 and again in 1808 went unanswered (as we shall see). When escalating Euro-Atlantic wars led to Napoleon's invasion of Spain, the fall of legitimate sovereignty, a summer of politics, and the coup that closed everything in 1808, the unity of power among oligarchs, regime officials, provincial elites, and leading professionals in Mexico City broke. The regime of mediation broke too. Many among the urban populace took to streets and plazas, expressing political views (as we shall also see). They never broke the social order with violent assaults on power. The city remained at peace—its people locked in dependence and fragmented by ethnic divisions.

The coup that imposed militarized powers backed by claims of popular sovereignty did set off debates that led to violent challenges to the regime and silver capitalism—not in the capital, but in outlying regions where mining mixed with agrarian capitalism, the productive core of the silver economy. The societal conflagration that took down silver capitalism and transformed a dynamic and rich, unequal yet stable New Spain into a struggling and conflictive Mexican nation began with the fall of the regime of mediation in Mexico City in 1808. Knowing the social history of power and production in the capital, a more political history of how regime mediation operated there before 1808, how Napoleon's invasion of Spain opened unprecedented debates, and how the September coup closed those debates and ended mediating rule is essential. The goal is to illuminate the central role of the mediating regime in sustaining New Spain's prosperity and stability, how it fell, and why the consequences proved radically destabilizing.

PART II

The Politics of Empire, 1765–1810

From Mediation to Revolution

CHAPTER 6

Time of Trial

Bourbon Reforms, Regional Risings,
and Regime Restoration, 1765–1771

~~ THE 1760S PROVED A KEY TIME OF TRIAL, CONFLICT, AND RESTORA-
tion in Mexico City and New Spain. As the Spanish Bourbon monarchy faced
years of warfare and mounting debts, reformers pressed new demands for
revenues. They sought more administrative ways of rule backed by new powers of coercion. In response, the men who led the Mexico City Council
demanded that their rights of petition and mediation be respected, insisting
that reforms be negotiated within the conciliar-judicial regime. While that
debate focused city politics, in the Bajío and other regions to the north, parallel demands for revenues and militia recruitment pressed on the men who
mined the silver that made New Spain rich and sustained Spain's empire.
They led working communities in riots that broke the peace and threatened
prosperity.

The powerful men who ruled Mexico City and silver capitalism remained
loyal to the regime—and to silver capitalism. In time, they raised rural militias
to contain the risings. By very different ways of resistance—Mexico City
councilmen demanding rights to petition and mediation; Bajío producers riot-
ing for fair earnings, lower taxes, and freedom from militia duties—key actors
in New Spain's silver economy showed the Bourbons and their reforming

agents that assertions of power backed by military force would destabilize silver capitalism. They negotiated a return to mediating rule—and silver production and Crown revenues soared into the nineteenth century.

The trials and restorations of the 1760s reset the regime and silver capitalism. Reforms continued, but from the 1770s through the 1790s they operated within the regime of corporate rights, conciliar consultations, judicial mediations, and limited military power while still focused on promoting silver production. After 1800, more intense wars led to greater revenue pressures in Spain and New Spain. The regime adapted to keep silver flowing—until Napoleon's 1808 invasion of Spain set off political conflicts in Mexico City that led to the September coup that locked military power at the core of the regime and broke rule by mediation. Two years later, the Bajío exploded in more widespread insurgencies. Political rebels demanded participations recently opened, then closed; popular communities took arms to claim redistributions in a search for social justice. Together, they set off conflicts that broke silver capitalism.

To understand the crisis of 1808, it is essential to see the stabilizing power of the regime of petition and mediation that ruled into the nineteenth century. The Bourbons' search for administrative rule backed by military power in the 1760s generated political conflicts in the capital and popular resistance in key mining regions—leading to negotiations that restored the regime of mediation. Silver capitalism held strong and stable from the 1770s into the early 1800s. The regime, the challenges of the 1760s, and the restoration that followed focus this chapter. The next recounts the politics of the surge of silver from 1770 to 1800. Then the analysis turns in depth and detail to the origins, course, and consequences of the crisis of 1808.

Empire of Mediation

The regime forged in the sixteenth century to integrate Spain's empire and the global economy of silver and trade it promoted proved remarkably enduring. Through centuries marked by wars with diverse rivals, Portuguese and Dutch, French and British, and despite a forced change in dynasty when Bourbons replaced Hapsburgs after 1700, the empire carried on. That persistence reflected the dynamism of the silver economy focused in the Andes from 1570 to 1650, then in New Spain after 1700, and the stabilizations enabled by a system of governance grounded in multiple corporations with diverse rights, integrated and balanced by judicial mediations. Across the empire, Spanish cities and towns had rights to councils, self-rule, local justice—and to petition and appeal to higher councils. Merchant financiers were organized in consulados, chambers with rights to self-rule, internal mediation of members' disputes—and appeal to higher authorities. And across the Andes and the Mesoamerican regions of New Spain, native communities reorganized as indigenous republics held rights to land, self-rule, petition to higher authorities, and appeal to higher courts.

Higher powers were represented by district magistrates (*alcaldes mayores*, sometimes *corregidores*) in county-sized jurisdictions across the empire, by high courts (audiencias) in major provinces, and viceroys who represented the king's justice in his American capitals—Lima and Mexico City, joined in the eighteenth century by Bogotá and Buenos Aires. General orders and high officials might come from Spain, but American councils, Spanish and indigenous, consulados, and others too knew they had rights to appeal and represent their interests locally to officials and audiencias in American capitals, even to councils in Spain. Ultimately they could appeal to the king's justice—a process that might take years. Most appeals and petitions resulted in outcomes negotiated by authorities in judicial roles. The system evolved and adapted for three centuries to keep the empire alive and silver capitalism strong.

Many will read the above paragraphs as an assault on known truth. The regime that ruled the Spanish empire for three centuries and kept its silver economy at the center of a vibrant commercial capitalism remains egregiously misunderstood. A conspiracy of misperception (unconscious?) has linked Latin American liberals, who since the nineteenth century have portrayed the empire as closed and backward, and Anglophone scholars, who persistently construct it as closed and despotic. Both link closure, backwardness, and despotism to Catholic traditions. The autonomies and representations, negotiations and mediations that shaped everyday governance—linked to Catholic religious legitimations—are either ignored or read as desperate appeals in the face of enduring authoritarian impositions.

J. H. Elliott's *Empires of the Atlantic World*, a massive and knowledgeable synthesis comparing the Spanish and British regimes in the Americas, brilliantly and powerfully exemplifies—and continues—the misreading.[1] Comparing mainland colonies of the two empires, he emphasizes the silver-producing cores of Spain's domains while downplaying the Caribbean slave colonies that drove Britain's American interests. Setting Britain's slave regime at the margins of his analysis while deemphasizing the rights and participations of the thousands of indigenous republics across Spanish America, Elliott portrays despotic imposition as the core of Spain's rule while asserting that representation and participation shaped Anglo-American ways.

Yet for decades before Elliott wrote, Anglophone scholars as distinguished as William Taylor, Woodrow Borah, and James Lockhart had documented that Spain's empire never imposed authoritarian power over its indigenous subjects. Instead, it granted them institutions of landed autonomy, local self-rule, and judicial appeal that enabled them to adapt, represent interests, appeal disputed decisions, and generally negotiate subordination during long centuries.[2] Years before Elliott published his synthesis, Alejandro Cañeque offered an analysis of the origins of viceregal power in New Spain, emphasizing representation, negotiation, and mediation.[3] Simultaneously, Annick Lempérière presented (in French) her pivotal study of corporate power and judicial mediations in late imperial Mexico City.[4]

The best scholarship on Britain's American empire long recognized the inherent contradictions of a regime that allowed participations to a few while holding so many enslaved.[5] A new understanding of Spanish governance in the Americas has escaped presumptions of authoritarian despotism to see a regime of participations, representations, and negotiations that extended rights and participations to Spanish Americans and indigenous majorities and ruled for three centuries primarily by judicial mediations. Recently, Regina Grafe and Alejandra Irigoin have focused on the eighteenth century and economic domains to broaden and strengthen our vision of how participations, representations, and mediations ruled in what they call a "stakeholders empire."[6] Spain's monarchy did not—could not—rule by coercive mandate; it negotiated the conflicts and contradictions inherent in the empire's social, cultural, and political diversity to sustain Spain's Americas and global commercial capitalism for three centuries.[7]

The regime that integrated Spain's empire came out of sixteenth-century encounters with indigenous American states, their destruction in the face of the smallpox and other devastating diseases carried across the Atlantic by Europeans, and the rise of silver and the global trades it stimulated after 1550. There was no overall design, just constant adaptations to a mix of calamities and opportunities by risk-taking entrepreneurs in search of profit and a monarchy in search of power and the revenues to sustain it.

Fearing that Europeans who imagined themselves "conquerors" might entrench themselves in power in the Americas, the regime worked from the 1540s to deny their rights to oversee native peoples via encomienda grants that sanctioned tribute taking and rotating labor services—grants that gave a European cast to indigenous ways of rule.[8] After 1550, authorities worked with clergy to reconsolidate rapidly shrinking native communities as indigenous republics—with local rights to land and self-rule. The end of encomiendas and the confirmation of native community autonomies ensured that New Spain would not include an entrenched noble estate parallel to those that endured in much of Europe through the eighteenth century.[9]

There were revealing exceptions. Cortés gained rights as Marqués del Valle de Oaxaca that included dominion over regions of the southern Valley of Toluca, the Cuernavaca basin, and Oaxaca. He and his heirs named local magistrates, rights to oversee justice parallel to those held by many European lords.[10] But those rights were unique in New Spain and limited by Cortés's heirs' decision to live in Europe. The men holding titles in Mexico City and elsewhere, so prominent in silver capitalism and dealings with the viceregal regime, gained labels of nobility in recognition of entrepreneurial success and contributions to imperial coffers—a few from the late sixteenth century, most in the eighteenth.[11] They had neither rights nor roles as a privileged estate. Thus the efforts to insert their interests at the height of the regime—often successful, thanks to their great economic power.

New Spain also lacked an indigenous nobility parallel to the *kurakas* so important to Spanish rule in the Andes. Regional lords earlier pivotal to Inca rule, kurakas (at times relabeled caciques) survived as hereditary noble intermediaries under the Spanish regime. They proved essential to Spanish rule and the rise of silver capitalism in the late sixteenth century, organizing labor drafts and delivering sustenance to Potosí as the mining center grew to 150,000 people. They mediated social stability across the Andes until the conflicts of the 1780s. Then, Tupac Amaru, a kuraka, led a massive rebellion around Cuzco. Pacification depended on kurakas and caciques still allied with the regime. Spanish dependence on kurakas—and the potential for kurakas to challenge Spanish rule—became clear in a decade of destabilizing violence.[12]

By 1600, New Spain had neither a European noble estate nor a stratum of native lords essential to Spanish rule (except for the caciques who held enduring if limited rights and roles in southern regions like Oaxaca, Chiapas, and Yucatán, far from the centers of silver capitalism). The regime had drawn surviving indigenous peoples into republics granted landed domains and rights to self-rule by councils of native notables. Similar rights were sanctioned for communities in the Andes, but there councils dealt as often with kurakas as with Spanish magistrates. In New Spain, native republics ruled themselves, dealing with Spanish district magistrates and the Indigenous Court in Mexico City when conflicts could not be resolved locally. In the heartland around the capital, indigenous republics sustained silver capitalism from the sixteenth through the eighteenth centuries, providing workers and staples to sustain mining centers and the city.[13]

The Hispanic peoples of New Spain concentrated in cities with their own councils. Led by powerful men who often purchased seats in times of Crown financial necessity, they oversaw local affairs: public works, craft guilds, city markets—and justice. They restored peace in times of crisis, as in Mexico City in the 1620s and 1690s. They held rights of petition and appeal to the Audiencia, the viceroy, the Council of the Indies in Spain, and ultimately to the king.[14]

The merchants so central to financing mines and sending silver into global trades gained their own chamber before 1600. The consulado set in Mexico City enabled merchants to negotiate disputes among themselves, petition the regime for rights and redress of grievances, and gain judicial resolution of conflicts they could not resolve internally. The consulados were not closed bodies that monopolized trade. They were chambers that all successful merchants and financiers joined, enabling them to limit and resolve conflicts and to press their interests before a monarchy that sought revenues—taxes, loans, and bequests—from those who profited most from silver capitalism. In the negotiation, the merchants of the Mexico City Consulado, a group of fluid membership, did rule the financing of mining and the delivery of silver into imperial and global trades for centuries. The Crown claimed soaring revenues; merchants-financiers gained opportunities to profit, autonomy in commercial justice, and access to press their interests in the councils of power.

In governance, the council led Mexico City, representing its interests before the monarchy. In trade, the consulado organized the city's merchants, promoting their profits and generating the revenues that were the monarchs' first interest. In indigenous communities, rural and urban, councils oversaw local lands, markets, justice, and religious life—and had favored access to courts that mediated conflicts within the indigenous world and with Spanish powers. Corporate autonomies and judicial mediations organized and integrated viceregal leaders, city governance, the imperial traders, and indigenous republics in the city and across New Spain.

The proclaimed goal was "el bien común"—the common good.[15] Ultimately the common good came at the intersection of diverse interests: the king sought to maximize silver production and the revenues it brought the regime; the city council aimed to maximize its autonomy and stabilize city life in an economy ruled by silver capitalists; the consulado's merchant financiers pursued profit by financing mines and joining in global trade; and indigenous republics worked to maintain self-rule and autonomies on the land in a region commercializing under the stimulus of silver. There was great potential for conflict and much to balance. There were also shared if unequal interests in the revenues, profits, and prosperity of silver capitalism and the stability needed to sustain it. Judicial mediation balanced those interests for centuries.

Notably, regime mediations stabilized New Spain for centuries without concentrated military power. Before 1520, the Mexica and other contenders for power in the Mesoamerican crucible of conflict had ruled by military force, as had the Incas as they extended power across the Andes. But Spanish rule came enabled by a depopulation that left ample resources for native survivors while silver delivered profit to entrepreneurs, revenue to the regime, and opportunity to many more. The new regime disarmed indigenous majorities—and saved costs by keeping Hispanic militia forces dispersed and limited. In that too, the regime in the Americas differed from monarchies in Europe. There, war and border defense mandated core militaries backed by militias. Force was available in times of conflict or resistance. In Spain's Americas, the absence of reliable, effective troops mandated reliance on mediation, making coercion a last, uncertain resort.[16] New Spain had no tradition of "martial life, there were, essentially, no regular military forces, there had never been direct participation in war."[17]

A final point about the regime, important to rights to petition and mediation over the centuries, and a key to the mobilizations in Mexico City in 1808:

corporate groups expected to be consulted on revenue questions and to participate in times of uncertain or contested sovereignty. The Castilian regime
came out of medieval traditions in which *cortes*—courts, assemblies, parliaments—gathered to confirm the rights of kings and to commit revenues in
exchange for respect for local autonomies and promises of justice. Iberian cities and towns with councils gathered periodically in cortes into the early sixteenth century. Then growing regime revenues generated in good part by gold,
silver, and other imperial flows allowed Carlos I (V as Holy Roman Emperor)
to rule at home and join in European wars without calling periodic Castilian
cortes and facing their demands for consultation and participation.[18]

Still, cortes continued to meet in the kingdom of Aragon (including
Catalonia and Valencia) into the seventeenth century—keeping the memory
and reality of the tradition alive. The Spanish councils of Cuzco and Mexico
City, former capitals of powerful Amerindian states, gained rights to join in
cortes and their deliberations. They were never called, but the rights were not
forgotten.[19] Spanish councils in New Spain were consulted on questions of
rights and revenues into the seventeenth century, when the Spanish Jesuit
Francisco Suárez wrote a treatise emphasizing that the sovereignty ultimately granted by God went first to the pueblos—cities and towns with
councils—who delegated it to monarchs in return for commitments to
deliver justice in the interest of the common good. The Stuart kings of
England banned Suárez's text as too radical for their monarchical goals. He
was taught across Spain's domains long into the eighteenth century—and
well remembered in Mexico City in 1808.[20]

The regime centered in Mexico City that governed New Spain and sustained silver capitalism to 1760 mixed corporate rights and regime mediations. There was no state, no church, no military—in any singular
institutional way. Everything was multiple. Diverse corporations worked
with diverse rights and regulations—and looked to diverse regime bodies to
respond to petitions and mediate disputes.[21] The homogeneous law that came
later to define states was neither imagined nor desired.[22] Forces of coercion
were minimal and multiple, mostly irregular militias and unreliable agents
of imposition. Their weakness reinforced the regime's reliance on mediation—and the broad legitimacy of its judicial ways of rule.

It was not a "model regime" that might be replicated elsewhere. It evolved
unplanned in a region where depopulation had left resources plentiful for the

populace while silver generated unprecedented riches for the powerful. New tensions came in the eighteenth century when renewed population growth began to press on limited resources, silver soared to generate new opportunities for profit, and wars escalated to create rising regime revenue demands. New Spain's population doubled from the 1680s to the 1740s—to hit a plateau. Silver production rose from just over 5 million pesos yearly after 1700 to over 12 million yearly after 1745—to hold at that high level to 1760. Then production fell by more than a million pesos in 1761—just as the costs and debts of the Seven Years' War struck the treasury of Carlos III, just enthroned in 1759.[23] He and his advisers, desperate for revenues, turned to administrative measures backed by new military powers. The attempt set off conflicts that disrupted silver production and blocked the creation of forces that might have backed more administrative rule in New Spain. The Bourbon dream of a state of assertion and coercion collapsed in the face of its disruption of silver capitalism—the necessary foundation of Spain's power in the world.

Bourbon Assertions, Bajío Risings, and Regime Adaptations, 1740–1770

If the Hapsburg regime that oversaw the rise of Spain's empire and silver capitalism emphasized diverse rights, corporate autonomies, and judicial mediations, the Bourbons who ruled after 1700 became famous for attempts to assert power from above. Their American subjects regularly resisted, accusing them of impositions, even of despotism. Their protests were carefully recorded in judicial processes energized to remind kings and reformers that ruling the empire and gaining its revenues depended on accepting diverse groups' rights to participate and petition, and on rulers' effective mediations—all to keep the peace and keep silver flowing, perhaps the ultimate, unstated definition of the common good.

Bourbon pressures on Mexico City began early in the 1740s. As the empire faced a conflict in the Caribbean that would soon turn to long battles over Austrian succession in Europe, Viceroy Conde de Fuenclara saw a Mexico City Council burdened by debts and unable to contribute to the rising costs of war. He insisted that with stronger finances, it might better serve the city and deliver more to the empire. He appointed an overseer of accounts, audiencia judge don Domingo de Trespalacios. The council saw imposition and loss of autonomy. The historic relationship between Crown and council was at stake: a council without control of financial resources could neither rule the city effectively nor engage in the classic role of bargaining rights for revenues with the monarchy. Trespalacios worked for years to restore council accounts, with some success (perhaps thanks to his close ties to the Condes de Santiago, the most honored of the capital's landed oligarchs). The council first protested his new role and powers. Then, as revenues rose and debts receded, it negotiated to strengthen its traditional rights to rule the city, represent its interests, and gain justice to balance the interests of council, city, and empire—all facilitated by the rise in silver production through the 1740s and its steady hold near then-historic peaks in the 1750s. No armed pressure was involved in the long negotiation.[24]

The more intense and costly Atlantic and European wars of 1757 to 1763 brought greater demands on imperial coffers. The Spanish Bourbons did not lose those wars, as is often asserted. They kept all their American domains— and added New Orleans and Louisiana. The British captured and held Havana and Manila for a year in 1762 and 1763—and returned them to Spain at war's end. Spain held its own, in good part thanks to New Spain's silver. Britain gained Canada, of limited economic or strategic value. France ceded Louisiana to Bourbon Spain, its dynastic family ally—and kept Saint-Domingue, the richest sugar-plantation colony of the time.

Arguably, the war proved a stalemate for Britain and France. It disrupted production and trade in Jamaica and Saint-Domingue, stimulating resistance by enslaved producers. After the war, new racial strictures returned both to new dynamism; both reclaimed their established roles as leading plantation colonies and engines of Atlantic capitalism.[25] But the cost of imperial stalemate was great. After the war, Britain and Spain pressed new revenue demands backed by military force in American domains.[26] From 1765 Britain imposed new taxes backed by armed power in its mainland colonies, setting off the conflicts that led to US independence. Spain pressed parallel demands for revenue and sought new military power in New Spain in the same years—and provoked conflicts that led to accommodations that kept Spanish rule in place and set silver capitalism rising to new heights.[27]

In 1765, the regime announced a new tobacco monopoly without consulting city authorities. It simultaneously sent troops to the capital and required the city to provide quarters and sustenance—without consultation. It demanded a militia census, aiming to draw more men to arms in the city. The council responded as "The Most Noble and Most Loyal City of Mexico,

Capital and Metropolis of the Towns and Cities of North America." The city saw itself as a metropolis, the capital of a North America constituted by cities and towns—meaning those with Spanish councils. It wrote as the first among the councils that ruled and represented North America, the Spanish domains from Central America to New Mexico, insisting that the tobacco monopoly, a revenue measure that reinforced Crown power and transformed local production and marketing, could not be implemented without consultation—or at least allowing the council to seek redress in light of the city's rights and interests. The lack of consultation and denial of rights of petition also made the demand to sustain troops unacceptable in the council's eyes.[28] It did not expect to make imperial policy—it did expect to be consulted and keep rights to petition for judicial redress when Crown acts impacted city powers and urban lives.

In a regime grounded in multiple councils and chambers, judicial in operation and thus negotiating in policy-making, impositions without consultations or rights to petition assaulted established ways and means. It its recent acts, the Bourbon regime treated the metropolitan council with no greater respect than "el vecino más plebeyo"—the most common citizen.[29] Several emphases are clear: the presumption that cities and their councils shared in governance and ultimately in sovereignty; the assertion that among Spanish cities of North America, the city of Mexico and its council held first rights to participate, petition, and ultimately appeal to the king, "el último juez"—the final judge.[30] Notably, those rights did not extend to plebeians.

Despite the council's protest, nothing could be done about the tobacco monopoly.[31] The displaced tobacco shops and stalls were mostly the province of women with no rights to guild organization or representation that the council could claim to defend. Little, too, could be done about troops that arrived unannounced and had to be quartered and fed.[32] Setting them loose in the city without food and quarters was no alternative to men devoted to order. The people of the city did prevent the taking of an effective militia census and the recruitment of new militias. Families refused to report the existence or whereabouts of eligible men, and the council had no interest in devoting funds to forces it might not control.[33]

Then in 1766, the Viceroy Marqués de Croix set new limits on the council's control of city revenues (just as Trespalacios gained promotion to the Council of the Indies in Spain). The council responded with petitions that

did reach Madrid despite the viceroy's attempt at immediate implementation. The regime of petition and mediation was not dead.

Meanwhile, in 1766 and 1767, violent conflicts erupted in key mining
centers north of the capital. While the city and its councilmen responded to
the tobacco monopoly, the placement of troops in the city, and claims on its
revenues, popular risings in nearby Real del Monte, the pivotal mining city
of Guanajuato in the Bajío, and in San Luis Potosí farther north reminded all
who contended for power and aimed to profit in New Spain that the political
peace and social stability essential to silver capitalism was more important
than the spats that divided them.

At Real del Monte, don Pedro Romero de Terreros, future Conde de
Regla, aimed to take maximum silver and profit after years of investment by
cutting the ore shares gained by the most skilled workers and the wages of
the rest. In 1766, while political debates roiled nearby Mexico City, they
rioted, killed a manager, and almost captured Romero before militias calmed
the conflict. Then audiencia judge don Baltásar Ladrón de Guevara negotiated a deal that gave workers most of what they demanded—and returned
the mines to production.[34] The same year, the announcement of tobacco and
playing-card monopolies in Guanajuato raised resentments of rising prices
on the pleasures of hard-working men facing lives of danger in the mines.
And those costs came with new taxes on foodstuffs and new demands for
militia enrollment. Workers rioted in the summer of 1766—and won locally
mediated resolutions. When the regime pressed local officials to reimpose its
demands on the workers who made New Spain rich, they rioted more vehe-
mently in 1767, holding the city center and stopping mining for months.[35]

Riots also spread across San Luis Potosí, again responding to new taxes
and other demands. There, the protests took a revealing political turn. Across
the region, rebel workers demanded the removal of immigrants, of gachupines, from office and trade. Rioters at the mining town of Guadalcázar even
called the Conde de Santiago, leader of Mexico City's landed oligarchs, to
become king of New Spain. Angry workers imagined an alliance of
Americans—landed oligarchs, regime officials, local councilmen, artisans,
shopkeepers, and workers—expelling arrogant, greedy immigrants from
Spain to create a more just New Spain.[36]

No local officials, provincial notables, mining or landed entrepreneurs,
and certainly not the Conde de Santiago, answered the call. Explicit at

Guadalcázar, implicit in other mining centers, the call from below for an alliance of Americans, powerful and poor, against Europeans found no adherents in the halls of power or the parlors of the oligarchs in the 1760s. Instead, the American Spanish mine operator, militia commander, and landed entrepreneur don Francisco de Mora mobilized an alliance of the powerful backed by provincial militias to crush the risings at Guadalcázar and across San Luis Potosí. Equally revealing, when workers already in arms in San Luis Potosí, Guanajuato, and elsewhere learned in the summer of 1767 that the regime planned to expel the Jesuits, the rioters offered to protect the priestly educators and preachers from arrest and deportation. The Jesuits chose to acquiesce in expulsion rather than challenge the alliance of power they had long sustained as educators, estate operators, and missionaries.[37]

The Conde de Santiago, don Francisco de Mora, and most of New Spain's Jesuits were American Spaniards. They shared a world of entrepreneurship and prosperity where the roles of European and American Spaniards might at times face conflict but ultimately merged to consolidate a domain of power unmatched in the Americas—power concentrated in Mexico City and in the provinces pivotal to silver capitalism. Powerful American Spaniards ignored the calls of a riotous populace to resist the assertions of the Bourbon regime. The risings were contained by militias led by American notables, manned by their provincial dependents, allowing the Bourbons' visitor general, don José de Gálvez, to follow with exemplary repression. The Conde de Santiago stayed rich and powerful in Mexico City. Don Francisco de Mora, honored as Conde de Peñasco, later married his daughter to don José Sánchez Espinosa, a Mexico City landed oligarch. Jesuits left for exile. The mines resumed operation, mineworkers returned to work—chastened, but with concessions on taxes and wages. In the shadow of those conflicts, authorities in the capital restored government by petition and mediation and silver production rose to new heights.

Righting the Regime: Reclaiming Mediation, 1769–1771
As peace returned to the mining centers that made New Spain rich and Mexico City powerful, in 1769 don Juan José de Areche, one of Gálvez's chief advisers, proposed that Viceroy Croix create a number of new seats on the Mexico City Council, perhaps three or four, to be "elected" by the viceroy. The proposal recognized that real power in the capital had risen above the

council. Proprietary councilmen of limited wealth, mostly modest landed proprietors with professional roles, needed reinforcement by more powerful men who might see imperial interests more clearly. The council had the right to lead public affairs, see to the common welfare, and provide justice in New Spain's capital, but its members lacked the wealth, power, and prestige to make those claims effective. Areche proposed that the viceroy appoint new "honorary" councilmen, chosen among the "outstanding" men of the city, among the oligarchs. Another newcomer would serve as *personero del común*, the people's representative—one voice to speak for the city's diverse majority. The council protested the creation of new seats without consultation and adamantly resisted the viceroy's power of appointment.[38]

This time Croix accepted the council's right of petition and quickly struck a bargain the council could accept. The council, not the viceroy, would elect three honorary councilmen yearly, each to serve a two-year term. Thus six would sit at all times, constituting a large minority. There would be a peoples' representative—one—also chosen by the council, not the people. It took years for the bargain to gain sanction in Spain, but it shaped the council from 1770. Through the decades that followed, proprietary councilmen of limited means, good education, and great aspirations repeatedly chose men on the rise, merchants and landlords, to join them for limited terms. Oligarchs learned the ways and means of the council; proprietary councilmen gained prestige in the shadows of their temporary colleagues and the powerful families they represented. Oligarchic power was confirmed. Oligarchs continued to pursue their interests primarily through marriages and other ties to high officials. Provincial elites on the council adapted to roles as subordinates, dependent on oligarchs who now sat with them for brief terms. Council power reconsolidated as an unequal alliance of oligarchs and provincials.

Defending American Spaniards' Rights in the Regime of Mediation

In the aftermath of these conflicts, negotiations, and consolidations, in 1771 the Mexico City Council wrote an often-cited representation asserting the rights of American Spaniards. In an immediate and obvious way, the proclamation was a loud statement of the council's right to petition—a right denied by reforming officials in 1765 and 1766, then (in the shadow of the conflicts in the Bajío) accepted in the compromise over honorary members in 1770, now utilized by a council that controlled its own membership and demanded to be heard on larger questions of power and participation.

The representation is famous because it has been taken as a statement of a presumed Mexican longing for independence. Of course, in 1771 the assertion of "Mexican" rights referred only to the city—no larger society claimed the name. A careful reading shows that the men who led the city, most American Spaniards, wrote to reassert their rights to autonomy, participation, and mediation within the empire. Ultimately, they insisted on American participation in rule by mediation. If armed force were needed to contain the populace, Americans would lead its use.

The council began by stating again that it addressed the king as "cabeza y corte"—head and court, thus capital city—representing the interests of "América Septentrional"—North America.[39] That was closer to true in 1771 than in 1765 after it fended off viceregal controls and integrated key oligarchs into the chamber. The reinforced council wrote to protest visions and policies based on "enlightened" thinking that denigrated Americans' intellectual and moral capacities and aimed to exclude American Spaniards from high regime offices and religious roles. They argued that the relegation of American Spaniards to "middling employments" was not only discriminatory, but "the route to the loss of America and the ruin of the state."[40]

Was this a veiled threat to declare independence five years before 1776? Improbably. It was first and foremost a reminder to the Bourbon king that his wealth and power depended on New Spain and its silver economy, that the alliance and integration of American and European Spaniards was essential to maintaining that economy, and that the link between New Spain and Spain was the key to the empire. A disruption of that alliance, that link, that prosperity, they warned, would ruin the monarchy built on the silver capitalism that fueled global trades and filled imperial coffers. The council proclaimed to the king and those who ruled in his name the lessons of the conflicts of 1765 to 1771: only shared participations among American and European Spaniards could keep the peace essential to silver capitalism.

Much of the long text argues against the prejudicial constructions of American character then spreading in Europe and used to justify proposed exclusions.[41] The council argued the discriminatory unfairness of such exclusions and detailed the long and enduring loyalty of American Spaniards, emphasizing Americans' ability and dedication to the monarchy.

The council called for unity and equality, opposing preferences for Europeans. Toward the end, it turned to narrate the periodic protests that had challenged power, peace, and prosperity in New Spain over the centuries—emphasizing that American Spaniards organized, funded, and led the militias that in moments of crisis kept the order essential to Spanish rule and transatlantic prosperity. American Spaniards had mobilized American forces to break the recent risings in Guanajuato and San Luis Potosí. The council emphasized the pivotal role of don Francisco de la Mora, now Conde de Peñasco, in raising and leading the militias that crushed resistance in San Luis Potosí.[42] Implicit in the text: military power in the Americas, limited to militias, belonged to the Americans who had long served the Crown's most valuable kingdom.

They would decide its fate—and if treated fairly, they would continue to show staunch loyalty to the Spanish Crown and the silver capitalism that profited so many. The proclamation insisted that American Spaniards were essential to Spanish rule in North America—that they were loyal, capable, and effective in implementing and defending that rule: "The world must know that Spanish Americans live the same nobility of spirit, the same loyalty, the same love for Your Majesty, the same zeal for the public good, as the most noble, faithful, cultivated peoples of Europe." Policies based on any other vision could only lead to "the most reprehensible injustice" and "unmaskable injury" to American Spaniards, Spain's empire, and implicitly to silver capitalism.[43]

The thrust of the document was to deny as absurd the "enlightened" constructions of Americans as incapable or disloyal. Their exclusion from high offices of Church and state could only be an indefensible injustice. Having stymied policies of administrative assertion backed by new military forces in the 1760s, the council aimed to block emerging policies of American exclusion and reclaim rule by collaboration between American and European Spaniards. It wrote to remind Bourbon reformers seen as grasping for power and revenues that they would break the transatlantic pact linking American and Iberian Spaniards at their ultimate risk. The pact, grounded in the regime of petition and mediation, made Spain's power and Americans' profit possible. Any break would bring peril to both.

The councilmen ended with a more radical suggestion: "It would serve Your Majesty well to order that the most honored ecclesiastical and secular officials serving in these regions should be chosen among Spaniards born here; and although to keep the link a few born in Spain may come to serve, for the most part they should be excluded from positions in the Indies—as they are preferred in the original Spain, with near complete exclusion of Americans."[44] After a broad assertion of American rights and roles in maintaining the empire, the council turned to provincial elites' core interests. As loyal and capable professionals, they deserved primary rights to positions in the religious hierarchy and regime bureaucracy. They asked for the same roles in New Spain that Iberians gained in Spain.

The proclamation of 1771 did not challenge the continuing flow of immigrants from Spain who came to join their merchant-uncles, claim wealth, and with success join the oligarchy. Every man in a position of power in Mexico City, whether ensconced at the heights of oligarchy or struggling to hang on among provincials, lived in the wake of ancestral immigrant success—distant or recent. Spanish immigrants sustained silver capitalism at its core: linking Spain and New Spain, renewing and integrating the Mexico City oligarchy, producing generations of risk takers who financed mining and sent silver into global trades. The most powerful of their descendants led the landed clans that anchored the oligarchy; their less favored heirs, cousins, and nephews—Americans all—might hold modest estates, earn professional degrees, and seek roles in regime offices and Church institutions, doing their part to serve the empire.

The American provincials on the Mexico City Council, after a process of protest, petition, and accommodation, now welcomed rising immigrant entrepreneurs to their chamber—a powerful minority chosen to sit temporarily by the proprietary councilmen, most American provincials. In the proclamation-petition of 1771, the council did not share the virulent anti-gachupín rhetoric that marked the angry calls of the popular rebels of 1767.

There was no search for American independence in the proclamation of 1771; there were defenses of autonomies—traditional autonomies that allowed diverse corporations, notably city councils, to press their interests and claim the king's justice. The call for American preference in New World offices would return the empire to ways that ruled from 1650 to 1750, sustaining silver capitalism through decades of challenge and resurgence. After the regime assertions of 1765 and 1766, the popular risings of 1766 and 1767, and the accommodations of 1770 and 1771, the council asserted the rights of

American Spaniards to meaningful roles in sustaining the regime of petition and mediation that ruled the empire of silver.

In defending the rights and roles of *American* Spaniards, the men of the Mexico City Council insistently defended *only* the rights of American *Spaniards*. They proudly emphasized how American Spaniards had controlled the native majority since the sixteenth century—and had recently mobilized to contain the workers of mixed ancestry who rose in the mining centers in 1766 and 1767. The council honored its pivotal role in ruling America Septentrional, North America, in the name of the Spanish monarchy—to sustain silver capitalism. It had no interest in challenging Spanish rule, disrupting silver capitalism, or mobilizing the majority of Americans, indigenous and mixed, who tilled the soil in native republics, worked at estates and mines, or labored in city shops and factories. The councilmen insisted on their rightful place of power within the city, the monarchy, and silver capitalism. In their proud assertions, they announced their success in blunting Bourbon demands and restoring of the regime of participations and petitions, negotiations and mediating justice. The Mexico City Council, now including oligarchs and provincials, saw the regime restored—and pressed for greater roles in its mediating rule.

CHAPTER 7

Carrying On

War, Silver Capitalism, and Social Peace, 1770–1800

~ THE JOUSTING OF 1765–1771 RESET THE POWER OF MEXICO CITY AND its council in New Spain, the empire, and silver capitalism. For decades after, the city carried on—silver rising to historic peaks, the commercial economy booming—while the powerful and the poor dealt with famine and plague at home and an Atlantic world wracked by wars and revolutions. New Spain's silver production rose from 12 million pesos yearly in the late 1760s to over 20 million in the early 1780s as the Atlantic powers fought the war that enabled US independence and Spanish power faced adamant uprisings that challenged silver capitalism high in the Andes. In New Spain, the devastating frost, drought, and famine of 1785–1786 drew silver flows back to 18 million pesos yearly, followed by a rise to over 23 million in the 1790s as France and Saint-Domingue generated revolutions that fueled another round of devastating, deadly, and costly wars. Through times of war and revolution abroad, famine and plague at home, New Spain's silver economy held strong to 1800—the pillar that sustained Spain's empire and expanding global trades.

So did the power of the oligarchy that ruled silver capitalism in Mexico City—where the silver pivotal to global commerce and imperial revenue was minted and taxed, accumulated and traded. China's demand and price rose again after 1770. So did Europeans' need for silver as Atlantic competition

127

stimulated wars and trade. New Spain's production rose to its highest level in history as wars peaked in the early 1790s and held there through difficult decades until 1809. There were policy challenges and trade disruptions along the way. But Spain's Bourbons, both Carlos III who reigned to 1788 and Carlos IV who faced wars and revolutions after 1790, had learned the lessons of the 1760s. Spain needed New Spain's silver to profit from global trades and compete in Euro-Atlantic power politics. To gain that silver, they had to let the oligarchy that ruled silver capitalism and the provincial elites who led councils in Mexico City, Querétaro Guanajuato, and other key cities carry on with the rights to petition, negotiate, and claim mediation that kept production going and silver flowing.

A series of episodes—too often portrayed as conflicts leading toward independence—reveal the persistence of mediation, silver capitalism, and New Spain's pivotal role in Spain's empire and global trades to 1800.[1] No group committed to silver capitalism looked to follow the United States into independence, a process that proved economically disruptive for decades.[2] When France and Saint-Domingue faced devastating and transforming revolutions in the 1790s, the power of silver capitalism kept oligarchs and provincials loyal in Mexico City and across New Spain—while majorities in the capital, mining centers, and the rural regions that sustained them remained at work.

Mexico City lived complex economic challenges, social negotiations, and political mediations during the decades after 1770. Throughout, oligarchs and provincials, Europeans and Americans, Spaniards all, focused on maintaining silver capitalism and social peace. Questions of internal military power held in the background until the early 1790s when new militias were founded—tied to corporations, oligarchs, and provincial elites. They reinforced the regime of mediation more than they concentrated coercive power in the regime. This chapter reviews the city's negotiation of peace and productivity in a world of conflict during the decades before 1800. It concludes by exploring the 1799 attempt by a few men to start a rising on the model of revolutionary France. They called a revolution and no one came. As the nineteenth century began, silver capitalism held strong.

Containing Reform, Keeping Silver Flowing, 1770–1790
From the first hard pressures by Bourbon reformers in the 1760s, promoting silver and the flow of pesos into Spain's Treasury and global trades was the

constant goal. A lull in production in the 1750s had coincided with the costly wars of 1757 to 1763—leading to the disruptive drive to raise revenues within the empire. New Spain generated over half of the empire's silver, trade, and revenues around midcentury. Most of the kingdom's specie stayed within imperial channels, flowing through Havana to Cádiz and via Acapulco to Manila—to be taxed and then traded for the finest products the world could provide. The imperial commercial system was never closed. It was controlled to maximize Spaniards' profits and regime revenues—while selling silver to the world beyond. In 1765, postwar reformers began to experiment with *comercio libre* (free trade), opening trade in diverse commodities across Spain's Americas and diverse Spanish ports. The core silver trade, the commerce that drove the empire, remained concentrated in New Spain, still ruled from Mexico City.[3]

Free trade, then and now, remains an ideal. But there is no trade without a state (or similar power) ready to define and protect property rights and transactions, and to adjudicate disputes—directly or through tribunals such as the consulados, the merchants' chambers that organized trade in Mexico City and other key cities of the empire. The Bourbon proclamations of free trade marked and masked policies aiming to promote trade in diverse products within Spain's empire while still regulating the flows of silver that stimulated everything and generated most revenues. Thus the first opening to "free trade" did not apply to New Spain. Its silver remained in limited, taxable channels; the Mexico City Consulado still organized trade and resolved disputes. Its merchant financiers continued to accumulate the capital essential to finance silver capitalism—and to fund the monarchy when it faced new and costly challenges, which came soon enough. The first Bourbon commercial reform was no reform at all in the silver metropolis. After the conflicts and disruptions of 1766 and 1767 in key mining regions, the rapid rise of silver output in the 1770s proved the benefit of leaving established ways of production and power, trade and mediation intact at the core of silver capitalism.[4]

By the early 1780s, the results of the first era of Bourbon reforms and the resistance that constrained them were clear. New Spain's silver production rose from under 12 million pesos yearly in the late 1760s to over 20 million yearly in the early 1780s. Alcabala sales tax revenues rose from under 800,000 pesos annually before 1775 to over 1.7 million annually after 1780. Mexico City

Council revenues jumped from under 110,000 pesos in 1768 to over 170,000 in 1785.[5] The reformers' attempt to create an administrative regime backed by coercive powers was blocked. Silver capitalism remained ensconced in Mexico City, its oligarchs still key powers and beneficiaries. Bourbon reforms did not drive the boom of the 1770s and 1780s; a restored and reinforced regime of mediation had resolidified the social stability that enabled merchant financiers to invest, mines to flourish, and diverse workers to work—responding together if unequally to the world's surging demand for silver.

In the late 1770s, the dynamic stability of Mexico City and New Spain's silver capitalism proved pivotal to Spain's empire—and to the creation of an independent United States. When Spain went to war against Britain in 1779, joining France in backing the rebels seeking independence in coastal North America, New Spain's silver proved essential. During the years of conflict, over 6 million pesos yearly flowed toward Havana to fund Spanish naval power and the fight for North American independence.[6]

In the run-up to a war that Spanish officials in Madrid and Havana saw coming once the Anglo-American continentals challenged British rule, officials in Mexico City collected donations totaling over 1.25 million pesos to fund the construction of warships in Havana. The consulado contributed 300,000; the community of mining entrepreneurs, then seeking sanction for an independent tribunal, gave another 300,000; the first Conde de Regla, then at the peak of his wealth, gave 200,000—funding a ship he insisted be christened Santa María de Regla. The city council and the Metropolitan Cathedral each gave 80,000 pesos, bringing the total contributed in the capital to 960,000—three-quarters of the donation. Among those based outside the city, the merchants of Cádiz gave 120,000; the rich bishopric of Valladolid (now Morelia), its revenues drawn from regions including Guanajuato's rich mines, sent 80,000.[7] Once war was formally declared in 1779, the consulado and the Mining Tribunal each contributed 100,000 pesos to the war effort in 1780.[8] After the Anglo-colonials fought Britain to a stalemate on land, France provided troops and a fleet and Spain sent 500,000 silver pesos to enable Washington's victory at Yorktown in the fall of 1781.[9] None of this could have been donated without the growth of silver and the accumulations it generated.

Still, the war had not ended and costs mounted. Mexico City merchant financiers and mining entrepreneurs donated another 150,000 pesos to help consolidate the victory in 1782 and 1783. Knowing the war would soon end and expecting silver to continue flowing strong, the regime turned to loans— some short-term and without interest, others long-term and bearing 5 percent returns. In the former, the regime collected another 1,314,800 pesos in Mexico City in 1782—led by the Conde de Rábago who loaned 102,000 pesos, don Antonio de Basoco and don Pedro Alonso de Alles who provided 100,000 each, followed by the Fagoagas who delivered 70,000. The young don José Sánchez Espinosa, just having acquired the estates that placed him among the richest of landed entrepreneurs, loaned 35,000 pesos.[10]

Later that year, the Crown solicited 1 million pesos in funds to be held for an indefinite term—with guaranteed interest of 5 percent yearly. Another short-term infusion would create an imperial debt that would provide guaranteed returns—based on continuing silver flows. The Mexico City Consulado solicited investments in royal bonds that were quickly oversubscribed. With 1.6 million pesos offered, the consulado could choose among those who would be "favored" with the opportunity. Members of the consulado claimed nearly half; religious institutions took more than a third; diverse investors gained the rest.[11] In total, the Crown collected over 4.5 million pesos in donations, advances, and loans at interest (about a third in each category) from those with wealth and power in Mexico City—beyond the regular revenues its booming silver capitalism provided—all to fund the independence of the United States.

Meanwhile, in 1780, while the war for US independence and its revenue demands carried on, Spanish power faced a very different and more threatening challenge in the Andes. The risings led by Tupac Amaru and other insurgents, usually but not always indigenous, threatened imperial rule and silver production in regions from Cuzco to the mining center of Potosí.[12] The challenge—and likely the costs—facing the empire doubled. With British ships inhibiting trade in the Atlantic (while the French and Spanish navies and North American merchants kept trade and merchandise flowing) how could New Spain's silver and imperial exchanges continue at a level to pay for both the war for independence in North America and the fight to suppress insurgency in the Andes? The problem was exacerbated as the indigenous uprisings cut already suppressed silver mining at Potosí.

Answers came in two trade shifts—both favoring Mexico City oligarchs and New Spain's silver capitalism. The mercury of Huancavelica that normally served refiners at Potosí was turned north to supply New Spain—ensuring that any limits of that essential ingredient imposed by British blockade on mercury from Almadén in Spain would be covered by shipments from the Andes. Equally important, the regime opened a Pacific free trade zone, enabling Mexico City merchants to purchase cacao in Guayaquil and deliver it to Acapulco, where it was traded for silks and cotton goods bought from China with New Spain's silver. The value of this trade to Mexico City merchants and to regime revenues is hard to establish precisely. Flows of cacao from Guayaquil to Acapulco were large—sufficient to profit key importers (enabling the Ycaza and Iraeta clans to join the ranks of the capital's oligarchs) and to elicit complaints from Caracas growers and traders. The shipment of silver from Acapulco to Manila was just shy of 2 million pesos in 1779 as war began in the Caribbean and the Andes remained at peace. Well over 4 million pesos went west in 1784 as the conflicts waned—to pay for a flood of Asian cloth and other goods that supplied New Spain and the Andes while the two conflicts raged.[13] The maintenance of Pacific commerce, fueled by New Spain's silver, was essential to keeping the Andean economy going and revenues flowing while local resources and forces focused on defeating the greatest indigenous challenge to Spanish power in the Americas.

In an irony that illuminates the paradox of the European empires and their Americas in the 1780s, New Spain's silver and the trades and concentrations of wealth it stimulated helped fund the containment of the Andean rebellions and British North American independence. The silver peso became the currency of the first American nation—renamed the dollar. In Mexico City, Spanish power, oligarchic rule, and everyday life carried on. In the 1780s, neither the British North American model of elite-led independence nor the Spanish South American example of multiethnic insurgencies found resonance or repetition in New Spain. There, silver capitalism carried on—reinforced by its success in funding the British North American war for independence and Spanish imperial counterinsurgency in the Andes.

Ultimately, the wars and negotiations to sustain Spain's power brought reinforcement to the powers concentrated in Mexico City. Since 1750, the Mexico City Consulado had proposed including New Spain's leading mine operators, creating a dominant concentration of corporate economic power in the capital. The regime resisted, fearing a center of power that would unbalance the mediations essential to silver prosperity and regime rule. In

1776, in the wake of the restoration of mediation in New Spain, as leading merchants and planters challenged British power in North America and Spanish leaders saw the war to come, Viceroy don Antonio María de Bucareli proposed founding a *tribunal de minería*. It would be separate from the consulado, though silver financiers might belong to both. Maintaining a division that would ensure the need for regime mediation, the proposed tribunal would reinforce the corporate organization of power that had long sustained silver capitalism—and often frustrated Bourbon reformers in Spain. But as wartime funding needs soared, Bourbon officials again learned to negotiate. They accepted the creation of the Mining Tribunal, using it to collect donations and loans even before it was formally sanctioned in 1783.

The years of North Atlantic war and South American counterinsurgency allowed mining entrepreneurs to gain their own corporation, named to emphasize its judicial role. It was based in the capital and had a director, three general deputies, and a dozen technical consultants. A dozen territorial deputies would represent mining districts: six from Guanajuato, three from Zacatecas, one to two from other centers. A corporation to serve and represent leaders of New Spain's key industry, it sat in the capital to deal with regime powers and consulado merchants, while extending its sway to wherever mining held strong. The tribunal would resolve disputes among its members; it could defend mining interests before the regime. It was a new and potentially powerful participant in the regime of mediation.[14]

And it was more. In addition to providing training for mining engineers and technical advice to mine operators, the tribunal included the Banco de Avío—an investment bank. It loaned more than 1.5 million pesos from 1784 to 1792, most to small operators near the capital. The great silver miners worked with the merchant bankers of the consulado until they could fund themselves with silver flowing from their own works. The tribunal lost 700,000 pesos in its financial experiment, closing down that part of its operation.[15] Still, it carried on to serve and represent mining and mine operators in the regime of mediation into the nineteenth century.

In 1782, as the threat of Tupac Amaru and the other rebels who rose in the Andean heartland surely reached Mexico City (discussed among the powerful in hushed tones) viceregal leaders joined the Mexico City Council in setting up a new judicial system for the popular barrios of the city. As guild organization and oversight declined, that traditional means of organization, representation, and mediation became available to ever fewer numbers in the city's growing population. The reform divided the city into eight new judicial districts overseen by High Court judges and council magistrates—usually men on the rise. Real mediation came from thirty-two ward magistrates, usually local craftsmen or shopkeepers charged to mediate disputes and contain petty crime. With an equal number of constables, they were to take censuses, regulate markets, maintain lighting—and generally keep policía, good order. These were not armed police forces—but magistrates and overseers aimed at bringing the regime of judicial mediation to city barrios more directly and effectively.[16]

As the North American and Andean conflicts ended with contrasting outcomes—the end of British rule in coastal North America; the reconsolidation of Spanish rule in Andean South America—in New Spain, silver capitalism and the regime of mediation were reinforced just in time to face their greatest internal crisis of the eighteenth century: the devastating drought, frost, and famine of 1785 and 1786. Across the highlands from the basins around Mexico City, through the Bajío, and into the north, two years of maize harvests were lost. Prices soared to four times normal levels. Tens of thousands died—and millions saw everything they had go to pay for the necessities of survival. Landed entrepreneurs profited selling stocks held from past years while joining in efforts to cushion the most devastating effects in the capital, the mining centers, and at their estates—the productive core of silver capitalism. They continued to feed the estate residents essential to future production and profits. They loaned funds to ship maize from the lowlands, where drought was limited and harvests better, to cities and mining centers. They led devotions calling on Guadalupe and other intermediaries for rain and relief. And after the crisis passed, they used the profits of dearth to expand irrigation, plant maize more securely, and profit as the staple essential to everything fell to prices still high by prefamine norms.[17] Oligarchs, provincials, and regime officials in Mexico City and provincial centers worked to limit the impact of the drought on silver capitalism. Mining production rose again in the late 1780s.

The famine past, in 1787, don José de Gálvez, now minister of the Indies in Spain, appointed intendants to lead New Spain's provinces—his last major attempt at reform. Modeled after officials named in the seventeenth century by Louis XIV to bolster Crown power across France, the Bourbons had introduced intendants in Spain and part of the empire earlier in the eighteenth century. While in New Spain as visitor general in the 1760s, Gálvez had asserted Bourbon demands for new powers and revenues, faced riots and political resistance, and learned to compromise. As minister of the Indies, he had negotiated the exchange of revenues for privileges that sustained the regime through the wars and insurgencies of the early 1780s. Now he hoped that new officials might assert regime power across the empire.

The experiment failed in Mexico City. There, don Fernando José Mangino gained appointment as superintendant, presumed to oversee the city and its council. He had served as director of the mint and overseer of ex-Jesuit properties in the 1760s and 1770s. He had formed close ties with don Pedro Romero de Terreros, New Spain's leading mine operator and landed entrepreneur. Already linked to the oligarchy that ruled silver capitalism when he became superintendant in 1787, Mangino was set to mediate among regime officials, oligarchs, and the city council. Yet that was the role already held by the viceroy. When the new position began to disrupt the balance of mediation reset after the conflicts of the 1760s, it was abolished. Mangino went to the Council of the Indies in Spain, overseeing American affairs— ready to help serve and preserve the interests of the Mexico City oligarchs essential to Spanish power.[18]

In New Spain's provinces, intendants became key mediators, integrating and balancing local interests and representing them before higher powers. In the pivotal mining center of Guanajuato, don Antonio de Riaño arrived in 1792, the city's second intendant. He focused on promoting and facilitating silver production. Working closely with financiers, mine operators, and silver refiners, he negotiated complex labor relations to keep production strong. He appointed local magistrates to promote social order. When smallpox threatened in 1797, Riaño brought the new science of inoculation to the mining center. Joining with local entrepreneurs and officials, the intendant made himself the center of a regional oligarchy—keeping silver, Guanajuato, New Spain, and Spain's empire strong into the nineteenth century.[19] Even the intendants, the Bourbons' signature administrative innovation, primarily reinforced the regime of petition, conciliation, and mediation.

Through the 1770s and 1780s, while New Spain funded the war for US independence and counterinsurgency in the Andes, reformers in Madrid negotiated with oligarchs and officials in Mexico City to stimulate silver production and the commerce it promoted. Except for the brief dip caused by the famine of 1785–1786, silver production held over 20 million pesos.[20] Total regime revenues taken in New Spain rose from under 10 million pesos yearly in the early 1770s to nearly 20 million just before the crisis of 1785, to hold near 18 million during and after the famine—still a substantial sum. Silver shipped from Veracruz in private hands held near 7.5 million pesos yearly in the 1770s to rise to only 8.2 million in the 1780s, the lesser rise in part reflecting the large shipments of silver sent across the Pacific, in part demonstrating the rise of regime revenues in times of wars. Still, silver, trade, and revenues grew together—keeping Mexico City and its oligarchs pivotal to the empire and a world of conflict and commerce.[21]

New Challenges: Free Trade, Revolutionary Reverberations, and New Militias

The Bourbon reforms—as contested and limited by the powerful and the people of New Spain—were succeeding. Direct taxes on silver and trade, the new tobacco monopoly, and increased tribute collection from the indigenous-mulatto majority drove revenues to rise faster than mining and trade—which still prospered. The turn from the 1780s to the 1790s would prove a watershed in Atlantic and world history—marked by the opening of the French Revolution in 1789 and the Haitian Revolution in 1791. In New Spain, those years brought "free trade," the reverberations of other peoples' revolutions, and a return to military recruitment. Policies imagined in Spain again threatened disruptions. And again, adaptations and mediations in New Spain kept silver capitalism strong.

To fund the US war for independence and counterinsurgency in the Andes, Gálvez had confirmed and even strengthened the concentration of economic power in Mexico City and its oligarchs. He was rewarded with soaring silver flows and revenues that funded Spain's costly triumphs in both conflicts. But after 1785, a modest decline in silver flowing from New Spain (about 10 percent) and a lamented (and apparently deeper) drop in imports from Spain (including, of course, goods from across Europe) brought reformers in Spain to consider opening trade with New Spain—within the empire. Gálvez died in 1787, just after implementing the intendancies. Without his cautions about potential disruptions, Carlos III's lead minister, the Conde de Floridablanca—who unlike Gálvez, had never experienced the complex power dynamics and social milieu of New Spain—promoted comercio libre for the empire's richest kingdom. He credited the rise in silver, trade, and revenues from the 1770s into the 1780s to free trade—though most came from New Spain where it did not apply. He blamed the decline of the late 1780s on the absence of open trade—though the dip of silver production resulted from New Spain's famine of 1785–1786, as did the decline in imports that came as families gave every peso they had to eat. By 1787–1788 silver was reviving, the prices of staples were falling, and imports were rising again.[22]

Ideological truth without knowledge of underlying complexities carried the day. Still, on a key question of trade tied to New Spain's silver, Floridablanca had to consult the consulados: the merchants of Seville and Cádiz, with most to lose, were wary of losing privileges; Barcelona, with much to gain, approved. The Mexico City Consulado resisted—pressing instead for cheaper mercury and lower taxes to stimulate mining and trade. All reported obvious self-interests. Floridablanca consulted in Madrid, too. Don Pedro Rodríguez Campomanes, head of the Council of Castile, did not oppose the reform but noted the danger of alienating or disrupting the powers in Mexico City—defending the Crown's ultimate interest. Soon after the death of Carlos III, Floridablanca announced "free trade" for New Spain—decreed on February 28, 1789.[23]

The reform had limited impact. Opening channels of trade within the empire did not limit—and perhaps favored—the concentration of financial and commercial power long set in Mexico City and now organized in both the consulado and the tribunal de minería. More immediately vexing in Spain and New Spain in the 1790s were reports of increasing violence in the revolutionary conflicts in France and Saint-Domingue. Bourbon powers and Atlantic empires faced unprecedented threats. In Spain and New Spain, silver and social stability remained essential goals among those who aimed to rule and profit.

Silver was flowing amply, jumping from 18.5 million pesos yearly in the late 1780s to over 23 million yearly in the early 1790s—the jump clear before any impact of open trade. So the regime focused on order. It began a new round of militia foundations, sanctioning new troops and taking broad censuses to help recruitment. Only Spaniards, mestizos, and mulattos might join in arms; the indigenous majority remained the object of social control—an object reinforced by memories of the Andean risings a decade earlier, while fears were inflamed by news of slaves in arms in nearby Saint-Domingue. Still, the new militias of the early 1790s were not regime-ruled forces. Rather, as funded and commanded by oligarchs and provincials in the capital and outlying regions, new militias aimed to keep the social peace in an enduring regime of mediation.

The censuses of 1791 and 1792 made key goals clear. They identified Spanish, mestizo, and mulatto men, designated as eligible for service at arms. They excluded indigenous men—long ago disarmed and still excluded from militia enrollment. The militias enrolled Hispanic men, mostly in cities and at northern estate communities. They faced limited military training, became subject to some military discipline, and gained separate corporate judicial rights—*fueros*. Within the Hispanic sectors of society, they created new armed forces—inside the regime of mediation. If the exclusion of indigenous men suggests that social control was a primary concern, the persistence of indigenous republics kept the regime of mediation the primary way of social integration in the center of New Spain in the 1790s.[24]

The militias were not centralized military forces. Most were sanctioned by Spanish councils, some by consulados and other corporations. Ultimate approval came from viceregal authorities who needed wealthy merchants and landed oligarchs to pay for mounts, arms, and uniforms. For that they gained sanction and command. The militias of the 1790s armed the established powers in the regime of mediation, making impositions from above less possible while announcing new fears and visions of social control aimed at the populace. While silver boomed and mediation held, the new militias proved neither effective nor disruptive.

Revolutionary Wars—And Keeping Silver Flowing, 1790–1800

In New Spain, the challenges of the 1790s came not from within, but without. The French and Haitian revolutions led to European wars that quickly became Atlantic. Trade was disrupted in a French Atlantic tied to Spain's specie and trades. When general war broke out in 1793, every belligerent coveted New Spain's silver—as Spain struggled to define its interests when Bourbons no longer ruled in France and revolutionary leaders promoted new participations that quickly became militarized. When Spain turned against its historic French ally in 1793, joining England to defend monarchy against the revolutionaries who executed Louis XVI, silver held high. It stayed strong when Spain shifted again to join France against England in the 1796 Treaty of San Ildefonso—leaving Spanish Atlantic shipping subject to British disruptions and depredations. Production held high as US merchants entered those trades as neutrals, profiting by carrying silver from Veracruz to Europe (often via US ports) and returning with manufactures. New Spain's silver flowed powerfully through the 1790s, holding at above 23 million pesos yearly in the face of revolutions, wars, shifting alliances, and trade disruptions.[25]

The free trade announced in 1789 to open New Spain to trade throughout the empire gave way in time of wars to more open trades that sent silver across contested (and long porous) imperial boundaries. No one debated the importance of silver and the Mexico City oligarchs who ruled financing, production, and trade in the empire's richest kingdom. The anonymous author of a 1792 report written in Madrid stated bluntly what all knew: New Spain's mines were "the richest revenue source of the Crown," stimulating "not just . . . all the nations of Europe, but the major nations of the globe." Mexico City merchants still financed trade between Cádiz and New Spain, Acapulco, and Manila—with extensions far beyond.[26] The Royal Mint in Mexico City kept its monopoly on coining and taxing pesos—guaranteeing Crown control of accounting and tax collection. Mexico City merchant bankers still financed mining at Guanajuato and elsewhere, delivered most silver to the mint, and sent what remained after taxes into global trades.[27]

One reform of the 1790s did appear to threaten Mexico City's merchant oligarchs: the 1795 founding of a new, potentially competing consulado in the Gulf coast port of Veracruz. Merchants there gained their own chamber to address shared concerns, to adjudicate local disputes, and to petition higher authorities. The proposal originated decades earlier; petitions of 1781 and 1788 were blocked by those committed to the powers concentrated in Mexico City. When authorities in Madrid revived the idea in the face of war after 1793, a powerful rejoinder came from don Fernando José Mangino—ally of the Condes de Regla, former mint director, and briefly superintendant in Mexico City, now sitting on the Council of the Indies in Spain, still speaking for Mexico City interests. His defense of its consulado delayed the founding of the Veracruz chamber another year—and reminded Madrid that whatever innovations came, the power of Mexico City could not be undermined. Spain lived by the wealth generated there.[28]

The merchants of Veracruz got their chamber in 1795. Why? It is essential to see that the new consulado, like the Mining Tribunal founded in the 1780s, did not challenge the regime of mediation but extended it, giving separate yet parallel rights to Veracruz merchants. Officially, the goal was to promote trade. Still, the timing is suggestive. Veracruz merchants gained rights and representation as war intensified in the Caribbean and revolution wracked Saint-Domingue. The sanctioning of the new consulado surely aimed to keep the merchants closest to island conflicts loyal to Spain and its interests—to stimulate and protect the silver that passed through Veracruz on the way to Atlantic ports and imperial treasuries at war.

The power of Mexico City was not challenged. All of New Spain's silver still passed through the capital. Mexico City financiers still ruled mining. Mexico City merchants still sent most private silver into trade—Atlantic and Pacific. Those who profited in finance, mining, and oceanic commerce still married their sons to landed heiresses, their daughters to aspiring immigrant merchants. All the reforms, all the wars, and all the revolutions had disrupted none of that. New Spain's silver capitalism had to thrive: it sustained Spain's imperial trades and revenues; it kept its Bourbons alive in global power politics.

Replicating the developments of the early 1780s, when Madrid needed revenues in the more conflictive world of the 1790s, it had one place to turn—the oligarchs of Mexico City. The merchants of Veracruz found good profits in Atlantic trades; they rarely entered the financing of silver that made the merchant oligarchs of Mexico City essential to Spain's empire.[29] From the outbreak of war in 1793 past 1800, when Madrid needed cash it turned to New Spain and Mexico City. Silver held high, and the trades it stimulated generated rising revenues. At key times, rich oligarchs again made large donations—contributions only they could provide. When the Crown needed more, it again sought loans, promising repayment at interest. Mexico City financiers, merchants, and oligarchs, again often organized by the consulado, led contributors. In support of Spain's alliance with Britain against revolutionary France in the early 1790s, they provided nearly 8 million pesos; in the conflict against England from 1796 to 1803, they delivered almost 7 million more.[30] No other city or oligarchy in the empire could generate such resources.

A growing portion of New Spain's silver passed to the Crown, leaving less for investment in mining and trade. Still, mining and trade carried on strong past 1800. Revenues flowed at peaks toward Europe—sometimes in Spanish ships; sometimes via British, then French allies; increasingly via US neutrals. Perhaps 40 percent of the silver flowing east from New Spain eventually reached Britain, the remaining 60 percent split between Spain and its French ally—increasingly in the latter's favor. The dual diversion to fund friends and foes was a problem for Madrid. The continuing strong flow of silver from New Spain showed all that silver capitalism carried on, pivotal to every economy, every empire, every army and navy—ultimately to a world economy at war.[31]

Imagining a Revolution—And No One Came

The endless negotiations of regime and reform, trade and finance make it clear that the men who ruled in Mexico City knew (as slowly and imperfectly as oceans allowed) that wars and revolutions made the world a dangerous, difficult, and uncertain place in the 1790s. While so many lived deadly struggles on distant shores, New Spain's oligarchs focused on mining, trade, and landed investment to profit while sending silver into global trades and imperial coffers. Mexico City provincials and professionals, officials and bureaucrats carried on, too, comfortable in lives less rich than the oligarchs', still favored in a city of diverse and often struggling producers. All knew the liberating political promises of Parisian revolutionaries and the liberating destructions of power and profit imposed by insurgent ex-slaves in Saint-Domingue. Few in the silver metropolis aimed to imitate either. Stability held into the nineteenth century.

A revolutionary plot that failed to start illuminates that entrenched stability. In the fall of 1799, authorities in Mexico City learned of a plan to attack the social order. A small group of conspirators angered by local exclusions and inspired by distant revolutions imagined an urban rising—and soon learned how few were ready to try revolution in the silver metropolis.

On October 8, don Teodoro Francisco de Aguirre met with his nephew, Cristóbal Orozco, a clockmaker, who "revealed that he was hot into a conspiracy of Creoles against Europeans." Don Pedro Portillo, a tax collector at the Plaza de Santa Catalina, led the plotters along with his brother, who held the same office at the Plaza del Volador. Two days later Aguirre went to the viceroy, don Miguel José de Azanza, saying he had agreed to join the plot in order to report on it to authorities. For a month Aguirre went to meetings, spying on his nephew and others.[32]

The conspirators had recruited Aguirre. Why he become an informant is clear in his first report. While the plotters claimed 26 adherents (in a city of near 130,000), Aguirre could identify only don Pedro Portillo and his brother, his own nephews (Orozco and his brother), a sergeant in the merchants' militia, and a few more as active participants: "all contemptible subjects, incapable of leading such an affair." Aguirre saw a small conspiracy doomed to fail. He reported that Portillo had rented a house from a "poor woman" on the Calle de Gachupines (a choice laden with irony) to hold clandestine meetings. On October 20, Aguirre reported that the plotters called themselves the "American National Convention"; Portillo claimed title as president and captain general; others imagined themselves lieutenant generals. They would ground military roles in an assembly. They swore to rid the city of "all the Europeans in government offices and trading houses, and assassinate them," aiming to compile a list of names and addresses. The anti-immigrant sentiments that drove rioters and rebels in northern mining towns in the 1760s now revived among the conspirators in the capital in the 1799. In Aguirre's report they styled themselves criollos, not americanos—the latter prevalent among the prosperous and powerful. The plotters resented the newcomers from Spain who found opportunities for prosperity and ascent in counting houses and regime offices—resentments deep enough the conspirators were ready to kill. Equally revealing, they drew inspiration from revolutionary France for an assembly asserting national sovereignty led by military men who would enforce compliance.

Too few to act, each plotter swore to raise fifty "partisans." Aguirre added that "they would free the prisoners in the jails, to increase the numbers ready to implement the killing." They also agreed to "fully respect religion and priests." If they followed French revolutionary precedent in styling themselves a National Convention, they proved deeply Spanish in committing to Catholicism and its priests. To fund the rising Portillo gave twenty pesos, the Orozcos ten, others only five. The plotters were not rich men. Aguirre reported all this and news that the next meeting was set for October 22. Azanza asked Aguirre to return with don Gregorio Martínez and don Manuel Yrrisarri, aides to the viceroy who would pose as new recruits.

They arrived to find but seven conspirators. The leaders read a document in a voice inaudible to Aguirre. Did they distrust him and his new colleagues?

In a louder tone "they lamented the oppression this country suffers, calling the rest to claim so-called liberty; they would soon try to acquire arms and find a way to take control of the viceroy and his palace." Men imagining themselves a popular assembly and claiming military rank aimed to topple the viceroy. The next day, Aguirre, Martínez, and Yrrisarri reported all this to the viceroy, now a target of the plot. They had learned of only eleven men involved: Portillo and his brother; the two Orozcos; the Portillos' shop clerk; Aguirre (did the viceroy's aides suspect he began as a real participant?); a sergeant of the Regimiento del Comercio; three others they could not name; and another militia sergeant from nearby Chalco. With this news Azanza assembled his ministers and set a plan "to cut such prejudicial seeds before they root."

The conspirators met next on November 9. Magistrate don Joaquín de Mosquera led a force that broke down the door and found six men around a table: don Pedro and don Antonio Portillo, Josef Orozco, don Josef Urriales, don Francisco Velasco, and don Joaquín Alegre. There were writing materials and copies of several *Gacetas de México*, the official periodical reporting news from Spain and New Spain. They claimed to be playing cards (*el monte*) and were quickly arrested. There were no weapons and no writings by those present. Later searches found nineteen machetes and five swords stored by Portillo, along with papers linked to an "American National Junta," a more traditional Spanish label, apparently favored by the plotters. (Had Aguirre used the word "Convention" to link them to despised French revolutionaries?) The men arrested led to another six conspirators, five silversmiths: Josef Agustín de Vargas, don Luis de Medina, Ygnacio Morel, Gerardo Soriano, and Cayetano González, plus Cristóbal Orozco, the clockmaker who had recruited his uncle Aguirre into the group. A total of twelve were jailed, some held in the Viceregal Palace, others in the prison of the Santa Hermandad. All confessed.

Statements made by eleven of the twelve (don Francisco Velasco was not deposed; was he, like Aguirre, an informant?) revealed a group of young men, most born in the provinces, struggling to live in the capital. They ranged from eighteen to thirty years in age, most in their mid-twenties. Only four were married. The Portillo brothers, unmarried small merchants and revenue collectors, were born in Toluca; so was Cayetano González, married and a guard at the plaza. The Orozco brothers, Josef, the elder at twenty-six, was single and "without employment"; the younger, Francisco Cristóbal, twenty-five, was married and a clockmaker—both from Zinacatepec, beyond Toluca, where the Intendancy of Mexico met Michoacán. Don Josef Urriales, the eldest at thirty, married and a guard stationed at Santo Tomás, was born in Valladolid, capital of Michoacán. Others had come from towns near the capital: Ygnacio Morel, a single merchant of twenty-five, was from Tacuba; Gerardo Soriano, from Azcapotzalco, distilled *aguardiente*, cane brandy, in the capital. Only three of twelve plotters were city-born: don Joaquín Alegre, the youngest at eighteen and single, worked as clerk for don Pedro Portillo; don Agustín Vargas, thirty and married, and don Luis de Medina, twenty-eight and a widower, were silversmiths.

The leaders and most of the dozen participants came from outside the capital, arriving as young men looking to make their way in the city. They had linked to city-born silversmiths (two honored as dons, likely masters, the others probably their dependents), men pursuing a historically prosperous craft. Why did these few men turn to conspiracy in the fall of 1799? We cannot know with certainty. But we begin to see the silver metropolis as a center of prosperity and imagined opportunity drawing three streams of migrants—a favored few from Spain, a few more Hispanics from New Spain's nearby provinces, and throngs of natives (most women) from communities in the same regions. All sought opportunity, or at least a chance, in a city of power, production, and polarity. Men from Spain famously succeeded; Hispanic men from New Spain struggled; the indigenous expected lives of service and survival—and seem to have found them. A handful of frustrated and angry Hispanic migrant men from nearby towns plotted revolution in 1799—joined by a few silversmiths.

That a dozen young Hispanic men plotted revolution in 1799 reveals their frustrations—and deep resentment of the gains made by immigrants from Spain. Small traders, tax collectors, a clockmaker, a distiller, and two urban guardsmen were not among the most marginal of the city's people. Still, most had not married; limited prosperity left them unable to claim the patriarchal ideal of household head. The master silversmiths, in contrast, pursued a craft of potential prosperity; both had married, one was a widower. All were españoles; they imagined a rising of americanos—only the informant Aguirre labeled them criollos, perhaps a pejorative used to focus the viceroy. Had wartime disruptions and revenue extractions made life tenuous for middling men without powerful protectors or secure employments? Petty trade, spirit selling, and clockmaking could be insecure. Tax collectors and guards might draw popular ire in the public square. What might draw silversmiths to radical risks? Had extractions of silver to pay for Europeans' wars made silver scarce and expensive for local craftsmen? Did uncertain times leave city households less able to buy silver wares? Perhaps, but we should not read too much into two master silversmiths drawing three apprentices into a plot that proved a fantasy.

If the conspirators did propose to call an American National Convention, as Aguirre claimed, they were responding to the French Revolution; the call for liberty shows them inspired by the ideals of the age. To gain allies, they would empty the jails; to force a hearing, they would find arms to capture the viceroy in his palace. Via *Gacetas de México* they knew the transatlantic world—through the eyes of New Spain's officials who shaped its contents. By 1799, news of French revolutionary promises of liberation and their often-violent implementations were currency in Mexico City—as the conspirators' rhetoric and plans showed.

If they knew of and were in part inspired by French revolutionary risings, they aimed for a very Spanish variant. Aguirre said they planned an American National Convention—a label sure to gain the viceroy's attention. The plotters' own voices and papers sought liberty via an American National Junta; they insisted on respect for Catholicism and the clergy. The clique of 1799 knew that however attractive the promises of French revolutionaries might be, attacks on the Church and clergy, on religion, were anathema in Mexico City.

Among the few conspirators of 1799, soaring ideals linked to particular interests—to be pursued by violent means. They aimed to round up all *europeos* employed in government offices and commercial houses. Anti-European sentiments were old in New Spain; the goal of *killing* immigrants was new. Did that reflect news of a French Revolution that seemed to raise killing in the name of liberty to new heights? The plotters knew they would find little support among powerful American Spaniards for an anti-European *jacquerie*. So they would empty the jails to gain numbers to purge the city of immigrants favored in regime offices and merchants' shops.

In a final report of March 1802, the Mexico City Audiencia's Criminal Chamber was dismissive of the conspirators.[33] The judges abhorred the idea of a "uprising" pitting "españoles americanos" against "europeos." Such divisive calls were "expressions so repugnant and hateful that they should be expunged from memory; such imagined enmity could only exist in the fantasy of men without principles or the education to see the damage to be done to those graced with finer qualities and to the community of our Sovereign's faithful vassals." The judges maligned the men who promoted such thinking as "untutored youths, many still minors, without the insight to consider the questions their raised." The plotters lacked substance. They were men "without roles in the Republic; without the help or protection of citizens of substance; incapable of forming ideas; doing mechanical work or humble jobs." The judges concluded that the conspirators lacked "any possibility of becoming a threat to be feared by the regime."

The court limited the conspirators' punishment to the thirty months they had been held in confinement. Released, they were instructed to keep good conduct. Anything more "would only promote the unjust idea of the imagined enemy." Despite the conspirators' dreams of violence, the court responded with traditional clemency for men seen as misguided and little threatening to the regime or the social order—the essence of conciliation and mediation. Still, the judges' final thought revealed that despite the minimal nature of the conspiracy and its quick containment, its ideas contained seeds of potential threat—another reason for clemency.

The 1799 conspiracy showed that a few American Spaniards, most migrants from country towns to the silver metropolis, held angry resentments against European immigrants. In that they shared views earlier revealed by northern provincial rebels in 1767—men who imagined that powerful Americans might join them in sedition. The men who joined the 1799 plot in the capital never imagined that oligarchs, provincial elites, leading professionals, or educated bureaucrats would join their purge of gachupines. Hispanic men from the provinces struggling to make it in the silver metropolis imagined a rising to eliminate immigrants from Spain—favored in social ascent and famously arrogant toward their American peers. Prosperous Americans showed no interest in the imagined revolution hatched on the Calle de Gachupines.

A dozen conspirators could recruit no more; their dreams of revolution were easily crushed; the regime showed remarkable clemency—in contrast to the plotters' dreams of mass killing in the name of liberty. In an Atlantic world wracked by wars and revolutions, as the century turned Mexico City remained a center of power, economic dynamism, social polarity—and enduring stability. Fueled by silver capitalism, integrated by a regime ready to mediate conflicts, the North American metropolis remained rich yet laden with inequities, at peace and at work, sending silver to the world to fund others' wars and everyone's trades.

CHAPTER 8

Toward Crisis

War, Revenue, Faction, and the Fall of the Monarchy, 1800–1808

⊸ AFTER 1800, SPAIN AND ITS EMPIRE REMAINED CAUGHT IN COSTLY wars, locked in alliance with Napoleon as Britain claimed control of the Atlantic. And Spain depended ever more on New Spain for revenue and trade. France demanded subsidies delivered in Spanish silver—its only major source of American revenues after the loss of Haiti in 1804. Yet Britain ruled the Atlantic after Admiral Nelson's destruction of the French and Spanish fleets at Trafalgar in 1805. All the warring powers coveted New Spain's silver, which continued to flow at historic peaks. How it crossed the ocean and who benefited became challenges driving escalating conflicts as imperial powers (and a young United States) fought to gain and transport silver.

Meanwhile, new programs in Spain, New Spain, and across the Americas aimed to take rising revenues for the embattled empire. Again, those demands focused on Mexico City—where silver and the wealth it spawned continued to concentrate. There, oligarchic power and regime realism combined to deflect collections onto provincial elites and emerging merchants. The great financiers, mining entrepreneurs, and agrarian capitalists carried on—while those just below struggled. The regime continued to mediate and silver flows held strong. But the coalition of elite power that linked oligarchs, provincial elites, and professionals to sustain silver capitalism faced new fissures.

The soaring costs of war in the 1790s had led the regime to forced sales of Church lands in Spain to generate new revenues. After a brief respite called by the Peace of Amiens late in 1802, when war resumed in 1804, costs and debts soared again and the program was applied in New Spain and the Americas. There, Church mortgages were called in by a program called the Consolidation of Royal Bonds beginning in 1805, as the British Navy destroyed the fleets at Trafalgar.

As the consolidation was debated and implemented in Mexico City, the challenge was to deliver its revenues to Europe. Wartime necessity led to complex deals that enabled US and British traders and financiers to ship specie to Europe. Britain claimed a growing share—as did France as the price of its alliance with Spain. As less of New Spain's silver flowed into Spain's coffers, political conflicts escalated in Madrid. New Spain's production held strong while silver dispersed to fund all sides in wars that would not end. Spain's monarchy cracked into factions contesting a dark imperial future. Carlos IV, his chief minister don Manuel de Godoy, and his eventual successor Prince Fernando fell into infighting over who should rule and how.

All the while, Spain depended ever more on New Spain's silver. Yet Britain ruled the seas and France claimed rising subsidies. More and more silver funded others' wealth and wars, leaving Spain a pawn in a violent Atlantic world. In October 1807, as Napoleon sent troops across Spain to invade Portugal, Spain's monarchy was rattled by an attempted coup aiming to depose Carlos and impose Fernando. In April 1808, as French forces marched into Madrid, a sequel at Aranjuez seemed to succeed. By May, Napoleon held both Spanish Bourbons captive in Bayonne. The fall of the Spanish monarchy to its invasive ally set the stage for Mexico City's summer of politics. Spain's empire and New Spain would never be the same.

War, Trade, and Revenues, 1800–1804

France and Britain faced off in constant wars beginning in 1793 (with a brief lull under the Peace of Amiens in 1802–1803). Spain joined Britain against French revolutionaries from 1793 to 1796; it shifted to sustaining France as revolutionary rule gave way to Napoleon's imperial ambitions. Throughout, Britain ruled the seas while France dominated the European continent. Spain's role was to supply New Spain's silver. That primary dynamic of war and revenue is clear. A less recognized yet no less important economic duality also shaped the Atlantic wars after 1790. Britain prospered to fund its war powers by promoting growing global textile trades that before 1810 depended on New Spain's silver.

British merchants operating in India sold rising quantities of the fine colored cotton goods made there in the late eighteenth century, sending them around the world—and notably to Africa, where Indian cloth was the primary product exchanged for the enslaved Africans shipped in rising numbers to Atlantic plantations. But British traders could not control production in India—which evolved in local relationships among merchant entrepreneurs and household producers. And to buy Indian cloth, British merchants needed silver—only available via trade with New Spain. Britain's alliance with Spain from 1793 to 1796 facilitated that trade—though it was formally restricted; Spain's shift to alliance with France aimed to inhibit Britain's access to silver—though it continued via US neutrals. As the 1800s began, Spain's ties to France limited Britain's access to New Spain's silver, inhibiting trades essential to British wealth and power.

Britain's famed industrial revolution had accelerated in mills around Manchester after 1780. Entrepreneurs innovated to make cotton cloth, enabling sales without dealing with South Asian producers and merchants, and without need for New Spain's silver. Emerging British industries competed with British India interests to sell in growing global markets. Before 1810, the silver-based trade in Indian cloth and sales of British-manufactured industrial cottons grew in parallel. In the first decade of the nineteenth century, New Spain's silver remained as important to Britain's prosperity as to Spain's Treasury and France's war effort. While Britain and Spain faced off in war, Britain and New Spain remained linked in trade.[1]

The years of British-Spanish alliance against revolutionary France from 1793 to 1796 had consolidated the link between the two leading Atlantic economies. Silver, trade, and revenues held strong between Spain and New Spain while Spain's debts soared. With Spain's return to alliance with France, British sea power disrupted trade and revenue transfers—leading Spain to open trade to neutral merchants and vessels from the United States. They often traded British goods for New Spain's silver. The American silver kingdom became increasingly pivotal to the economies, trades, and revenues of all the empires at war—and the young United States, too.[2]

Seeking a solution to rising debts, the government of Carlos IV looked for revenues not dependent on transatlantic flows. In 1798 it created the Caja de Amortización, the Redemption Fund. Church institutions in Spain had long funded religious, charitable, educational, and hospital activities with land rents. The new act required that lands be auctioned, the proceeds paid to the fund, with the monarchy promising to pay 3 percent of the value to sustain Church activities. The Treasury would gain an immediate boost in revenues—aiming to pay off the *vales reales*, royal bonds issued since the war against England in support of US independence. The Church lost properties and became dependent on the monarchy and its Treasury for funding.[3]

There is irony in this trajectory of war, debt, and the search for solutions by taking Church wealth. The French Revolution began in 1789 when Louis XVI's treasury could not pay its debts built in support of the US war for independence. Seeking new revenues, he called the Estates General. It became a revolutionary assembly, and after 1793 turned to expropriating Church wealth to sustain the revolution and its wars. Most Spaniards staunchly opposed that turn against the Church, widely seen as an assault on Catholic truth, opposition that helped mobilize them in the war against revolutionary France in 1793. Spain too had built debts in support of the US war for independence—mostly through bond sales. The war against France from 1793 to 1796 increased those debts and made the payment of interest increasingly difficult. So Carlos IV and Godoy turned to claiming Spanish Church wealth to pay debts in large part created by a war to defend the French Church from revolutionary depredations. Carlos insisted that his program was not an expropriation and not an attack on Catholicism. He promised to sustain the Church.

From 1798 through 1804 the Redemption Fund (and its successor from 1800, the Consolidation Fund) collected sums equivalent to 40 million pesos, half in redeemed bonds.[4] Old obligations dropped, but new revenues were not enough to keep overall debts from rising. Regime creditors gained lands concentrated in the south of Spain.[5] The Church saw 15 percent of its property in Castile (3 percent of total property) sold to private buyers. It was not stripped of wealth. Still, property changed hands rapidly in times of war, fueling economic disruptions.

Heated political debates and new economic uncertainties spread across Spain. As war continued through 1802 debts rose; interest owed to bondholders, old and new, and to Church institutions, too, became hard to pay. The

Peace of Amiens brought a respite from war, a revival of trade, and new dynamism to New Spain's silver economy. Any chance at a strong revival in Spain, however, vanished in the face of the dearth and disease that plagued central and southern regions from 1803 to 1805. The resumption of war in 1804 brought rising costs, new military catastrophes, economic dislocations, and political polarization in Spain. As debts soared, a struggling monarchy turned again to New Spain, seeking greater revenues.

By 1804, the once-rich French colony of Saint-Domingue had become free Haiti. Hundreds of thousands of formerly enslaved people turned to sustaining families on the land, all but ending plantation production and leaving France without revenue from the Americas. Napoleon had little choice but to focus on extending power across continental Europe. Britain ruled the sea and faced exclusion from the European markets essential to home industries and colonial produce. War resumed, and Spain was drawn into a contradiction without solution. It remained France's ally, promised Napoleon large subsidies—and faced British assaults at sea.

Everything turned at Trafalgar. The 1805 destruction of the combined French and Spanish fleets left both powers landlocked—with devastating consequences for Spain. During three centuries, its power depended on American silver and the trades it generated; suddenly, in a time of war and soaring costs, it had no fleet to protect trade with New Spain and its other American domains. Spanish traders turned again to neutral shipping, most from the United States. British forces challenged neutral ships—except when they delivered silver to British merchants and financiers. Robert Oliver, an Irish immigrant who had arrived in Baltimore in 1783, shipped nearly 20 million pesos from New Spain between 1804 and 1808; the English-Spanish firm of Gordon and Murphy nearly half as much. They supplied the silver kingdom's strong demand for fine cloth and other goods, mostly from British sources; they earned rich profits for delivering silver to Britain, Spain, and Napoleon. Silver still flowed near the peak levels of the 1790s. But it increasingly benefited US and British traders, and France via subsidies. Spain faced a deepening revenue crisis.[6]

Seeking Consolidation, Creating Faction: New Spain, 1805–1808
Spain's Atlantic trade was blocked, home production faced deepening dislocation, and the Treasury emptied as it faced rising obligations to Napoleon

and the bondholders who had funded years of costly conflicts. Mounting discontent from aristocratic factions excluded from power at court and a populace struggling to get by focused on Godoy, Carlos IV's "favorite" minister. Godoy's political failings and personal excesses were magnified as he was blamed for selling Spain to Napoleon. As war resumed in 1804, it was clear that the alienation of Spanish Church properties, with all its disruptions, would not cover wartime costs and mounting debts. So Godoy and Carlos turned to a parallel program for Spain's Americas—focused inevitably on New Spain. Another Consolidation of Royal Bonds would call in ecclesiastical wealth, again delivered to the Treasury in exchange for promises of interest to sustain Church activities. But in New Spain, Church wealth was mostly in loan funds, not land. Most loans were long-term mortgages that borrowers expected to hold indefinitely while paying interest. In New Spain, a consolidation would expropriate capital—taking land only when capital could not be redeemed.

The economic and social consequences would depend on implementation—which depended on one more round of regime mandates and resistant petitions, negotiations, and mediated outcomes. In perhaps the last major success of the mediating regime in New Spain, the great oligarchs deflected the most draining, disruptive consequences of the consolidation onto men of lesser wealth—provincial landlords and emerging merchants. It was a success with divisive consequences. The oligarchy and silver capitalism held strong, but the larger coalition that sustained them faced new divisions.

Don José de Iturrigaray arrived to serve as viceroy in Mexico City in 1803, appointed by Godoy and Carlos IV, who saw a strong representative of Crown interests in difficult times. A son of Spain's northern gentry, a provincial elite in the terms used here for New Spain, Iturrigaray's father had entered the Crown service and held posts in the port of Cádiz, the commercial link to New Spain and the empire. Don José chose a military career, faced battle in France from 1793 to 1795, and rose to the rank of general, to be appointed military commander at Cádiz as the new century began. There he married doña María Inés de Jaúregui, daughter of General don Agustín de Jaúregui, viceroy in Lima during the difficult years from 1780 to 1784 when the uprisings around Tupac Amaru challenged Spanish power from Cuzco to Potosí.[7]

Arriving in Mexico City during the Peace of Amiens, Iturrigaray knew his first task was to promote mining and the flow of silver to Cádiz—as

Crown revenue and as specie to fuel trade. Soon after taking office, he visited Guanajuato. He built close ties with leading American mining magnates, don Ignacio de Obregón and the Marqués de San Juan de Rayas at Guanajuato, along with the second Conde de Regla, then struggling to revive the Real del Monte mines that had made his father the richest man in the Americas. Iturrigaray was famously attentive to the flow of mercury; mined at Almadén in the Sierra between Madrid and Cádiz, it was essential to refining midgrade ores in older mines, a key to silver production and tax accounting. For his efforts, the viceroy gained fees, gratuities, or bribes—depending on one's perspective.[8] Like so many before him, he profited promoting the industry essential to Spain's imperial survival.

In the summer of 1805, with renewed warfare pressuring trade and revenues, Iturrigaray received orders to implement the Consolidation in New Spain. A committee led by the viceroy and including Archbishop don Francisco Javier Lizana y Beaumont announced the program in August. Capital on loan from religious institutions was called in; to sustain religious life, interest of 5 percent would be paid on redeemed funds. The program seemed ingenious: borrowers would pay back loan funds, which would pass immediately to the Treasury. Ecclesiastical lenders would receive 5 percent interest over time—the same rate they normally received from mortgage loans. The Crown would gain; the Church would lose nothing (thus viceroy and archbishop could collaborate). But most borrowers would be hard pressed to find cash to redeem mortgages—and then would find capital scarce for future enterprises.[9]

Petitions quickly followed, demanding mediation. The Mexico City Council, voice of the North American metropolis, took the lead in September. Now integrating landed oligarchs in a body still ruled by landed provincials, one of the former, the Marqués de Santa Cruz de Inguanzo, took the lead in defending the interests of all. The council understood the differential impact of the consolidation: it noted that two-thirds of miners and merchants would be hurt, as would nine-tenths of estate operators. Among the latter, the tenth that would not suffer were the landed oligarchs who held half the estates that sustained Mexico City and silver capitalism. Knowing that concentration, the council defended the interests of often-indebted provincial elites, struggling miners, and lesser merchants. The powerful would escape or get by.[10]

Figure 8. The Mexico City Cathedral. Photograph by the author.

The Mining Tribunal added its own petition. Led by don José Mariano Fagoaga, powerful in finance and trade, mining and landed entrepreneurship, the corporation that spoke for silver miners also noted that nine-tenths of estate operators would suffer. There was not enough cash to redeem all mortgages. Calling them in would create a crisis of capital that would cripple the economy of New Spain and limit its ability to pay revenues to the Crown.[11]

Iturrigaray quickly replied that the consolidation was policy and he did not seek the opinions of the council or the tribunal—just as Croix had responded in 1766 to council petitions. The viceroy was pleased to learn that the consulado, the merchants' chamber, the third key corporation established to speak for power to power in the capital, had decided to take no position. Its leaders communicated privately that they would not add to the "impediments to implementing His Majesty's mandate," but would "work as they could to bring the greatest success to His Majesty's policy."[12] Why the merchants' chamber stood back demands analysis.

The merchants of the consulado had substantial ties to Church-linked financing. Three sodalities, sanctioned by the archbishopric and organized to serve factions of merchants linked by common origins in Spanish homelands, provided religious and social services funded by lending capital at interest. The Charitable Bank of the Blessed Sacrament had over 800,000 pesos on loan in 1805, half in mortgages, half in commercial investments. Among the mortgages, one created in 1782 invested 200,000 pesos in the northern estates of the family of the Condes de Regla, a sign of oligarchic solidarity with a family holding mining and landed properties valued over 6 million pesos. Two other mortgages invested 40,000 pesos in estates of other major landed clans. Most of the rest were loans of 12,000 pesos or less to provincial elites.

The Charitable Bank loaned the other half of its capital in commercial advances, mostly to the consulado to finance tax collection contracts and tobacco monopoly operations. Two loans, a mortgage for 22,000 pesos and a commercial advance of 70,000—10 percent of the bank's capital—went to the Consulado of Veracruz (the feared rivalry had become a financial dependency). The Charitable Bank loaned funds to solidify links to landed oligarchs, provincial elites, their own consulado, and its Veracruz ally.[13] The Sodality Bank of Our Lady of the Rosary also had over 800,000 pesos out on loan in 1805. Among its borrowers were Fagoagas; the Regla family; the mining entrepreneur don Diego, Conde de Rul; and don José Sánchez Espinosa, the great agricultural entrepreneur who had taken a mortgage to help purchase a pulque hacienda in the 1790s. Most loans to individuals ranged between 70,000 and 20,000 pesos, funding a few oligarchs, several provincial elites, and emerging merchants, including don Gabriel de Yermo, who owed 28,000 pesos. The Sodality of the Rosary placed about 20 percent of its capital in commercial-institutional loans to the consulado, the Royal Treasury, and the Mexico City Council.[14]

The Sodality of Our Lady of Aránzazu had less capital, about 270,000 pesos on loan in 1805. Its loans tended to be smaller, often funding emerging merchants. About 40 percent of its capital funded ventures of the consulados of Mexico City and Veracruz. Aránzazu's activities over time show capital of just under 60,000 pesos in 1760 growing to over 100,000 by 1770, then jumping to 210,000 in 1780. Growth to 229,000 pesos in 1790 and 235,000 by 1800 came with increasing loans to the consulados, as institutional funding absorbed more capital while regime revenue claims rose. When consolidation officials demanded accounts in 1805, the sodality's loans had risen to 270,000 pesos. The merchants' religious-charitable banking held strong, linking them to oligarchs, provincial elites, the larger merchant community, and key regime institutions.

Why, with so much capital at stake, did the consulado stand back from the debates on the consolidation? Perhaps because the sodality banks, formally Church institutions, would see capital called in from their creditors while gaining interest payments from the Treasury. As a long-time recruiter and contributor of loans to the Crown, the consulado had a strong interest in bond repayment—the goal of the consolidation. Perhaps members were divided: emerging merchants relying on loans might be hurt; established financiers with ample capital would not—and might well invest in embargoed estates. Taking no institutional stand, the merchants' chamber could stand quietly in support of Crown policy—and await negotiations sure to come.

Late in November the politics of the consolidation took another turn. Nearly seventy "cultivators and leading men of the province of Mexico," not just near the capital but including regions from the sugar basin just south around Cuernavaca to the rich Bajío plains north around Querétaro, signed a petition of opposition. They insisted that draining the convent capital that funded 90 percent of commercial growers would "destroy the hatchery of golden eggs" and undermine their ability to pay taxes, sustain silver production, and contribute as they always had to the exceptional needs of the Crown.[15]

This petition was different. It did not come from an established corporation with sanctioned rights to address the Crown. It represented the assembled voices and interests of a powerful segment of New Spain's oligarchy—leading landed entrepreneurs, including many major merchant financiers and mine operators who had invested in commercial estate. Most lived in Mexico City; others in Querétaro and nearby provincial centers. Oligarchs had reached out to include numerous provincial elites in the capital and beyond. A powerful interest group without official corporate sanction demanded a hearing, expanding the politics of mediation. Two Fagoagas signed, as did the Conde de Santiago and the Conde de Regla (a close ally of Iturrigaray). So did don Diego, Conde de Rul, with major mining and landed interests around Guanajuato and across the north. The Mariscal de Castilla, the leading landed proprietor around San Miguel and Dolores signed, as did don José Sánchez

Espinosa and his son, now Conde de Peñasco, leading proprietors from the capital to Querétaro and San Miguel—and dominant across San Luis Potosí to the north.

These were men who could not be ignored. They were joined by larger numbers of the less rich and powerful—including don Gabriel de Yermo, a rising merchant, struggling to establish himself in sugar around Cuernavaca and as a purveyor of aguardiente (cane brandy). He held the *abasto* contract to supply meat to the capital—bringing dealings with great grazers in the Bajío and farther north, dealings that required ample capital he had gained in loans from ecclesiastical banks.[16] Through the fall of 1805, petitions challenging the consolidation also poured in from dispersed provinces, some formally from councils, some informally from groups demanding a voice. Notably, don Manuel Abad y Quiepo wrote for the cathedral chapter, cultivators, and merchants of Valladolid—the bishopric including Guanajuato's mines and rich estates across the Bajío bottomlands. To the standard complaints about the drain of capital, he added a new emphasis: a few men with capital would gain embargoed estates and further concentrate landed power. Querétaro corregidor don Miguel Domínguez made the same point in his long representation of the interest of entrepreneurs there.[17]

The consolidation mobilized the politics of petition in unprecedented strength and new diversity. Iturrigaray could allow no appeal to authorities in Spain; their need for revenues was desperate. He played his part in the politics of mediation by negotiating compromises that enabled a partial implementation that sent ample new funds to the Crown while limiting the impact of collections and disruptions on the most powerful oligarchs and the silver capitalism they led. Provincial elites and rising merchants paid.

The evidence is in the implementation. From 1805 to 1808 the consolidation collected 10.5 million pesos across New Spain, half in the Archbishopric of Mexico that included the capital, Querétaro, and surrounding regions. New Spain paid two-thirds of the 15 million pesos taken across Spain's Americas, a fair indicator of the silver kingdom's dominant importance. To put the extraction in the context of New Spain's economy, silver production then averaged nearly 23 million pesos yearly. The 10.5 million pesos taken over three years was a significant addition to Crown revenues—yet not a devastating blow to silver production, which held high to peak at over 26 million in 1809.

The consolidation was implemented by committees: a general committee led by Iturrigaray oversaw local committees that did the work of demanding accounts from Church-linked lenders, calling in their capital, and then negotiating to gain as much as seemed possible—and political. Most of the negotiations focused on payment deals, allowing mortgage holders with little cash to pay what they could over time. There is evidence that many powerful men were spared. Others less eminent, notably don Gabriel de Yermo, felt targeted.[18]

The sodality banks linked to the consulado paid little: of the more than 800,000 pesos on loan in 1805 by the Charitable Bank of the Blessed Sacrament, only 200,000 went to the consolidation in three years of collections; of the 270,000 pesos in loan capital of the Aránzazu Sodality bank, just over 50,000 were collected in the same period. A 22 percent collection rate brought revenues yet limited the hit on the banks and their borrowers. The over 800,000 pesos in loan capital of the Sodality of Our Lady of the Rosary appears to have fully escaped the consolidation. If that was the case, overall extractions from consulado-linked banks held near 12 percent.[19] Quiet negotiation served the chamber and its leading merchants very well.

Collections from oligarchs were limited in a different way: titled landlord-borrowers paid just under 350,000 pesos, 7 percent of total collections in the capital. Yet they controlled at least half of the value of landed properties tied to the capital and its markets. The consolidation proved a most regressive tax, targeting lesser landowners and commercial borrowers, sparing the most powerful. Among the latter, the Conde de Regla paid most, 86,000 pesos. The great miner-landlord, still struggling to revive Real del Monte and a close ally of Iturrigaray, appears to have paid off all his Church-linked loans. Still, they were less than three percent of properties valued over 3 million pesos—not including his mines. The Conde de la Cortina, a consulado merchant investing in the land, paid 72,000 pesos, again a small hit on landed wealth over 1 million. Two long-established landed oligarchs also paid large sums: the Mariscal de Castilla delivered 64,000 pesos linked to lands in the Bajío; the Marqués de San Miguel de Aguayo paid 42,000 pesos on his vast holdings across the far north. Finding cash might be difficult for oligarchs with lands locked in entails they could not sell; still, payments were small in the context of vast holdings.[20]

Don José Sánchez Espinosa held rich estates entailed as an obra pía and seemingly liable to disentailment; he owed nearly 70,000 pesos to Our Lady of the Rosary. He signed the landlords' petition of November 1805—and in some invisible way, the negotiations that followed exempted the priest-oligarch, who ruled a clan including his son the Conde de Peñasco and his vast northern holdings. Neither father nor titled son appeared in the payment accounts; they never mentioned the consolidation in extensive business or personal correspondence. Their holdings held intact when the program ended in 1808.[21] Mediations far from the public eye kept the powerful free of the hardest demands of the consolidation.

Collections focused on the convent banks that loaned funds to sustain provincial elites, draining capital from the landed-professional clans in Mexico City, Querétaro, and elsewhere that relied on mortgages to fund estate operations—and to hold places at the edge of power. Many arranged payment over time and still struggled to pay. Some, including Father Miguel Hidalgo at San Miguel, saw estates embargoed. The consolidation also hit a few emerging merchants hard. The largest payments, totaling nearly 122,000 pesos, came from a partnership that had borrowed convent capital to start a business to transport silver. Famously don Gabriel de Yermo owed 197,000 pesos; he paid 86,000, 44 percent, and saw his sugar estate embargoed.[22] His experience was not typical, but it epitomized the frustrations of newer merchants dreaming of rising to eminence as silver boomed yet revenue demands prejudiced men with little capital.

The consolidation reminded all of the declining power of Spain's monarchy in the face of wars led by British and French regimes fighting for Euro-Atlantic dominance. It demonstrated again the pivotal importance of New Spain's silver—and the continuing viability of the regime of mediation that kept Spain and New Spain together. The Bourbons gained new revenues; Mexico City oligarchs carried on; silver production held strong. Still, the revenue program generated fissures in the larger social coalition that sustained silver capitalism in New Spain. Always dependent and insecure, provincial elites became more insecure; emerging merchants saw capital dwindle as the Crown claimed more silver for endless wars. The fissures would become fractures in 1808, when provincial elites and emerging merchants took opposite sides in the summer of politics and then the coup that closed new participations and old mediations.

While he negotiated the consolidation to claim revenues, sustain power, and prejudice the least among the powerful, Iturrigaray continued to support

mining in alliance with leading miners and financiers. Then in 1806, he tried
to implement an old but unenforced Crown directive that would break the
rule of established leaders in the consulado and open space for emerging
merchants—precisely those prejudiced by the consolidation and the scarcities of capital it accelerated. Was the viceroy trying to mollify with new participations those he prejudiced with painful collections? Iturrigaray argued
that he was fulfilling orders from Spain; the consulado's established leaders
petitioned for relief; the petition reached Madrid—where officials dependent
on silver capitalism assured its most powerful merchant financiers the right
to rule Mexico City's consulado.[23] Oligarchy was restored.

Whatever Iturrigaray's aims, his intervention in consulado governance
first alienated the powerful merchants who had backed him in implementing
the consolidation—and largely gained exemption from collections. Any allegiance from emerging traders proved short-lived when higher authorities
blocked the opening and returned the powerful to power. The regime of petition and mediation again sustained the powerful interests that kept silver
capitalism strong. Yet fissures were piling on fissures.

Monarchy in Crisis: Napoleon and the Spanish Bourbons, 1807–1808
The extraordinary revenue programs that hit ecclesiastical wealth in deeply
Catholic domains revealed to all the depths of the difficulties that endless
wars imposed on Spain—and the continuing pivotal importance of New
Spain's silver to Spain, all the belligerents, and global trades. "All Europe . . .
had a stake in sustaining Spain's colonial system"—while Europe's war's corroded Spain's imperial regime.[24] When France resumed war against Britain
in late 1803, Napoleon demanded a subsidy from Spain in lieu of troops it
could not provide and ships it could not spare from the essential task of protecting Atlantic trade and silver shipments. Britain had allowed neutral shipping in the war of 1797 to 1801, keeping silver flowing. In 1803 it aimed to
block neutrals—except when they delivered silver to British interests. The
destruction of the French and Spanish fleets at Trafalgar in 1805 ensured that
neither could carry specie to Europe, forcing covert deals that profited a few
and diverted rising flows to Britain. While New Spain's silver production
held strong, Spain's revenue programs—resented in Spain and New Spain—
could not cover rising expenses, soaring debts, and the subsidy Napoleon
demanded.[25]

Wartime revenue challenges led to a crisis of legitimacy that wracked Spain's Bourbon monarchy. By the fall of 1806, Napoleon grappled with a deepening contradiction that threatened his ambitions to power. He knew, as one report to his advisers stated, that New Spain was "the center of the world's commerce." With the loss of Haiti, its rich trades and revenues, Spanish silver became more essential to France's economy and war efforts. Yet Spain's naval power had vanished, leaving a regime unable to protect trade and deliver silver. Napoleon concluded that Spain's Bourbons had to become his dependent pawns—or they had to go.[26] Unannounced, the goal of controlling or replacing Carlos IV and Prince Fernando guided French policy in Iberia in the critical years of 1807 and 1808. The larger goal was to make Spain's Americas, especially New Spain, French protectorates to benefit French trade and Napoleon's revenues.[27]

The policy began to unfold in public on October 1, 1807, when French troops crossed the Pyrenees and entered Spanish territory on their way to Lisbon. The announced goal was to claim Portugal and the revenues of its empire, notably Brazil. Weeks later, Carlos and Godoy signed the Treaty of Fontainebleau, granting Napoleon permission to cross Spain to assault Britain's last continental ally. Napoleon acted; the Spanish monarchy adapted. Facing "financial, commercial, and strategic pressures," Napoleon mobilized "the arrogance of power as the ideals of the French Revolution became imperialist." He had worried about Spain's Bourbons as "allies" since they joined Britain against revolutionary France in 1793. Despite the renewed alliance with France in 1796, Napoleon never trusted Carlos IV not to turn again to Britain, a shift that would deliver access to silver and open a second front on France's southern border. While French troops drove toward Lisbon, reports reached Madrid that the emperor's goal was to occupy Spain.

Carlos and Godoy agreed to France's military march to Portugal knowing they could not stop it. They could acquiesce or admit Spain's military impotence. Godoy tried to shape Spanish policy in the face of impossible contradictions: London ruled the seas; Paris distrusted the deals that sent New Spain's silver to Britain—the only way to deliver Spain's subsidy to France. "In 1807 and 1808 the prize for the two most powerful states in Europe and the Atlantic was the Spanish empire in the Americas, in particular New Spain's silver." So Godoy juggled the inescapable dilemma of Spanish power: Madrid's blatant impotence tied to New Spain's wealth in silver.

Napoleon plotted to oust the minister and perhaps replace Carlos with a young Fernando he imagined more malleable.[28]

As French troops marched to Portugal, Spain's regime began to crumble. Cracks had developed as policy and revenue challenges mounted. Some still saw Spain's fate tied to France; nationalists imagined adapting reforms from French revolutionary models to shore up Spain's power. Others saw Napoleon as predatory and imagined that a turn toward Britain might bring strength— or at least better access to New Spain's silver. All knew that either ally would seek a growing share of the silver all coveted. Those debates overlay divisions between an aristocratic party that had been edged out by Charles III and Charles IV, and the gentry professionals (parallel to the Mexico City provincials) they recruited to promote reforms they proclaimed as enlightened, yet had failed to slow Spain's decline.[29]

The aristocratic party provoked a crisis at the Escorial, the king's retreat northwest of Madrid, on October 27, 1807. Papers came to light linking Fernando to a plot to depose Godoy and force stronger ties to Napoleon by marrying the recently widowed Spanish prince to a Bonaparte. The coup aimed to oust Godoy and force greater dependence on France; if Carlos objected, he might be deposed to make Fernando king—tied to Napoleon by marriage. Key members of the aristocratic faction led by the Duque del Infantado took part. Carlos and Godoy learned all this as French troops marched on Spanish soil. The prince was confined to quarters; more probing revealed dealings with Napoleon that threatened the rule of Carlos and Godoy.[30]

On October 30, Carlos had the *Gaceta de Madrid* publish details of the plot and announce Fernando's arrest—exposing divisions within the royal family and the regime to the political public. Further investigation confirmed that Fernando and the aristocrats, at whose initiative was unclear, aimed to take power and tie the regime to Napoleon. Then, trying to limit the damage to a crumbling monarchy, Carlos announced Fernando's confession and a conditional pardon based on a promise of reformed behavior. Aristocratic conspirators faced closed trials and internal exile, removing them from palace intrigues. Napoleon's role stayed secret—at his insistence.[31]

The Spanish public learned of sharp conflicts within the royal family, a plot linking Fernando and aristocrats aiming to oust Godoy—but not Fernando's overtures to Napoleon. With the revelation and Fernando's house arrest, Carlos and Godoy remained in power as French troops entered Portugal. Napoleon offered Godoy a small kingdom in southern Portugal for his helpful service. All adapted to Napoleon's pressure and invasion. What alternative did they have? But Godoy was reviled, blamed for all Spain's difficulties. Fernando, his readiness to serve Napoleon kept secret, gained rising honor as "El Deseado"—the desired one, the prince who might save Spain from the doom that encircled as Britain ruled the seas and France invaded.[32] Myth trumped truth as crisis deepened.

Napoleon's invasion of Portugal proved slow. When troops finally entered Lisbon on November 30, Prince Regent João was on board ship, ready to move with his court and regime to Brazil, escorted by British warships. Napoleon might have Portugal; he would not gain the revenues of its empire, which would flow to Britain. On landing at Salvador in Brazil's northeast plantation zone in January 1808, before settling in to rule from his new capital at Rio de Janeiro, João decreed the opening of Brazil's trade to all allied and neutral shipping—favoring Britain and excluding France and Spain.[33] Brazil, rising prosperity as sugar and slavery revived in the shadow of revolutionary slaves' destruction of Haiti's plantations, would serve British power.

Meanwhile, Godoy, having blocked Fernando's plot to become Napoleon's Bourbon agent in Spain, tried his own negotiations with the invading emperor. Could he prevent the rumored occupation of Spain? Whatever the minister's dreams, the invasion came. Napoleon needed a stable, dependent Spain—and access to New Spain's silver. The farce at the Escorial proved that neither Carlos and Godoy nor Fernando and his aristocratic allies could deliver stability or silver. Portugal's empire now delivered to British hegemony, the French emperor mounted an invasion aimed at Madrid and its Bourbon monarchs. Desperate for New Spain's silver and trade, Napoleon could not allow Spain's fractious Bourbon's to continue to rule.[34]

Late in December of 1807, multiple columns of French troops crossed the Pyrenees to take Burgos, San Sebastián, and Pamplona; others marched toward Barcelona. This was no spur-of-the-moment decision, but an orchestrated plan to occupy Spain, formally an ally. By mid-March there were thirty thousand French troops in Portugal and seventy thousand in Spain north of the Ebro. Napoleon intended to make Spain a dependent state, by negotiating with flailing Bourbons if possible, by force and regime replacement if not. His ultimate aim was economic control of Spain and its empire. To compete with Britain, he needed the trade and revenues of New Spain. Advisers convinced him that key Spanish leaders called *ilustrados*, the enlightened, would back French rule as a way to reform the regime and hold the empire.[35] No one addressed the obvious question of how France and Spain, fused under Napoleonic rule, might keep access to New Spain's silver and larger American trades in a post-Trafalgar world. Britain ruled the Atlantic.

In March, with troops occupying most of northern Castile, Napoleon sent forces under his brother-in-law Joachim Murat to take Madrid. Again, nothing went as Napoleon planned. Troops foraging for supplies fueled resentments among local populations. Godoy was widely blamed for inviting a French occupation. Napoleon worried that Carlos would follow João in fleeing to America, keeping his throne while delivering silver and trade to England. Godoy proposed such a move in early March, refused by Carlos who saw such a flight as a betrayal of Spain.[36]

In mid-March, a dysfunctional and conflict-laden court and royal family were at their palace at Aranjuez, a day's ride south of Madrid. Had they gone to escape the French troops approaching the capital? Were they en route to Seville and perhaps America, ready to abandon Spain to keep the empire? Were they divided, uncertain, and keeping options open? Probably. Whatever the plan, on the March 18, a clique of Fernandista aristocratic allies now led by the Conde de Montijo raised a crowd in nearby towns and pressed a riot that drove Godoy into hiding. The next day he resigned, followed by Carlos's abdication. The aristocrats and their crowd proclaimed Fernando king. The option of an American Bourbon empire based in New Spain closed. Fernando claimed the mantle of Spanish nationalism and returned to Madrid. He entered with an escort of grandees to public acclaim—only to learn that Murat would not deal with him without instructions from Napoleon. The emperor concluded that Fernando was too unreliable to serve as an effective tool. To serve French interests, it was time for a new regime in Spain.[37]

Like the plot at the Escorial in October, the March coup at Aranjuez solved nothing. The accession of El Deseado brought a brief public euphoria. The aristocrats who engineered the coup imagined exercising new influence. Many favored a turn toward Britain—impossible with French troops in Madrid. Ilustrados of less exalted origins saw an opening to reforms modeled on French precedents—in opposition to French domination. The necessity of the empire and the impossibility of its maintenance plagued every Spanish faction and interest. Carlos and the ousted Godoy saw the need for New Spain and the Americas—but Carlos would not abandon Spain to keep the wealth of empire. Fernando hoped to reign under Napoleon, providing a mask of Bourbon legitimacy to deliver American silver to shore up French power. Napoleon's first interest in Spain, with or without a Bourbon ally, was New Spain's silver. All flailed while Britain ruled the Atlantic; when silver sailed it was in British ships, or those Britain sanctioned.

As French troops consolidated control of northern Spain and Madrid in late April, Napoleon invited Fernando, Carlos, Godoy, and the entire royal family to Bayonne, just over the border in southern France. Their acceptance demonstrated that the Bourbons no longer ruled. Napoleon would set the next steps in a process aimed at regime change. As May began and more of the royal family left Madrid for confinement in exile, a riotous rising rattled Madrid. On May 2, a crowd mobilized by pro-Fernando nationalist military officers took to the streets and plazas of the Spanish capital to insult French troops and demand the return of El Deseado. It was not a spontaneous rising but a political riot orchestrated by don Pedro de Velarde, an artillery officer tied to the family of the Marqués de Herrero, the judge who married a daughter of the Conde de Regla, gained great wealth, and rose to sit in the highest councils of empire in Spain. Velarde and his allies aimed to denounce French rule and Fernando's captivity. Over four hundred died in the rising, most at the hands of the French repression made famous in Goya's *Third of May 1808* painting.[38]

Also on May 2—as part of the same orchestrated plan—magistrates at Mosteles, a town on the outskirts of the capital, called councils across Spain to join in juntas to address the questions of sovereignty left open by the Bourbons' captivity. The Madrid risings were not an exercise in spontaneous popular radicalism, but a mobilization of popular groups to back a call for regime renewal in the established Spanish tradition. If vacated, monarchical sovereignty returned to the pueblos—towns with councils. It was the role of the councils to call assemblies, culminating in traditional cortes, to reestablish sovereignty. The Madrid risings revealed that for many political Spaniards, Napoleon's capture of the royal family had vacated sovereignty. No replacement dictated by the French emperor could be legitimate. The pueblos—that is, the councils—of Spain must act to resolve the crisis.

During the same days of early May, Fernando and Carlos were in Bayonne negotiating abdications. Fernando abdicated to his father on May 5; Carlos abdicated to Napoleon on May 10; by then the events of Madrid were widely known. Both accepted pensions and comfortable exiles in France to escape the impossible challenges of ruling Spain and keeping its empire while caught between French armies and British navies. Napoleon named his brother Joseph Bonaparte king of Spain and its Americas: José I. Don Miguel José de Azanza, who as viceroy in New Spain had easily ended the imagined rising of 1799 and now sat on the Council of Castile, led a faction of officials ready to back the imposed newcomer. They dreamed of a return to order.[39]

French troops and local allies kept José in Madrid through the coming months and years. But the news of Aranjuez, the Bayonne captivity, the May 2 uprisings, the call for councils to meet in juntas, the Bourbon abdications—all in a month's time—set off an unprecedented political crisis and opening across Spain. In key provincial capitals including Cartagena, Valencia, Seville, Badajoz, Oviedo, Santander, and Zaragoza, local notables assembled crowds, distributed arms from local army depots, and called on councils to assert allegiance to Fernando and, given his captivity, to form juntas grounded in traditional local rights. The aim was to resist French rule and work toward a new regime. People powerful and poor, devoted to an imagined, desired Fernando who would defend Spain, preserve the empire, and never collaborate with Napoleon, struggled to reclaim sovereignty and their sovereign.[40]

Power in Europe had long been more militarized than power in Spain's Americas. French revolutionaries proclaimed popular rights and liberties in the 1790s—and mobilized unprecedented military powers to defend them and the revolutionary nation against internal enemies and outside powers. In 1808, Napoleon mobilized postrevolutionary military forces grounded in claims of French national sovereignty to assert power in Spain. He toppled the monarchy—and provoked resistance that turned to Spanish traditions of the sovereignty of the pueblos while beginning to arm the people. How else to resist Napoleon's armies? Old ways of rule were becoming new, linking diverse ways of popular sovereignty to militarized power. What began in Spain would soon resonate in New Spain—with unintended consequences for both.

For two years, diverse juntas and then a regency contested power in Spain while fighting French armies that first slowly, then steadily moved south—by 1810 leaving only the isolated port of Cádiz, Spain's link to its Americas, free of French rule. A cortes gathered there to write a liberal constitution proclaimed in 1812—honoring Fernando and aiming to retain the empire. But in the summer of 1808, the main drama shifted to the city of Mexico, capital of New Spain and pivot of silver capitalism. If provincial capitals in Spain claimed the right to form juntas and join in remaking sovereignty, should not the capital of the American kingdom that sustained the empire gain equal participation? A new politics mixing Spanish traditions, old mediations, and new mobilizations debating ways of popular sovereignty tried to find a resolution for the richest region of the Americas in the summer of 1808—until a military coup transformed politics and power there, too.

CHAPTER 9

Summer of Politics, 1808

Contesting Power and Popular Sovereignties

✦ THE SUMMER OF 1808 BROUGHT TRANSFORMING POLITICAL CON-
flicts to the city named Mexico. The consolidation debates had focused political people there on the challenges of war and its draining costs. As 1807
ended they began to hear fragmented reports about Napoleon's invasion of
Iberia and rumors about the Escorial affair. The spring of 1808 brought news
of the French turn on Madrid. Then official channels began to report an
evolving crisis. On June 9, the *Gaceta de México* announced the jailing of
Godoy and the abdication of Carlos at Aranjuez. Viceroy Iturrigaray,
appointed by Carlos and Godoy, called celebrations of Fernando's accession.[1]
Public ceremonies proclaimed El Deseado king. Then on June 22, the *Gaceta*
revealed that French troops were in Madrid—insisting they came as allies to
solidify the French-Spanish alliance. The claim lost credence, if it had any,
when the *Gaceta* of June 25 reported the popular risings in Madrid—but not
the captivity of the Bourbon kings. Thanks to commercial letters and sailors'
tales, official news came surrounded by a haze of uncertain, often contradictory rumors.

What followed in the summer of 1808 in Mexico City defies synthesis.
News and rumors mixed in uncertain waves. Established corporations and
people with diverse interests, rights, and expectations reacted as they

could—often in changing ways to changing reports that soon enough changed again. It was a summer of deep debates and transforming changes that can only be understood as it was lived, in a narrative of uncertain learning and less-certain adaptations.

July Debates: Seeking Continuity in Times of Uncertainty

When documents arrived from Madrid stating that Napoleon's brother, proclaimed José I, would rule Spain and the empire and defend their independence (certainly not from France), the men who ruled New Spain and its capital faced new challenges. They hesitated to publish the decrees announcing Bonapartist rule. On July 15, the viceroy met with the city council (recognizing that with the break of sovereignty, he had to consult the pueblo?). In a tumultuous session, they decided to print Napoleon's missives, which appeared in the *Gaceta* the next day.[2] Debates continued. The viceroy and the council (opponents in the consolidation debates) searched together for an interim sovereignty tied to established local institutions; the Audiencia and the consulado (the viceroy's allies in the consolidation) saw any interim sovereignty as a threat to their interests—and to ties with Spain.

As the *Gaceta* published news that opened every political question, viceroy and council met again on July 16. The council remained a bastion of provincial elites, led by legal men such as don Francisco Primo de Verdad and don Juan Francisco de Azcarate. They were joined in 1808 by don Juan José Fagoaga and don Manuel Francisco Sánchez de Tagle, both of established silver-banking families, and the Marqués de Uluapa and the Marqués de Santa Cruz de Inguanzo, men of leading landed clans. In days of looming challenges, oligarchs and provincials came together in the council, reinforcing its right to represent the capital of New Spain. On the July 19, led by First Magistrate Fagoaga, the council wrote to Iturrigaray proclaiming the captured Carlos still sovereign—and claiming a de facto autonomy in alliance with the viceroy, his ministers, and the judges of the Audiencia. They would rule until Carlos regained his freedom and throne. With the viceroy's consent, the council challenged the rights claimed by Napoleon and just announced in the *Gaceta*. New Spain would not serve France. The text is revealing:

"The most Noble, most Loyal and Imperial City of Mexico, Metropolis of North America," lamented and rejected the fall of Spain's legitimate king.

Figure 9. The Mexico City Council Hall. Photograph by the author.

"This horrid abdication, involuntary, forced, and made in a moment of conflict, has no effect on the most respected rights of the nation." Even if the Bourbons accepted abdication, any succession arranged by Napoleon was void: "The Spanish monarchy is the patrimony of its sovereigns, founded by the Nation." Only the nation set rules of succession; the council denied a king's right to alienate sovereignty. But what constituted the nation? An abstract sovereignty, as proclaimed in revolutionary France, or something more ancient, grounded in Spanish history?

Should a monarch vacate the throne, "by his absence or impediment, Sovereignty resides in and represents the entire kingdom, the classes that form it, and most particularly in the Superior Tribunals that govern, administer justice, and in the corporations that carry the public voice . . ." Quickly, the abstract nation became embodied in established judicial institutions and the councils that spoke for cities. "Mexico in representation of the Kingdom as its metropolis, and for itself, resolutely sustains the rights of our August

Monarch Carlos IV." The council of New Spain's capital, representing North America, recognized only the sovereignty of Carlos IV. Fernando's coup and coronation, celebrated a month earlier, were rejected on news of the captivity. For the moment, the viceregal regime would carry on seeking "the public and common interests of the Fatherland, the good of the Nation, and its happiness, with conspicuous love for and deep loyalty to our august Sovereigns." Any who did not accept continuing viceregal rule and council oversight in the face of the captivity "is declared a traitor to King and State."

The councilmen ended with a volley of rhetorical flourishes. First they insisted: "We feel pain as Mexicans who cannot fly across the ocean to unite with our Fathers to back our King and defend the Monarchy. . . ." Though they remained in America, far from peninsular conflicts, "no city in the world like Mexico, capital and metropolis of New Spain, represented more faithful vassals." Their last insistence: how fortunate that "Divine Providence" had brought don José de Iturrigaray to lead them as viceroy in such trying times. Formally, the proclamation was addressed from the council to the viceroy.[3]

The proclamation seems clear: established institutions would rule New Spain in the absence of a legitimate sovereign in Spain. Viceroy and Audiencia, offices of government and revenue collection, intendants and city councils, district magistrates and indigenous republics would carry on as always. It was a declaration of continuity, claiming autonomy until events in Spain became clearer. Yet the proclamation of abstract loyalty and institutional continuity was laden with language that revealed a contested and fluid politics just below the surface. The text offered three different bases for sovereignty. First, sovereignty belonged to the nation (a French revolutionary notion). The Mexico City Council claimed to represent that abstraction—calling it, the nation, to back established powers in support of anti-French insurgency.

Then in a quick rhetorical slide, the 1808 proclamation immediately insisted that the nation was embodied in the tribunals of government and justice and the councils that led cities and towns. In that turn, the councilmen looked to the established Spanish presumption of the sovereignty of the pueblos—now fused with the regime of petition and mediation. Was it confusion, division, or subtlety that linked the potentially revolutionary sovereignty of the nation to the long-established sovereignty of the pueblos, now recast as the councils linked to established institutions of higher justice? When the council concluded that Viceroy Iturrigaray—sent by Divine Providence (yet appointed by the captive Carlos)—would lead tribunals and councils through times of uncertainty, their goals (or dreams?) become clearer. Established powers, the viceroy, ministers and judges, and councils representing oligarchs and provincial elites, American and immigrant Spaniards, would unite to lead New Spain and defend Spain.

The council called for consensus in continuity with rhetoric laden with contradictions and potential conflicts. A nation might escape control of established tribunals, as France had done so recently. In Spain, the sovereignty in the pueblos, cities and towns with organized councils, was an old and conservative tradition. In New Spain, councils had never joined in cortes—which convened rarely in Spain after 1660. The council of New Spain's capital alone had negotiated subsidies and other revenue questions—taking a role parallel to a cortes.[4] In July 1808, the council reasserted its right to speak like a cortes—calling viceroy, ministers, and judges to join it while asserting that the viceroy led by Divine Providence. Traditionalism in time of uncertainty led to unprecedented innovations.

One innovation that might have found sanction in tradition was avoided. If pueblos with councils were the ultimate recipients of divine rights to sovereignty, empowered to assemble in cortes to debate key questions, what was the role of New Spain's indigenous republics? There were over four thousand such republics with councils, most around the capital and in regions south.[5] They held domain over local lands and had rights to self-rule and to appeal to viceregal justice. A focus on the sovereignty of the pueblos might draw native republics into political conversations. The men of the Mexico City Council in 1808 could not accept such participation. So they adapted tradition to serve their interests in a very different New World: they linked the rights of their council to viceregal institutions. The goal was participation by Spanish pueblos in a continuing regime of petition and mediation. Spanish councils would engage High Court judges, the viceroy, and his ministers. Native republics would stay separate and subordinate.

While viceroy and council called for unity in continuity, broadsides posted on streets and plazas inflamed relations between Americans and immigrant Spaniards. Divisions lurking in the barrios took the public square. The councilmen appeared to avoid the question. Yet when they referred to the people of Spain as "our fathers," they addressed that chal-lenge—if obliquely. In a patriarchal society, and New Spain was deeply patri-archal, fathers and sons must live in mutual respect. Early on, fathers must rule; later, sons would claim independence to become a new generation of patriarchs, honoring their fathers while striking out on their own.[6] Offering Spain as the land of "our fathers" rhetorically opened the way for New Spain to claim its majority. The monarchy and Spain, the father and his homeland, were honored. But with the king in captivity, the regime—the father—was disabled. Was a homeland occupied by French troops nearing death? If so, the sons must claim independence. Such questions had to be considered, at least in worried conversations among the powerful.

For the moment, viceroy, judges, and ministers would rule in the name of the king and Spain—the father. New Spain's councils and chambers, duti-ful sons, would carry on—loyal to Carlos and Spain, at least in rhetoric. The regime would carry on, operating between council and viceroy in Mexico City, struggling to mediate new, uncertain, and contested realities. All this was negotiated among men sanctioned to participate in the regime of peti-tion and mediation.

July 29: The People Act—Taking the Streets to Proclaim a King

The council's recognition of Carlos IV and proclamation of continuity grounded in established institutions held but ten days. At 5:30 on the morn-ing of July 29, a broadsheet posted across the city declared Fernando VII king. There followed a day of mass mobilization, parades, cannonades, masses, and embraces of El Deseado by the powerful—all demanded, it appeared, by an excited, mobilized populace. The people, it seemed, took to the streets to overturn the proclamation of the powerful. A new politics began parallel to the events of May 2–3 in Madrid, except in Mexico City, the people won—for a time.

Between the 19th and the 29th, commotion and debates had continued in streets and plazas, in the council chamber and in the viceroy's offices. On the 26th, the radical friar don Melchor de Talamantes had stood before the council to read a proposal pressing for de facto independence; he would recognize no sovereign in Spain in such tumultuous times. The *Gaceta* planned to publish on the 29th a report that Valencia had risen against the French and declared an armistice with the British, news already known to the viceroy, audiencia judges, consulado leaders, and likely among councilmen and others too.[7] New visions imagining independence, new news confirming widening and continuing conflicts in Spain, and evidence of a new British role set the context for the day of mobilization that opened a new politics in Mexico City.

The events of the 29th were detailed in the *Diario de México*, an independent periodical backed by American audiencia judge don Jacobo de Villaurrutia and written by don Carlos María de Bustamante, an American journalist and ideologue. He reported the rising of July 29 as a great show of unity. Careful reading suggests more complex developments. Many among the urban populace did take to the streets demanding recognition of Fernando and backing Spain's fight against Napoleon. In Bustamante's telling, the powerful then stepped forward to acquiesce, following a crowd they could not contain.

Many among the populace did take the streets and plazas that day, but the mobilization came preceded by a printed broadside announcing a clear political goal: recognition of Fernando. Men with access to arms and artillery joined them in the streets—firing volleys while the throngs remained peaceful. As had happened in the March coup at Aranjuez (that also proclaimed Fernando) and in the May 2–3 risings in Madrid, the July mobilization in Mexico City was provoked, shaped, and led by political men aiming to use popular pressure to force change.

After the posters proclaimed loyalty to Fernando, "a great artillery cannonade and the tolling of church bells" called people to the streets and a new politics. Only military men could orchestrate the firing of cannon; only clerics could coordinate the ringing of bells. In response, people flocked to the plaza in front of the Viceregal Palace. There Iturrigaray and several of his ministers came out, said Bustamante, "to receive the *vivas* of the noble and loyal pueblo of Mexico." Facing the crowd, the viceroy proclaimed Fernando king—again.[8] Then, Bustamante insisted: "The same pueblo took the artillery to offer another volley" in adamant support of "Spanish arms." Clearly, the crowd had been raised to pressure the viceroy. Artillery fire before and after his acquiescence showed that this "pueblo" had allies in the military. Many surely were pleased to join in proclaiming El Deseado king. But unknown men with printing presses and cannon shaped popular actions that pivotal day.

The next scene revealed much: "Amid the fierce vehemence and enthusiasm of the volley, a part of the pueblo carried a portrait of the beloved

Figure 10. The Viceregal Palace. Photograph by the author.

FERNANDO to the royal palace, without the troops able to keep order in the crowd. The audiencia judge don Josef Arias Villafañe and the First Magistrate of this Most Noble City don Josef Juan de Fagoaga came down to the first landing of the great staircase to accept the portrait, carrying it amid the multitude to His Excellency the Viceroy, who received it with most loyal satisfaction." The people handed the portrait of Fernando to leaders of the Audiencia and the city council, who presented it to the viceroy—in another attempt to show unity, this time linking the people, the council, the judges, and the king's representative. Iturrigaray set the image on the balcony facing the plaza, standing with his ministers who together "showed their jubilation by tossing a large number of pesos, it appeared two thousand."

If lettered men with allies with access to artillery called the people to press the viceroy to proclaim Fernando, the people were ready to join. Men of the crowd, not the troops, entered the palace with Fernando's portrait, to be met and joined on the great staircase by a High Court judge and the powerful merchant financier then serving as the city's first magistrate. They

joined the viceroy in placing the portrait on the balcony: a common front for
El Deseado. Why scatter 2,000 pesos (a peso was most of a week's wages for
city workers)? Was it an attempt to both reward the crowd and deflect it from
further political assertions?

If so, it did not work. After the portrait ruled on the balcony for a time,
"the pueblo asked for its return, to parade it triumphally through the city."
The judge Villafañe and other "gentlemen of the city" returned the portrait
"to the pueblo" and the crowd "carried it through all the streets of the capital." They crossed the square to demand that the archbishop say mass to
honor their new sovereign. "Then they continued through diverse streets,
churches, convents, and public squares with the most passionate vivas; even
the women tossed their shawls and overskirts in the air in signs of joy. VIVA
FERNANDO VII, death to the Emperor of the French. Thus the expression
of patriotism, the focus of Mexican loyalty; the object of passionate desire. . . .
Acclamation and vivas continued all day: the joyous and sonorous Cathedral
bells, by demand of the pueblo, escaped the rules and kept ringing." The
populace took control of bells across the city—which rang all day. The people, men and women, took the portrait of their king first to the viceroy, next
to the archbishop, then to the streets—taking over the bells that announced
religious truth and regime sovereignty. The people of Mexico City—the
pueblo mexicano—installed Fernando VII as their king.

When the viceroy, council, and first junta had proclaimed continuity in
the name of Carlos IV on July 19, they knew that both potential sovereigns
had been captured and could not rule. But they had not published that pivotal news. Did the men who orchestrated the great rising on the 29th know
that? Probably—or at least many had heard rumors. Did the people who
rushed to the streets to acclaim Fernando know he was held captive and
could not rule? That seems less probable. The prince was little known in New
Spain, beyond being the young heir apparent. He was honored as the legitimate heir to sovereignty in the regime of petition, mediation, and justice—
and for not being Carlos or Godoy, who had reigned while difficulties
mounted.

When the people took to the streets and plazas of Mexico City on July 29,
they acted with limited and uncertain information. Cajoled and joined by men
at arms, they called themselves "el pueblo" to make Fernando "el rey." They
rejected the adapted sovereignty of "los pueblos" that led the viceroy, council,

and other established corporate powers to proclaim their own continued rule in the name of Carlos. The people of Mexico City claimed sovereignty as "the people" to demand that the viceroy, Audiencia, and council rule in the name of Fernando. Why?

Bustamante noted in passing that "The statues and portraits of Napoleon have been burned by the pueblo . . . in just enthusiasm." Clearly, some in the city had imagined joining a Napoleonic Spain, enough to have statues and portraits of the emperor set about. The people proclaiming Fernando not only crushed that option, they showed those who presumed to rule that if continuity of rule was to persist in New Spain, the authorities in Mexico City would carry on not by their own presumption, but by the will of the people of the capital.

That statement made with rowdy emphasis, those who had drawn the crowd to proclaim Fernando and gain the viceroy's and council's acquiescence turned toward reinforcing order. "At noon, more than six thousand men marched to the royal palace in military order, European and American countrymen together repeating the vivas His Excellency received from his balcony. An equal troop of all classes assembled in the Alameda, putting green branches in their hats and showing their joy."

European and American Spaniards marched together in good—almost military—order before the viceroy, demonstrating the solidity of the Euro-American alliance essential to power in New Spain. Had military men set them in order? The less exalted gathered at the Alameda, blocks to the west, away from the Spaniards and the viceroy. Were the provocateurs who raised the people unsure of the populace that showed such energy proclaiming Fernando? Did the urban throngs at the Alameda wonder if the time had come to be more assertive? Finally at four in the afternoon, the groups combined, now eighteen to twenty thousand strong, to again parade Fernando's portrait before the palace. The city was illuminated all that night. This was not the normal proclamation of a new king, orchestrated by the authorities. Insisted Bustamante: "It must be said that Mexico has not seen a day like this for many centuries." The political participation of the populace was unprecedented, as was the role of ideologues and military men in calling, orchestrating, and containing that participation. A diverse people asserted sovereignty on the streets of Mexico City that July day in 1808, in part drawn out by military men—and ready to show military strength to get their way.

Iturrigaray, swept along by the day's events, had to demonstrate solidarity with the crowd. "His Excellency the Viceroy left accompanied by his wife for the Sanctuary of Our Lady of Guadalupe, to give her thanks for the great favor of the day. El pueblo followed in a great throng, all with shared enthusiasm." Did Iturrigaray head toward Guadalupe's sanctuary to show solidarity with the people, her staunch devotees? That was his proclaimed intent. But the road to Guadalupe was also the road to Veracruz, and to Spain or exile. Did he imagine that if the throngs did not calm and return to work, allowing their rightful rulers to rule, he might journey on away from the capital and a kingdom he was no longer certain he could lead? That seems probable, too. By joining the pilgrimage to Guadalupe, the crowd kept control of their leader—while together they honored New Spain's guiding patroness.

Then Bustamante, who began by reporting that el pueblo—the people in general—had risen to proclaim Fernando, returned to the classic Spanish understanding of sovereignty: "Great God, Sovereign Father of los pueblos in whose hand rests the destiny of Kings." God granted sovereignty to towns with councils; they sanctioned kings. In the 1770s, Anglo-American radicals promoted the sovereignty of the people—el pueblo in Spanish; in the 1790s, French revolutionaries proclaimed the sovereignty of the nation—*la nación*. Spanish tradition gave sovereignty to the pueblos—towns led by councils, a less radical formulation that aimed to constrain monarchical powers. Bustamante reported that the crowds of July 29 were mobilized with revolutionary abstractions, then contained by a return to Spanish tradition: el pueblo rose to proclaim the popular favorite as king; los pueblos then asserted rights to established ways—in support of Fernando and against French usurpation. Could that tenuous balance of concepts and powers hold in the silver metropolis?

Bustamante concluded his first report, constructed in the commotion of a day and night of exalted mobilizations, emphasizing that the alliance of Spain and New Spain must persist—and that devotion to Guadalupe was key to keeping the populace dedicated to that outcome: "Immortal God, in You alone trust the two Spains—what other Israel: look favorably on our arms and we fear nothing, not even the abyss conjured before us." He added: "Mexicans: you have the joyous opportunity of an august intercessor whose protection is infallible. In this precious image of Holy Mother of Guadalupe you have locked your fate. She has promised to hear you constantly; continue your supplications and vows and be sure that an illustrious victory will come and bring you happiness." He called for unity in devotion to Guadalupe—and in the union of the two Spains against Napoleon. Was it also a call to leave the streets and let their betters in the Euro-American alliance of Spaniards lead in most uncertain days?

On July 31 Bustamante offered a second report, still honoring the rising, now seeing it as less spontaneous. He saw an "agreeable commotion" that thrilled "every good Spaniard."[9] He insisted that "the enthusiasm was everywhere, without exception" and estimated the mobilized "troop of the populace" at fifty thousand—a number that included women and constituted nearly half the city's population. He added: "Despite so much tumult, there was not the least disorder, there was no need for patrols because everyone was *militar* [a soldier, or a militant?]. Into the evening diverse troops of the populace stayed in the principal points of the city, maintaining their joy with games and music." Everyone was military, and military men were in the streets to join the throngs, not contain them. Bustamante also revealed detail that showed advanced planning: the men of the "ball game at San Camilo" mounted a "magnificent carriage" to carry Fernando's portrait accompanied by martial music. The carriage was "hauled by el pueblo" accompanied by torch-carrying men on horseback. On street corners across the city, poems, proclamations, and inscriptions everywhere honored Fernando.

Bustamante now reported, too, that the day after the first risings, on the 30th, the Conde de Santiago joined the festival of adulation. Clearly, he was not part of the planning—nor had he joined the ritual of acquiescence at the palace on the first day. A day later he joined the viceroy and others in accepting the mandate of the crowd and its promoters. Bustamante knew the import of the Conde's participation—if a day late: "The House of the Conde de Santiago, always unique in appreciation and loyalty to our Sovereigns, has expressed itself with magnificence in these days. The day before yesterday, the royal portrait was set from eleven in the morning until four in the afternoon in one of the principal balconies, set beside the royal standard on velvet cloth. When el pueblo returned to reclaim the portrait, the conde in person, accompanied by his sons and family, came down to deliver it personally." The display of Fernando's portrait by the Conde de Santiago, his family long at the head of the city's landed oligarchy, confirmed American and oligarchic

devotion to El Deseado. The conde's return of the portrait to the people recognized their new rights in questions of sovereignty.

Negotiating to Contain the People, July 30–August 7
After two days of popular assertions provoked and in part guided by
unknown hands, at 9:00 p.m. on July 30, Viceroy Iturrigaray convened the
Real Acuerdo, the highest council of government in New Spain, in a rare
Saturday evening session. The gathering included the judges of the
Audiencia and other top ministers and officials of the royal administration,
along with the Mexico City Council and leaders of the consulado, the university, the Protomedicato (College of Physicians)—and the governors and
magistrates of the *parcialidades de naturales*, the capital's indigenous
republics. The meeting of the Real Acuerdo became Mexico City's first
junta, drawing a wide array of established corporate leaders aiming to contain the people.

The previous day's events were not a traditional recognition of a new
king, but a rising that challenged the established order. Those who expected
to rule now met to decide what, if anything, to do. While the assembled
notables deliberated, "an immense pueblo held the plaza outside." When the
gathered officials proceeded to the cathedral, the crowd followed: "perhaps
there never was such large attendance in the magnificent temple."[10]
Throughout, "El pueblo continued proclaiming its loyalty, rejoicing in numbers impossible to count, offering a variety of entertainments in throngs
overflowing with joy impossible to describe." The crowd surrounded and
constrained those who ruled with exhortations of loyalty. They ensured that
from the powerful through the populace, all were ready "to bury themselves
in the rubble of their homes before they would subject themselves to a slavery
imposed by the monster of ambition"—meaning Napoleon. The risings of
July 29–30 in Mexico City paralleled and showed solidarity with the risings
of May 2–3 in Madrid. Fortunately for the people of Mexico City, there were
no French troops to shoot them down. Some among the political, the military, and the clergy had called the rising; they had participated in and
patrolled the proclamation of Fernando—an early and nonviolent fusion of
popular and military power. Many among the powerful—the viceroy, the
Conde de Santiago, and more—looked on in fearful wonder, proclaimed solidarity with the people, and worried about what might come.

With the people surrounding their deliberations, the men of the junta that gathered on the evening of July 30 resolved to send "the troop of the populace in parade to the Sanctuary of Most Holy María de Guadalupe, to offer her the most exalted devotion, and give her thanks for the protection she has given our cause, freeing us from enslavement to the monstrous enemy of religion," again referring to Napoleon. As the people announced new power, the powerful looked again to Guadalupe for protection from Napoleon—and from the throngs in the streets.

The great march to Guadalupe occurred on the morning of July 31, the capital still in commotion. That afternoon, the viceroy and his wife paraded through the city carrying Fernando's portrait, backed by a cavalry guard of two thousand.[11] He aimed to affirm his devotion to the new sovereign (questioned by many given his appointment by Carlos IV and recognition of him on July 19)—and to show his potential coercive power. That evening, the men of the ballgame at San Camilo paraded again; the same evening the Regimiento del Comercio, the militia of the merchants' consulado, marched in devotion to Fernando for the first time. Now, it seemed, every major interest had joined the people's proclamation—and the people and the military seemed to mix in everything. Bustamante ended the third *Diario* report devoted to the risings with an exhortation to the city's youth: "Young people: if your noble efforts show resolve, . . . Victory awaits us." Clearly, young men had led in the popular mobilization. With Fernando proclaimed king yet held captive, with the French enemy an ocean away, and with Britain in control of the sea, what was the goal of the necessary resolve?

In a time of dissolution, divisions and mobilizations led to calls for unity and resolve. But to what end? That was far from clear. Meanwhile, a complex and uncertain relationship between military power and popular assertions became evident: some among the military or militias joined in calling people to the streets; the people successfully pressed the recognition of the captive Fernando on the powerful; the powerful then turned to military demonstrations to show the people they would not rule uncontested. Rule by mediation was cracking; the powerful and the people met in the streets—each showing that coercion was in play. Still, these were demonstrations of potential force. Armed assertions were yet to come.

On August 5, Bustamante opened the next *Diario* with a poem submitted by an anonymous reader:

The name gachupín is extinguished; that of criollo also buried,
that of indio and others are no longer thought because Fernando has
united us.

It went on:

In the troops of VIVAS that have formed, the plebian and noble unite;
The rich leave vanity behind, marching with the poorest side by side.[12]

Here was a new and radical call to unity. Oligarchs had long promoted
unity among Spaniards, Americans and immigrants, while divisions distin-
guishing nobles and commoners, Hispanic and native peoples, rich and poor,
and diverse corporate groups had shaped society and organized the mediating rule that sustained New Spain's power and prosperity. Bustamante's pub-
lication of a call to homogenized unity was understandable after days of
mobilizations. Still, an end to distinctions might also announce the demise
of the regime of rights and mediations that had long sustained stability in the
capital and kingdom of silver capitalism.

Of course decades of war and then Napoleon's intrusion had already
provoked the conflicts and uncertainties Bustamante and his readers faced.
The poetic call to a new unity was proposed as way forward—a way in which
the old politics of corporations, petitions, and mediations might no longer
serve. The urgency of the message suggests that fissures were coming to the
fore in the throngs that proclaimed Fernando. The call to unity aimed to
dampen disunities as the powerful negotiated with the populace in search of
a route through uncertainty.

In the same *Diario* of August 5, Bustamante finally set in print what the
powerful had known for weeks: there had been "previous notices of the violent
abdications of our Kings in favor of the Emperor of the French." Both Carlos
and Fernando were captive, both had abdicated by force, neither could rule.
The July 19 proclamation of the powerful declared their intent to rule in the
name of Carlos, without acknowledging his captivity. The risings of the 29th
insisted that the people of Mexico City would only recognize Fernando. The
powerful could acquiesce, because they knew neither would rule—news that
surely was spreading before Bustamante made it fully public. The certain
absence of a sovereign in Madrid could only open new uncertainties.

In that context, Bustamante's *Diarios* of August 5, 6, and 7 kept retelling
and amplifying the tale of the risings, adding new details while calling for
unity and downplaying divisions.[13] On the 8th he reported an unprecedented
development: the night before, the city illuminated and celebrations everywhere, "for the first time a small troop of women was seen, dressed in white
with shawls worn backward, marching in line." Bustamante quickly turned
to others' proclamations of loyalty to Fernando—but women marching on
their own very much troubled him. Had some of the thousands laboring in
the tobacco factory found a political voice? With people in the streets, including women parading as women, good order was in jeopardy.[14]

Finally, Sunday came and the men who expected to rule found some
relief. There was another great procession to Guadalupe, carriages of the rich
mixed among the many on foot. That "the troop of women" went along still
troubled Bustamante. But all in all, it was a pilgrimage in unity to honor and
thank Guadalupe. Everyone proclaimed "VIVA FERNANDO VII."

The rest of the day saw orderly marches through the city, culminating in
a great spectacle in front of the palace. The parade included "a boat built by
the natives of Coyoacán and San Agustín de las Cuevas, drawn by more than
four thousand men, escorted by a committee of the citizens of those pueblos
who came on horseback. The governors sat in the vessel attending the portrait of our monarch, carrying torches that illuminated his visage."[15] Order
seemed restored. Men from nearby native republics marched as *naturales* led
by their governors to honor Fernando. (Did they also assert their right to join
in the sovereignty of the pueblos?) As Sunday ended, the city seemed right
again. The powerful and their political allies who expected to rule had faced
an urban populace that took the streets to proclaim their preferred sovereign. In the end they negotiated a solution: together they would serve a captive sovereign, honored as a mythical redeemer. Could a solution mediated
in the streets hold?

August Days: Mobilizing Power to Contain the People

The men most committed to power and silver capitalism worried throughout. On August 1, in the heat of popular exaltations, the Mining Tribunal
wrote to the viceroy. It represented leading mining interests linking European
and American Spaniards: don Fausto Elhuyar, a European, had promoted
Crown interests in mining in New Spain for decades; the Marqués de San

Juan de Rayas and don Ignacio de Obregón were Americans with rich mines in Guanajuato, both close to Iturrigaray. The three did not always agree, but they could not ignore events of recent days. Recognizing the fait accompli imposed by the crowds, the tribunal insisted that the ferment of the 29th "filled loyal inhabitants of the capital with extreme joy and contentment."[16] The day before the demonstrations, the tribunal had met and committed to defend "the just rights held by the Royal Family of the Bourbons in these domains"—no monarch preferred. Now it accepted the people's insistence on Fernando.

Also before the risings, the tribunal had proposed to forge one hundred pieces of field artillery and fund companies of eight men each to man them. Commanders would come from among the students at the Mexico City mining college. The original plan for the artillery was to bolster the defense of New Spain in support of "the energy, valor, and heroic constancy of our unfortunate brothers in Europe." Now on August 1, "circumstances"—surely meaning the people in the streets—still called for armed force. The tribunal asked to meet with Iturrigaray.

So much had changed in a few fateful days. On the July 28, the tribunal pledged to defend the Bourbon line; on August 1 it followed the crowd and swore to defend Fernando, asking that he "prosper for many years for the good and happiness of the Spanish nation in both hemispheres." Loyalty to Fernando must ground continuing bonds linking European and American Spaniards, the alliance of power that sustained silver capitalism. The people should desist in political assertions—and perhaps new artillery would help.

The viceroy looked to political means toward the same end. On August 5, Iturrigaray wrote to the Real Acuerdo, the core group of high judges and ministers that counseled his rule. He aimed to confirm the July 19 proclamation, meaning continuity of institutional rule in New Spain in the absence of a monarch in Spain. Now facing "the most grave events of the day"—the crowds that ruled the city's streets and plazas—it was time to call a "general junta" of "tribunals, corporations, and persons . . . in imitation of those in Seville and Valencia."[17] News of widening resistance to French armies and devotion to Fernando had come with reports of juntas organizing resistance and asserting sovereignty across Spain. Iturrigaray called the highest officials in New Spain to join him in following that model. The only recent change in New Spain was the continuing spectacle of the people in the streets of the

capital. Calling a formal junta might capture, deflect, or direct their unpredictable energies.

The officials of the Real Acuerdo wrote back the next day. They argued
that the July 19 commitment to rule by established powers remained sufficient. They accepted the people's insistence on Fernando as "our legitimate
Sovereign." They emphasized the real uncertainty of his reclaiming the
throne anytime soon—if ever. Should he return, a junta was irrelevant;
should he not, a junta of uncertain legality would to lead to unpredictable
outcomes. Thirteen of fourteen ministers concurred that no junta should be
called in New Spain.[18]

Iturrigaray was ready for the Acuerdo's resistance. He shot back with a
long rebuttal: a junta was essential "for the preservation of the rights of His
Majesty; for the security of the kingdom; for the satisfaction of its inhabitants; and for the organization of the provisional government that may be
needed to address questions of revenue and sovereignty as circumstances
change."[19] This was a radical turn, recognizing that no legitimate power
would soon return to rule in Spain and that the people of New Spain, at least
in the capital, had inserted themselves irrevocably into the politics of uncertain times. Iturrigaray insisted that it was the insertion of the people into
politics that made a junta essential.

He went on: to defend the continuity of power and the unity of the two
Spains, it was necessary to protect "navigation, commerce, and mining."
Ultimately, the goal was to sustain silver capitalism. Its persistence in uncer-
tain times required a junta that might lead to a provisional government. In a
broadening vision, Iturrigaray called for a "congress" to consider whether
New Spain needed a "Governing Junta" to counsel him in changing times.
He promised to continue consulting the city council, the Real Acuerdo, and
the Consejo de Guerra (the military authorities)—while he pressed them to
approve an assembly that might override their advice and limit their powers.
The threat of popular power drove divisions among the powerful.

The same day, the consulado, the merchants' chamber representing the
mostly European Spaniards who ruled trade and finance in New Spain,
wrote to Iturrigaray to express deep concerns. As representative of the world
of commerce "it had the satisfaction . . . of having joined with all the classes
of the State in honoring with demonstrations of good will and friendship the
heroic actions of the Spaniards of our Peninsula, and proclaiming don

Fernando VII our august Sovereign." But amid that restrained satisfaction in unity with Spain and the people of the city, the merchants "have learned with pain that some have posted on the corners of this city seditious papers directed at breaking the close union that is the soul of society and the most faithful guarantee of the success of all undertakings." [20]

The merchants of the consulado stated clearly what Iturrigaray and the ministers of the Real Acuerdo suggested in veiled ways: during the mobilizations of July 29 and after, amid proclamations of unity in defense of Fernando, shouts and placards insulted gachupines. The crowds challenged the unity of American and European Spaniards—the social cement of silver capitalism. The merchants, targets of the insults, reacted with anger and fear: "We know well that these products, vile and not worthy of printing, are generated by confused minds and malign hearts, people unfortunately never absent in even the smallest populations."

No one should minimize the threat: "We are certain that most common people, and surely all sensible men, detest the abominable introduction of the spirit of division and disunion in the republic; but such positive thinking, though it tempers in part our discontentment, cannot fully contain the insults of a *popular rebellion* against the members of our corporation and all persons of power—who must lose in the face of such insults. We demand a rapid and effective remedy." The viceroy must act "to cut out at its origin the cancer that threatens to spread in this body politic, to extinguish the fire of discord that having started as a small spark can spread to cause the gravest ruin if a rapid response does not bring active precautions."

Merchants, great and small, were worried. They heard anti-gachupín voices in the streets as they nervously joined in proclaiming Fernando king. They saw flyers threatening worse posted on street corners. And they feared the worst: popular rebellion. They knew the history of anti-European sentiments in New Spain, sentiments long contained by the Euro-American alliance of power that unified the oligarchy, incorporated provincial elites, and sustained silver capitalism. They also knew how in revolutionary times, first in Paris, then in Saint-Domingue, urban crowds and enslaved people had broken historic containments to destroy old powers and ways of wealth. They saw the beginnings of such rebellion in the streets of Mexico City and insisted it could not persist. They challenged the viceroy but did not offer a solution.

August Debates

While the Mining Tribunal forged artillery, officials of the Real Acuerdo opposed any assembly, and merchants insisted the populace be contained, a few aimed toward unprecedented ends. Reflecting on all that had happened in Spain and New Spain, notably on the Mexico City risings of July 29, Fray Melchor de Talamantes printed a broadside promoting an "American national congress." The date it appeared is not certain, but it came after the rising of the 29th and aimed to guide the assembly Iturrigaray called to meet on August 9.

Talamantes was a Mercedarian friar and priest; born and educated in Lima, he had served officials there and in New Spain, including Iturrigaray. He had contacts with great miners like don Ignacio de Obregón, the leading merchant financier don Antonio de Basoco, and many more in the regime, the oligarchy, and among provincial elites. He knew their interests and dilemmas. A powerful intellectual, Talamantes represented himself. He had offered his views to the Mexico City Council on July 26, then to the viceroy amid the risings of that began on the 29th.[21] He was surely not among the promoters of that day of mobilization: he opposed recognizing any captive sovereign, and he feared popular power. He was politically radical yet socially cautious.[22] He asserted that the congress "must exercise all the rights of sovereignty"—easily read as a call for independence. Yet his was a very conservative call. The first acts of the congress should be to confirm the viceroy in office as captain general of "the kingdom" and all other officials in their current roles. When vacancies came, as they inevitably would, the assembly should fill open offices. Again, the first goal was continuity.

Talamantes did propose reforms: he would end the jurisdiction of the Inquisition except among the clergy, which would remain subject to doctrinal control. Everyone else would gain new freedoms of religious and civil discourse—freedoms already being exercised and long past control. Less liberating, he proposed a new tribunal to intercept all correspondence with Spain; it would read letters, proposals, appeals, and other messages, holding what it judged pernicious, delivering only what it found acceptable—that is, in the interests of New Spain's authorities.

His view of proper relations between Spain and New Spain came in a set of economic proposals. Anyone living in Spain while holding entailed properties in New Spain would lose them. The Cortés family heirs would lose their sugar holdings around Cuernavaca; local merchants or oligarchs would surely gain. Talamantes would also cancel all private debts owed to Spain—favoring struggling merchants. The consolidation would end; those who had paid would be compensated. Talamantes aimed to stop the drain of silver from New Spain to Spain, shoring up silver capitalism and the place of provincial elites in it. New Spain's economy, still the richest in the Americas, should serve New Spain. He would reduce the tithes that sustained the bishops and restore the ecclesiastical banks that financed provincial elites' and aspiring merchants. He would free commerce, mining, agriculture, and industry from "the shackles" imposed by ties to Spain. With no effective regime in Madrid, the friar proposed that established officials and institutions remain in place, that reforms restore the position of provincial elites, and that silver capitalism be liberated to serve the interests of New Spain first. An economic break was implicit in his vision—as many surely saw.

And while open to a break with Spain, Talamantes called for sending an ambassador to the United States to seek alliance and assistance. He added that any recognition of a sovereign ruler of "Spain and the Indies" be delayed until the final session of New Spain's American Congress. He saw the people's July 29 proclamation of Fernando as done with "speed and restlessness." Talamantes preferred careful deliberations to decide on any recognition. If the congress did recognize a King of Spain and the Indies, that king must recognize all the acts and appointees of New Spain's Congress. He would oversee dual, essentially independent kingdoms, a proposal parallel to the vision that concluded the Mexico City Council's 1771 memorial.

Talamantes clearly aimed to extract New Spain from the conflicts consuming Spain—and New Spain's wealth. He saw the July 29 actions of the people in the streets as tying New Spain to those conflicts and their costs. He distrusted the populace, whether independent or manipulated. He sought alliance with the United States, a neutral nation eager to trade with New Spain, itself disrupted and angered by the trade wars between Britain and France. New Spain and the United States might make a North American bloc until Europeans settled their differences. He could not predict the outcome of Europe's wars or the conclusions of New Spain's American Congress. In the interim, the congress should rule New Spain—as decided by established power holders, not as imposed by people in the streets.

Talamantes imagined breaking ties with Spain—and the flow of silver to its crumbling regime. Did he see the inevitable reaction of many merchant financiers based in Mexico City? Reinforced by immigrant flows from Spain, they ruled trades that extended to Cádiz and Manila and worlds beyond. Their capital financed the mines that sustained global commerce. Repeated marriages into American landed clans cemented oligarchic unity and financed the agrarian capitalism that sustained Mexico City, the mines, and the commercial and industrial cities essential to silver capitalism. Breaking ties to Spain would shake the social order of silver capitalism and its capital city. Oligarchs listened—but they did not follow Talamantes's lead.

In direct opposition to Talamantes, don Ciriaco González Carbajal, the senior American judge on the High Court, thus a member of the Real Acuerdo, wrote to Iturrigaray on August 7. He argued that New Spain did not need a junta because, unlike in Spain, legitimate institutions of government survived and continued to function. A junta would open the world of sovereignty and power too much. He feared "that a multitude of voices, enabled by circumstances that must be avoided, may come to agree on something that perhaps is not right"—a perfect, if oblique, description of how most of the powerful saw the popular proclamation of Fernando—"and if not executed with the ardor those voices expect may result in more inevitable wrongs." To contain popular assertions, the viceroy must rule as always. Only if Spain fell to "the French nation" might a junta be in order in New Spain. Recent news showed that Spanish resistance held.[23] The American judge advised the European viceroy to rule without a junta open to too many voices.

As debate engulfed the political city, on August 8 the Real Acuerdo tried a last attempt to block the junta. Thirteen ministers insisted that the laws of the Indies required that the viceroy continue to rule counseled by the Real Acuerdo. They opposed any mobilization of the populace, a vision shared by all political actors. They opposed a junta, fearing it would open debates and bring the people into play. And they opposed any break with Spain, instead calling Iturrigaray to "respect and obey the authority of the Supreme Junta of Seville, or any other that legitimately represents our beloved Monarch, don Fernando VII."[24]

Iturrigaray aimed for a junta parallel to those rising across Spain—sharing equally in the reconstitution of a transatlantic sovereignty.

Talamantes promoted a sovereign American congress ready to seek American alliances, focused on promoting American interests, and open to a break with Spain. The viceroy and the friar saw New Spain as an equal kingdom in a transatlantic monarchy but differed on how to respond to the current crisis. The Real Acuerdo insisted on New Spain's subordination to the Junta of Seville, or any junta that consolidated rule to lead resistance in Spain. Debate focused on whether New Spain was an equal kingdom or a colonial dependency. Behind that question lurked powerful interests.

Talamantes's call to break economic ties with Spain sent the (mostly European) merchants of the consulado into convulsions. They feared losing everything. If a break came, British naval power, shipping, and merchant capital would rule the Atlantic unfettered. What role would remain for immigrant merchants from Spain seeking their fortunes in New Spain? Mining interests could adapt more easily; they formed a Euro-American bloc controlling production of the world's most valuable commodity. Surely they could finance mines and find markets in a world under British hegemony. Agricultural entrepreneurs, oligarchs and provincials too, mostly Americans, knew that their markets were internal and linked to the dynamism of silver. They would be fine as long as silver thrived. Powerful interests, all tied to silver, faced distinct challenges if a junta met and opened the question of New Spain's tie to Spain.

Rejecting the positions of González Carbajal and the Real Acuerdo, Iturrigaray convened the junta in the "Main Salon" of the Viceregal Palace on August 9.[25] The gathering included many who opposed its meeting, notably the ministers of the Real Acuerdo, including the judges of the High Court. Also present were the men of the Mexico City Council (staunch backers of the gathering), diverse high officials of the royal bureaucracy, leading miners and merchants (whose consulado opposed the meeting), along with powerful landed oligarchs and the governors of the indigenous parcialidades of San Juan Tenochtitlan and Santiago Tlatelolco—a small concession to a broader sovereignty of the pueblos. An opening proclamation rejected Napoleon and refused obedience to any emissary he might send. It asserted loyalty to Fernando VII, rejecting Talamantes's call for delay. It made no mention of the juntas struggling to organize resistance in Spain. Loyalty to the captive Fernando resolved nothing; the question of relations between the Juntas of Spain and New Spain remained key—and unsettled.

The list of signatories to that opening consensus decree was an impressive array of power: regime leaders, ecclesiastical authorities, and entrepreneurial powers. The viceroy and the leaders of the Audiencia and Real Acuerdo signed: Iturrigaray first, González Carbajal third, Archbishop don Francisco de Lizana y Beaumont, seventh. The great merchant banker and city magistrate don Josef Juan de Fagoaga came soon after, followed by great landlords such as the Marqués de Castañiza, the Marqués de San Miguel de Aguayo, and down the list but pivotally present, the Conde de Santiago Calimaya. The leaders of the Mining Tribunal, don Fausto Elhuyar, the Marqués de Rayas, and don Ignacio de Obregón signed; so did the Conde de Regla and the dominant merchant financier of the day, don Antonio de Basoco, who eschewed both title and landed investment. All signed (and likely sat) interspersed together, along with lawyers including don Francisco Primo de Verdad, and emissaries from Jalapa near the coast. Toward the end, the governors of the capital's native parcialidades signed. Absent were the voices at the extremes, Talamantes and the officers of the consulado. The former rejected ties to a Spain in disarray; the latter demanded an affirmation of dependence on Seville's Junta.

On August 11, after long meetings and unrecorded debates, Iturrigaray published more platitudes about devotion to Fernando and resistance to Napoleon and any invasion that might threaten New Spain.[26] On the 12th, the viceroy issued a proclamation stating that the gathering recognized none of the juntas then emerging in Spain. Talamantes quickly responded that such a position left the viceroy to rule without check; the friar insisted that a larger junta of New Spain must assemble to provide essential oversight.[27] Both asserted that New Spain would govern itself while the situation in Spain remained fluid and contested, offering de facto declarations of independence, neither with a clear map of the future.

Instead, everyone kept the fiction of loyalty to Fernando and to an imagined monarchical Spain, while no monarch ruled there or in New Spain. On the 13th, the *Gaceta de México* published an announcement signed by First Magistrate don Josef Juan de Fagoaga for the City Council: at three that afternoon, a solemn procession of dignitaries of council and Church would again proclaim Fernando king.[28] Popular acclamation on July 29th was not enough—or too threatening. Now it would be done right: by established leaders as a message to the people. Could platitudes and parades heal divisions among the powerful, calm popular spirits, and solidify rule by local authorities loyal to a captive king an ocean away?

We know much about the diverse and often contradictory public statements and private views of those imagining power during the heady days of uncertainty in August 1808. We know, too, that the diverse people of the city were often in the streets, parks, and plazas, drawn to acclaim visions of sovereignty that opened new political possibilities. As the populace pressed its own visions, many among the powerful felt threatened. The city was alive with rumor and debate. Still, we know little about popular views. Two glimpses offer openings to an emerging popular politics—mostly operating as talk, yet focused on the pivotal issues of the times.

In the days after the August 9 junta, with its heated discussions of sovereignty and alternative possibilities, a Franciscan priest, Miguel Zugástegui, was overheard in heated conversation in a café on the Calle de Reloj, near the city center. Someone had lamented that the junta had not committed to send people and funds to support the juntas rising to fight Napoleon in Spain. Zugástegui answered that not even a half real (a sixteenth of a peso) should leave New Spain, "because it remains independent" with Fernando held prisoner in Bayonne. The friar added that he had heard two city councilmen, including the landed Marqués de Uluapa, propose that Iturrigaray name himself king as José I of New Spain (taking the label claimed by Napoleon's brother in Spain). When challenged that talk calling the viceroy to become king (whether by the councilmen or the friar) deserved prosecution and incarceration, the friar answered that the council had ample money to spread among the people—who would surely rise to slit the throats of the judges who insisted on loyalty to the Spain's juntas.

The conversation was reported to authorities, still led by Iturrigaray. Zugástegui was cautioned and ordered to confinement in his convent.[29] Apparently the friar's café outburst was worth investigating and potentially subversive—but not worthy of more than a limited rebuke. Were his ideas extreme or just common in days of political contest and public controversy?

A more radical conversation occurred as a group of artisans and small merchants gathered for mass at the cathedral one Sunday morning later in August. José Morales, a tailor, and Vicente Acuña, a merchant, approached the great temple with other friends when Morales saw Pedro Salinas—for whom he had done some work. Morales reported that Salinas and others were talking about "the events of the day" when Acuña stated that if "there is no king" then a descendant of Moctezuma should "return to the throne." How? "He would call the plebeians of the pulquerías . . . and the barrios, . . . giving out money and pulque so they would head out drunk and proclaim a king in the Plaza." Acuña did not see a people ready to proclaim a native king, only sufficiently malleable and drunk to be used in the effort.

Acuña then added, according to Morales, that he had met with the son of "doña Andrea the fruit seller," a descendant of Moctezuma. Acuña confirmed the conversation—but insisted that he had only said that in the absence of a king in Spain, there would be talk of crowning a native monarch. Nor did the merchant deny suggesting calling the people to the plaza—but only to hear their views. These second conversations were not reported to authorities until after the September coup; thus there was no response in the heady days of August when they occurred. Still, they reveal that when everything was open and in debate, public ruminations included artisans and merchants well below the heights of power, including some who could imagine that the fruit seller's son, don Dionisio Cano y Moctezuma might become an indigenous king.[30]

That Moctezuma's descendant lived by buying produce at Chalco and delivering it to the city for his mother to sell reveals how far native royalty had fallen (yet still prospered in limited ways). That don Dionisio was imagined a candidate for kingship by a group of artisans and traders who also imagined raising a drunken populace to sway debates about sovereignty reveals how open and imaginary those debates had become. Both Iturrigaray, the viceroy, and don Dionisio, the fruit seller's son, could be imagined as king of New Spain. Raising the native barrios could be both promoted and feared as the way to change.

While such conversations swirled through the city, on August 20, Iturrigaray wrote a letter addressed to the Junta of Seville, with copies to juntas at Valencia and Zaragoza, stating that at present there was no basis for New Spain to recognize any of Spain's many juntas. The letter was still held by postal officials at the port of Veracruz, its contents likely read and shared with local officials and traders, when a ship landed on August 26 with two emissaries from Seville. They had been sent to gain New Spain's allegiance and silver by whatever means they could. With little settled in the Mexico

City Junta of August 9–11, everything became open, uncertain, and increasingly conflictive with the landing of the Seville Junta's emissaries.[31]

August Becomes September: Emissaries, Juntas, Congresses, and Fractures

The Seville Junta claimed supremacy over the others mobilizing regional resistance in Spain. It had two advantages in that effort: distance from Madrid and France's armies, and rule over Andalusia and Cádiz, whose merchants were Spain's link to New Spain and its silver. The men asserting power in Seville knew that link could only be consolidated by recognition in New Spain. They sent the two emissaries with instructions to gain that recognition in Mexico City—by persuasion, by negotiation, by political intrigue, and by toppling the viceroy, if necessary.

They were an interesting pair. The younger, Colonel don Manuel Francisco de Jaúregui was Iturrigaray's brother-in-law and cousin. He had joined in the coup at Aranjuez, then settled in Seville to seek Spain's interests as he could. The elder, don Juan Jabat, was a naval officer of long service in the greater Caribbean, experience that had brought conflicts with Iturrigaray over smuggling. They were a good-emissary/bad-emissary pair: Jaúregui, as family, stayed in the viceregal residence where he lobbied his brother-in-law; Jabat lodged with the highest-ranking judge of the Audiencia, seeking allies in the Real Acuerdo—aiming to pressure the viceroy.[32] They came with eight hundred quintals of mercury, essential to refining silver, and a promise of three thousand more. Mercury mined at Almadén north of Seville was Spain's key contribution to New Spain's silver economy. Jaúregui and Jabat were sent to negotiate, to pressure if necessary, backed by a reminder that only Seville could supply mercury, only its junta could sustain silver capitalism.[33]

The emissaries arrived in Mexico City on August 29. Still, Iturrigaray would recognize no Spanish junta. Seville's ties to British commercial and naval interests worried him. An alliance to defend Spain from Napoleon could easily become a British monopoly of New Spain's silver and trade. Yet de facto autonomy would also serve British naval and commercial power. Was the viceroy covering something—or just looking for a delay?

Iturrigaray convened another junta on August 31. All the players were there, plus Jaúregui and Jabat, allowed to make the case for Seville. After much discussion and debate, recognition gained approval by nearly two to one, including many of the pivotal powers of silver capitalism: Basoco, Fagoaga, Pérez Gálvez, and the Mariscal de Castilla and Marqués de Aguayo, too. The delivery of mercury was perhaps persuasive. But before the decision could be printed, news arrived from London that the junta at Oviedo also claimed supreme status and had strong backing in England. Everything, again, was unclear. Iturrigaray called the junta back the next afternoon, September 1. With Jabat and Jaúregui excluded, heated debates focused on the limits of Seville's primacy. Leading audiencia judges tried to keep the decision of the day before; the financial oligarchs who ruled silver capitalism proved their power by shifting back to Iturrigaray's position of nonrecognition—of autonomy. They carried the vote.[34]

The same day a brief circular called provincial Spanish councils across New Spain to prepare to send delegates to join the Mexico City Council in urgent talks on "the present circumstances." The next day, Iturrigaray wrote to the Real Acuerdo asking its counsel on a larger assembly including councils across New Spain. On September 3, the Acuerdo objected: "The revolution begun in 1789 in France ended in setting the wicked Napoleon on that august throne, the cause of the vexations that surround us and our current dilemmas; all that has no origin other than the convocation of the junta there called the estates and here a cortes. That junta destroyed the Monarchy and carried the unfortunate Louis XVI to the gallows."[35]

Later that day, the viceroy wrote to the Junta of Seville, stating again that no recognition was coming. He sent copies to magistrates across New Spain and to Lima and Manila, too. Then Mexico City's politics moved behind closed doors and intensified. Jabat claimed to have seen a plan for an American congress and pressed the Real Acuerdo for Iturrigaray's removal. On September 5, the viceroy wrote in his own hand to the ministers, proposing (not quite offering) his own resignation and replacement by Field Marshall don Pedro Garibay. The viceroy emphasized the need to end the factional fighting provoked by Jabat and Jaúregui.[36]

With that note in his opponents' hands, on September 6 Iturrigaray announced what they had to see as a provocative act. He pardoned the common criminals held in city jails across the realm. He excluded some egregious offenders, but many more would gain release. It was an age-old custom for new monarchs to pardon prisoners; Fernando could not act, so Iturrigaray acted in his stead. The viceroy would be king in the absence of the king.[37]

Again proclaiming continuity lodged in tradition, Iturrigaray freed men who might back him if conflict returned to the streets.

The next day the Audiencia was ready to accept the viceroy's resignation but uncertain about a successor. The city council pressed him to stay on, fearing a rising that might break "the public calm." On September 8, the viceroy decided to stay, supported by the council and the Marqués de San Juan de Rayas. On the 9th Iturrigaray called another junta that again denied recognition to Seville, proposed a larger congress of New Spain (despite Archbishop Lizana's opposition), and set aside the viceroy's proposed-then-withdrawn resignation.[38] Was Iturrigaray's private offer to resign, public release of prisoners, and acquiescence to council pleas to remain for fear of popular risings an orchestrated threat to the Real Acuerdo? Perhaps.

Politics hardened in the halls of power. Jabat pressed for a coup, hoping for backing by the Real Acuerdo, the military, and part of the commercial community. At the same time, don Jacobo de Villaurrutia, a senior American judge on the Audiencia, worked on a rationale for the congress to come. Family and interest tied Villaurrutia to the Fagoagas and Basoco, too. After years in the imperial service, he'd earned respect in the heights of Mexico City's oligarchy and among lettered professionals like don Carlos María de Bustamante. He aimed to represent the interests of the oligarchs and regime officials who ruled silver capitalism; he met regularly with Talamantes. Yet ultimately, he too spoke for himself. As an audiencia judge, he responded to his colleagues' opposition to a congress by emphasizing that the court's first role was judicial. It was not empowered in matters of "politics, state, and war"—domains demanding critical decisions in times of war and broken sovereignty.[39] A congress was needed to deal with England, keep peace with the United States, and fend off France. It would serve in place of the Council of the Indies, the leading policy body and final mediator in the regime of petition and mediation.[40]

In a September 13 text, Villaurrutia insisted that the role of the Real Acuerdo was only advisory. To make policy in the absence of a sovereign, New Spain required a Junta of Ayuntamientos, a meeting of sovereign pueblos that should not recognize any of the juntas then claiming sovereignty in Spain: "all seek the same end, which is to remove the yoke, exterminate the enemy, and reclaim the sacred person of our sovereign." But in the heat of conflict, the many juntas of Spain had not determined which was supreme.

"In the present situation, America cannot recognize, should not recognize, any of them."[41]

New Spain would support Spain and its liberation struggle. "It is agreed by uniform consent that we will give the Metropolis [Spain] all possible help from the funds of the public Treasury, or the Royal Accounts [which were they?] . . . so necessary for Spain's redemption. We only await the good administration of those domains [Spain]." Villaurrutia promised that New Spain would keep silver flowing, sending revenues to fight Napoleon—when Spain's governance found order. But how could such order come in the face of French occupation and fragmented political and popular responses.[42] The American judge focused on New Spain's right to an assembly: "The example of the provinces of Spain authorizes the convocation . . . of juntas, supreme, general, and local . . . whether by demand of the people or of higher officials." New Spain could do what so many in Spain had already done:

The convocation of the kingdom is also more and more necessary to affirm and consolidate tranquility by gathering our spirited voices, offering new ways of thinking, and ensuring that those promoting discord see that it is better, more convenient, and more just to discuss with reason and cede to the majority. The unprecedented events in Europe and the sensation they have caused in the spirit of the inhabitants of America have awakened and excited ideas and desires that have changed as the news has changed. As there are none practiced in the discussion or planning of politics and legislation, unfortunately for the majority those without talent or judgment, and without education, agitate and propose pernicious notions, as has happened everywhere, because the illusions of innovations dazzle and seduce the multitude. Everywhere there are people of discontentment, many ill-intentioned and jealous, and all needy, who imagine bettering their fortune in another order of things—or in our very disorder: the people at the bottom, whether due to docility or to having nothing to lose, are disposed to wrong impressions.[43]

The judge worried and warned that debates were widening among the people, who acted without clear knowledge, good order, or regular obedience. A junta was needed to organize debates, reach conclusions, and calm spirits. His was a very modern understanding of the operation of representative institutions. They would create limited participations to enable the powerful to seek a way forward in trying times—while containing the assertions of the populace and perhaps maintaining rule by conciliation and mediation.

A junta could be called by the "pueblos," towns with councils, or by "superior authorities." Villaurrutia backed a junta called by the viceroy, the highest authority in New Spain—the king's representative—to gather the pueblos, Spanish towns with councils. The judge deflected the concern of the Real Acuerdo, rejecting "the examples they cite, especially of the revolution of the estates in France. No one can know or predict ... what the meeting of the proposed congress might bring, including some inconveniences, as happens in all human affairs."[44] Could the recognition of uncertainty in times defined by uncertainties convince men committed to closing debates?

Villaurrutia, like Talamantes, aimed to inhibit popular influence: the congress would have a president, a general counsel, and a secretary; two judges of the High Court; two representatives of the cabildos; two for the secular clergy; two for the regular orders; two for the titled nobility; two for "el estado general"—the populace (with no recognition of ethnic differences or rights); two for the military; one for the Inquisition; one for mining; one for commerce; one for the *hacendados* (great estate operators); one for the university; *el gobernador del estado* or his representative; and a *fiscal real*.[45]

The shift from legitimation to implementation again proved creative—and limiting if one believed in the sovereignty of the pueblos. A congress called to represent sovereign pueblos would give them but two total delegates. Villaurrutia aimed to use traditional sanction to call a congress very different from a Castilian cortes. New Spain's Congress would represent established regime and religious powers, the men who ruled silver capitalism, and the Euro-American alliance. Most regime officials and leading merchants were European; most miners, landlords, and titled nobles (mostly mining and agricultural entrepreneurs) were American. Their representation sought unity at the heights of power. Allowing but two men to represent all of New Spain's city councils, bastions of provincial elites, would highlight the power of the Mexico City Council and leave others with marginal roles. The populace, vast and fragmented across New Spain, would gain two representatives (chosen how?), present but effectively powerless.

Here was a proposal for a junta, an assembly, or a congress of New Spain; different proponents offered different labels. It would gather the powerful and their professional allies, allowing city councils and the populace a token presence. Thousands of indigenous republics, pueblos with councils, would gain no formal role—presumably represented by the two popular delegates. The Junta General de Nueva España would consider the prospects and policies of the silver kingdom in time of imperial breakdown. The goal was to preserve power and sustain silver capitalism. Debate would focus on ties to a Spain occupied by Napoleon in a world at war.

As September began, politics in Mexico City had changed irrevocably. Bourbon sovereignty had broken. The politics of petition and judicial mediation was dissolving. People and groups, sanctioned and unsanctioned, petitioned—sometimes in text, sometimes in the streets. No power could mediate. Bourbon kings sat captive in Bayonne; José I disputed supremacy in Madrid with juntas rising across Spain—all desperate for New Spain's silver. Could any power mediate or resolve escalating conflicts over how to repair broken sovereignty? In New Spain, Viceroy Iturrigaray split from the majority in the Real Acuerdo; Villaurrutia split from his colleagues on the Audiencia. The Mexico City Council joined the viceroy and Villaurrutia in calling an American congress, aiming to delay recognition of any junta in Spain. Most audiencia judges, the larger Real Acuerdo, and many merchants insisted on recognizing Seville's junta; its emissaries lobbied hard and delivered mercury. Many at the heights of the oligarchy remained uncertain. They aimed to preserve silver capitalism, but no one knew how.

People in the streets of the capital had demanded recognition of Fernando—a symbolic affirmation of loyalty to Spain. Debates escalated in plazas, on streets, and in taverns. Officials and oligarchs with interests to protect feared rowdy mobs that honored Fernando yet threatened gachupines. In the public debates among those who presumed to rule, calls for unity among Americans, immigrant Spaniards, and those still in Spain held strong. In fluid rhetoric that simultaneously aimed to sanction popular sovereignty and limit popular participations, political men juggled calls to the pueblos (the towns) rooted in Spanish traditions, the pueblo (the people) reminiscent of Anglo-American abstractions, and the nation—a French revolutionary innovation that sanctioned powers of state in the name of abstract people. Creative innovations came when calls to the sovereignty of the pueblos sanctioned assemblies of regime officials and oligarchic powers, while limiting the representation of Spanish towns and excluding thousands of pueblos with native councils. Ultimately, claims of popular sovereignty aimed to contain popular power.

The Mexico City Council called for a congress; the viceroy proposed to resign, emptied the jails, decided to stay on—and prepared to call a congress that would open every question and draw provincial cities to the politics focused in the capital. For the emissaries from Seville, most audiencia judges, military leaders, and a segment of merchants, that opening could not be. They aimed to close politics, tie New Spain to Seville's junta, and keep silver flowing to its fight against Napoleon.

CHAPTER 10

September Coup, 1808

Military Power and Imagined Revolutions

↝ LATE ON THE EVENING OF SEPTEMBER 15, 1808, A GROUP OF MORE than three hundred militiamen, most tied to the city's commerce and trades and led by don Gabriel José de Yermo, marched into the Viceregal Palace and captured Iturrigaray, forcing a resignation they expected to be sanctioned by key leaders of the Audiencia and the military.

The next day, the Real Acuerdo proclaimed: "Inhabitants of Mexico of all classes and conditions: Necessity is not subject to regular laws. El Pueblo has taken control of His Excellency the Viceroy; it has demanded his removal for reasons of utility and common necessity; last night it called the illustrious archbishop and other authorities to the Real Acuerdo, which ceded to urgency and recognized the removal of the viceroy. Rule has devolved, in accordance with the royal order of 30 October 1806, to Field Marshall don Pedro Garibay."[1]

That brief statement not only announced the overthrow of the viceroy; it confirmed a radical transformation of regime power and politics. It addressed the inhabitants of the capital—the only place then named Mexico. And it addressed residents of all classes and conditions—recognizing neither corporate rights nor distinctions. It announced the end of rule by established law—due to unprecedented emergency. More radically, it stated that "the people" had captured the viceroy—an act in the "common necessity." During the summer of politics, diverse groups had paraded military force, even symbolically fired cannons, to press visions and interests in times of debate. The September coup built on that developing fusion between armed power and claims of popular sovereignty. Now armed power toppled the established viceroy and set a new leader in his place. Both Iturrigaray and Garibay were military men. But Iturrigaray had been named by a legitimate monarch and ruled by established ways of conciliation and mediation. Garibay came to power by armed imposition—a militarized accession aimed to end mediations.

The Coup: Plans, Goals, and Consequences

The proclamation implied that it was after the coup, after the people's act, that the Real Acuerdo (minus the deposed viceroy) met with the archbishop and other unnamed authorities, conceded to necessity and the people in arms, and formally removed the viceroy. They named in his place a high military official—as mandated, they insisted, by order of a Bourbon regime that no longer ruled. The judges and other officials that met as the Real Acuerdo not only announced and sanctioned the overthrow of the viceroy, they announced the end of the regime of mediation that had ruled New Spain and silver capitalism for three centuries. The summer of politics had rattled the politics of mediation. The coup replaced the king's representative with a military officer—by force sanctioned as an act of the people.

The coup was not spontaneous. The Seville emissaries came with instructions that included removing Iturrigaray as a last resort. Their conversations with leading audiencia judges and high military officials intensified after the first of September, as plans for a congress continued while Iturrigaray talked of resigning, then released prisoners and stayed on. By September 14–15, it seemed clear—at least to those committed to recognizing the Seville Junta—that Iturrigaray was not about to resign, and that he intended to call a congress backed by leading men of Mexico City's oligarchy and by the Mexico City Council, an assembly that would at least minimally convoke provincial elites and claim to speak for New Spain.[2] Viceroy, oligarchs, and councilmen aimed to tap and transform traditional rights of the sovereignty of the pueblos to preserve their established powers and silver capitalism—holding open the option of taking New Spain and its rich economy out of a Spanish empire in disarray.

The plotters insisted that New Spain's silver must flow to Seville—if inevitably on British ships in the post-Trafalgar world. They too aimed to preserve silver capitalism while locking it to funding the fight against Napoleon. Support for the coup was never unanimous in any group. Jabat, the military representative of Seville, kept military commanders at the center of the planning. While most of the Audiencia's judges joined in the ouster, they knew that Villaurrutia and regent don Pedro Catani were opposed, so they kept them out of the conversations. The consulado divided: don Martín Ángel Michaus, an immigrant trader of some substance, allied with the Condes de Santiago and invested in Cuernavaca sugar property, reported the coup plans to Iturrigaray, adding that leading financiers and traders including the pivotal don Antonio Basoco, don Gabriel de Yturbe y Iraeta, don Joaquín Colla, don Diego de Agreda, don Ángel Puyade, and don Tomás Murphy all stood opposed. The coup did not represent a united consulado; it was backed by a frustrated faction of less-established merchants.[3]

Don Gabriel José de Yermo, an immigrant merchant with sugar properties, the contract to supply the capital's slaughterhouses, and massive debts made impossible by the consolidation that embargoed his estate, took the lead in finding support for the coup in the consulado. He built a coalition of men aiming to rise and seeing their way blocked if the link to Cádiz and Seville was broken. He raised a segment of the merchants' militia, along with militiamen recruited among city bakers, hog butchers, and leather workers—tradesmen Yermo had struggled to supply. In total, just over 330 armed men, led by a few merchant-officers, invaded the palace on the evening of September 15 to take the viceroy—in service of an alliance of high military commanders and High Court judges.[4] Yermo and his militiamen were key actors in invading the palace and taking the viceroy, a public performance that allowed the more powerful men who planned and sanctioned the coup proclaimed an act of the people to remain less visible.

That a faction of the powerful were in charge became clear the next morning when the judges and ministers of the Real Acuerdo immediately sanctioned the overthrow, backed by the archbishop. Equally important and less often recognized, when the coup was announced to the people of the city, its streets and plazas were occupied by military units with cannon ready, backed by militias drawn from distant provinces—including the San Luis

Potosí regiment led by don Félix Calleja and a troop from Michoacán including don Agustín Iturbide.[5]

If a small corps of urban militiamen played the people in arresting the
viceroy, high regime officials proclaimed and sanctioned the coup, backed by
a powerful show of military force. Not only did armed power force a change
in leadership and a reversal of policy at the top of the viceregal regime, the
lead role of the audiencia judges in planning, proclaiming, and implementing the change announced the end of the regime of mediation: the highest
judicial mediators in New Spain planned a coup and ensured that no appeal,
no mediation, could follow.

On the morning of the 17th, people arriving at the Parián, the luxury
market in the plaza in front of the Viceregal Palace, faced a political message posted anonymously to denounce the coup: the merchants of the
Parián were "the people" who had toppled the viceroy. A day after defenders of the coup announced that "the people" had deposed the viceroy,
unknown others proclaimed that "the people" who had made the coup
were traders profiting in luxuries.[6] Neither statement was accurate.
Disaffected merchants led militiamen who implemented a coup planned
and backed by established military and judicial powers. Two emphases
came to the fore in public discourse: military power ruled and claimed to
represent the people. Who the people might be, and what they might do,
remained debated.

Later on the 17th, the Audiencia and Acuerdo met again to defend the
coup. They still insisted that "el pueblo" had provoked their actions: "el
pueblo of the capital asked permission to enter and make diverse requests
concerning the public calm." There had been calls on the 16th to reinstate
Iturrigaray; defenders of the coup insisted that the pleas came from men
loyal to the deposed Godoy, that they must not be heard, and that Garibay
should rule. The deposed viceroy's ties to Godoy, blamed for Spain's crisis,
came into public play. The Real Acuerdo emphasized that "military commanders" seconded by "eight colonels," backed Garibay. Finally, adding his
voice to those of "el pueblo" and the military commanders, frigate captain
don Juan Jabat, commissioned by the Supreme Junta of Seville, acknowl-
edged "the great satisfaction of all with the loyalty, vision, and skill of His
Excellency don Pedro Garibay. The Supreme Junta of Seville desired only a
leader who would rule and keep the peace in this kingdom [New Spain]."

The Audiencia and the Real Acuerdo agreed in a revealing way: "in the circumstances of the day, he [Garibay] is the leader most ready to calm and unite our spirits, who will be obeyed with pleasure by military men and the paisanos [from Spain], and other classes of people, allowing the recruitment of more volunteers ready to defend the kingdom, drawing more abundant donations and other contributions to assist metropolitan Spain—the considerations that must prevail."[7]

By the 17th, it was clear that an alliance of military commanders, high officials, and judges had recruited frustrated merchants and a small force of militiamen, most from Spain, to play the people and topple the viceroy. In the process, the judges joined in gutting the regime of mediation that their predecessors had long maintained to sustain silver capitalism. They sanctioned a new politics—forced by necessity, they insisted—in which military men, again, most from Spain, would rule the heights of power and set policy. All would obey. Mediation ceded to coercion in the name of the people.

There were, of course, precedents. Bourbon officials had tried to impose a new administrative rule backed by military force in the 1760s—and succeeded in provoking resistance that disrupted silver capitalism. They relied on local militias to control the resistance, imposed a visible repression—and then backed away from militarized power. In the 1790s, in the times of French and Haitian revolutions, new militias were raised, but they reinforced New Spain's oligarchs and provincial elites more than the regime, limiting any attempt at rule by armed imposition. Then in Mexico City's political summer of 1808, public shows of force sometimes reinforced and sometimes countered popular participations—but no armed assertion turned the course of politics and regime rule until the September coup. Then, a militia force parading as the people toppled the viceroy, backed by High Court judges and military commanders who set a show of armed force in the capital's streets and plazas, ready to repress any resistance that might come when the people heard the news the next morning. The regime of mediation was overthrown; rule by force in the name of the people had begun.

September 17: Calling the Pueblos and an Indio King—And No One Came

After the coup and the proclamations that quickly sanctioned it, the alliance oligarchs and councilmen that had backed the viceroy and plans for a congress acquiesced. There was no mobilization in defense of Iturrigaray, his

allies, or their plans for more autonomous New Spain to keep silver capitalism alive while awaiting a clear outcome of the conflicts in Spain. Had the
show of military force in the capital on September 16 carried the day?
Perhaps. But the men who backed Iturrigaray—leading merchant financiers,
top mining entrepreneurs, and great landlords, Europeans and Americans
together—were committed first to silver capitalism.

They had no interest in prolonged conflicts that might disrupt the economy and keep the populace mobilized. The alliance of military and merchant
forces that made the coup promised to sustain silver capitalism in service of
Seville and the fight against Napoleon. The Seville Junta had allied with
Britain, a strategic necessity. The alternative of autonomy under Iturrigaray
backed by a congress also aimed to keep silver capitalism strong—without a
tie to Seville or any junta in Spain. British power, ships, and merchants were
essential to getting New Spain's silver into Atlantic circuits; British power
would be reinforced either way. The future of New Spain and silver capitalism remained unclear—either way.

What was clear was that continued political divisions and popular mobilizations would disrupt the economy that all participants in the politics of
power in Mexico City knew had to continue. As news filtered in after the
coup of the Spanish victory at Bailén on July 16–19, where forces loyal to
Seville blocked France's march to the south, oligarchs began to see backing
Seville as a reasonable course, better than provoking continuing conflict. So
most acquiesced.

Still, rumor and debate buzzed across Mexico City in the days after the
coup, ferment provoked and legitimated by proclamations that the coup
was an act of "el Pueblo." Once the pueblo was mobilized, even rhetorically,
who might act in its name became an open question. Since the parades of
July 29, factions of the political and the powerful had called people to the
streets, calling for change—or continuity—in their name. Others worried
about raising mobs that might claim to be sovereign. On September 15, a
clique of the powerful sent armed men, proclaimed the people, to topple
the viceroy. On the 17th, while the Real Acuerdo, military men, and agents
from Seville met to consolidate and legitimate the new order, something
very different was proposed in the name of the people: "A plan of insurrection with the goal of crowning one of the Governors of the Parcialidades
de Indios."[8]

The leader was said to be don José Luis Rodríguez Alcanedo, a master silversmith. The plot was said to include the Conde de Valenciana, the Conde de Peñasco, and the Governors of San Juan Tenochtitlan and Santiago Tlatelolco—two men of the oligarchy and two leaders the capital's indigenous republics. An unnamed informant revealed the plot to Viceroy Garibay on the 20th. Rodríguez and his wife, doña María Gertrudis Acuña, faced quick arrest. The two counts and the two governors were summoned to appear. No rising had come; still, the craftsman who reportedly led the plot was jailed—as was his wife. The noblemen and indigenous governors were important enough—in different ways—to be treated with caution and respect.

The Conde de Peñasco, grandson and heir to the lands and title of the landed militia commander who had contained the risings of the 1760s in San Luis Potosí, son of the powerful landed priest-oligarch don José Sánchez Espinosa, appeared first, immediately on September 20. In sworn testimony he stated that he had gone out on Saturday, September 17, seeking a medallion honoring "Nuestro Rey"—Our King. He did not say, but presumably he meant Fernando VII. Entering Rodríguez Alcanedo's shop, the conde saw what he wanted and commented on "the news"—the ousting of the viceroy. The silversmith offered a "thought." As "the merchant gachupines have taken control of all armaments, in time they will do as they please with all of us." So he proposed that: "we meet privately with the Governors of Santiago and other republics, making them see the current circumstances, and that they need to take a lead in calling the Indios of the Pueblos to join in building ditches and outer ditches around the city, closing the entrances and exits to prevent [the gachupines'] departure and blocking the delivery of necessities—forcing by hunger their surrender and disarmament." The pueblos, plural, would be mobilized—this time the indigenous majority. The proposal continued: "This done, we should crown an indio and remove all gachupines from their positions."

There is so much to consider here: the merchant gachupines had taken arms to overthrow the viceroy. Even after the judges and ministers of the Real Acuerdo joined military commanders and the archbishop to sanction the coup, greedy immigrants in arms gained blame. More important, Peñasco and the silversmith saw that the new rulers controlled all the armaments in the city. The coup set foundations for rule grounded in a monopoly coercion. The regime of petition and mediation had given way to a state of coercion. And because a few had claimed a monopoly of coercion, the only recourse for opposition was to raise the pueblos, the indigenous republics in and around the capital, build trenches and barricades to keep the offenders in and sustenance out—starving the city into submission, forcibly dispersing offensive gachupines, and crowning an indio king. It was a plan that understood how Mexico City and New Spain had changed—and imagined a social revolution, grounded in established native republics, to call and sustain a new, indigenous monarchy.

An unprecedented coup stimulated unprecedented notions of resistance: if anger against greedy gachupines ran deep among middling American Spaniards (as suggested in the failed conspiracy of 1799 that also looked to silversmiths), the call to raise the indigenous pueblos, sanction their participation in sovereignty, and draw them to build barricades was new. New too was the call to crown an indigenous king. Rather than kill gachupines, as the 1799 plotters proposed, the 1808 plan would force them out of the capital. Newcomers might still come from Spain, "on condition that when they wish to marry they will be required to marry indias." Instead of marrying landed American heiresses, as a few so famously did, gachupines would join with native women—a social descent in the eyes of Spaniards, yet a social amalgamation parallel to those so common in the city. The irony of the plot: native pueblos would call an indio king while despised immigrants would marry native women. Peñasco related all this in matter-of-fact detail—as a conversation he happened upon in a silver shop. He said he knew nothing about involvement by the Conde de Valenciana.

The Conde de Peñasco, don Mariano Sánchez y Mora, was the older of two sons of don José Sánchez Espinosa, one of the capital's great landed oligarchs, with holdings from the edge of the city, through the Bajío, and across San Luis Potosí. Don José had married the daughter of the Conde de Peñasco, the San Luis Potosí miner turned landed entrepreneur who led the militias that put down the risings of 1767 across the north. Don José Mariano inherited his grandfather's title and estates, properties ruled by don José until early 1808, when the patriarch retired to let his titled son, then in his late 20s, lead the family and run its landed empire.[9] Father and son had signed the oligarchs' petition against the consolidation in 1805; they lost little, if anything.

Called to testify, the young patriarch offered that he went out the day after the coup seeking a medal to show his devotion to the captive Fernando—the least offensive of political acts. In the silversmith's shop he struck up a conversation with a craftsman who, according to Peñasco, chose to share a plan surely seditious in the eyes of those who ruled after the coup—a plan that Peñasco absorbed so clearly, he could narrate its detail without interruption. New authorities of uncertain legitimacy had to investigate. Neither they nor Peñasco doubted Rodríguez's role. But why would he spontaneously share the plot with a young oligarch? The first reports indicated that not only Peñasco, but an equally young and inexperienced Conde de Valenciana were also involved. His father had built a silver empire on Guanajuato's richest mines. The young conde had inherited wealth and title to live the most privileged of lives in the capital—while his half-brother, don Antonio de Obregón, ran the mines and sat on the Mining Tribunal. Had two young men with titles and privileged wealth joined a radical plot?

American Spaniards had long imagined finding legitimacy in the native past, grounding their right to rule New Spain in a Mexica regime long fallen.[10] Had the young noblemen led or joined a plot that aimed to go beyond metaphor and crown a Mexica king? Did they presume they would dominate the new king—and imagine dominating native pueblos? Peñasco's father had profited for decades operating La Teja, an estate just west of the city. Father and son knew the estate's dependence on village workers to raise the produce that fed the city. Did young Peñasco imagine calling them to politics, expecting to organize their participations, as his father's managers used their labor? Such imaginings seem more likely the product of the naïve nobleman than a working silversmith—the latter surely stronger on anti-gachupín sentiments.

Wondering where all this came from, later on the 20th the investigators questioned the young Conde de Valenciana. He admitted knowing the silversmith Rodríguez Alcanedo for four years, but only through his "craft work." Valenciana described Rodríguez as "a man of ill intent and bad conduct; without a word of truth in his dealings and contracts." Always angling to take what was not his, Rodríguez could not be trusted. The count swore that he had no role in or knowledge of the details of "a project of infamy that appeared badly planned." Valenciana thus admitted having learned of the plot and insisted that he rejected any involvement. Peñasco relayed details, admitting he had listened intently. Both young noble oligarchs deflected blame onto the craftsman.

September 20: More Popular Conspiracies and Nativist Dreams

Such conversations might have appeared just that—conversations among a frustrated silversmith and two rich young noblemen in the aftermath of a coup that made the future of Mexico City and New Spain uncertain. But later on September 20, the day the conversations of the 17th were reported, the silversmith and his wife arrested, and the two noblemen questioned, a more public conversation was reported to wary authorities. They began to fear wider opposition and suspect a more worrisome plot.[11]

Around ten on the morning of the 20th, José Bustamante and Julián Rojas, shoemakers, and Ignacio Rivera, a tinsmith, were crossing the San Antonio bridge when they faced two men demanding their money or their lives. When the three artisans proved ready to resist, the robbers announced that the confrontation was a test—to see if the three men were brave. The "robbers" revealed themselves as Vicente Acuña, a merchant, and José Morales, a tailor. They offered their three victims money to join in spreading news of a plot to right the wrongs of September 16: if the recruits would raise resistance in the barrios of Santa María, San Pablo, and La Palma, Acuña and Morales would recruit followers in San Juan Tenochtitlan, the large indigenous *parcialidad.*

Morales, the tailor, then told of a plan that recognized that power had turned to military force sanctioned by popular rights. He would recruit *la gente* (the people) to form a regiment of twenty companies—just as the gachupines had done. The real people's regiment would go to the palace, gain the gachupines' confidence, enter, overwhelm the despised immigrants, and offer them a choice: disarm and live, fight and die. Then, having ousted the gachupines who made the coup, the armed gente would go to the convent of Belem, free Iturrigaray, and return him to his role as viceroy. Morales said he had a *compadre* raising men in San Juan Tenochtitlan.

At that point, the merchant Acuña interrupted his partner's telling of a careful (if improbable) plan. The merchant insisted that it was better to just call the populace to take up knives and clubs, set fires across the city, force the ouster of the gachupines, and free the viceroy. Acuña claimed to have thirty men ready to join; the recently accosted artisans should help recruit more. Morales, perturbed, cut off his partner; uncontrolled destruction was not the plan, the tailor insisted. At that point, the three artisans agreed to join the movement, spread the word, and come to a meeting later in the day.

Instead, they went immediately to the palace and reported the encounter to the sergeant at arms. Later that day (likely while authorities questioned Peñasco and Valenciana), the three artisans went to the meeting, joined by an officer of the Provincial Regiment of Mexico City—disguised as another shoemaker recruited to join the plot. Only Morales and his family were present. When he began to spin fantastic tales of rights to rule, the officer in disguise revealed himself, arrested Morales, and began a search for Acuña that would last ten days.

On the evening of September 20, four days after the coup, officials of the coup-imposed government had news of two plots, both calling for popular risings to oust them by force, one linking young noblemen and artisans and aiming to crown an indigenous king; the other linking a merchant and diverse artisans and calling to mobilize diverse peoples including the indigenous barrios—aiming to free Iturrigaray. The similarities suggested wider conversations and perhaps a larger movement; the differences and uncertainties perhaps indicated little more than widespread talk and discontent. That the silversmith Rodríguez was married to an Acuña, and that she was arrested, suggested that the plots—or at least the conversations—were linked. Authorities fragile in power continued investigating.

The next day, September 21, the governors of the parcialidades appeared. First came don Manuel Santos Bargas Machuca, governor of Santiago Tlatelolco. Asked if he knew the "silversmith Rodríguez," Bargas answered "that he has no memory of knowing nor having known the individual in question, nor of having dealt with others about issues related to the government of the day." It was an equivocating reply—I do not recall—punctuated by an insult to the authorities as the government *of the day*. It was a sworn denial laden with deflection and disrespect.

The governor of San Juan was slow to appear, though his chambers were much closer to the center (see map 1)—another sign of disrespect? He first sent his son with a note claiming delay due to heavy rains. Finally, after 6 p.m., don Eleuterio Severino Guzmán, Governor of San Juan Tenochtitlan, arrived. The scribe recorded: "he says he does not know the individual in question"—meaning Rodríguez. Guzmán added that he had discussed current events with no one, except to report to "High Court judge don Guillermo de Aguirre" about "the revolutions we are facing." The Governor of San Juan Tenochtitlan, ruler of the largest indigenous republic in the Americas, denied conversations about politics and then remembered reporting on ongoing "revolutions" to a powerful judge. Guzmán denied contact with Rodríguez or knowledge of any plot. Were other "revolutions" afloat? Surely the investigators worried that the governor was referring to the Acuña-Morales plot.

The brief questioning of the indigenous governors suggests that the investigators believed they were not involved—or that they were too pivotal to keeping peace in the barrios to alienate. We cannot know, but it seems likely that Rodríguez, Peñasco, and perhaps Valenciana had discussed recruiting the governors to an American alliance against a post-coup regime built to defend European interests. If they were approached, the capital's indigenous governors had rejected the plan. Had Guzmán reported the contact to the judge, thus setting off the inquiry? His late, brief, and oblique formal testimony raises that possibility.

On the 22nd, the investigators interrogated Rodríguez again, this time in his cell in the Royal Jail. He described himself as don José Luis Rodríguez Alcanedo, born in Puebla, *patrón del arte de platería*, forty-six years old, and married to doña María Gertrudis Acuña. If interrogators wondered if she was kin to the blustery merchant conspirator still on the loose they gave no hint. They did ask Rodríguez if he had any knowledge of "the Europeans involved in the imprisonment of His Excellency, Viceroy don José Iturrigaray" or any related plans or discussions. The aim of freeing the viceroy was a goal of the Acuña-Morales plot, not mentioned in Rodríguez's conversation reported by Peñasco. The interrogators were looking for links between the plots—without sharing that they knew about both sets of seditious conversations. Rodríguez answered that "he had joined in nothing in particular; he had no plan." Then he suddenly recalled that on the night the viceroy fell, don Manuel Villaseñor, an employee at the mint, had talked of a rising. Rodríguez was ready to implicate others (and suggest wider opposition) to defend his innocence while insisting he had no role or interest.

The same day that the authorities interrogated the silversmith Rodríguez, Acuña fled the city to a village near Tlalnepantla, just north. He later claimed to have gone to attend to business, but a priest there reported a revealing encounter. When the clergyman asked the merchant why he had come, Acuña said that he was a wanted fugitive because he was a friend of Talamantes, the radical friar who had been arrested along with Iturrigaray. The authorities proved little interested in a link between Acuña and an intellectual in the autonomy movement.[12]

They were concerned with plots to raise the barrios and crown an indigenous king—notions that seemed to link the two reported conspiracies. The investigators sought out people who knew Rodríguez. All swore that the silversmith had stood back from the conflicts of the day. Such corroborations could be true, or statements by allies protecting Rodríguez and themselves. Investigators were not convinced. On the 25th they returned to Rodríguez's cell to interrogate him about his brother, don José Ygnacio Rodríguez Alcanedo; at the time of the coup, he was in Mexico City, staying at the Mesón de Santo Tomás. Had his brother known of or spoken about a plot? The silversmith insisted his brother had come to the capital for work linked to a botanical garden planned for Puebla. They had barely spoken: another deflection, not a denial.

The investigators then got to the point. They accused Rodríguez of lying to cover the plot to crown a native king—aiming to link the silversmith to Acuña and Morales. The silversmith denied the accusation. Then interrogators shared Valenciana's testimony that Rodríguez lacked character. Rodríguez answered that he and Valenciana had disputed a payment of 300 pesos for curtains (drapes inlaid with silver?). The craftsman implied that the rich Valenciana was taking revenge for a business spat, blaming the silversmith for a plot that did not exist.

There the first investigations stalled—Rodríguez Alcanedo in jail, the two condes free, yet facing suspicion. Acuña was captured on September 30. He had returned to the city, to be turned in by the artisans who had earlier reported the encounters of the 20th. October inquiries focused on the reported plan to raise the people and crown a native king. Investigators learned that Morales was married to Gertrudis Tezozomocoa, a name suggesting roots in the parcialidades. They learned that Acuña and Morales were heard in precoup conversations at the cathedral talking of emptying the pulquerías and prisons to raised crowds and name a descendant of Moctezuma as king. They discovered Acuña's dealings with doña Andrea the fruit seller and her son don Dionisio Cano y Moctezuma—the vegetable trader who might be imagined king. Facing such revelations, the presumed conspirators turned to mutual recriminations. Acuña accused Morales of bragging about links to a noble official in San Juan Tenochtitlan and of proposing the idea of a popular regiment to invade the palace.

As no rising came and the city remained at peace, the investigators looking into the two reported plots carried on slowly. In February of 1809, Rodríguez again denied involvement in anything political, calling Peñasco an acquaintance who came to the shop to buy a medallion. Questioned again, Peñasco's memory got fuzzy; now he remembered little. Workers in Rodríguez's shop confirmed that the patrón and Peñasco talked for half an hour on the day in question, but only about the medallion and never in private. Was that true, cover for their employer, or protection for themselves as participants in seditious conversations?

Continuing on into March, investigators believed that something seditious was discussed in the silver shop—but no action taken. They documented ties between Rodríguez and Peñasco, at least the design and making of the medallion honoring Fernando VII—itself a political act. On March 20 they recalled Valenciana, who stood by the truth of his first account. When the judge stated that details had proven wrong, Valenciana suddenly remembered that around the time of the coup, he too had contracted with Rodríguez to strike "a medal of Our Lady of Guadalupe" that he had sent to Guanajuato. Both rich and titled young men had visited the silversmith in the aftermath of the coup. Both had medals made that were symbols of New Spain's autonomy. The coincidence confirmed the judges' suspicions, but they had little hard evidence to move a case forward. The file went to Spain for review. Rodríguez won release in November of 1809, after a year in jail on suspicions that could not be proven.

Also in March of 1809, judges in the Morales-Acuña case concluded that there was a plot to raise a mob and crown a native king, that Acuña was its primary author, Morales a full participant, and that both deserved execution—commuted to remittance to Spain (along with the record of the Peñasco-Rodríguez plot). After the coup, judges saw real threats and a need to investigate; they also preferred to keep public knowledge limited.[13]

What can we draw from this record of reports, inquiries, and denials? There were conversations about a plot between Rodríguez and Peñasco; the young noble stated that much. Valenciana probably was approached, but held back; the city's native governors, likely contacted, had no interest. Peñasco's clear first narrative shows that he and Rodríguez, and perhaps others, concluded immediately after the coup that the alliance of military leaders, judges, and merchants had set coercion at the foundation of regime power— and that the only way to challenge that power was to raise the indigenous pueblos. The merchant Acuña and the tailor Morales shared a similar vision—whether by contact with Rodríguez (via his Acuña wife?), by common response to ideas floating in the city, or by coincidence, we cannot know. All believed that only native leaders could raise the urban parcialidades (Acuña and Morales) or the nearby pueblos (Peñasco and Rodríguez)— and all dreamed of an indigenous king, a notion floating around the Cathedral before the coup. Morales and Acuña would call the people to arms—the former in organized companies, the latter in a riot that would set the city aflame. Rodríguez and Peñasco would raise the pueblos to control city sustenance and starve gachupines into submission. All had concluded that only a mobilization of the pueblos could counter the power of those who had taken power by force of arms—and claimed to be el pueblo.

The governors of the parcialidades insisted they had neither knowledge nor interest in any of this—and the authorities believed them. The governors were essential to the social order in the capital. Without ample evidence or strong cause for suspicion, neither present in the fall of 1808, regime officials faced risk in challenging such men. There is also reason to suspect that the governors were more interested in holding their established power in the parcialidades than in challenging the new and uncertain powers above them.

If investigators were ready to accept the role of the two young noblemen as unproven, the Conde de Peñasco's father, the great landed capitalist and priest don José Sánchez Espinosa, drew his own conclusions. He was certain his wayward son had gone beyond the bounds of acceptable behavior and took steps to discipline him. Sánchez Espinosa had built an agricultural empire, profiting amply supplying food and drink to Mexico City, staples to Querétaro and Guanajuato, wool to Querétaro obrajes, and meat to Mexico City and Querétaro. In April 1808, the priest, patriarch, and entrepreneur, advancing in age, had turned management over to his son, the Conde de Peñasco.[14]

Then on September 29, soon after the coup and as plot investigations widened, Sánchez Espinosa announced to his managers that he had retaken control of his estates and businesses—and sent his son, the Conde de Peñasco, away to live on a pulque estate near Otumba, past the ancient pyramids at Teotihuacan.[15] The powerful priest-patriarch stripped his titled son of all power over family affairs and sent him away, far from investigators, from politics, and from any chance to make problems for the businesses that kept the clan at the heights of the oligarchy. Sánchez Espinosa had worked for decades to amass land, profits, and power. Now his son had jumped into the most contentious politics in the most fragile times. Young Peñasco surely acted from a mix of idealism and naiveté. His father saw foolishness risking everything he had built and banished his titled son to languish in rural isolation, far from the capital. If he wanted to hide behind indigenous power, let him cower in the shadow of the pyramids. Peñasco's dream—and his father's reaction suggests it was his dream—proved impossible. Still, the exchange between the naïve nobleman and the working silversmith offered a clear analysis of the regime remade by the September coup: power taken by armed forces proclaimed the people could only be countered by people asserting their own power by force.

Defending the State of Coercion

In the face of the reports of the two plots and the wider discontent they indicated, the makers of the coup knew they had to defend their intervention to close the option of an autonomous New Spain—in the process breaking the regime of mediation. The need became ever more clear when it became known that on the day after the coup (while Peñasco and Rodríguez met), don Gabriel de Yermo had handed officials of the Real Acuerdo a list of demands for concessions tied to his personal economic interests: the end of the consolidation, tax reductions on cane brandy and the production and sale of sheep and wool. It became easy to conclude that the coup of "the people" aimed to serve a faction seeking to join the powerful.[16]

So the higher authorities that had planned and backed the coup turned to continuing legitimations. On September 24, the Audiencia wrote the Junta of Seville to affirm its loyalty and explain its role in a coup "so great and extraordinary."[17] The judges reported being surprised by the coup, swept along by events. "From one in the morning on, the houses of all the ministers of this tribunal were surrounded by armed gente (people), reporting that they had captured His Excellency Viceroy don José Iturrigaray." Armed men had captured the viceroy, removing him from office. Only then did the judges join the larger Real Acuerdo to accept the coup. Aiming to deflect responsibility, the judges confirmed Peñasco's emphasis that the "people" who made the coup were armed men. The ideological fusion of the people and the military marched forward.

After the coup, the judges were "directed by the same armed people." Under duress, they insisted, they sent for the archbishop and other senior clerics: "The streets and the royal palace, outside and within, were occupied by the same armed people, paisanos from Spain. They held the staircase and the hallways and the court chamber too, insisting on the removal of the viceroy and the appointment of Field Marshall don Pedro Garibay. So we agreed, calling the commander, who was charged to command." That done, all the military and political leaders, prelates and chambers gathered to learn of the extraordinary event. They learned that at eleven in the morning of the 16th, the same day, "all would meet in the salon of the royal palace to honor the new supreme leader and offer him obedience. That was done by all, and by the native republics in the customary way."[18] In their new telling, the judges of the High Court did not lead or plan the coup. They faced armed men, paisanos from Spain, who captured the viceroy and forced them to name a preselected replacement, Garibay. Why did the judges try to hide their leading role in the coup when writing to the Seville Junta that was its primary beneficiary?

They continued their narrative. On the morning of the 17th (while Peñasco and Rodríguez imagined an alternative way forward) the judges took up regular business. Soon after convening, they learned that "el pueblo" was outside and asking to enter. A spokesman for the crowd demanded that there be no further consideration of leadership; Garibay must be confirmed. "A few military commanders were present and more kept arriving; on hearing the demand of the pueblo, they supported it." In the face of assertive commanders backed by armed people, the Audiencia again confirmed Garibay. The judges concluded reiterating their loyalty to Fernando and "union with Spain"—a union more promising as news confirmed that Napoleon's march south toward Seville had stalled at Bailén, and that the prolonged siege of Zaragoza meant that the French would not easily rule Spain's north.[19] Did the military intrusion into the Audiencia chamber lead the judges to worry that their own powers, long built on consultation and mediation, were being marginalized? Were they becoming unsure of the coup they had made and decide to deny their early involvement, claiming that armed people had forced everything?

On October 4, Garibay addressed "All the Inhabitants of This New Spain." He first recognized the "Supreme Junta of Seville," stating that it had risen out of "the great events that have happened in the Metropolis since the month of October of 1807," all the conflicts since the failed coup at El Escorial. He condemned "the machinations of the Emperor of the French" and praised "the sacrifices and heroic efforts" of the many in Spain fighting to reclaim the rights of the captive Fernando. He concluded insisting that "as we share one king, one interest, one happiness, and one religion, the Supreme Junta exhorts us to unite in our efforts to sustain a cause so great and so just."[20]

Garibay lamented that the sea prevented the people of New Spain from taking on the "glorious sacrifices" of fighting Napoleon, yet they must join the "heroic enterprise." He called them to: "reveal your generosity, support the peninsula, open your treasures, and send them without delay." If the message was not clear: "There they give their blood, here you can give your riches." Garibay called all to the Euro-American alliance—yet he referred to the people of New Spain not as *us*, but as *you*: the people of the peninsula "demand your help as a loving father who turns to his caring and compassionate sons." Garibay returned to the patriarchal metaphor, earlier mobilized to hint at the possibility of New Spain's adulthood, of its autonomy. The new viceroy insisted that the father lived and required the sons' energetic services—or at least their silver:

"Gather up your riches, assemble your silver, reject all that is useless and superfluous, limit your comforts, economize on your expenses and deliver the rest to the public treasuries . . . Form associations of corporations, communities or guilds: name persons to receive great or small amounts; offer whatever you produce if you do not have money, and once you have given generously, know you have saved our King, our Holy Religion, and our homeland." All this Garibay addressed to "most faithful Americans." In his call for unity against Napoleon Garibay first used language that separated Americans and Europeans, then called on the established corporations essential to the old regime, and at the end proclaimed unity in a shared king, religion, and fatherland. Set in office by a coup made by men from Spain aiming to hold power in New Spain, he struggled to find language to unite a transatlantic Spanish community.

His next decree, issued October 6, revealed troubling uncertainty. Since taking command, Garibay aimed to promote "tranquility and public peace." Unfortunately, "a few restless spirits, malignant and rebellious types still work to disturb and seduce people of peaceful souls, not only in this city but in the other provinces, by means of anonymous postings, lampoons, and infamous libels." If the powerful and privileged had acquiesced to the coup and most were ready to sustain Spain against Napoleon, if the imagined revolution linking oligarchs and indios had come to naught, many among the populace still proclaimed public opposition. Troubling interventions were reaching the provinces. With the backing of the Real Acuerdo, Garibay pardoned all previous postings of public libels, offered anonymity to those who reported future postings, and promised criminal prosecution of future culprits.[21] He offered a last mediation, backed by a promise of stern discipline.

In his public pronouncements Garibay emphasized the seditious activities of those who posted anonymous broadsheets and talked too freely in taverns and public squares. He also faced conflict with Yermo, the man who led the troops that forced the coup. Yermo had asked for economic concessions and honors for his troop, labeled the Patriots of Fernando VII. When Garibay refused, he feared a second coup against his own post-coup rule. So he called a regiment from Celaya (in the Bajío) to the capital. When it arrived to disband Yermo's patriots on October 15, Yermo resisted and fears of a second coup mounted. Then Yermo called for a procession to Guadalupe and a celebration of the new regime there, aiming to bring tradition and popular acclaim to the new government—and perhaps to himself. Again, Garibay refused.[22] Did he fear Yermo, the consequences of calling so many people into public space, or both?

Amid all that continuing uncertainty, and only after the judges of the Audiencia and the new viceroy had offered their versions and legitimations, did the full Real Acuerdo offer its vision—published on October 16, precisely a month after it sanctioned the coup. The gathering included most judges of the Audiencia, several financial officials, one leader of the merchants' chamber, don Fausto Elhuyar of the Mining Tribunal, the head of the College of Lawyers, and others. The meeting included men who had joined in Iturrigaray's juntas, opposed their decisions and direction, and later backed the September coup. They shaped a story to justify that action.[23]

The men who met as an expanded Acuerdo (almost a junta?) knew they
had to take the story back to the pivotal meetings and debates of early
August. They offered their own, self-interested history of the two months
that transformed politics and regime power in New Spain. They began by
stating that on August 6, they received a call to a meeting without a clear
agenda. The gathering opened on August 9 with don Francisco Verdad y
Ramos—the villain of the tale—announcing that sovereignty had "returned
to el pueblo." Such claims, "seditious and subversive," were questioned by
others demanding to know who represented the people. Verdad reportedly
answered: "the existing authorities." During the debates that followed, men
opposed to Verdad's premise of a return of sovereignty to the legally constituted authorities accused him of the radical new doctrine of the sovereignty
of "el pueblo." They argued that such a doctrine would give sovereignty to
indigenous pueblos and descendants of the Aztec kings (an emphasis reconstructed with knowledge of the post-coup plot?). The Acuerdo recreated precoup debates to make Verdad and Iturrigaray appear radical in ways they
were not. Why? The viceroy had been toppled and was a captive on his way
to Seville. Verdad, the voice of the council and its search for institutional
continuity had been jailed—to die in captivity in early October in very suspi-
cious circumstances.

The Acuerdo then turned to the junta of August 31. It argued that debates
then focused on whether to call a "General Junta of the entire kingdom" or to
recognize the Junta of Seville. City magistrate and merchant don José Juan de
Fagoaga and audiencia judge don Agustín de Villaurrutia, Americans both, led
the call for the general junta. Iturrigaray joined them. The men of the Acuerdo
noted (correctly) that the majority preferred to recognize Seville. Facing defeat,
a frustrated Iturrigaray promised this would be the last junta.

Yet he assembled the group the next day, September 1—again, the report
complained, with no agenda—to consider papers just arrived from the junta at
Oviedo. Iturrigaray felt vindicated in his refusal to recognize Seville and his
call for a junta general: "Gentlemen, we have verified what we announced yesterday; Spain lives in anarchy; all the juntas are supreme—none should be
obeyed." It was a persuasive rationale. Backed by the men of the Mexico City
Council, the viceroy argued that they should recognize no junta in Spain,
insisted there be no other business, and closed the meeting. The next morning,
September 2, he sent messages asking all participants to send written votes on

the questions of the previous two days: whether to recognize the Junta of Seville and whether to call a junta of the entire kingdom.

Ballots were tallied at a junta of September 9. As they were read, voices shouted in frustration. When it was clear that the vote favored the junta general, opponents called for discussion of who should be represented—only the city councils or "other classes." As debate escalated, the opposition railed at Iturrigaray: "If discussing just the possibility of a Junta of the Kingdom generates such division, what will happen if it meets?" Opponents insisted that no action come until the viceroy consulted the Real Acuerdo—knowing it opposed a general junta. Others insisted: "if we don't call the cities, they will meet on their own." And provincial juntas would open fragmentations like those consuming Spain.

The Acuerdo then recalled a session behind closed doors. Asked if he had proposed stepping down, the viceroy answered that he had thought of resigning, "because I am sixty-six years old, tired, and the challenges of the day are beyond my capacities." Having heard that the Seville Junta planned to replace all appointees of the "old government," he considered stepping aside. Verdad then rose to argue that the viceroy must remain or there would be "incurable damage to religion and the state." A few others spoke briefly, followed by "a profound silence for six or eight seconds"; then Iturrigaray announced: "Gentlemen, let us turn to other things." Discussion closed. The men of the October Acuerdo insisted that the assembly expected Iturrigaray to resign in the next days. When he did not, they had their rationale for the coup.

The report is selective, aimed to justify the coup. While offering much detail, some not available in other sources, the October report leaves out the pivotal shift by Basoco and the men who ruled the financial heights of silver capitalism from support for Seville on August 31 to backing Iturrigaray and the General Junta in early September. The great men of finance had subsequently acquiesced in the coup; they remained essential to the regime and silver capitalism; so they were left out of the report.

In a revealing irony, the backers of Seville first accused Verdad of placing sovereignty in "el pueblo." Then they mobilized merchants and militiamen to implement a coup—declaring that they were "el pueblo." Every faction involved in the summer of politics and the coup of 1808 feared the populace, yet in moments of crisis every faction claimed to be, serve, or represent the people. In its October report, the Acuerdo did not emphasize that aspect of the coup. In the aftermath of the coup, with conspiracies imagining popular risings and lampoons posted all around while armed factions debated which should serve as "the people," had men committed to established power decided to erase the people from the summer of politics?

By mid-October the coup had held. The plots to raise the native pueblos and appoint a native king found no resonance—beyond rumor and fear. The last legitimate viceroy was under house arrest and headed to Seville. Verdad was dead. Other authorities had sanctioned the coup or acquiesced in its outcome, helped by continuing reports that Napoleon's armies had been held north of the Sierra Morena. Andalucía remained free and Seville remained the base of opposition to the French invaders. Napoleon had taken key armies from Iberia to help him reassert power in Eastern Europe. Life in Mexico City settled toward an approximation of normality.

The Coup—And the Revolution that Did Not Come:

The events of September 15–20 and the debates that followed did not resolve the political uncertainties facing New Spain. They did break the last remnants of established imperial legitimacy, end the primacy of rule by mediation, set military force as the base of regime power—and make the people a basis of sovereignty, to be proclaimed by all factions when it served their interests. All that had changed—yet nothing was settled.

Before the coup, as news and rumors of Bourbon family divisions, Napoleon's invasion, rising political and popular oppositions, and the conflicts over supremacy in the fight to reclaim Spain all filtered into Mexico City, politics took on new life in the capital of New Spain. Established powers declared commitments to continuity yet divided over whether to honor Carlos or Fernando as news came that both were held captive. In the absence of a sovereign, Spanish tradition returned sovereignty to the pueblos—towns with councils. Did that mean calling a junta in Mexico City, a larger assembly (a cortes?) for New Spain, or backing a junta in Spain? By August, two factions coalesced: one, led by Viceroy Iturrigaray and the Mexico City Council, drew support from landed oligarchs, the provincial elites who ruled the council, and many mining entrepreneurs. It moved toward rule by a local junta and a policy of watchful waiting—to eventually propose an American congress that might exercise effective autonomy in the name of the deposed and captured Fernando VII. The other faction coalesced around audiencia judges, other high officials (the Real Acuerdo), and military commanders who demanded loyalty to Spain despite the uncertainty about who ruled there—better, amid the certainty that no power, group, or faction ruled there. By late August military commanders pressed for loyalty to a Seville Junta that claimed supremacy, yet remained one of many contenders for power in Spain.

The great merchant financiers who led the consulado and financed mining and global trade formed the key swing interest. As news of changing events in Spain came in bursts through the summer, the financiers at times backed the viceroy and the council, forming a solid bloc in defense of silver capitalism, ready to wait to find policies that would serve its preservation. At other times, the financiers, nearly all immigrant Spaniards, leaned toward the men dedicated to sustaining Spain. In early September, Iturrigaray, the council, and the core of landed and mining oligarchs were ready to call an American congress. When don Antonio Basoco and the financiers turned to back that coalition, the men demanding loyalty to Seville saw their days numbered. They mobilized their one advantage, military power, to topple the viceroy and force allegiance to Seville. The coup tied New Spain's silver to Seville, guaranteeing immigrant Spaniards at least chances at power and opportunity in governance and trades.

After the coup discontent spread in many quarters of the city, but few proved ready to challenge the government imposed by the new concentration of coercion. The few who did imagine popular risings from September 17–20 saw that only the pueblos could challenge the armed power committed to Seville. Their visions of the coup offered revealing analyses of times to come: politics grounded in military powers proclaiming the people sovereign. Still, their calls to raise the pueblos and proclaim an indio king went unanswered.

The viceroy, Verdad, Talamantes, and a few more were jailed. Their allies among the great financiers, mining magnates, landed oligarchs, and provincial elites remained free. None acted to oppose the coup. The people of the city, Spanish, mixed, and indigenous, so recently in the streets to proclaim Fernando VII sovereign, stayed home and at work. The post-coup plotters, with their differing mixes of perceptive vision and improbable idealism, imagined a revolution in the name of the pueblos, the indigenous pueblos in and around the city—and no one came. No one offered to become an indigenous king—to rule as Moctezuma's heir.

Great financiers, mining magnates, landed oligarchs, and provincial elites were ready to claim new participations in trying times—as long as those participations kept the few in power and did not disrupt silver capitalism. If only a popular rising could topple the militarily imposed regime, the oligarchs would acquiesce in the coup. They knew that silver capitalism could not thrive without them. They knew that the men who made the coup and the new regime, and the Seville Junta, too, remained dependent upon silver. The oligarchs were confident they would not lose in any major way. They preferred stability to participations they could not control. So, it seems, did the governors of the city's indigenous republics. They showed no interest in a plot that called the pueblos to take the streets and build barricades, opening conflicts none could control. If the silversmith Rodríguez, the merchant Acuña, and a handful of artisans were open to rattling power, they found no support above (beyond Peñasco and perhaps Valenciana) or below in a city of hierarchical power, social fragmentation, and economic dynamism.

Mexico City, like most cities, was a center of exchange, drawing silver from mining regions nearby and far to the north, minting the world's currency, sending it into Atlantic and Pacific trades, and drawing back luxuries that announced the capital's power. Like all cities it depended on sustenance drawn from without. Dependence on trade and sustenance defines cities; disruption of either threatens urban power, prosperity, and survival.[24] The essence of Peñasco's plot (and don José Sánchez Espinosa believed it was his son's plot) called outlying pueblos to strangle the city. Who in the city, but a young and naïve landed oligarch, would do that?

The regime imposed by the coup survived to send silver to Seville via British ships at peak levels through 1809 and into 1810. Yet the post-coup rulers never consolidated power or legitimacy. The years after the coup brought endless political debates, strong silver production, drought that prejudiced life from the capital through the Bajío, and after a brief respite, the decline of the Seville Junta's power in Spain. Two years to the day after the Mexico City coup used military power proclaimed "the people" to force the continued delivery of silver to Spain and the fight against Napoleon, a mass uprising in the Bajío, the mining and agricultural core of silver capitalism, challenged those who ruled in the capital and the economic concentrations that prejudiced everyday lives in the mines and on the land. Neither silver capitalism nor Spain's empire would survive the challenge of a people in arms— exercising force in their own interests.

CHAPTER 11

The Fall

From Silver Capitalism to Social Revolution, 1808–1810

◆ AFTER A SUMMER OF UNPRECEDENTED UNCERTAINTIES, MOBILIZA-
tions, debates, and then the coup that imposed a new regime and way of rule,
political life in the capital seemed to calm—at least at the heights of power.
New authorities held on, silver flowed at peak levels, and the Seville Junta did
what it could to fight Napoleon through the rest of 1808 and into 1809. Still,
difficulties lurked: did the silver that peaked in 1809 serve the fight against
Napoleon or flow to diverse British interests? In Mexico City, popular discontent fueled by anonymous posters, often accusing gachupines of playing
the people in imposing the coup, continued to worry Garibay and allies still
fragile in power into 1809. Later that year, provincial leaders in Michoacán,
west of the capital and near the Bajío so pivotal to silver, met to discuss rights
to political participations blocked by the 1808 coup. In the spring of 1810, talk
of rights and juntas moved to Querétaro, a key commercial city linking the
capital and Guanajuato's mines. And while political uncertainties simmered,
from September of 1808 to September of 1810 drought stalked the land. How
could authorities of debated legitimacy and little committed to mediation
deal with rising scarcities that again enabled landed oligarchs to profit while
the people so recently and loudly declared sovereign faced desperation and
destitution?

Silver rose and stability held through 1809. Then escalating conflicts exploded in insurgencies in September of 1810. Authorities set in power by armed force faced a people in arms. Unprecedented violence drove political conflicts begun by provincial elites while tens of thousands took arms to claim the necessities of survival in the core regions of silver capitalism. The regime of mediation disabled by the coup of 1808 dissolved in political and social violence beginning in 1810. Silver capitalism broke quickly. As conflicts continued, Spain's empire fell as New Spain became Mexico in 1821.

Recognitions

News of the coup that ousted Iturrigaray traveled fast. While reports and rumors of plots to raise the people of the capital rattled Garibay and his allies, support for the coup and the leaders it imposed came quickly from the Veracruz City Council. The Gulf port was a bastion of merchant interests tied to Seville and Cádiz. Its council wrote to Garibay on September 18, recognized him as viceroy, and emphasized "the jubilation in this city, staunch in exalting the patriotism of the city of Mexico." The coup promised "the tranquility of this precious kingdom and the happiness of the peninsula." Tranquility was code for order. Stability in New Spain would allow maximum support for the fight against the French in Spain—a fight built on popular mobilizations there. The merchants of Veracruz credited "the Mexican public and the authorities that concurred" with stabilizing New Spain to sustain a Spain in arms. Of course, the "public" that made the coup was a small group of militiamen led by angry merchants, most immigrants from Spain; primarily peninsular authorities concurred in a coup they had planned to keep themselves in power. The myth of a people's coup was spreading, useful to immigrants, merchants, and military men aiming to preserve their roles in a cracking imperial order.[1]

On September 22, the commanders of the military garrison at Jalapa, strategically inland and upland from Veracruz, also wrote to Garibay with recognition, but greater reserve. There was no reference to the public; the coup was credited to the Real Acuerdo and the archbishop. The act was received "with respect and submission due the integrity, justification, and wisdom of those authorities . . . in the hard and thorny circumstances of the day." The commanders at Jalapa would respect the coup; they had no interest in crediting the people.[2] Did they already know of the reports of popular ferment discovered in the capital on the 20th?

The Zacatecas City Council, a bastion of mining interests tied to the commercial axis that linked Mexico City and Seville, showed no reticence proclaiming support for the coup on September 23. It addressed Garibay and the Real Acuerdo to honor "a pueblo truly great and generous." The men of Zacatecas went on to praise "the heroism of the pueblo mexicano; . . . it will astound modern nations to know its civilization and culture; it will bring desperation to the Emperor of the French" who sees New Spain as "the richest prey in the universe." The result: "jubilation and . . . joy without limits in old and New Spain, to see all the intrigues that threaten their political and religious existence thwarted, and to know that the ties that have united them so happily for three centuries have been tightened."[3] The myth of a people's coup had gone north, there amplified by the power of silver capitalists. The people of Mexico City claimed their place in the world of civilized and cultured nations. The prey would stop Napoleon the hunter and keep Spain and New Spain together.

Such proclamations of support would continue to come from men of power committed to sustaining Spain and profiting from silver capitalism. While most people in the capital knew that the pueblo credited with the coup was a self-selected group of armed immigrants committed to keeping their own powers and roles in the link with Spain—and to defending Spain from French rule—the powerful across New Spain, European and American Spaniards alike, knew that the key to everything was the preservation of silver capitalism.

Silver, the Mining Tribunal, and the Question of Mercury

While politics still held the stage in the capital, on October 5 the intendant of Guanajuato, don Juan Antonio de Riaño, wrote a long report to the Real Acuerdo aiming to bring the economy back into focus.[4] The leading official at New Spain's premier mining center offered proposals to counter Yermo's post-coup demands. While Yermo sought concessions that might relieve revenue burdens on a struggling merchant trying to become a landed entrepreneur, Riaño emphasized the need to sustain the commercial foundations of silver capitalism. The intendant proposed seeking greater revenues from sectors of the economy stimulated by silver (unstated—there should be no new taxes on silver). He called for streamlined collection of the Alcabala sales tax on internal trade and the tithe impacting commercial cultivators; he proposed limits on proprietorship in offices, aimed against the provincial elites who ruled city councils. He would raise taxes on urban real estate, again hitting provincial elites. Riaño aimed to deflect revenue demands from mining and the heights of commerce toward provincial trade and urban real estate. Silver and trade between Spain and New Spain should not be burdened.

Riaño was aware of the emerging shifts in the global economy that might challenge the primacy of silver and favor a rising British–Anglo-American axis in the Atlantic world. He knew the innovations that were transforming North America: the rise of industrial cotton factories in England and the drive of cotton and enslaved labor across the Mississippi. He called for the promotion of cotton cultivation and the distribution of cotton gins in Texas and for opening its ports to deliver the staple to the world—including New Spain's textile producers. He called for defense of New Spain's northern borders from a United States recently expanded by the purchase of Louisiana in 1803. And Riaño proposed the abolition of slavery: few slaves remained in New Spain, and he insisted that the expansion of cotton should not revive bondage.[5]

In the days after the September 1808 coup, Riaño had a moment of vision in a world of conflict and change. Born in Spain, he had served in Spanish New Orleans in the 1780s, marrying a daughter of its planter elite. Family ties kept him up on the expansion of cotton. From the 1790s, he saw cloth makers across Guanajuato find protection and prosperity in years of war and trade disruption. Now, the post-coup alliance with Britain would open New Spain to a flood of cloth, threatening producers across the kingdom. Expanded cotton cultivation in Texas would lower costs for New Spain's cloth makers. Did he dream of an economy in which Guanajuato's vibrant silver mines would stimulate rising cotton manufacturing in New Spain? Could cotton flourish in Texas without the degradations of slavery? If so, a powerful economy of silver and cotton might thrive—a prospect perhaps not impossible in 1808.[6]

While focused on promoting silver and imagining a cotton economy without slavery, Riaño said nothing about the deepening pressures plaguing people across Guanajuato and the Bajío as silver boom mixed with profiteering from drought. The agrarian capitalism that sustained silver capitalism was not questioned by its promoters and beneficiaries in the fall of 1808. For that lack of foresight, shared by New Spain's oligarchs and most provincial elites in the capital and across the Bajío, Riaño would pay with his life when insurgent masses besieged Guanajuato and its granary, the alhóndiga, in September of 1810.

The Mining Tribunal followed Riaño in focusing on silver. Two representations, one unofficial, one official, came from the tribunal late in November of 1808. They detailed the centrality of silver in production, politics, and trade; the potential for disruption brought by recent political divisions; and the challenge of supplying essential mercury after Napoleon's invasion of Spain. On November 25, 1808, don Marcelo José de Amat and don Juan Antonio de Terán wrote to the Junta of Seville, to "show their loyalty, love and obedience to the Sovereign."[7] They followed the post-coup loyalist custom of addressing the collective junta as their singular sovereign. They claimed to write for the tribunal, the corporate body that promoted mining in New Spain. But only two of five directors signed. They began: "No time in past centuries has brought more admirable acts nor more lamented catastrophes; . . . never have we seen enthroned a more admirable King than Your Majesty, nor treachery more abominable than that of the fierce enemy that batters us now." Nothing had broken the loyalty of the Mining Tribunal.

Yet many believed otherwise. "Thus the case: The Viceroy of this Kingdom don José Iturrigaray, as a result of the news of the removal of Your Majesty from your Domains, convoked juntas to which two subjects who belong to our General [Mining] tribunal were named, . . . the General Administrator the Marqués de Rayas and the director don Fausto de Elhuyar." Amat and Terán went on: "As the questions and issues to be discussed in the Juntas were not known in advance, the corporations could not prepare their participants, nor could the latter prepare and coordinate their votes, leaving them free to act as individuals in every Junta debate." Amat and Terán wrote to separate themselves and the tribunal from Rayas and Elhuyar's opposing roles in recent politics.

Why soon became clear. "One question stirred most debate: if representatives of all the cities, villas, and towns of the Kingdom should be called to meet as a Supreme Junta? The majority voted No, but there were contrary votes, one by the Marqués de Rayas who pressed his view with ardor. Still, all worked to the same goal, which was to keep these domains for our Holy Religion, in their ancient loyalty to our legitimate and beloved Sovereign, and to defend them from our common enemy. Only the means differed." The authors aimed to minimize support for the junta general—and Rayas's role in promoting that option.

The Marqués de San Juan de Rayas, an American, director of the Mining
Tribunal, and head of one of Guanajuato's oldest mining families, had backed
the call for a supreme American junta. So did the Conde de Regla and other
leading mining entrepreneurs. Elhuyar, European and a Crown appointee,
held opposed. After the coup, Amat and Terán wrote to separate themselves
from Rayas and the proposal for a supreme junta in New Spain: "From the
moment we knew of the question, we two took the view opposite the Marqués
de Rayas." They also insisted the Marqués never spoke for the tribunal,
"whatever the director proposed, the view of the tribunal remained uncertain." The tribunal as a corporation had written to the viceroy insisting that
the votes of both Rayas and Elhuyar were *particulares*—personal. That
emphasized, Amat and Terán turned to defending Rayas, still a key leader of
the tribunal and of mining in New Spain.

"The goal of the Marqués was sound, his loyalty and love for the throne
well known. We always believed the same of the others who shared his opin-
ion. Time and subsequent actions that reveal the truth, have confirmed those
commitments. But because part of el Pueblo saw contrary designs and bas-
tard judgment, . . ." the controversy cast a shadow on the full tribunal.
Carefully, Amat and Terán suggested that those justifying the ouster of the
viceroy imagined disloyalty among Rayas and others who supported the call
to create a supreme junta in New Spain. That shadow of disloyalty tarnished
the tribunal. At the time, they had written to Iturrigaray opposing Rayas's
view, arguing that "the proposed General Representation should not be convoked, primarily because it could lead to mobilizations in the pueblos, uncertain projects, efforts to promote them, leading to grudges, flights of fancy,
and a proliferation of parties—always to be feared in times of revolution and
restlessness."

Two high officials of the Mining Tribunal confirmed, again, that the
junta gathered by Iturrigaray and the Mexico City Council, including leaders
of the tribunal, discussed calling the pueblos—towns with councils—to participate in a *junta suprema*. And they emphasized, again, that the proposal
led to fears of uncontrollable popular mobilizations—unthinkable among
the powerful. Rayas had backed the call to the pueblos to assemble in a junta;
but once the idea was rejected, he joined the rest in more limited goals. Amat
and Terán wrote to separate themselves from Rayas's moment of ardor, to
defend his ultimate loyalty, and to insist that the tribunal remained most

loyal and devoted to the sovereign—now the Seville Junta. They concluded: "Oh that His Majesty returns to throne you now occupy, . . . we your loyal vassals ask that with ardent desire!" Amat and Terán wrote to legitimate the Mining Tribunal in the eyes of the junta ruling in the king's name. If the conflicts of the summer of 1808 seemed settled in November, passions remained heated. Memories of debates and participations were contested; important men worried about others finding them on the wrong side of past (and present?) divides.

The next day, November 26, 1808, the full tribunal wrote a petition that made clear why its legitimacy was essential.[8] It was addressed to "The Supreme Governing Junta of Seville" and signed by all five members of the tribunal: the Marqués de San Juan de Rayas, don Fausto de Elhuyar, don Marcelo José de Amat, don Ygnacio de Obregón, and don Juan Antonio de Terán. Obregón was the entrepreneurial leader of the family that owned the Valenciana mines, half-brother of the Conde de Valenciana implicated in the September 17th plot to call an indio king.

The official petition aimed to show unity by honoring "our heroic resolve to resist the tyrannical yoke of the French, . . . sacrilegious and inhuman monsters of nature, . . . authors of the most detestable excesses and crimes. . . . The brilliant efforts of those who resist the French have brought joy and consolation to the loyal inhabitants of these domains." The tribunal offered honor to "all the provincial governing Juntas, Supreme and Subaltern." By honoring the Seville Junta and all others, the men of New Spain's Mining Tribunal were recognizing obliquely their own earlier divisions. Then they turned to their primary business: mining and mercury.

"Finally we have gained the peace and free navigation of the seas negotiated with the English government; and soon we will see the full provision of all the goods we have lacked because of the war." As British ships and traders brought rising imports, the Mining Tribunal did not worry about New Spain's cloth industry. They went on: "Our Miners" are especially grateful to "the Supreme Junta" that "with the greatest speed has aided them with the product most essential and necessary for the success of their businesses, mercury." Thankfully, 5,260 quintals had landed at Veracruz, just as scarce supplies threatened production. Yet they quickly added that "those 5,260 quintals of mercury are far from fully covering the current necessities of our members, given the shortages they suffered in recent years." The result was "transcendental harm to the Public and the Royal Treasury." The tribunal spoke for a "public" of mine operators and workers essential to regime revenues. Mercury had been scarce in years of wars and trade disruption when British naval power had limited deliveries to America. Now, with British allies, the tribunal insisted that "all the mercury held in the warehouses of the peninsula must be shipped immediately to our domains."

The petition concluded with a promise that was also a threat. "With the mines restored to the flourishing state they reached in recent years, the income of the Royal Treasury will rise . . . and the men of this body and those in all the other activities that depend directly or indirectly on mining will be able to show the vibrant sentiments of loyalty, love, and prosperity they wish to their Mother Country—with greater fullness than the anguished situation of the day permits." After praising the Seville Junta for sending some mercury, the men of New Spain's Mining Tribunal demanded more. If it came and mining returned to its previous prosperity, Treasury receipts and mining profits would soar, all New Spain would prosper, and loyalty to Seville's Junta would deepen. Left unsaid, yet clear to any reader: without mercury New Spain's profits, prosperity, and loyalty to the junta would wane.

The Mining Tribunal promised loyalty wrapped in a challenge: could the Seville Junta, or any other body in a Spain wracked by war and insurgency, produce sufficient mercury and ship it to New Spain to keep silver capitalism strong and the tie to Spain alive? The summer of politics had divided the leaders of the tribunal; in November they united to challenge the Seville Junta, the beneficiary of the September coup: provide mercury or see Spain and New Spain split apart—surely delivering New Spain's silver to Britain and Spain to Napoleon.

1809: The Last Year of Silver Capitalism

1809 proved a very good year for New Spain's mining and revenues sent to Seville: silver production peaked at over 26 million pesos—well above the 23 million pesos that had been the average through the 1790s and into the 1800s.[9] And silver crossed the Atlantic easily, as the tie between the post-coup regime and the Seville Junta was cemented by alliance with Britain. After Trafalgar, only British ships could cross the ocean with such rich cargo. From December of 1806 to March of 1808, before the coup, New

Spain's silver had sailed in British warships on contract to British-linked merchant houses that claimed important shares for their services. The diversion of specie to British hands helped draw Napoleon's invasion of Spain. After the coup, from December 1808 through 1809, silver shipments were larger, all on Spanish ships and consigned to recipients including el rey (the junta), the Cádiz consulado, and Spanish merchant houses (most in Seville or Cádiz)—protected by a British Navy keen to prove its commitment to a new Spanish ally.[10] For a year, the coup achieved key goals: sending silver to Seville, enabling merchants to profit in Spain and New Spain.

Challenges remained. Early in 1809, Viceroy Garibay learned that Treasury offices at most mining centers lacked funds to buy silver and ensure it was minted, taxed, accounted for, and shipped through official channels. The result was that "foreigners," often agents of British merchants, traded unminted silver for merchandise, often British textiles, diverting silver to England. In response, the Mexico City Consulado agreed to release a total of 1.5 million pesos, "to buy silver from mine operators . . . so they can release their metal and quickly pay the rising costs of their business, without having to discount their silver." New "rescue banks" would finance mines and profit miners, financiers, and the regime.[11]

Mercury was as important as financing to maintain silver flows, and it too returned to ample levels. In late July of 1809, the Mining Tribunal, still led by Rayas and Elhuyar, wrote to the Supreme Junta with profuse thanks for its commitment to deliver more than fifty thousand quintals to New Spain. It was "one of the greatest proofs of the love of Your Majesty for all your Vassals, and especially for mining in this kingdom."[12] Ample mercury sustained mining and silver revenues and solidified the loyalty of those who ruled silver capitalism in New Spain. The tribunal named don Miguel de Lardizábal y Uribe, a native of New Spain living in Seville and serving the junta, to represent its interests.[13] In September of 1809, the junta was working to ensure that iron was available to miners and that mercury was distributed fairly among refiners.[14]

The soaring silver production of 1809 fueled a year of booming trade. During the crisis year of 1808, New Spain exported through Veracruz just under 14.6 million pesos' worth of goods and specie. Of that, 4.4 million pesos was silver destined for Spain, 2.1 million went to other regions of the Americas (mostly to Cuba to sustain the Spanish Caribbean, some surely reaching the United States), and 5.4 million headed to "foreign ports"—some to the United States, most to Britain. Over 80 percent of New Spain's exports remained silver, and nearly half left for non-Spanish ports. Imports held at 10.4 million pesos, creating an apparent trade surplus, yet mostly marking revenues sent to sustain Spain and the empire. Imports from Spain were just under 2.4 million pesos, including 650,000 accounted as foreign goods (mostly cloth) sent via Spanish ports. European goods arriving from other ports in the Americas reached 500,000 pesos (again mostly cloth). And foreign ports sent 2.6 million pesos of cotton cloth (mostly British); 1.3 million pesos of linens (often French); 100,000 pesos of woolens; and 30,000 pesos of silks.[15] Half of imports were cloth, much from Britain. In the political year of 1808, mining carried on and trade held strong. Much of the benefit went to British and US merchants, British and French producers.

In 1809, the tie between Britain and Seville in place, political peace holding in New Spain, and resistance solid in Andalusia, trade through Veracruz exploded. Exports doubled from 14.4 million to 28.3 million pesos, imports from 10.4 million to 20.4 million pesos; 8 million pesos were taken as revenues. How much funded Seville and how much its British ally is unclear. It was a good year to mine silver or engage in trade. Exports as always were mostly silver: 16.3 million pesos went to Spain, meaning Cádiz and Seville; 5.45 million went to American ports (again to sustain the empire and pay for trade with the United States). If silver exports slipped to 78 percent of total trade, 75 percent of that specie now went to Spain to profit merchants and fund the war against France. New Spain was doing its part to finance Spain's fight for independence.

Among the imports drawn in 1809, 10.25 million pesos' worth were counted as Spanish goods sent from Spain, joined by 6.9 million pesos' worth of foreign goods (mostly British cloth) shipped through Spanish ports. Another 1.65 million pesos of imports came from Spain's American colonies, matched by 1.62 million pesos of foreign goods arriving via American ports. While silver exports doubled and flowed to Spain to fund resistance, imports of cloth from foreign, mostly British sources rose from 5.2 million pesos in 1808 to 8.52 million pesos in 1809.[16] The British alliance was essential to resist Napoleon; it protected Spanish shipping at sea—yet brought a flood of cloth that diverted 30 percent of New Spain's silver to Britain and assaulted a textile industry essential to hundreds of thousands of families across New

Spain. Riaño's dream of a silver boom combined with a strong cotton industry in New Spain proved impossible in time of war and alliance with Britain.

The 1809 peaks in silver production and trade kept commercial activities in Mexico City and across New Spain at near-historic high levels.[17] Those who financed and operated mines could profit nicely; those who worked in the mines and the refineries continued to face threats to life and health to gain exceptionally high wages. But those who worked directly in mining were a small minority—in the pivotal Bajío, perhaps twenty-five thousand in a population of over five hundred thousand. Most people depended on urban industries, crafts, and trade, and especially on agriculture to sustain their families. The boom in silver and trade brought profit to the financier-merchants of Mexico City; it sustained prosperity among many artisans and shopkeepers in the capital and Bajío cities and towns—while prejudicing cloth makers. Calculations of nonmining commercial activity in the Bajío show that total production had risen from the late 1780s to peak from 1801 to 1805. It then declined from 1806 through 1809 as war disrupted so much.[18]

Exploitation without Mediation: Profiteering from Drought

As silver boomed through 1809 while wider commercial activity slipped in New Spain, the agricultural sector that sustained silver mines, cities, and the rural majority faced polarizing pressures. The drought that began in the summer of 1808 and struck from the heartland around Mexico City through the Bajío deepened to plague the region through 1809 and into 1810. Maize became scarce and costly. Dearth struck consumers, urban and rural; families paid ever more of their limited incomes simply to eat. Meanwhile, scarcity brought opportunities for soaring profits to the entrepreneurs who ruled commercial cultivation. Following long-proven strategies, they held vast surpluses from previous years of good rains. When drought brought rising prices, they took peak profits by feeding desperate people—and sustaining the silver economy.[19]

The drought, dearth, and profiteering of 1808 to 1810 were not unique. The famine of 1785 and 1786 was deeper, more costly, and more deadly across the core regions of silver capitalism. The scarcity and profiteering of 1808–1810 were different because they began during the crisis of sovereignty that challenged the Spanish empire and persisted as mediating rule disintegrated in New Spain. In 1808, proclamations of the rights of the people were everywhere while maize, the people's staple, became scarce and expensive. During 1809, politics calmed, silver production soared, and trade boomed. Still, New Spain's textile industry faced assault from imports while drought deepened, maize prices soared, and landed entrepreneurs took historic profits. The people were proclaimed sovereign while they faced hunger laced with insecurities.

In the capital and elsewhere, the alhóndigas (public granaries) tried to increase maize supplies and restrain prices. Outside the city, in regions where indigenous republics shared the countryside with commercial estates, native councils negotiated release from tribute payments to cushion the cost of maize. In this time of crisis, the landed republics still claimed gains from the remnants of the mediating regime. In the Bajío, where the rural majority lived as tenants and workers on commercial estates, republics were scarce. Those who leased land were left without crops. Men who earned monthly salaries and maize rations carried on with limited difficulty. But growing numbers dependent on seasonal wages found work scarce as crops withered and maize prices soared. The dearth that mounted during 1809 brought visible profits to landed oligarchs, rising costs to mine operators as demand for silver rose, and life challenges to the majority that sustained the capital and silver capitalism.[20]

Political and social peace held through 1809. Silver boomed; drought was a recurring challenge expected to wane. Public discourse—in council chambers and barrio taverns, rural churches and village markets—focused on the fight to oust the French, redeem the promise of Fernando, and restore a precarious empire. Still, to people struggling to eat while sustaining silver capitalism and the fight against Napoleon, the blatant profiteering of a few stood in sharp relief against the struggles of the many so recently proclaimed sovereign.

Uncertain Politics, Provincial Juntas, Collapse in Spain, and the Turn to Insurgency

Through 1809, the coup of 1808 seemed to have restabilized New Spain, locked it to the Seville Junta, made Britain an essential ally in war and trade, and sent silver production to new heights. Seville depended on New Spain's silver to finance what had become Spain's war for independence. The great merchant financiers who had stood back from the coup and then adapted to its outcome flourished. Don Antonio Basoco and other financiers profited enough to send contributions of from 200,000 to 50,000 pesos each, in total over 1 million pesos, to an effort to which their profits and prospects were now fully committed. The wealth of New Spain again sustained the power of Spain, now locked together in a fight for survival.[21]

Yet politics never fully calmed in Mexico City and New Spain after the coup and the flurry of challenges and worries that followed. The military men and judges who led the coup had agreed to appoint Field Marshall Garibay as viceroy. Yermo, the struggling merchant and militia officer who had led the force that played the people and captured Iturrigaray, expected honors, influence, and favors. Garibay resisted, and Yermo complained to Seville that he was not gaining deserved recognition. Don Juan Gabriel Jabat, the commander who had represented the Seville Junta in bringing together the forces that made the coup, saw Yermo as grasping, Garibay as an "Angel of Peace" who consolidated power and pacified the city after the coup. The junta received conflicting complaints and reports of enduring spats among judges, officers, and other officials through the end of 1808 and into 1809. The divisions likely looked more troublesome in Seville—struggling to survive in the face of French threats—than in Mexico City, where silver capitalism and everyday life carried on.[22]

In February of 1809, the junta decided to replace Garibay with Mexico City Archbishop don Francisco Javier de Lizana y Beaumont. He had supported the coup and seemed a more moderating presence. The news of Garibay's ouster, however, did not arrive in New Spain's capital until July. In the interim, squabbles persisted—as did investigations into presumed conspiracies that might threaten the powers in place. On February 11, a naval pilot visiting the capital reported hearing a conversation in which a Franciscan priest, don Miguel Zugástegui, talked of plans by High Court judges Aguirre and Borbón to draw defense forces back from the coasts and deliver New Spain to the French, rather than let "sus patriotas"— autonomists—rule. Zugástegui then reportedly claimed that leading citizens of Mexico City were ready to turn the kingdom into a republic, and that within months blood would flow in the streets (presumably gachupín blood). The Franciscan was promptly arrested. Longstanding links to the radical Talamantes and a history of incendiary public comments going back to the weeks before the coup kept him jailed. Zugástegui's defense that he only repeated talk common across the city did not help his cause—or calm the authorities' nerves.[23]

On the same day the friar was overheard and arrested, the judge Aguirre received an anonymous letter (later revealed to have been written by militia captain don José María Falces) calling the Marqués de San Juan de Rayas a "malicious creole rogue," an "anti-European" holding *tertulias* (meetings) discussing the overthrow of "the legitimately constituted authorities." Rayas was said to be backed by his equally radical wife and her kin and by the great merchant, banker, landlord, and city magistrate don José María Fagoaga. Rayas's primary anger was said to be with Aguirre—who was warned of potentially dire consequences. Even when Falces admitted to a recent spat with Rayas and that most of his "news" reflected well-known divisions from the heady days before the coup, his report raised worries. Rayas had agreed to attend to Iturrigaray's financial and family interests after the coup. Yet whatever he believed, Aguirre could not act against Rayas, who remained pivotal to the Mining Tribunal and the silver flowing amply to support the junta in Seville.[24]

Worries mounted among officials of uncertain legitimacy. Later in February, the barber José Palacios reported conversations overheard in San Agustín de las Cuevas, a retreat south of the city, talking of attempts to remove Garibay and allied judges. Garibay appointed a special court of inquiry led by magistrate don Juan Collado and backed by captain don José María Arango, who was charged to build a force to apprehend, guard, and transport political prisoners, and funded by a 3,000 pesos allotment. Political justice became militarized.[25]

In April, one José María Aguilar reported walking through the Alameda earlier in the year and hearing talk of removing all europeos from official positions, replacing them with criollos, and organizing a junta in the city—long after such questions were supposedly settled by the coup.[26] Soon after the report, Garibay prohibited the sale and use of "hand presses," the small portable presses that allowed the rapid production, posting, and distribution of so much the authorities found objectionable. In June he enlarged the court prosecuting "treasons" to a three-judge panel.[27] Business was apparently growing.

Worried authorities kept investigating. Yet they feared the consequences of public inquiries and punishments. So they investigated, sentenced a number of presumed incendiaries—Acuña and Morales, Talamantes and Zugástegui—to death, then commuted their sentences and sent them off to

Seville. They followed Iturrigaray, who had demanded and gained a full hearing of the charges against him. Talamantes and Zugástegui got to the fortress of San Juan de Ulúa, an island in the harbor off Veracruz, where they died of yellow fever. Lesser threats, Acuña, Morales, and others, were held in the upland fort at Perote until passage could be arranged. They made it to Seville, where they were kept until later released. Several would join the fight for autonomies in New Spain after 1810.

On July 19, 1809, the decree replacing Garibay with Archbishop Lizana y Beaumont arrived in the capital. Lizana was expected to be more of a "conciliator." Could he recreate legitimate mediating rule, stabilize New Spain, and keep silver flowing to Spain? He could try. But the old ways and legitimacies were gone. Seditions kept coming to officials' ears. By late September, Lizana had appointed a new tribunal charged with prosecuting what was called the "French party"—any opponent of rule by Seville now presumed to back Napoleon. Continuing "seditious rumors" were to be uncovered and prosecuted.[28] The price of illegitimacy grounded in militarized impositions was a turn from mediation to paranoia.

Under Lizana, political discontent began to rise in key provinces. Valladolid was capital of the Intendancy of Michoacán, a region mixing Tarascan communities to the south and west with commercial estates supplying the Bajío and its mines just north. Its bishopric oversaw the core of the Bajío, including the Guanajuato mines and surrounding estates—from which it drew tithes. A group of provincial elites, landowners and professionals, including commanders of the militias founded or fortified in the 1790s, began to meet in August of 1809.

They knew of the plans a year earlier to call a congress that would have given them a voice in remaking sovereignty. They knew how the coup that mobilized military force in the name of the people blocked their participation. Michoacán militias had been drawn to the capital to contain the people on September 16, 1808. As news from Europe and Mexico City brought glimpses of continuing conflicts and new ferment, a year later they gathered to discuss rights and roles. They talked of challenging the regime imposed by the coup. They envisioned a junta to defend New Spain from French rule—as they feared the men of Mexico City would not. The Valladolid plotters saw traditional rights in the sovereignty of the pueblos. They considered military assertions to topple the post-coup regime in Mexico City. Divisions and debates ensured they had not acted when leaks to local authorities led to the arrest of key participants in December 1809. Sent to Mexico City, they faced interrogation. Lizana, seeking a return to mediation, released most with admonitions to obedience.[29] The archbishop-viceroy and the Valladolid plotters all opposed French rule.

The new government carried on under Lizana into 1810. Peak flows of silver delivered profits to the powerful in New Spain and essential revenue to Seville. But the alliance between Spain and New Spain, better, between Seville and Mexico City, began to erode when Napoleon's troops routed Spanish forces at Ocaña, near Toledo, south of Madrid, on November 19, 1809. A march to the south followed. By February 1810, "the situation in Spain was desperate"; French troops occupied Seville and the junta once recognized as supreme fled, leaving a regency clinging to the peninsula at Cádiz.[30] There, a faction tied to merchants in New Spain ousted Lizana on February 22—news not known in Mexico City until May 8. In the interim, less-certain rumors and reports arrived telling of the advance of French forces and the demise of the Seville Junta—with definitive news of the latter coming only in April. By May 1810 it was clear that there was no junta in Seville—and no viceroy in Mexico City. A self-designated regency in Cádiz, subject to merchant power there, would lead the fight against Napoleon. The Audiencia would struggle to rule in Mexico City, with no viceroy to mediate or impose.[31] Could sovereignty and government be any closer to absolute vacancy? What legitimacy was possible?

In May, the Cádiz Regency named don Francisco Javier de Venegas viceroy of New Spain. A general who had led the fight to delay the French march to the south and helped set the remnant regime in Cádiz, his rule would maintain the military hue of the regime. He did not arrive in Mexico City until September 14, 1810.[32] Before he could begin to assess conditions in New Spain, the Bajío exploded in insurgency two days later, led by provincial elites declaring allegiance to the captive Fernando while calling the people to arms to save a monarchy presumed about to fall to Napoleon.

Provincial Politics and Unimagined Insurgencies

After the search for a junta at Valladolid in the fall of 1809 did not prosper, the news from Europe became more devastating during the spring of 1810. When it became clear in May that the Seville Junta had collapsed, that New

Spain was without a viceroy, and that the record flow of silver in the previous year had funded no known triumph, a second group of provincials began to meet at Querétaro, a key commercial center linking Mexico City, Guanajuato, the Bajío, and regions north—the primary axis of silver capitalism. Again, the goal was to discuss a junta that might speak for the Spanish cities of New Spain in defense of Fernando and against any attempt to impose French rule. Don Miguel Domínguez, an American who had protested the consolidation in 1805, remained corregidor, the royal magistrate at Querétaro. He hosted meetings that drew the leading merchant, landlord, and councilman don Pedro Septién along with artisans, shopkeepers, and others. Men who had plotted at Valladolid and notables from Guanajuato towns came too, including San Miguel landlord and militia commander don Ignacio de Allende and the priest-landlord don Miguel Hidalgo from the outlying parish at Dolores.

Most agreed on the need to defend New Spain from the French—in the name of Fernando; there was broad interest in the right to call a junta, to mobilize the sovereignty of the pueblos. Debate focused on a call to arms. Some provincial militia commanders, like Allende, were ready to raise forces to back a junta. Others, including Domínguez and other powerful Querétaro provincials, were less sure of a turn to arms or the people.[33] The goal was to defend New Spain, silver capitalism, and the social order. The question was how.

As participants sought wider support: "between September 9 and 15, denunciations flooded the authorities."[34] A potential turn to arms and the people worried many; they reported contacts to separate themselves from the planning. On the evening of September 15, two years after Yermo led militiamen to topple Viceroy Iturrigaray, local commanders loyal to the post-coup regime rounded up the "conspirators" they could in Querétaro, including Domínguez, Septién, and others. Domínguez's wife, doña Josefa Rodríguez, la corregidora, remained free and sent word to Allende at San Miguel that the group had been broken. Seeking to stay ahead of men coming to arrest him, Allende rode north to Dolores. He and Hidalgo spent a night debating what to do. In the morning, as people gathered for Sunday mass, Hidalgo called them to rise in defense of Fernando and true religion—and against Napoleon.

Hidalgo and Allende expected support from a core of militiamen in the local regiments founded in the 1790s. Allende and a few allies commanded units they could mobilize, perhaps fifteen hundred men. The Grito on Sunday morning in Dolores addressed a gathering of diverse people who had assembled for mass—local notables, shopkeepers, and artisans, along with mulattos, mestizos, and Otomí who lived herding livestock and working the land at outlying estates. Within hours, uncounted thousands joined Hidalgo and Allende on a march southward. At the sanctuary of Atotonilco, a center of penitential devotion just north of San Miguel, they found a banner honoring Guadalupe in the basement and made it their flag. The Virgin called to calm crowds in the capital in 1808 became the symbol of a people in arms in 1810.[35]

When the growing rebel mass arrived in San Miguel, thousands more joined. A week later they held Celaya, with insurgent throngs then estimated in the tens of thousands. Before September ended, they took Guanajuato. Local elites led by Intendant Riaño sought refuge in the city granary, the alhóndiga. They paid with their lives in the fortress that stored the silver city's sustenance, a massive symbol of the mediating regime that no longer kept the people at peace and at work. From the start it was clear that the people in arms had their own visions and goals. They defended Fernando and attacked gachupines—Spanish immigrant officials and traders, long resented, and now hated after they had posed as the pueblo to lead the coup that denied the sovereignty of the pueblos and broke the regime of mediation.

Yet the populace in arms in the Bajío also and insistently attacked haciendas, whether owned by Americans or Europeans, emptying granaries to feed themselves and families still hungry on the eve of the next harvest. The people demanded justice and sustenance.[36] They fought for what the regime of mediation had long promised and often delivered. Now, after the coup and two years of hunger without effective mediations, with promises of popular sovereignty tied to armed force in the air, and with newly inflamed hatreds of gachupines everywhere, people across the Bajío took arms to assert their interests—in the name of the captive Fernando.

By the summer of 1810, Spanish power was collapsing in Spain, despite record flows of New Spain's silver the previous year. Officials in Mexico City were locked in a relationship that sent wealth to a dying regime. Seeing that, provincials in the Bajío, the productive core of silver capitalism, aimed to create juntas, joining the Spanish tradition of recreating sovereignty as it appeared about to break for a second time in Spain. When the authorities set in power in Mexico City by the 1808 coup broke a Querétaro movement already stymied by worries about calling the people to arms, a few outlying provincials took the risk of making just such a call. The number and diversity of those who responded astonished everyone.

Political men did not fully understand the unprecedented life challenges that had struck people across the Bajío during the previous decades. After the great drought, famine, and profiteering of 1785 and 1786, from the 1790s on landed entrepreneurs had imposed declining wages, rent increases, and evictions on rural families. Incomes fell, insecurities spread, and working men struggled to provide family sustenance—challenging claims to household patriarchy. Mine operators at Guanajuato pressed to maximize silver flows and profits by cutting workers' ore shares, wages, and food rations.[37] The drought, famine, and profiteering that began in 1808 layered onto those predations while political elites in the capital proclaimed the people sovereign— and then gachupines took arms to impose a coup, insisting that *they* were the people.

A perfect vortex of provincial elite frustration, social polarization, popular grievance, and ideological expectation generated the explosion of 1810. The rains cooperated. That September the first good maize crop in two years stood ripe in fields across the Bajío, free for the taking by men with starving families, called to arms to defend a captive king. To the people, sovereignty and the common good began with sustenance.

What followed is well known. The Hidalgo revolt rose and fell in four months, its leaders captured, tried, and executed. It spawned a mix of political and popular insurgencies that endured through the next decade. Quickly grasping their ultimate interests, the powerful men of Mexico City and Querétaro united to fight political and popular insurgents, aiming to protect silver capitalism and sustain Spanish rule—or at least rule by the alliance of Spaniards, American and European, that had long benefited from New Spain's silver economy. They failed. By 1812, silver production had dropped to half the level of 1808–1809, to hold low for the rest of the decade and long after. The Spanish regime fell in New Spain in 1821—toppled in the end by the military men (led by don Agustín Iturbide, American son of an immigrant from Spain) who had fought since 1808 to defend Spain, silver capitalism, and the coup that set them in power.

Mexico was born in political and social violence, every faction proclaiming a vision of popular sovereignty backed by armed power. In that conflictive process, the silver economy and regime of mediation that for centuries had made New Spain wealthy, stable, and central to global capitalism were destroyed.[38] The Mexican nation that emerged would be plagued by violence and instability unknown in New Spain before the crises and transformations of 1808–1810.

Popular Politics and Coercive Powers

Mexico and the World

ON SEPTEMBER 15–16, 1808, AFTER NAPOLEON HAD BROKEN THE Spanish monarchy in May and people in Mexico City lived a summer of demonstrations and debates seeking popular sovereignty, military men led a coup that toppled the viceroy who ruled in the capital of silver capitalism. They ended centuries of rule by mediation and turned the regime toward reliance on organized violence—while claiming to be and serve the people. On September 15–16, 1810, a clique of provincial elites in the Bajío, the productive center of a still-booming yet socially polarized silver capitalism, called the people to arms to demand political participations. Thousands took arms in a search for food, social justice, and more independent lives on the land. Political crisis led to social revolution.

The goals of the two turns to violent power could not have been more different. The Mexico City 1808 coup aimed to end political and popular participations and lock New Spain and its booming silver economy in service of Spain's fight against Napoleon. In 1810, provincial elites in the Bajío demanded political participations—and opened the way for a struggling populace to take arms in search of sustainable lives. The means were the same: violence in the name of the people. In two fateful years, politics changed irrevocably—with transforming political, economic, and social consequences.

From 1810 on, violence contested everything that mattered in New Spain: power and production, politics and social relations, ideology and culture, and more.[1] After the defeat and collapse of the brief Hidalgo revolt, men at arms—José María Morelos, Vicente Guerrero, and many others less famous—led a fight for political participations that in time became a drive for independence (inflamed by anger against the gachupines who played the people in the 1808 coup). During the same years of conflict after 1810, people working the land in diverse communities—most anonymous to history, yet sure they were the people—fought to gain a different kind of independence: autonomies of sustenance on the land.[2]

In the face of those violent risings, political and popular, the regime remade by the 1808 coup found staunch backing in the Mexico City oligarchy and among most provincial elites; they built loyal militias into a military machine to fight insurgents demanding political independence and popular autonomies. Even the now-chastened Conde de Peñasco took a command against those who challenged the rule of property after 1810.[3] When popular communities took arms against landed power, he and his father, the landed priest-oligarch don José Sánchez Espinosa, had much to lose. Violence became the essential means to defend power and profit.

In the face of simultaneous wars to defeat French armies in Spain and defend Spanish power, property, and silver capitalism in New Spain, a cortes met in Cádiz to write a new constitution for the empire in 1812. Clinging to the last bit of land under Spanish rule in the peninsula, desperate political men worked to forge a new regime that could hold the empire together and mobilize its resources to fight Napoleon. They proclaimed liberal rule and promised electoral rights to the people on both sides of the Atlantic. They gave homogenous rights to individual men, ending the regime of multiple corporate rights and diverse mediations that had long integrated Spain and its dominions and stabilized silver capitalism. Written to sustain Spanish armies in Spain, New Spain, and beyond, the 1812 Cádiz Constitution tied an abstract popular sovereignty to universal male electoral rights, all to sustain military powers.[4] The regime of mediation would be replaced by a new state.

When Napoleon fell and Fernando regained his throne in Spain, he abrogated the liberal Constitution and the rights it promised. He did not return to rule by mediation. Instead, he reinforced military power, aiming to win the continuing war against insurgents in New Spain. Leading political rebels were killed or contained by 1815; popular insurgents in the Bajío held off counterinsurgency campaigns until they accepted pacifications that consolidated lives on the land after 1818. Then, just as New Spain seemed to calm, in 1820 military men in Spain, led by Colonel Rafael Riego, refused to sail to fight Simón Bolívar in South America—unless Fernando reinstated the Constitution. They would not be the military force of the regime unless it promised rights to the people. Fernando, his rule dependent on armed forces, acquiesced.[5] The link between popular sovereignty and military power at the core of the original Hispanic liberalism was set—and clear to all who would see.

When the military men who had led the fight against insurgencies, political and popular, in New Spain learned of the return to Cádiz's liberal promises of political participations (including indigenous peoples, but excluding those of African ancestry—to keep Cuba in the empire), staunch royalist don Agustín Iturbide returned to arms to forge a union with insurgent survivor Vicente Guerrero (a mulatto), to break with Spain and declare a Mexican monarchy in 1821. At the head of troops—most royalist, others once insurgent, for a moment reuniting European and American Spaniards—they claimed Mexican independence as a monarchy proclaimed in service of the people.[6] Mexico was born in a crucible of people in arms.

In the process, the decade of armed political and social conflicts destroyed silver capitalism. The coup of 1808 aimed explicitly to preserve and promote silver production to sustain Spain against Napoleon. Mining and trade boomed for two more years, until insurgencies in the Bajío surrounding the Guanajuato mines and in the Mezquital near Real del Monte brought it down. By 1812, silver production was cut in half by risings that corroded silver production at Guanajuato, Real de Monte, and elsewhere.

The long popular insurgencies that transformed life and work in the Bajío responded to decades of deepening challenges to everyday life among producing families: predations imposed on the populace by capitalists driving to profit in a world of uncertainty after 1790.[7] Impositions by mine operators and agrarian capitalists deepened from 1808 as drought and famine brought profiteering from desperation—amid widening proclamations of popular rights followed by the coup that militarized power and stymied mediation. Capitalist predations, proclamations of popular sovereignty, and a coup that blocked regime mediations merged to set off the insurgencies that brought down silver capitalism—and then Spain's empire.

For a decade, silver mined at half the levels sustained before 1810 funded counterinsurgent campaigns, with little left to send to Spain. Nothing remained for investment in mines and infrastructure.[8] Mining did not revive after independence in 1821. Silver yields stayed depressed into the 1840s, constraining the commercial economy and limiting government revenues. Meanwhile, the military that rose to contain insurgents and then founded the nation remained and demanded to be paid. The revenue deficits that plagued the national state after 1821 resulted from depressed silver production and revenues while military costs (minimal in New Spain) held high.[9] While entrepreneurs searched for a new economy in the wake of the fall of silver capitalism, militarized political factions proclaiming variants of popular sovereignty crippled Mexicans' attempts to consolidate a national regime for decades.

Mexico City's summer of politics and coup of 1808 was followed by a decade of uncivil wars, political and social, locking in a politics of militarized power grounded in claims of popular sovereignty—the essence of the states proclaimed modern that rose to organize and contest the new, increasingly industrial world forged in the nineteenth century. In Mexico the unplanned and contested rise of such a state came tied to the collapse of a once dynamic, globally important silver capitalism. The new nation that came out of the conflicts of 1808 to 1821, briefly a Mexican monarchy, then a republic from 1824, searched simultaneously for a new polity and a new economy. Politicians fueled hatred of gachupines to mask the underlying economic collapse, revenue shortfalls, and military impositions.[10] Meanwhile, communities on the land took proclamations of popular sovereignty seriously, worked to serve their own needs and goals, and periodically took arms to contest divided, weak, yet often intrusive state powers.[11] Mexico began in a long conflict shaped by diverse claims of popular sovereignty tied to assertions of armed power—all begun in the summer of 1808 in Mexico City.

The historic invasions, mobilizations, and conflicts that broke New Spain's regime of mediation, took down silver capitalism, and brought Spain's imperial collapse came as a key, perhaps culminating, episode in a larger Atlantic process of state making amid economic transformations. In the later sixteenth century, the Dutch Republic proclaimed popular rights while mobilizing military forces to escape Spanish Hapsburg rule—and to press imperial-commercial powers across the globe.[12] In the middle of the

seventeenth century, armed factions fought for power in England while facing popular mobilizations. Oliver Cromwell led military forces that ousted
monarchical powers for over a decade in a process that mobilized and then
contained groups such as the Levellers demanding popular rights—all while
England accelerated militarized imperial expansions. In North America,
new assertions of regime power mixed with risings of native peoples and
poor Englishmen—set first to fighting each other, then leading to new
accommodations with colonists, violence against natives, and a turn toward
enslaved Africans to force labor and profit the few. The restored English
monarchy of 1660, reinforced by the Dutch invasion that set William and
Mary on the throne in the "Glorious Revolution" of 1688, was indelibly
marked by the theories of popular sovereignty promulgated by John Locke.[13]
Such celebrated proclamations of popular sovereignty should not blind us to
their grounding in armed power—and service as legitimations.

The eighteenth century brought new British expansions in search of
profitable trade, always backed by military power. That drive led to the Seven
Years' War of 1757–1763, creating the costs and debts that led to revenue
demands backed by military assertions in North America in 1765. Colonials
resisted by demanding rights as Englishmen; cycles of British armed assertion and colonial resistance led to a declaration of independence proclaiming
popular sovereignty—and aiming to draw enlistments in armies fighting
British power. Independent popular risings proved limited in British North
America because so many were held in slavery—the other coercion too often
at the heart of the rise of popular sovereignties. Slaveholding General George
Washington was acclaimed founding father of a United States proclaiming
the people sovereign.[14]

Soon, France's military support for the US war for independence created
debts its old regime could not pay. In 1789, the monarchy called the Estates
General seeking funds. Conflicts over rights and powers escalated into a revolution that brought rising political violence, popular assertions, and new
proclamations of popular sovereignty—rights of man imagined as liberty,
equality, and fraternity (insistently male). A volatile mix of military power
and popular sovereignty marked revolutionary France until Napoleon made
power fully military and sovereignty popular only in rhetoric.

Meanwhile, as French revolutionaries debated popular rights, attempts by
diverse peoples in Saint-Domingue to claim such rights in a society 90 percent

enslaved led to new and different violent conflicts that in time ended slavery there. As Saint-Domingue became Haiti, armed men escaping slavery kept popular power real; they built autonomies on the land, pushing back against rulers dreaming of keeping plantation production alive. A testy balance between armed people strong on the land and military rulers seeking a state sustained by commercial revenues shaped the difficult formation of a Haitian nation forged by armed powers claiming and contesting popular rights.[15]

After the loss of Saint-Domingue and its revenues and the destruction of his navy at Trafalgar, Napoleon provoked the invasion of Spain that set off the transatlantic crises of Spain and New Spain in 1808. Again, invasion, armed political conflicts, and popular risings mixed in conflicts in which militarized powers and proclamations of popular sovereignty fused. The republics of Spanish America gained independence in variants—often radically different variants—of the processes detailed here for New Spain's becoming Mexico. Proclamations of popular sovereignty coincided with the rise of militarized powers across the hemisphere.[16] And links binding military power to assertions of popular sovereignty rooted in the Cádiz Constitution extended far beyond the Americas. Military insurgents pressed the Cádiz liberal model across Mediterranean Europe and into Russia in the 1820s.[17] Demands for popular sovereignty spread, tied to and backed by military power—all within political and imperial contexts grounded in the contested history of capitalism.

As Spain's empire began to consolidate the gains of early silver capitalism after 1550, the Dutch mixed popular rule and military assertions to escape Spanish rule and take their own imperial role in early capitalist expansions. The violent politics and popular legitimations of Cromwell's England produced Navigation Acts that aimed to claim a British role in world trade then dominated by Spanish, Portuguese, and Dutch merchants. The war that led to a US independence framed in promises of popular rights also imagined a more prosperous place for mainland British America in an Atlantic capitalism led by Caribbean plantation regimes.

France fell into revolution in 1789 in good part because its military attempts to hold a place in Atlantic capitalism proved too costly to sustain. The enslaved people of Saint-Domingue took advantage of the conflicts and promises of revolutionary Paris to take arms against the predations inherent in lives as enslaved producers in France's engine of plantation capitalism.

And facing the loss of Haiti, Napoleon mobilized military power built on revolutionary dreams to invade Spain. Seeking the wealth of New Spain's silver, he broke Spain's empire, provoked conflicts mixing popular claims and armed powers that undermined silver capitalism, all leading to a Hispanic liberalism that mixed dreams of popular rights grounded in spreading armed powers across widening regions grappling with the rise of a new industrial capitalism built on an inseparable mix of liberations and coercions.[18]

In the age of wars and revolutions that rattled the Atlantic world from the 1770s to the 1820s, new states emerged to shape "modern" industrial capitalism. Monarchies grounded in diverse corporations, open to diverse laws, ruling by mediations backed by limited concentrations of coercion gave way to states proclaiming popular sovereignty, insisting on homogeneous law, enforced by concentrations of coercion.[19] Participations set in claims of popular sovereignty mixed with coercive, often militarized powers in complex and diverse ways. Throughout, popular sovereignties and armed powers rose together and remain inseparable.

The promoters of "democratic capitalism" imagine regimes in which the people rule—with military and police power in the background. Yet close examinations of the complexities of history, past and present, reveal that popular rights and participations have repeatedly faced constraints imposed by coercive powers claiming legitimacy as expressions of popular sovereignty. In 1808, the people of Mexico City, the powerful few and a diverse majority, found themselves at the center of a pivotal transformation. Provoked by Napoleon's military assault on Spain's monarchy, they dreamed of popular participations—to face military closure followed by a decade of violent conflicts that destroyed silver capitalism and ended their time as the leading metropolis in the Americas. A long, hard, and conflictive rebuilding followed, searching for a new regime set in popular sovereignty while militarized powers held strong—and for a new place in a world being remade by a new industrial capitalism.[20]

Notes

Abbreviations

AGI	Archivo General de Indias, Seville, Spain
AGN	Archivo General de la Nación, Mexico City, Mexico
AHN	Archivo Histórico Nacional, Madrid, Spain
CSC	Condes de Santiago Calimaya Papers, Biblioteca Nacional, Mexico City, Mexico
DM	Diario de México
GC	García Collection, Benson Latin American Collection, University of Texas at Austin
GM	Gazeta de México
HDC	Hernández y Dávalos, J. E., *Colección de documentos para la historia de la guerra de independencia en México de 1808 a 1821*, 5 vols. (1877–1882, reprinted, Mexico City: Sistema Postal de la República Mexicana, 1977).
JSE	José Sánchez Espinosa Papers, Benson Latin American Collection, University of Texas at Austin
PCR	Papeles de los Condes de Regla, Washington State University Library, Pullman, Washington
PCRb	bound volumes in PCR
PCRun	uncatalogued materials in PCR
WBS	W. B. Stevens Collection, Benson Latin American Collection, University of Texas at Austin

Preface

1. On the wider processes of change across the Americas, see Tutino, *New Countries*.
2. On slavery, independence, and economic expansion in the United States, see Morgan's classic *American Slavery, American Freedom*; and Baptist's powerful *Half Has Never Been Told*.

3. On the contradictions of the Haitian Revolution, see Dubois, *Avengers of the New World*.

4. On the contradictions of Cádiz liberalism in a fragmenting empire, see Breña, *El primer liberalismo*.

Introduction

1. As I finished this work, Elías Palti published *An Archaeology of the Political*. That important and innovative study sets Spanish political traditions in a broad comparative context from the seventeenth century to contemporary times, with an emphasis on movements toward Spanish American independence in the early nineteenth century. His study came to me too late to fully engage here. I would suggest that this inquiry is a local yet pivotal case study of processes Palti engages more broadly. We converge in emphasizing that conceptual visions are best understood as they inform and/or legitimate practices—I would add conflicts, a particular kind of practice. I hope readers will engage our two studies as part of an important larger conversation.

2. Stein and Stein, *Crisis in an Atlantic Empire*.

3. This is the culminating focus of Tutino, *Making a New World*.

4. For an analytical survey of the politics of 1808 to 1821 and the conflicts that turned New Spain into Mexico, see Ávila, *En nombre de la nación*. For a more recent and still political view, see Rodríguez, *We Are Now the True Spaniards*. On provincial conflicts after 1810, Van Young, *Other Rebellion*, remains essential. For a brief synthesis in English, see Tutino, *Mexican Heartland*, chapter 5.

5. The intersection and inseparability of these processes is the focus of Tutino, *New Countries*.

6. My understanding of the US war for independence is shaped by Edmund Morgan's two classic studies: *American Slavery, American Freedom* and *Inventing the People*. For a narrative that makes clear the interplay of military power and political ideology, see Countryman, *American Revolution*. For a new view that emphasizes that as the world industrialized and the United States became more prosperous and "democratic," it depended for decades on a "war capitalism" grounded in the enslavement of the producers in its leading economic sector, see Baptist, *Half Has Never Been Told*; and Beckert, *Empire of Cotton*.

7. On the origins, course, and ramifications of the French Revolution, Furet, *Revolutionary France*, is most useful. On the Haitian Revolution, the reigning synthesis is Dubois, *Avengers of the New World*. On the mix of popular power and military force during and after the Haitian conflict, see Fick, "From Slave Colony to Black Nation."

8. For a recent example, see Klooster, *Revolutions in the Atlantic World*.

9. See Tutino, *Making a New World*; and Giráldez, *Age of Trade*.

10. Kamen, *Empire*, offers a synthesis that emphasizes global reach and flexibility.

11. On profit-seeking inequity as the essence of capitalism, see scholars ranging from Braudel, *Civilization and Capitalism*, to Piketty, *Capital in the Twenty-First Century*. Piketty adds that unconstrained inequities may destabilize capitalism.

12. The role of the state in stabilizing capitalism has been a key concern in Marxian debates (see Poulantzas, *Political Power and Social Classes*) and liberal orthodoxies (see North, Wallis, and Weingast, *Violence and Social Orders*).

13. The vision lives in a new and more historically sophisticated version in Elliott, *Empires of the Atlantic World*.

14. Made powerfully clear in Crosby, *Columbian Exchange*.

15. See Taylor, *Magistrates of the Sacred*; Hughes, *Biography of a Mexican Crucifix*; and my synthesis in Tutino, *Mexican Heartland*.

16. This is an emphasis of Tutino, *Making a New World*, reinforced in Tutino, *Mexican Heartland*.

17. This is another emphasis of Tutino, *Making a New World*; see also Guevara Sanginés, *Guanajuato diverso*.

18. This was detailed in Archer, *Army in Bourbon Mexico*.

19. A vision countered by many of the works grounded in indigenous language sources and that culminated in Lockhart, *Nahuas after the Conquest*; and by Tutino, *Making a New World* and *Mexican Heartland*.

20. Borah, *Justice by Insurance*; Taylor, *Drinking, Homicide, and Rebellion*; and Owensby, *Empire of Law*.

21. Cañeque, *King's Living Image*.

22. Grafe and Irigoin, "A Stakeholder Empire." An early version much influenced *Making a New World*.

23. Sánchez de Tagle, *Del gobierno y su tutela*.

24. Lempérière, *Entre Dios y el rey*.

25. See Collins, *State in Early Modern France*.

26. On the impact in China, see Lin, *China Upside Down*.

27. See Tutino, "Capitalist Foundations."

28. In *The Dead March*, Peter Guardino also emphasizes that the economic disparity between a powerful United States and a struggling Mexico led to the outbreak and outcomes of the Mexican-American War. He sees the disparity, however, as a colonial legacy; I emphasize that it came from the complex conflicts of 1770 to 1830—notably the fall of silver capitalism as New Spain became Mexico and the rise of the "war capitalism" grounded in slavery in the United States. On the latter, see Baptist, *Half Has Never Been Told*; and Beckert, *Empire of Cotton*.

29. See Tutino, "Americas in the Rise of Industrial Capitalism"; on monopolies of coercion and popular participations in the rise of modern capitalism, see North, Wallis, and Weingast, *Violence and Social Orders*.

Chapter 1

1. This synthesis of the pre-Hispanic city relies on Clendinnen, *Aztecs*; Hassig, *Trade, Tribute, and Transportation*; and Palerm, *Obras hidráulicas prehispánicas*.

2. On Mexica religion and expansion, see Padden, *Hummingbird and the Hawk*; and Conrad and Demarest, *Religion and Empire*.

3. Hassig, *Trade, Tribute, and Transportation*. Katz, "Rural Rebellion," details the risings against late Mexica power.

4. Clendinnen, *Aztecs*, emphasizes legitimacy within the metropolis; Padden, *Hummingbird and the Hawk*, details illegitimacy and resentment among conquered peoples.

5. This is explored in Mundy, *Death of Aztec Tenochtitlan*.

6. This analysis follows Crosby's classic *Columbian Exchange*.

7. The process is followed in Mundy, *Death of Aztec Tenochtitlan*.

8. Ruiz Medrano, *Reshaping New Spain*, is the best study of early government.

9. Calnek, "Conjunto urbano."

10. The rise of silver capitalism in the basins around Mexico City is the focus of Tutino, *Mexican Heartland*, chapters 1–3.

11. On early mining at Taxco, see Enciso Contreras, *Taxco en el siglo XVI*; on Pachuca, see Cubillo Moreno, *Los dominios de la plata*. On the Mexico City Mint, see Castro Gutiérrez, *Real Casa de Moneda*.

12. On northern mining and its links to Mexico City, see Tutino, *Making a New World*.

13. On people of African ancestry in Mexico City, see Velázquez Gutiérrez, *Las mujeres de origen africana*.

14. This transformation is detailed in Tutino, *Mexican Heartland*, chapter 2.

15. The challenge of water and the impact of the *desague* are detailed in Candiani, *Dreaming of Dry Land*.

16. On power and politics in the early seventeenth-century city, see Israel, *Race, Class, and Politics*; and Hoberman, *Mexico's Merchant Elite*.

17. On political life in the city under Spanish rule, see Torres Puga, "La ciudad novohispana"; Israel, *Race, Class, and Politics*, deals with the riotous politics of 1624 in revealing detail.

18. On the cultural shift in the city, see Poole, *Our Lady of Guadalupe*; Sousa, Poole, and Lockhart, *Story of Guadalupe*; and Brading, *First America*.

19. On Sor Juana, see Paz, *Sor Juana*; on intellectual ferment of the age, see Leonard, *Baroque Times in Old Mexico*.

20. See Cope, *Limits of Racial Domination*; and Silva Prada, *La política de una rebelión*.

21. On New Spain's silver and the rise of Bourbon power, see Tutino, *Making a New World*, chapter 3.

22. See Walker, *Tupac Amaru Rebellion*; and Serulnikov, *Revolution in the Andes*.

23. On the rural transformation that sustained the city, see Tutino, *Mexican Heartland*, chapter 3.
24. This synthesizes the foundational analysis of Florescano, *Precios del maíz*.
25. On the epidemic and its impact, see Molina del Villar, *La Nueva España y el Matlazahuatl*, and her *Diversidad socioétnica*.
26. See Tutino, *Making a New World*, chapter 4; and Castro Gutiérrez, *Nueva ley y nuevo rey*.
27. The essential history of these conflicts is Castro Gutiérrez, *Nueva ley y nuevo rey*. My analysis in the context of silver capitalism is in Tutino, *Making a New World*, chapter 4. In the sugar islands of the British and French Caribbean, the war created disruptions that provoked attempts at slave resistance, followed by harsh new racial impositions. The trades in sugar and enslaved peoples soared through the postwar decades as both engines of New World capitalism energized after the war and its disruptions. See Burnard and Garrigus, *Plantation Machine*.
28. See Tutino, *Making a New World*.
29. This is emphasized in Tutino, *Mexican Heartland*, chapter 1.
30. The term is from Beckert, *Empire of Cotton*.
31. See Owensby, *Empire of Law*.
32. See Tutino, *Making a New World*, chapter 4, and Lempérière, *Entre Dios y el rey*.

Chapter 2

1. The continuing dynamism of silver and its importance to Atlantic trade and war are detailed in Marichal, *La bancarrota del virreinato*, an important study that emphasizes the collapse after 1808.
2. See Brading, *Miners and Merchants*, and Tutino, *Making a New World*.
3. On militias, see Archer, *Army in Bourbon Mexico*, and Vinson, *Bearing Arms for His Majesty*.
4. See Castro Gutiérrez, *Real Casa de Moneda*, 43, for minting levels, and 62–65 for the silver bankers' roles; silver production levels are in Tutino, *Making a New World*, 550.
5. On eighteenth-century mint output, see Castro Gutiérrez, *Real Casa de Moneda*, 120; on mining, Tutino, *Making a New World*, 550.
6. The classic study of this shift is Burkholder and Chandler, *From Impotence to Authority*.
7. The identification of this pattern came in Brading in *Miners and Merchants*.
8. For Mexico City estate entrepreneurs operating properties in the Bajío, see Tutino, *Making a New World*, chapters 5 and 7; for those working estates near the capital, see Tutino, *Mexican Heartland*, chapter 3.
9. Brading, *Miners and Merchants*, 40; Ladd, *Mexican Nobility at Independence*; "Ynstancia de don Ygnacio Leonel Gómez de Cervantes . . . 1793," G257 in GC-BLA Collection.

10. On Mier and the Santiagos, PCR: V. 109, 1 Mar. 1788; 14 Mar. 1788; V. 115, 20 Mar. 1795; V. 123, f. 46, 9 Jun. 1801; V. 124, f. 69, 6 Mar. 1802; f. 49, 23 Jun. 1802; f. 58, 13 Jul. 1802; V. 125, f. 3, Jan. 1803; V. 129, f. 4, 8 May 1805; also GM, 4 Jun. 1804. On the Santiago family under women's rule, see Tutino, "Power, Class, and Family." On profiteering in Mexico City's food supply, the essential study is Florescano, *Precios del maíz*.

11. Tutino, *Making a New World*, 283.

12. See Brading, *Miners and Merchants*, 117; Lohman Villena, *Los Americanos*, II, 338; Romero de Terreros, *Antiguas haciendas*, 103–106; Romero de Terreros, *Testimonios relativos*, 7–8; JSE, V. 213, n. 410, 5 Nov. 1800; PCR, V. 123, f. 52, 21 Jun. 1801; PCR, uncatalogued materials, "Ynventario de . . . la Casa del Señor Conde de Santa María de Regla (c. 1782), f. 65; DM, 21 Mar. 1813, 11 Dec. 1815.

13. Couturier, *Silver King*.

14. This early career is reconstructed from PCRun, 1765, "Testamento de don Manuel Rodríguez de Pedroso"; PCRun, 1767 "Testimonio de . . . don Joseph Julián Rodríguez García de Arellano"; PCRb (bound volumes), "Condado de Jala . . . 1836."

15. Rodríguez de Pedroso's trades are in PCRun, 1765, "Testamento de . . . d. Manuel Rodríguez de Pedroso." On Mexico City merchants' dominant roles in the Manila trade, the key study is Yuste López, *Emporios transpacíficos*; on cacao and Caracas, see Arcila Farías, *Comercio entre Venezuela y México*, 40; on cochineal and Oaxaca, the classic study is Hamnett, *Politics and Trade*, now complemented by Baskes, *Indians, Merchants, and Markets*; on mining production and labor, see Tutino, *Making a New World*, chapters 3 and 6.

16. These roles are detailed in PCRun, 1770, "Méritos del . . . Conde de San Bartolomé de Jala."

17. PCRun, 1765, "Testamento de . . . d. Manuel Rodríguez de Pedroso."

18. Brading, *Miners and Merchants*, 186.

19. PCRun, 1765, "Testamento"; Fernández de Recas, *Mayorazgos de Nueva España*, 289–97.

20. PCRun, 1765, "Testamento"; *Gaceta de México*, 3 May 1785; AGN, Padrones, V. 12, f. 144, 1792; AGN, Bienes Nacionales, V. 1844, exp. 3, 1797; Calderón de la Barca, *Life in Mexico*, 215–33.

21. PCRun, 1765, "Testamento"; AGN, Bienes Nacionales, V. 1844, exp. 2, 1778; AGN, Padrones, V. 12, f. 144, 1792; PCRb, "Condado de Jala . . . 1836"; Romero de Terreros, *Antiguas haciendas*, 147.

22. PCRun, 1765, "Testamento"; PCRun, 1767, "Testimonio"; AGN, Bienes Nacionales, V. 1844, exp. 2, 1778; PCRb, "Condado de Jala . . . 1836," fol. 17, 33–34.

23. PCRun, "Testamento"; AGN, Bienes Nacionales, V. 1844, exp. 1778; AGN, Intendencias, V. 61, exp. 345, f. 317–19; PCRb, "Condado de Jala . . . 1836," f. 42.

24. PCR, V. 62, 1762; V. 64, 14 Apr. 1764; PCRun, 1765, "Testamento"; AGN, Bienes Nacionales, V. 1844, exp. 2, 1778; PCRb, "Condado de Jala . . . 1836," f. 17.
25. Conflict and resolution are in PCRb, "El Condado de Jala . . . 1836," f. 36–37, 42–42, 105–106, 108–10.
26. This is clear throughout Yuste López, *Emporios transpacíficos*.
27. PCR, V. 82, 1777; AGN, Bienes Nacionales, V. 1844, exp. 2, 1778; AGN, Intendentes, V. 65, exp. 411, f. 343, 1778; Fonseca and Urrutía, *Historia general de Real Hacienda*, 3:411.
28. Sánchez Espinosa's career at the pinnacle of power is detailed in Tutino, *Making a New World*, chapter 5.
29. Romero de Terreros, *Una casa del siglo XVIII*.
30. Brading, *Miners and Merchants*, 183–85; Couturier, *Silver King*.
31. PCRun, "Ynventario de . . . la Casa del Señor Conde de Santa María de Regla," 1782, f. 48–50; PCRb, "Testamento del Señor Conde de Regla, Cuenta de División . . ." 1782, f. 25–27; Romero de Terreros, *Testimonios relativos*, 28.
32. The strike is noted in Tutino, *Making a New World*, 235–36, and detailed in Ladd, *Making of a Strike*.
33. PCR, V. 46, 9 Sep. 1775; V. 52, 18 May 1775; 17 Feb. 1779; PCRb, "Posesión de . . . San Javier, " 1777; PCRb, "Testamento, Cuenta, del Sr. Conde de Regla," 1782; Brading, *Miners and Merchants*, 64–66.
34. On Herrera's marriage into the Regla clan, PCR, V. 120, 11 Oct. 1788; Romero de Terreros, "Los hijos de los primeros," 192–93; *Gaceta de México*, 19 Dec. 1801; On Herrera's and Tepa's persuasive representation of Mexico City oligarchs, their kin, and others, see Brading, *Miners and Merchants*, 43, 46–47.
35. Romero de Terreros, *Testimonios relativos*.
36. Property values are for 1782 at the time of inheritance. See PCRb, "Testamento, Cuenta," 1782; that estate profits in cereals averaged over 6 percent, in pulque closer to 8, is shown in Tutino, *Mexican Heartland*, chapter 3.
37. PCRun, "Ynventario."
38. Lafuente Ferrari, *El virrey Iturrigaray*, 144–52; Romero de Terreros, "La Condesa escribe," 458–67.

Chapter 3

1. On the challenges faced by the late eighteenth-century Church in New Spain, see Taylor, *Magistrates of the Sacred*; and Voekel, *Alone Before God*.
2. This pattern is detailed in Brading's essential *Miners and Merchants*.
3. This cross section of the stratified landed elite summarizes Tutino, "Creole Mexico," 15–47.
4. Tutino, "Creole Mexico," table 4.1, 195.
5. For González, see WBS, V. 134, f. 8, 8 Mar. 1781; AGN, Vínculos, V. 20, no. 1, ff. 1, 2, 13, 80; for Rodríguez, see WBS, V. 134, f. 1, 6 Feb. 1781; f. 3, 11 Oct. 1782; f. 7, 13 Jan. 1769; f. 13, 27 Nov. 1784; f. 76, 13 Jun. 1788; f. 85, 26 Aug. 1786.

6. JSE, V. 213, n. 76, 15 May 1784; V. 215, n. 67, 18 Dec. 1784; AGN, Padrones, V. 12, f. 144, 1792; V. 5, f. 317, 1793; GM, 23 Oct. 1799.

7. PCR, V. 124, f. 22, 8 Apr. 1802; GM, 5 Mar. 1818.

8. AGN, Vínculos, V. 54, n. 1, ff. 27–33; V. 55, n. 10, 19 Oct. 1798; no. 21, 28 Sept. 1795; GM, 20 Oct. 1784.

9. For the Santiagos, PCR, V. 124, f. 69, 6 Mar. 1802; for the Fagoagas, PCR, V. 127, 9 Feb, 1804; also see PCR, V. 121, f.14, 17 Jan. 1800 for the Vivancos; and PCR, V. 124, f. 7, 28 May 1801 for the Cervantes y Padilla.

10. For three examples, see PCR, V. 110, 15 Nov. 1788 for the Leal y Gamboa; PCR, V. 123, f. 5, 11 Jan. 1801 for the Ojedas; PCR, V. 123, f. 94, 24 Nov. 1801 for the Cano Moctezuma.

11. For the Mota Sanz notice, PCR, V. 123, f. 21, 27 Feb. 1801.

12. AGN, Vínculos, V. 53, n. 10, f. 22; no. 5, f. 1, ff. 33–55; V. 54, n. 1, f. 198; n. 2, f. 1; no. 11, f. 43–44.

13. AGN, Vínculos, V. 53, n. 11, f. 43.

14. AGN, Vínculos, V. 53, n. 11, ff. 39, 44; GM, 3 Mar. 1797.

15. AGN, Vínculos, V. 53, n. 9, ff. 22–24; n. 5, ff. 13, 16; V. 54, n. 1, ff. 83, 119; V. 55, n. 10, 5 Jan. 1801.

16. Alamán, *Historia de Méjico*, 1:45.

17. The sample data is reported in Tutino, "Creole Mexico," table 1.2, 28.

18. This contradiction was documented originally and brilliantly by Florescano in *Precios del maíz*.

19. Ladd, *Mexican Nobility at Independence*.

20. Tutino, *Making a New World*, chapter 5.

21. Tutino, "Hacienda Social Relations in Mexico," table IV, 508.

22. PCR, V. 106, 11 Apr. 1785; V. 121, f. 99, 27 Aug. 1800; V. 118, f. 27, 24 Apr. 1799.

23. On the Obra Pía allocation, JSE, V. 214, n. 99, 27 May 1808; for solicitations, see JSE, V. 213, n. 155, n.d., c. 1787; n. 249, 12 Apr. 1793; no. 451, 16 Jul. 1802; V. 214, n. 48, 15 Jul. 1806; n. 87, 1 Mar. 1808.

24. JSE, V. 213, n. 394, 19 Apr. 1800.

25. AGN, Bienes Nacionales, V. 550, 12 Aug. 1801; GM, 20 May 1801.

26. JSE, V. 213, n. 33, 2 Jun. 1781; n. 127, 21 Oct. 1786; n. 220, 29 Jun. 1792; n. 337, 12 Apr. 1798; n. 341, 29 May 1798; n. 358, 20 May 1799; n. 446, 7 May 1802.

27. PCR, V. 124, f. 29, 16 Mar. 1802.

28. PCRb, "Testamento, Cuenta"; PCRun, "Ynventario," ff. 12, 14, 15, 39; PCR, V. 108, f. 58, 20 Sep. 1785; Couturier, "Hacienda de Hueyapan," 98; DM, 11 Mar. 1813; GM, 27 Oct. 1821.

29. PCR, V. 106, 11 Apr. 1785.

30. PCR, V. 120, 11 Oct. 1788; V. 172, 29 Mar. 1819; V. 189, 25 Apr. 1820; PCRun, "Ynventario," ff, 13–14; JSE, V. 215, n. 80, 7 Apr. 1785.

31. JSE, V. 213, n. 150, 10 Oct. 1787; no. 160, 3 Jun. 1789; n. 226, 25 Sep. 1792; V. 215, n. 90, 26 Nov. 1793.

32. JSE, V. 213, n. 226, 25 Sep. 1792; n. 228, 10 Oct.1792.

33. JSE, V. 213, n. 410, 5 Nov. 1800; n. 528, 10 Sep. 1805; n. 530, 19 Oct. 1805; n. 544, 27 Dec. 1805; V. 214, n. 14, 26 Jan. 1806; n. 93, 3 Jun. 1808; on the takeover conflict, Tutino, *Making a New World*, 275–76.

34. To avoid reproducing a long paragraph of citations to Sánchez Espinosa's correspondence with his managers from 1779 to 1811, see Tutino, "Creole Mexico," 230, note 69.

35. JSE, V. 213, n. 174, 20 Nov. 1789.

36. JSE, V. 213, n. 51, 28 Sep. 1782; PCR, V. 81, 5 Apr. 1777; V. 95, 27 Nov. 1782; V. 97, 30 Jun. 1783; V. 99, 23 May 1783; V. 111, 26 Feb. 1791; CSC, "Libro de data del Condado de Santiago, 1794; GM, 3 Sep. 1796.

37. PCR, V. 118, f. 60, 15 Jul. 1799; f. 63, 20 Jul. 1799; V. 121, f. 47, 1 Dec. 1800; f. 180, 10 Sep. 1800; V. 123, f. 19, 17 Feb. 1801; f. 63, 28 Aug. 1801; V.124, f. 45, 12 Jul. 1802; f. 25, 24 Apr. 1802; f. 49, 16 Jun. 1802; f. 78, 2 Sep. 1802; V. 125, f. 7, 12 Feb. 1803; V. 127, f. 1, 28 Jan. 1804.

38. PCR, V. 123, f. 21, 27 Feb. 1801; f. 5, 11 Jan 1801.

39. PCR, V. 75, 7 Apr. 1775; 30 Apr. 1775; V. 80, 18 Jan. 1779; V. 89, 15 May 1780; V. 90, 27 Sep. 1780; V. 92, 18 Jan. 1781; V. 93, 5 Apr. 1781; V. 95, 4 Nov. 1782; V. 109, 14 Feb. 1788; V. 111, 26 Feb. 1791.

40. PCR, V. 118, ff. 12–13, 17 Feb. 1799; f. 29, 24 Apr. 1799; V. 121, f. 25, 21 Feb. 1800; V. 124, f. 23, 19 Apr. 1800; V. 125, f. 8, 3 Mar. 1803; V. 1217, f. 14, 1 Sep. 1804; V. 129, f. 13, 14 Nov. 1805; f. 15, 23 Nov. 1805.

41. I detailed her administration in Tutino, "Power, Class, and Family."

42. PCRun, 1767, "Testimonio"; CSC, "Libro de data . . . del Condado de Santiago 1794"; PCR, V. 121, f. 42, 22 Mar. 1800.

43. Among many examples, see PCR, V. 118, f. 47, 19 Jun. 1799; f. 69, 6 Mar. 1802.

44. PCR, V. 124, f. 69, 6 Mar. 1802; Palacio also signed for another member of the inner circle in 1801: PCR, V. 123, f. 7, 28 Dec. 1801.

45. PCR, V. 121, f. 42, 22 Mar. 1800.

46. PCR, V. 124, f. 13, 20 Feb. 1802; f. 81, 29 Sep. 1802; V. 125, f. 16, 22 Jun. 1803; V. 140, 18 Mar. 1809.

47. PCR, V. 118, f. 99, 6 Nov. 1799.

48. See Tutino, *Mexican Heartland*, chapter 4–5.

Chapter 4

1. This is evidenced throughout Tutino, *Making a New World*, for the Bajío and regions north.

2. The classic study of the city's native republics is Lira, *Comunidades indígenas*. For analysis of the republics in 1800, see Granados, "Cosmopolitan Indians."

3. González Angulo, *Artesanado y ciudad*; Kicza, *Colonial Entrepreneurs*; and Pérez Toledo, *Población*.

4. González Angulo, *Artesanado y ciudad*, 85–87, 186–87.

5. Kicza, *Colonial Entrepreneurs*, 189, 209–11.
6. Kicza, *Colonial Entrepreneurs*, 209–11.
7. On spinning, weaving, and clothing the family as pivotal women's roles in pre-contact Tenochtitlan, see Clendinnen, *Aztecs*; on women's cloth making in a nearby village under Spanish rule, see Cline, *Colonial Culhuacan*.
8. On the coming of sheep, see Melville, *Plague of Sheep*; on the woolen industry, see Salvucci, *Textiles and Capitalism*, and Miño Grijalva, *Obrajes y tejedores*.
9. I explore the obrajes, weavers, and spinners of Querétaro and the Bajío in *Making a New World*. The same pattern is evident for Mexico City in González Angulo, *Artesanado y ciudad*; Kicza, *Colonial Entrepreneurs*; Salvucci, *Textiles and Capitalism*; and Miño Grijalva, *Obrajes y tejedores*.
10. The numbers are reported in Kicza, *Colonial Entrepreneurs*, 209.
11. I detail the Spanish intrusion into indigenous sectors in Tutino, *Mexican Heartland*, chapter 3.
12. Kicza, *Colonial Entrepreneurs*, 209, 224.
13. Kicza, *Colonial Entrepreneurs*, 209.
14. González Angulo, *Artesanado y ciudad*, 111–13.
15. Kicza, *Colonial Entrepreneurs*, 210.
16. Kicza, *Colonial Entrepreneurs*, 211.
17. Kicza, *Colonial Entrepreneurs*, 211.
18. Kicza, *Colonial Entrepreneurs*, 211.
19. This analysis depends on Castro Gutiérrez, *Real Casa de Moneda*.
20. See discussion and diagrams in Castro Gutiérrez, *Real Casa de Moneda*, 102–21.
21. Castro Gutiérrez, *Real Casa de Moneda*, gráfica 5, 143, for weekly labor fluctuations; cuadro 7, 144, for permanent and replacement workers; cuadro 8, 147, for daily wages; cuadro 9, 148, for piece rates; anexo I, 223–25 for administrators' and skilled overseers' salaries.
22. Castro Gutiérrez, *Real Casa de Moneda*, 152–74; on advances and obligations in the commercial economy of the Bajío, see Tutino, *Making a New World*.
23. Castro Gutiérrez, *Real Casa de Moneda*, gráfica 4, 139, and anexo 4, 232–39.
24. See Deans-Smith, *Bureaucrats, Planters, and Workers*; and González Gómez, *El tabaco virreinal*.
25. González Gómez, *El tabaco virreinal*, 118; Deans-Smith, *Bureaucrats, Planters, and Workers*, table 20, 176.
26. Deans-Smith, *Bureaucrats, Planters, and Workers*, table 25, 192–93; also 180–82, 220–26.
27. Deans-Smith, *Bureaucrats, Planters, and Workers*, tables 29–30; 211–12.
28. This discussion builds on Allen, *British Industrial Revolution*; Parthasarathi, *Why Europe Grew Rich*; and Tutino, "Americas in the Rise of Industrial Capitalism."

29. The information we have comes from the work of Miño Grijalva, first in "El camino hacia la fábrica," 135-48; then in *Obrajes y tejedores*, 244-46, 252-55.

30. My analysis of native barrios synthesizes the complex vision of Granados in "Cosmopolitan Indians."

31. Granados, "Cosmopolitan Indians," table 3.1, 168.

32. Granados, "Cosmopolitan Indians," 520.

33. These numbers are detailed and discussed in Granados, "Cosmopolitan Indians," tables 6.6-6.9, 446-61, for cloth producers; and tables 6.12-6.21, 476-97 for the rest.

34. The figures for the traza are from AGN, Padrones, Vols. 101, 103, 104, 105; they were compiled by Luis Fernando Granados and graciously shared with me from his unpublished work.

Chapter 5

1. Kicza, *Colonial Entrepreneurs*, table 2, 3.

2. Pérez Toledo, *Población*, tabla II.2.3, 102.

3. I detail this in Tutino, *Making a New World*, 302-16.

4. Pérez Toledo, *Población*, tabla II.1.6, 90; tabla II.2.10, 120.

5. Pérez Toledo, *Población*, tabla II.1.5, 90; tabla II.2.9, 117.

6. I detail these pressures in Tutino, *Mexican Heartland*, chapter 3.

7. Pérez Toledo, *Población*, 90, 118-19.

8. See Pérez Toledo, *Población*, 28-30; and Haslip-Viera, *Crime and Punishment*, 47.

9. Viqueira Albán, *Relajados o reprimidos?*, 21-22.

10. Haslip-Viera, *Crime and Punishment*.

11. This is my reading of Viqueira Albán in *Relajados o reprimidos?* His emphasis on the enclosure of popular religion in the vecindades parallels Pizzigoni's discovery that in the face of similar constraints on public festivals, families turned to household altars and saints in the Valley of Toluca. See *Life Within*. In both cases, public constraints of popular expression led religion indoors.

12. Lempérière, *Entre Dios y el rey*, 65-71.

13. Both cases are detailed in Lempérière, *Entre Dios y el rey*, 62-68.

14. This is a key focus of Florescano, *Precios del maíz*.

15. The system of profit and the extremity of 1785-1786 are also in Florescano, *Precios del maíz*.

16. The relief program is reported and lauded in GM, 18 Apr. 1786; the construction of profiteering in times of scarcity as charity is detailed in Tutino, *Making a New World*, 296-99.

17. PCRb, "Méritos," lists junta members; the larger relief effort is detailed in Cooper, *Epidemic Disease*.

18. PCRb, "Méritos."

19. PCRb, "Méritos"; Testimonio, 48-50.

20. Tutino, *Making a New World*, 420-22.

Chapter 6

1. Elliott, *Empires of the Atlantic World.*
2. See Taylor, *Drinking, Homicide, and Rebellion*; Borah, *Justice by Insurance*; and Lockhart, *Nahuas after the Conquest*: studies that detail rights and negotiations, adaptations and survival—and nothing approaching despotism.
3. Cañeque, *King's Living Image.*
4. Lempérière, *Entre Dios y el rey*, originally appeared in French in 2004.
5. The classic works of Morgan—*American Slavery, American Freedom* and *Inventing the People*—make that clear.
6. Irigoin and Grafe, "Bargaining for Absolutism," and Grafe and Irigoin, "A Stakeholder Empire."
7. The origins of this regime are seen Cañeque, *King's Living Image*; and Owensby, *Empire of Law.*
8. This is explored in Ruiz Medrano, *Reshaping New Spain.*
9. This key point is emphasized by Lempérière in *Entre Dios y el rey*, 81.
10. The exception was brilliantly studied by Bernardo García Martínez in *El Marquesado del Valle.*
11. See Ladd, *Mexican Nobility at Independence.*
12. The reliance of Spanish power in the Andes on enduring kurakas is emphasized in Stern, *Peru's Indigenous Peoples*; and Spalding, *Huarochirí.* On kurakas in the conflicts of the 1780s, see Serulnikov, *Revolution in the Andes*; and Walker, *Tupac Amaru Rebellion.*
13. On indigenous councils in the Andes, their relations with kurakas, and importance to Potosí, see Mumford, *Vertical Empire.* On indigenous republics and their roles at the foundations of silver capitalism in New Spain, see Tutino, *Mexican Heartland*, chapters 1–3. On regime justice and native republics there, see Borah, *Justice by Insurance*; and Owensby, *Empire of Law.*
14. See Israel, *Race, Class, and Politics*; and Silva Prada, *La política de una rebelión.*
15. See Cañeque, *King's Living Image*; Owensby, *Empire of Law*; and Lempérière, *Entre Dios y el rey.*
16. This is a key emphasis of Lempérière, *Entre Dios y el rey.*
17. Sánchez de Tagle, "Las reformas del siglo XVIII," 196.
18. The classic study of the containment of council power in Spain is Haliczer, *Comuneros of Castile.* On the monarchy in Spain during the formative years of New Spain, see Domínguez Ortiz, *El antiguo régimen.*
19. Cañeque, *King's Living Image*, 66–76.
20. On Suárez's enduring influence, see Breña, "Cádiz Liberal Revolution," 81–82.
21. This is emphasized by Lempérière, *Entre Dios y el rey*, 33–34, 40, 71, and throughout.
22. On modern states' searches for homogeneity and their limits, see Scott, *Seeing Like a State.*
23. Production figures are in Tutino, *Making a New World*, table D.1, 550.

24. This episode and Trespalacios's role are detailed in Sánchez de Tagle, *Del gobierno y su tutela*; my interpretation, as in all that follows, integrates Sánchez's innovative understanding of the city council and its dealings with the regime with my analysis of the rise of oligarchic rule as outlined in part 1.

25. This is a key emphasis of Burnard and Gerrigus, *Plantation Machine*.

26. On parallel postwar policies and outcomes, see Lempérière, *Entre Dios y el rey*, 21. I compare why British policies led quickly to independence in North America while Spanish assertions led to riots, compromises, and stabilizations in the Bajío in *Making a New World*, chapter 4.

27. On the Bajío and British North America, again see Tutino, *Making a New World*.

28. Sánchez de Tagle, *Del gobierno y su tutela*, 58–59.

29. This is the main thrust of Sánchez de Tagle's essential new analysis of the council in *Del gobierno y su tutela*, stated clearly beginning on 17–18 and developed throughout.

30. Sánchez de Tagle, *Del gobierno y su tutela*, 37.

31. See Deans-Smith, *Bureaucrats, Planters, and Workers*.

32. On the Bourbons' military assertions, see Archer, *Army in Bourbon Mexico*.

33. Sánchez de Tagle, "Las reformas del siglo XVIII," 196–97.

34. The key study is Ladd, *Making of a Strike*.

35. The essential study of the conflicts at Guanajuato and across San Luis Potosí is Castro Gutiérrez, *Nueva ley y nuevo rey*. José de Gálvez's report on the risings is in Gálvez, *Informe sobre las rebeliones*; additional local detail and documents are in Rionda Arreguín, *La Compañía de Jesús*.

36. I detail this in *Making a New World*, 238–41, based on sources made available by Castro Gutiérrez in *Nueva ley y nuevo rey*; and Gálvez, *Informe sobre las rebeliones*.

37. Again, this is detailed in Tutino, *Making a New World*, chapter 4.

38. This discussion synthesizes the detailed analysis in Sánchez de Tagle, *Del gobierno y su tutela*.

39. The document is reproduced in HDC, vol. 1, 427–55. In his title to the document, Hernández y Dávalos asserted that the text called for preferences for criollos. Reading the document reveals no use of the term criollo and a demand for equality between American and European Spaniards, preferences for none.

40. HDC, vol. 1, 428.

41. On enlightened assaults on American character, see Brading, *First America*; on the policy of exclusion, see Burkholder and Chandler, *From Impotence to Authority*.

42. HDC, vol. 1, 450.

43. HDC, vol. 1, 452.

44. HDC, vol. 1, 454.

Chapter 7

1. Ties between Spain and New Spain are explored in detail in Stein and Stein, *Apogee of Empire* and *Edge of Crisis*.
2. On the struggles of the United States after independence, see McCoy, *Elusive Republic*.
3. Stein and Stein, *Apogee of Empire*, 69–80.
4. This is clear in Brading, *Miners and Merchants*, and Tutino, *Making a New World*, 300–51.
5. Mining figures are in Tutino, *Making a New World*, table D.1, 550; Alcabala receipts are in Sánchez Santiró, "La modernización conservadora," 319. City council receipts are in Lempérière, *Entre Dios y el rey*, 291, 297.
6. Stein and Stein, *Apogee of Empire*, 263, note 158, 408.
7. Valle Pavón, *Donativos, préstamos y privilegios*, 25–47; cuadro 1, 46.
8. Valle Pavón, *Donativos, préstamos y privilegios*, cuadro 2, 52.
9. Chávez, *Spain*.
10. Valle Pavón, *Donativos, préstamos y privilegios*, cuadro 2, 52; cuadro 12, 127–28.
11. Valle Pavón, *Donativos, préstamos y privilegios*, 142–52; cuadro 14, 147.
12. See Serulnikov, *Revolution in the Andes*; and Walker, *Tupac Amaru Rebellion*.
13. This is my reading and interpretation of the detailed materials presented and discussed in Valle Pavón, *Donativos, préstamos y privilegios*, 81–122; the figures for silver shipments are on 121. On the broader development of the Pacific trades that peaked in these crucial years, see Bonialian, *Pacífico hispanoamericano*.
14. The foundation of the tribunal is outlined in Lempérière, *Entre Dios y el rey*, 313–19. The links between sanction and wartime funding are detailed in Valle Pavón, *Donativos, préstamos y privilegios*, 35–42.
15. The tribunal's loan capital is explored in Sánchez Santiró, "La modernización conservadora," 296–97.
16. This reform is discussed in chapter 5, via sources in notes 8 and 9 there.
17. This sketch synthesizes materials in Florescano, *Precios del maíz*; Tutino, *From Insurrection to Revolution*, 74–80; Tutino, *Making a New World*, 352–402; and the discussion of urban relief in chapter 5 here.
18. Tutino, "Creole Mexico," 102–3; and Brading, *Miners and Merchants*, 207.
19. On the intendant reform and Guanajuato, see Brading, *Miners and Merchants*; on Riaño, mining entrepreneurs, and the social order in Guanajuato, see Tutino, *Making a New World*, 300–51, 420–22.
20. Tutino, *Making a New World*, app. D, table D.1, 550.
21. This synthesizes materials in Stein and Stein, *Apogee of Empire*, 261–66, notes 154–59, 407–8; and Tutino, *Making a New World*, 316–20, app. D, 548–57.
22. Stein and Stein, *Apogee of Empire*, 266–72.
23. This is detailed in Stein and Stein, *Apogee of Empire*, 272–304.

24. On the military, see Archer, *Army in Bourbon Mexico*; on corporate rights, see McAlister, *Fuero Militar*; on a key provincial militia, see Sánchez de Tagle, *Por un regimiento*; for a detailed exploration of militia censuses, see Tutino, *Making a New World*, chapter 7. On the specter of Saint-Domingue, see Granados, *En el espejo haitiano*; on indigenous republics and social peace in the rural heartland, see Tutino, *Mexican Heartland*, chapter 3.

25. The shifting alliances are detailed in Stein and Stein, *Edge of Crisis*, 3–54; the silver levels are in Tutino, *Making a New World*, app. D, table D. 1, 550.

26. These debates are detailed in Stein and Stein, *Edge of Crisis*, 91–129, quote on 117.

27. This is a very brief summary of the conclusions of Brading in his classic study *Miners and Merchants*.

28. Stein and Stein, *Edge of Crisis*, 131–40.

29. Stein and Stein, *Edge of Crisis*, 160.

30. Valle Pavón, *Finanzas piadosas*, cuadro 8, 67–68.

31. On silver and trade, see Stein and Stein, *Edge of Crisis*, 162–87. On revenue diversion, see Marichal, *La bancarrota del virreinato*.

32. The file on the report, investigation, and resolution is in AHN, Madrid, Consejo de Indias, vol. 21061, exp. 458. f. 12–30. First, report, 10 Oct. 1799, f. 12v–13v.

33. AHN, Madrid, Consejo de Indias, vol. 21061, exp. 458. f. 29–30; 27 Mar. 1802.

Chapter 8

1. On Britain, see Allen, *British Industrial Revolution*; on the global transformation, see Beckert, *Empire of Cotton*; on New Spain in the industrial transformation, Tutino, "Americas in the Rise of Industrial Capitalism."

2. This analysis synthesizes the vast research and complex vision of Stein and Stein, *Edge of Crisis*, 206–57.

3. The policy goals of creating the fund are detailed in Stein and Stein, *Edge of Crisis*, 277–307; details of implementation in Spain are in Herr, *Rural Change and Royal Finances*, another key study too few have engaged.

4. These are my calculations based on Herr, *Rural Change and Royal Finances*, appendix F, 778–80.

5. Herr, *Rural Change and Royal Finances*, table 5.2, 122; map. 5.1, 130.

6. This is detailed in Stein and Stein, *Edge of Crisis*, 319–72; on Oliver see Bruchey, *Robert Oliver*.

7. On Iturrigaray's origins, see the brief sketch in Stein and Stein, *Crisis in an Atlantic Empire*, 299–302; the classic biography is Lafuente Ferrari, *El virrey Iturrigaray*. On the South American risings, see Serulnikov, *Revolution in the Andes* for a superb overview; on Tupac Amaru and the risings around Cuzco, see Walker, *Tupac Amaru Rebellion*.

8. Stein and Stein, *Crisis in an Atlantic Empire*, 302–11.

9. The most detailed analysis of the consolidation in New Spain is Wobeser, *Dominación colonial*. Stein and Stein depend on her work in *Edge of Crisis*, 308–18. Now Valle Pavón, in *Finanzas piadosas*, has examined the program from the perspective of merchants and the consulado. I rely on their research and analyses in all that follows. Interpretations are mine.

10. Valle Pavón, *Finanzas piadosas*, 76–81.

11. Valle Pavón, *Finanzas piadosas*, 81–82.

12. Valle Pavón, *Finanzas piadosas*, 82–83.

13. Valle Pavón, *Finanzas piadosas*, cuadro 3, 46–47.

14. Valle Pavón, *Finanzas piadosas*, cuadro 4, 50–51.

15. Valle Pavón, *Finanzas piadosas*, 88–90.

16. Valle Pavón, *Finanzas piadosas*, 88–104; signatories are listed in cuadro 2, 91–94.

17. Valle Pavón, *Finanzas piadosas*, 104–10; on Domínguez and Querétaro, see Tutino, *Making a New World*, 436–42.

18. Details on implementation are in Wobeser, *Dominación colonial*.

19. See Wobeser, *Dominación colonial*, cuadro 30, 155; cuadro 33, 158; and apéndice 10, 356–86.

20. Wobeser, *Dominación colonial*, cuadro 48, 192.

21. See Tutino, *Making a New World*, 263–99.

22. Wobeser, *Dominación colonial*, 182–87; cuadro 43, 183.

23. Valle Pavón, *Finanzas piadosas*, 151–59.

24. The quote is from Stein and Stein, *Edge of Crisis*, 398; the analysis that follows depends on their detailed research and perceptive analysis of transatlantic politics.

25. Stein and Stein, *Edge of Empire*, 397–429.

26. Stein and Stein, *Edge of Crisis*, 424–25; quote on 426.

27. Stein and Stein, *Edge of Crisis*, 437–38.

28. Stein and Stein, *Edge of Crisis*, 438.

29. Stein and Stein, *Edge of Crisis*, 438–39.

30. Stein and Stein, *Edge of Crisis*, 439–40.

31. Stein and Stein, *Edge of Crisis*, 444–47.

32. Stein and Stein, *Edge of Crisis*, 447–48, 453.

33. Stein and Stein, *Crisis in an Atlantic Empire*, 16–19.

34. The oft-repeated presumption-assertion that the escape of the Portuguese Crown to Brazil led to a spontaneous decision to invade Spain is untenable in light of the Steins' and others' new and detailed research. If the goal was Iberian stability and access to New Spain's silver, the Portuguese regime's escape was predictable and acceptable—and occupation of Spain all but inevitable, if ultimately unsuccessful in delivering New Spain's silver to Napoleon.

35. Stein and Stein, *Crisis in an Atlantic Empire*, 19–23.

36. Stein and Stein, *Crisis in an Atlantic Empire*, 25–32.

37. Stein and Stein, *Crisis in an Atlantic Empire*, 33–38.
38. Stein and Stein, *Crisis in an Atlantic Empire*, 77–83.
39. Stein and Stein, *Crisis in an Atlantic Empire*, 86.
40. Stein and Stein, *Crisis in an Atlantic Empire*, 96.

Chapter 9

1. Stein and Stein, *Crisis in an Atlantic Empire*, 203.
2. Stein and Stein, *Crisis in an Atlantic Empire*, 204–6.
3. AHN, Madrid, Consejo de Indias, México, vol. 21663, exp. 661. The proclamation is reproduced in HD-CDHI, vol. 1, 475–85.
4. This is detailed in Cañeque, *King's Living Image*, 66–76.
5. Tanck de Estrada, *Pueblos de indios*.
6. This is detailed in Tutino, *Making a New World*, and in chapters 2 and 3 here.
7. Stein and Stein, *Crisis in an Atlantic Empire*, 206–8.
8. DM, 30 July 1808; reproduced in HDC, vol. 1, 495–96.
9. DM, 31 July 1808; reproduced in HDC, vol. 1, 496–98.
10. DM, 31 July 1808; in HDC, vol. 1, 497–98.
11. DM, 1 Aug. 1808; in HDC, vol. 1, 498–99.
12. DM, 5 Aug. 1808; in HDC, vol. 1, 499.
13. DM, 5, 6, 7 Aug. 1808; in HDC, vol. 1, 499–503.
14. DM, 8 Aug. 1808; in HDC, vol. 1, 503.
15. HDC, vol. 1, 503–5.
16. HDC, vol. 1, 505–6.
17. HDC, vol. 1, 506–8.
18. HDC, vol. 1, 509–10.
19. HDC, vol. 1, 508–9.
20. HDC, vol. 1, 511.
21. Stein and Stein, *Crisis in an Atlantic Empire*, 234–55.
22. HDC, vol. 1, 494.
23. HDC, vol. 1, 512–13.
24. HDC, vol. 1, 509–510.
25. HDC, vol. 1, 513–516.
26. HDC, vol. 1, 513–17, 516–18.
27. Ávila, "Nueva España, 1808–1809," 140–43.
28. HDC, vol. 1, 518–19.
29. Zárate, "Gobierno precario," 98–100, details the conversation and limited response.
30. Zárate, "Gobierno precario," 90–93, details the testimony related to this conversation.
31. Stein and Stein, *Crisis in an Atlantic Empire*, 256–57.
32. Stein and Stein, *Crisis in an Atlantic Empire*, 257–66, explore this in greater detail.

33. Stein and Stein, *Crisis in an Atlantic Empire*, 263.
34. Stein and Stein, *Crisis in an Atlantic Empire*, 266–73.
35. HDC, vol. 1, 529–31.
36. Stein and Stein, *Crisis in an Atlantic Empire*, 276–80.
37. HDC, vol. 1, 534–35.
38. Stein and Stein, *Crisis in an Atlantic Empire*, 279–86.
39. Stein and Stein, *Crisis in an Atlantic Empire*, 288–91.
40. Stein and Stein, *Crisis in an Atlantic Empire*, 291–92.
41. The full text is in HDC, vol. 1, 583–90.
42. HDC, vol. 1, 583–84.
43. HDC, vol. 1, 586–87.
44. HDC, vol. 1, 588.
45. HDC, vol. 1, 589.

Chapter 10

1. HDC, vol. 1, 592.
2. Stein and Stein, *Crisis in an Atlantic Empire*, 334–36.
3. This synthesizes the detailed discussion in Stein and Stein, *Crisis in an Atlantic Empire*, 327–36.
4. On Yermo, see Stein and Stein, *Crisis in an Atlantic Empire*, 336–46; and Valle Pavón, *Finanzas piadosas*, 160–206.
5. Stein and Stein, *Crisis in an Atlantic Empire*, 248–349.
6. Zárate, "Gobierno precario," 49.
7. HDC, vol. 1, 593–94.
8. The file compiled by the authorities is in AHN, Consejo de Indias, México, vol. 21209. It includes materials dating from 20 September 1808 to February 1810. I will not keep citing quotes all from the same source.
9. For Sánchez Espinosa and the family history, see Tutino, *Making a New World*, 263–99.
10. This is a key message of Brading's *First America*.
11. The Acuña-Morales plot is detailed in Zárate, "Gobierno precario," 73–95.
12. Zárate, "Gobierno precario," 78–81.
13. This is emphasized by Zárate in "Gobierno precario," 122–29.
14. All detailed in Tutino, *Making a New World*, chapter 5.
15. This shift is detailed in Sánchez Espinosa's fall 1808 letters, all in JSE.
16. Zárate, "Gobierno precario," 142, 176–82.
17. HDC, vol. 1, 605.
18. HDC, vol. 1, 603–5.
19. On the war in Spain, see Esdaille, *Peninsula War*; Fraser, *Napoleon's Cursed War*; Tone, *Fatal Knot*; and Cayuela Fernández and Gallego Palomares, *La guerra de independencia*.
20. HDC, vol. 1, 607–8.

21. HDC, vol. 1, 608–9.
22. Zárate, "Gobierno precario," 142–48.
23. HDC, vol. 1, 617–24; a heading suggests an Audiencia document; the text confirms a product of the Real Acuerdo.
24. In a brilliant essay, Eric Van Young showed that during the wars for independence that followed after 1810, insurgency marked diverse rural regions—never the cities, beyond brief explosions; see "Islands in the Storm."

Chapter 11

1. HDC, vol. 1, 596–97.
2. HDC, vol. 1, 599–600.
3. HDC, vol. 1, 600–601.
4. HDC, vol. 1, 609–15.
5. On the expansion of slavery through Louisiana, see Rothman, *Slave Country*; on the demise of slavery in Guanajuato and the Bajío before 1810, see Tutino, *Making a New World*.
6. Riaño's dream should be read in the context of the ongoing transformations in Louisiana detailed in Baptist, *Half Has Never Been Told*, and the post-1810 reconstruction detailed in Tutino, "Americas in the Rise of Industrial Capitalism."
7. AGI, Seville, Mexico, vol. 2248, 25 Nov. 1808.
8. This petition is in AGI, vol. 2248, dated 26 Nov. 1808.
9. Tutino, *Making a New World*, appendix D, table D.1, 550.
10. Trujillo Bolio, *El péndulo marítimo-mercantil*, cuadro 7, 136–41.
11. AGI, Mexico, 2249, Madrid, 5 Feb. 1809.
12. AGI, Mexico, vol. 2248, 28 July 1809, Mexico City.
13. AGI, Mexico, vol. 2248, 1 Aug. 1808, Mexico City.
14. AGI, Mexico, vol. 2248, 12 Sept.; 27 Sept. 1809, Seville.
15. Lerdo de Tejada, *Comercio exterior de México*, no. 21, "Balanza . . . 1808."
16. Lerdo de Tejada, *Comercio exterior de México*, no. 22, "Balanza de 1809."
17. These figures are based on calculations in Tutino, *Making a New World*, appendix D, tables D.2–D.5, 551–54.
18. On the decline of regional commerce after 1805, while mining boomed, see Tutino, *Making a New World*, appendix D, especially table D.6, 554.
19. On drought and profit in Mexico City, see Florescano, *Precios del maíz*; on 1808–1810 in the Bajío, see Tutino, *Making a New World*, 397–412; for the basins around the capital, see Tutino, *Mexican Heartland*, chapter 4.
20. This is an emphasis in all of part 2 of Tutino, *Making a New World*.
21. Stein and Stein, *Crisis in an Atlantic Empire*, 429, 435, 443.
22. Zárate, "Gobierno precario," 147–52.
23. Zárate, "Gobierno precario," 99–101.
24. Zárate, "Gobierno precario," 102–4.

25. Zárate, "Gobierno precario," 97, 114–116.
26. Zárate, "Gobierno precario," 98.
27. Zárate, "Gobierno precario," 117.
28. Zárate, "Gobierno precario," 117–18.
29. These events are well known, but too often seen as a "conspiracy for independence." For an early account in English, see Hamill, *Hidalgo Revolt*, 97–101; for a recent synthesis in light of the latest historiography and their own research, see Stein and Stein, *Crisis in an Atlantic Empire*, 593–613.
30. Stein and Stein, *Crisis in an Atlantic Empire*, 461, 467.
31. Zárate, "Gobierno precario," 164–65.
32. Stein and Stein, *Crisis in an Atlantic Empire*, 593–99.
33. On the Querétaro gatherings, see Hamill, *Hidalgo Revolt*, 101–16; and Tutino, "Querétaro y los orígenes de la nación mexicana."
34. Hamill, *Hidalgo Revolt*, 117.
35. Hidalgo and the revolt he led remain a focus of debate. For the most comprehensive analysis to date, see Herrejón Peredo, *Hidalgo*.
36. The political course of the revolt is detailed in Hamill, *Hidalgo Revolt*; its social bases and estate targets are emphasized in Tutino, *From Insurrection to Revolution*. For recent perspectives, see Granados, *En el espejo haitiano*; and Tutino, "De Hidalgo a Apatzingán."
37. All detailed in Tutino, *Making a New World*, part 2.
38. The complex route from 1810 to 1821 is outlined in Tutino, *Mexican Heartland*, chapter 5.

Conclusion

1. The best synthesis of the complex and conflictive politics that turned New Spain into Mexico is Ávila, *En nombre de la nación*. On regional politics and indigenous participations after 1810, see Van Young, *Other Rebellion*. For a brief analysis, see Tutino, "Soberanía quebrada." For a larger, complex exploration that shares many of my emphases on the conflictive politics of being Spanish, while less focused on questions of economic power and popular insurgency, see Rodríguez, *"We Are Now the True Spaniards."*
2. On political and popular insurgencies, see Tutino, "De Hidalgo a Apatzingán."
3. All this will be detailed in Tutino, *Remaking the New World* (in progress for Duke University Press).
4. For a comprehensive analysis of the Cádiz process, see Breña, *El primer liberalismo*; for a concise synthesis, see Breña, "Cádiz Liberal Revolution"; on implementation, impacts, and limits in New Spain, see Tutino, "Soberanía quebrada."
5. Stites, in *Four Horsemen*, analyzes this shift in Spain and its impact across the Mediterranean and into Russia.
6. For a synthesis of events leading to 1821, see Tutino, *Soberanía quebrada*.

7. The predatory turn is the focus of Tutino, *Making a New World*, part 2, 261–492.
8. On Bajío insurgency and its impacts: Tutino, "The Revolution in Mexican Independence."
9. The key study is Hernández Jaimes, *La formación de la hacienda pública*.
10. Sims, *Expulsion of Mexico's Spaniards*, explores these conflicts after 1821.
11. These are primary themes of Tutino, *Mexican Heartland*, parts 2 and 3.
12. For a strong synthesis see Israel, *Dutch Republic*.
13. Analyses begin with classics such as Hill, *Century of Revolution*. On ramifications in North America, see Morgan, *American Slavery, American Freedom*; and Webb, *1676*. On the long trajectory from England in the 1640s to the United States in 1787, the essential study is Morgan, *Inventing the People*.
14. For an introduction to these complexities, read Countryman, *American Revolution*, in the context of Morgan, *Inventing the People*. For a detailed synthesis, see Wood, *Radicalism of the American Revolution*.
15. For a comparative analysis that emphasizes how international conflicts set off the French Revolution, see Skocpol, *States and Social Revolutions*. On the inseparable yet different French and Haitian revolutions, see Furet, *Revolutionary France*, and Dubois, *Avengers of the New World*. On Haiti's post-independence struggles, see Fick, "From Slave Colony to Black Nation."
16. See the essays in Tutino, ed., *New Countries*.
17. This is the clear message of Stites, *Four Horsemen*.
18. A powerful emphasis of Beckert's *Empire of Cotton*.
19. This is the classic view of Max Weber, who saw modern states as grounded in legitimate monopolies of coercion. I would suggest they sought monopolies of coercion legitimated by popular sovereignties. Weber's long-prevailing view is updated in North, Wallis, and Weingast, *Violence and Social Orders*.
20. That difficult search is a primary focus of Parts 2 and 3 of Tutino, *Mexican Heartland*.

Bibliography

Alamán, Lucas. *Historia de Méjico*, 5 vols. 1849–1852. Reprint, Mexico City: Editorial Jus, 1972.

Allen, Robert. *The British Industrial Revolution in Global Perspective*. Cambridge: Cambridge University Press, 2009.

Archer, Christon. *The Army in Bourbon Mexico, 1760–1810*. Albuquerque: University of New Mexico Press, 1977.

Arcila Farías, Eduardo. *Comercio entre Venezuela y México en los siglos XVII y XVIII*. Mexico City: Colegio de México, 1950.

Ávila, Alfredo. *En nombre de la nación*. Mexico City: Taurus, 2002.

———. "Nueva España, 1808–1809." In Breña, *En el umbral de las revoluciones*, 129–43.

Ávila, Alfredo, and John Tutino. "Becoming Mexico: The Conflictive Search for a North American Nation." In Tutino, *New Countries*, 233–77.

Baptist, Edward. *The Half Has Never Been Told: Slavery and the Making of American Capitalism*. New York: Basic Books, 2014.

Baskes, Jeremy. *Indians, Merchants, and Markets: A Reinterpretation of the Repartimiento and Spanish-Indian Relations in Colonial Oaxaca, 1750–1821*. Redwood City, CA: Stanford University Press, 2000.

Beckert, Sven. *Empire of Cotton: A Global History*. New York: Knopf, 2014.

Bonialian, Mariano Ardash. *El Pacífico hispanoamericano: política y comercio asiático en el imperio español, 1680–1784*. Mexico City: Colegio de México, 2012.

Borah, Woodrow. *Justice by Insurance: The General Indian Court of New Spain*. Berkeley: University of California Press, 1982.

Brading, D. A. *The First America: The Spanish Monarchy, Creole Patriots, and the Liberal State, 1492–1867*. Cambridge: Cambridge University Press, 1993.

———. *Miners and Merchants in Bourbon Mexico, 1763–1810*. Cambridge: Cambridge University Press, 1973.

Braudel, Fernan. *Civilization and Capitalism: 15th to 18th Centuries*. 3 vols. Translated by Sian Reynolds. New York: Harper and Row, 1982–1984.

Breña, Roberto. "The Cádiz Liberal Revolution and Spanish American Independence." In Tutino, *New Countries*, 71–104.

———. *El primer liberalismo español y los procesos de emancipación de América, 1808–1824*. Mexico City: Colegio de México, 2013.

———, ed. *En el umbral de las revoluciones hispánicas: el bienio, 1808–1810*. Mexico City: Colegio de México, 2009.

Bruchey, Stuart. *Robert Oliver: Merchant of Baltimore, 1783–1819*. Baltimore, MD: Johns Hopkins University Press, 1956.

Burkholder, Mark, and D. S. Chandler. *From Impotence to Authority: The Spanish Crown and the American Audiencias, 1687–1808*. Columbia: University of Missouri Press, 1977.

Burnard, Trevor, and David Gerrigus. *The Plantation Machine: Atlantic Capitalism in French Saint-Domingue and British Jamaica*. Philadelphia: University of Pennsylvania Press, 2016.

Calderón de la Barca, Fanny. *Life in Mexico*. Edited by Howard and Marion Fisher. Garden City, NY: Prentice-Hall, 1966.

Calnek, Edward. "Conjunto urbano y modelo residencial en Tenochtitlan." In *Ensayos sobre el desarrollo urbano de México*, edited by Calnek et al., 11–65. Mexico City: Secretaría de Educación Pública, 1974.

Candiani, Vera. *Dreaming of Dry Land: Environmental Transformation in Colonial Mexico City*. Redwood City, CA: Stanford University Press, 2014.

Cañeque, Alejandro. *The King's Living Image: The Culture and Politics of Viceregal Power in Colonial Mexico*. New York: Routledge, 2004.

Castro Gutiérrez, Felipe. *Historia social de la Real Casa de Moneda de México*. Mexico City: Universidad Nacional Autónoma de México, 2012.

———. *Nueva ley y nuevo rey: reformas borbónicas y rebeliones populares en Nueva España*. Zamora: Colegio de Michoacán, 1996.

Cayuela Fernández, José Gregorio, and José Ángel Gallego Palomares. *La guerra de independencia: historia bélica: pueblo y nación en España, 1808–1814*. Salamanca: Editorial Universidad, 2008.

Chávez, Thomas. *Spain and the Independence of the United States: An Intrinsic Gift*. Albuquerque: University of New Mexico Press, 2002.

Clendinnen, Inga. *Aztecs: An Interpretation*. Cambridge: Cambridge University Press, 2000.

Cline, S. L. *Colonial Culhuacan: A Social History of an Aztec Town*. Albuquerque: University of New Mexico Press, 1986.

Collins, James. *The State in Early Modern France*. 2nd. ed. Cambridge: Cambridge University Press, 2009.

Conrad, Geoffrey, and Arthur Demarest. *Religion and Empire: The Dynamics of Aztec and Inca Expansionism*. New York: Cambridge University Press, 1984.

Cooper, Donald. *Epidemic Disease in Mexico City, 1763–1813*. Austin: University of Texas Press, 1965.

Cope, Douglas. *The Limits of Racial Domination: Plebian Society in Colonial Mexico City, 1660–1720*. Madison: University of Wisconsin Press, 1994.

Countryman, Edward. *The American Revolution*. Rev. ed. New York: Hill and Wang, 2003.

Couturier, Edith. "Hacienda de Hueyapan: The History of a Mexican Social and Economic Institution." PhD diss., Columbia University, 1965.

———. *The Silver King: The Remarkable Life of the Conde de Regla in Colonial Mexico.* Albuquerque: University of New Mexico Press, 2003.

Crosby, Alfred. *The Columbian Exchange: Biological and Cultural Consequences of 1492*. Westport, CT: Greenwood Press, 1972.

Cubillo Moreno, Gilda. *Los dominios de la plata: el precio del auge, el peso del poder— las reales de minas de Pachuca a Zimapán, 1552–1620*. Mexico City: Instituto Nacional de Antropología y Historia, 2006.

Deans-Smith, Susan. *Bureaucrats, Planters, and Workers: The Making of the Tobacco Monopoly in Bourbon Mexico*. Austin: University of Texas Press, 1992.

Diario de México. Mexico City, 1805–1817.

Domínguez Ortiz, Antonio. *El antiguo régimen: los reyes católicas y las Austrias*. Madrid: Alianza Editorial, 2007.

Dubois, Laurent. *Avengers of the New World: The Story of the Haitian Revolution*. Cambridge: Harvard University Press, 2005.

Elliott, J. H. *Empires of the Atlantic World: Britain and Spain in the Americas, 1492– 1830*. New Haven, CT: Yale University Press, 2007.

Enciso Contreras, José. *Taxco en el siglo XVI: sociedad y normatividad en un Real de Minas novohispano*. Zacatecas: Universidad Autónoma de Zacatecas, 1999.

Esdaille, Charles. *The Peninsula War: A New History*. London: Palgrave MacMillan, 2003.

Fernández de Recas, Guillermo. *Mayorazgos de Nueva España*. Mexico City: Porrúa, 1965.

Fick, Carolyn. "From Slave Colony to Black Nation: Haiti's Revolutionary Inversion." In Tutino, *New Countries*, 138–74.

Florescano, Enrique. *Precios del maíz y crisis agrícola en México, 1708–1816*. Mexico City: Colegio de México, 1969.

Fonseca, Fabián de, and Carlos de Urrutía. *Historia general de Real Hacienda*, 3 vols. Mexico City: n.p., 1845–1853.

Fraser, Ronald. *Napoleon's Cursed War: Popular Resistance in the Spanish Peninsula, 1808–1814*. London: Verso, 2008.

Furet, Francois. *Revolutionary France, 1770–1880*. Translated by Antonia Nevill. Oxford: Blackwell's, 1988.

Gálvez, José de. *Informe sobre las rebeliones populares de 1767*. Edited by Felipe Castro Gutiérrez. Mexico City: Universidad Nacional Autónoma de México, 1990.

García Ayluardo, Clara, ed. *Las reformas borbónicas, 1750–1808*. Mexico City: Fondo de Cultura Económica, 2010.

García Martínez, Bernardo. *El Marquesado del Valle: tres siglos de régimen sensorial en Nueva España*. Mexico City: Colegio de México, 1969.

Gazeta de México. Mexico City: 1728–1739, 1784–1822.

Giráldez, Arturo. *The Age of Trade: The Manila Galleons and the Dawn of the Global Economy*. Lanham, MD: Rowman and Littlefield, 2015.

González Angulo Aguirre, Jorge. *Artesanado y ciudad a finales del siglo XVIII*. Mexico City: Fondo de Cultura Económica, 1983.

González Gómez, Carmen Imelda. *El tabaco virreinal: monopolio de una costumbre*. Querétaro: Universidad Autónoma de Querétaro, 2002.

Grafe, Regina, and Alejandra Irigoin. "A Stakeholder Empire: The Political Economy of Spanish Imperial Rule in the Americas." *The Economic History Review* 65:2 (May 2012), 609–51.

Granados, Luis Fernando. "Cosmopolitan Indians and Mesoamerican Barrios in Bourbon Mexico City." PhD diss., Georgetown University, 2008.

———. *En el espejo haitiano: los indios del Bajío y el colapso del orden colonial en América Latina*. Mexico City: Ediciones Era, 2016.

Guardino, Peter. *The Dead March: A History of the Mexican-American War*. Cambridge, MA: Harvard University Press, 2017.

Guevara Sanginés, María. *Guanajuato diverso: sabores y sinsabores de su ser mestizo*. Guanajuato: Ediciones La Rana, 2001.

Haliczer, Stephen. *The Comuneros of Castile: The Forging of a Revolution, 1475–1521*. Madison: University of Wisconsin Press, 1981.

Hamill, Hugh. *The Hidalgo Revolt: Prelude to Mexican Independence*. Gainesville: University Press of Florida, 1966.

Hamnett, Brian. *Politics and Trade in Southern Mexico, 1750–1821*. Cambridge: Cambridge University Press, 1971.

Haslip-Viera, Gabriel. *Crime and Punishment in Late Colonial Mexico City, 1692–1810*. Albuquerque: University of New Mexico Press, 1999.

Hassig, Ross. *Trade, Tribute, and Transportation: The Sixteenth-Century Political Economy of Mexico*. Norman: Oklahoma University Press, 1985.

Hernández Jaimes, Jesús. *La formación de la hacienda pública mexicana y las tensiones centro-periferia, 1821–1835*. Mexico City: Colegio de México, 2013.

Hernández y Dávalos, J. E., ed. *Colección de documentos para la historia de la guerra de independencia en México de 1808–1821*. 3 vols., 1877–1882; rpt. Mexico City: Sistema Postal de la República Mexicana, 1977.

Herr, Richard. *Rural Change and Royal Finances in Spain at the End of the Old Regime*. Berkeley: University of California Press, 1989.

Herrejón Peredo, Carlos. *Hidalgo: maestro, párroco e insurgente*. Mexico City: Fomento Cultural Banamex, 2011.

Hill, Christopher. *The Century of Revolution, 1603–1714*. 3rd. ed. New York: Norton, 1980.

Hoberman, Louisa. *Mexico's Merchant Elite, 1590–1660: Silver, State, and Society.* Durham, NC: Duke University Press, 1991.

Hughes, Jennifer Scheper. *Biography of a Mexican Crucifix: Lived Religion and Local Faith from the Conquest to the Present.* New York: Oxford University Press, 2009.

Irigoin, Alejandra, and Regina Grafe. "Bargaining for Absolutism: A Spanish Path to Nation-State and Empire Building." *Hispanic American Historical Review* 88:2 (2008), 173–209.

Israel, Jonathan. *The Dutch Republic: Its Rise, Greatness, and Fall, 1477–1806.* Oxford: Oxford University Press, 1998.

———. *Race, Class, and Politics in Colonial Mexico, 1610–1670.* Oxford: Oxford University Press, 1975.

Kamen, Henry. *Empire: How Spain Became a World Power.* New York: Harper Collins, 2004.

Katz, Friedrich. "Rural Rebellion in Pre-Conquest and Colonial Mexico." In *Riot, Rebellion, and Revolution: Rural Social Movements in Mexico,* 65–94. Princeton, NJ: Princeton University Press, 1988.

Kicza, John. *Colonial Entrepreneurs: Families and Business in Bourbon Mexico City.* Albuquerque: University of New Mexico Press, 1983.

Klooster, Wim. *Revolutions in the Atlantic World: A Comparative History.* New York: New York University Press, 2009.

Ladd, Doris. *The Making of a Strike: Mexican Silver Miners' Struggles in Real del Monte, 1766–1775.* Lincoln: University of Nebraska Press, 1988.

———. *The Mexican Nobility at Independence, 1780–1826.* Austin: University of Texas Press, 1976.

Lafuente Ferrari, Enrique. *El virrey Iturrigaray y los orígenes de la independencia de México.* Madrid: Consejo Superior de Investigaciones Científicas, 1941.

Lempérière, Annick. *Entre Dios y el rey, la república: la Ciudad de México de los siglos XVI a XIX.* Translated by Ivette Hernández Pérez Verti. Mexico City: Fondo de Cultura Económica, 2013.

Leonard, Irving. *Baroque Times in Old Mexico: Seventeenth-Century Persons, Places, and Practices.* Ann Arbor: University of Michigan Press, 1960.

Lerdo de Tejada, Miguel. *Comercio exterior de México desde la conquista hasta hoy.* 1857; rpt. Mexico City: Banco Nacional de Comercio Exterior, 1967.

Lin, Man-Huang. *China Upside Down: Currency, Society, and Ideology, 1808–1856.* Cambridge, MA: Harvard University Press, 2007.

Lira, Andrés. *Comunidades indígenas frente a la Ciudad de México: Tenochtitlan y Tlatelolco, sus pueblos y barrios, 1812–1919.* Zamora: Colegio de Michoacán, 1983.

Lockhart, James. *The Nahuas After the Conquest: A Social and Cultural History.* Redwood City, CA: Stanford University Press, 1993.

Lohman Villena, Guillermo. *Los americanos en las órdenes nobiliarias, 1529–1900.* Madrid: n.p., 1947.

Marichal, Carlos. *La bancarrota del virreinato: Nueva España y las finanzas del imperio español, 1780–1810.* Mexico City: Fondo de Cultura Económica, 1999.

McAlister, Lyle. *The Fuero Militar in New Spain.* Gainesville: University Press of Florida, 1957.

McCoy, Drew. *The Elusive Republic: Political Economy in Jeffersonian America.* Chapel Hill: University of North Carolina Press, 1980.

Melville, Elinore. *A Plague of Sheep: Environmental Consequences of the Conquest of Mexico.* New York: Cambridge University Press, 1991.

Miño Grijalva, Manuel. "El camino hacia la fábrica en México: el caso de la 'fábrica de indianillos' de Francisco de Iglesias." *Historia Mexicana* 34:1 (1984), 135–48.

———. *Obrajes y tejedores de Nueva España, 1700–1800.* Madrid: Instituto de Cooperación Iberoamericana, 1990.

Molina del Villar, América. *Diversidad socioétnica y familias entre las calamidades de siglo XVIII.* Mexico City: CIESAS, 2009.

———. *La Nueva España y el Matlazahuatl.* Zamora: Colegio de Michoacán, 2001.

Morgan, Edmund. *American Slavery, American Freedom: The Ordeal of Colonial Virginia.* New York: Norton, 1975.

———. *Inventing the People: The Rise of Popular Sovereignty in England and America.* New York: Norton, 1988.

Mumford, Jeremy. *Vertical Empire: The General Resettlement of Indians in the Colonial Andes.* Durham, NC: Duke University Press, 2012.

Mundy, Barbara. *The Death of Aztec Tenochtitlan, the Life of Mexico City.* Austin: University of Texas Press, 2015.

North, Douglass, John Wallis, and Barry Weingast. *Violence and Social Orders: A Conceptual Framework for Interpreting Recorded Human History.* New York: Cambridge University Press, 2009.

Ortiz Escamilla, Juan. *Guerra y gobierno: los pueblos y la independencia de México.* Rev. ed. Mexico City: Colegio de México, 2013.

Owensby, Brian. *Empire of Law and Indian Justice in Colonial Mexico.* Redwood City, CA: Stanford University Press, 2008.

Padden, R. C. *The Hummingbird and the Hawk: Conquest and Sovereignty in the Valley of Mexico, 1503–1541.* New York: Harper, 1970.

Palerm, Ángel. *Obras hidráulicas prehispánicas en el valle de México.* Mexico City: Instituto Nacional de Antropología y Historia, 1973.

Palti, Elías José. *An Archaeology of the Political: Regimes of Power from the Seventeenth Century to the Present.* New York: Columbia University Press, 2017.

Parthasarathi, Prasannan. *Why Europe Grew Rich and Asia Did Not: Global Economic Divergence, 1600–1850.* New York: Cambridge University Press, 2011.

Paz, Octavio. *Sor Juana, or the Traps of Faith.* Translated by Margaret Sayers Peden. Cambridge: Harvard University Press, 1990.

Pérez Toledo, Sonia. *Población y estructura social de la ciudad México, 1790–1842.* Mexico City: Universidad Autónoma Metropolitana, 2004.

Piketty, Thomas. *Capital in the Twenty-First Century.* Translated by Arthur Goldhammer. Cambridge, MA: Harvard University Press, 2014.

Pizzigoni, Catarina. *The Life Within: Local Indigenous Society in Mexico's Valley of Toluca, 1650–1800.* Redwood City, CA: Stanford University Press, 2013.

Poole, Stafford. *Our Lady of Guadalupe: The Origins and Sources of a Mexican National Symbol.* Tucson: University of Arizona Press, 1995.

Poulantzas, Nicos. *Political Power and Social Classes.* London: Verso, 1975.

Rionda Arreguín, Isauro. *La Compañía de Jesús en la provincia guanajuatense, 1590–1767.* Guanajuato: Universidad de Guanajuato, 1990.

Rodríguez, Jaime. *"We Are Now the True Spaniards": Sovereignty, Revolution, Independence, and the Emergence of the Federal Republic of Mexico, 1808–1824.* Redwood City, CA: Stanford University Press, 2012.

Rodríguez Kurí, Ariel, ed. *Historia política de la Ciudad de México (desde su fundación hasta el año 2000).* Mexico City: El Colegio de México, 2012.

Romero de Terreros, Manuel. *Antiguas haciendas de México.* Mexico City: Editorial Patria, 1956.

———. *Una casa del siglo XVIII en México: la del Conde de San Bartolomé de Jala.* Mexico City: n.p., 1957.

———. "La condesa escribe." *Historia Mexicana* 1:3 (1952), 456–67.

———. "Los hijos de los primeros Condes de Regla." *Memorias de la Academia Mexicana de Historia* 3:2 (1944), 187–204.

Romero de Terreros, Pedro José. *Testimonios relativos de la legitimidad de sangre y nobleza.* Mexico City: n.p., 1803.

Rothman, Adam. *Slave Country: American Expansion and the Origins of the Deep South.* Cambridge, MA: Harvard University Press, 2005.

Ruiz Medrano, Ethelia. *Reshaping New Spain: Government and Private Interests in the Colonial Bureaucracy, 1535–1550.* Translated by Julia Constantino and Pauline Marmasse. Boulder: University Press of Colorado, 2012.

Salvucci, Richard. *Textiles and Capitalism in Mexico: An Economic History of the Obrajes, 1539–1840.* Princeton, NJ: Princeton University Press, 1988.

Sánchez de Tagle, Esteban. *Del gobierno y su tutela: la reforma a las haciendas locales del siglo XVIII y el Cabildo de México.* Mexico City: Instituto Nacional de Antropología y Historia, 2014.

———. *Por un regimiento, un régimen: la formación del Regimiento de Dragones de la Reina en San Miguel el Grande.* Mexico City: Instituto Nacional de Antropología y Historia, 1982.

———. "Las reformas del siglo XVIII al gobierno: la ciudad, su policía, su gobierno." In García Ayluardo, *Las reformas borbónicas,* 164–224.

Sánchez Santiró, Ernest. "La modernización conservadora: el reformismo borbónico y su impacto sobre la economía, la fiscalidad y las instituciones." In García Ayluardo, *Las reformas borbónicas,* 288–336.

Scott, James. *Seeing Like a State: How Certain Schemes to Improve the Human Condition Have Failed.* New Haven, CT: Yale University Press, 1999.

Serulnikov, Sergio. *Revolution in the Andes: The Age of Tupac Amaru.* Translated by David Frey. Durham, NC: Duke University Press, 2013.

Silva Prada, Natalia. *La política de una rebelión: los indígenas frente al tumulto de 1692 en la Ciudad de México.* Mexico City: Colegio de México, 2007.

Sims, Harold. *The Expulsion of Mexico's Spaniards, 1821–1836.* Pittsburgh, PA: University of Pittsburgh Press, 1990.

Skocpol, Theda. *States and Social Revolutions: A Comparative Analysis of France, Russia, and China.* Cambridge: Cambridge University press, 1979.

Sousa, Lisa, Stafford Poole, and James Lockhart, eds. and trans. *The Story of Guadalupe: Luis Laso de Vega's Huei tlamahuicoltica of 1649.* Redwood City, CA: Stanford University Press, 1998.

Spalding, Karen. *Huarochirí: An Andean Society under Inca and Spanish Rule.* Redwood City, CA: Stanford University Press, 1984.

Stein, Barbara, and Stanley Stein. *Crisis in an Atlantic Empire: Spain and New Spain, 1808–1810.* Baltimore, MD: Johns Hopkins University Press, 2014.

———. *Edge of Crisis: War and Trade in the Spanish Atlantic, 1789–1809.* Baltimore, MD: Johns Hopkins University Press, 2009.

Stein, Stanley, and Barbara Stein. *Apogee of Empire: Spain and New Spain in the Age of Charles III.* Baltimore, MD: Johns Hopkins University Press, 2003.

———. *Silver, Trade, and War: Spain and America in the Making of Early Modern Europe.* Baltimore, MD: Johns Hopkins University Press, 2000.

Stern, Steve. *Peru's Indigenous Peoples and the Challenge of Spanish Conquest: Huamanga to1640.* Madison: University of Wisconsin Press, 1982.

Stites, Richard. *The Four Horsemen: Riding to Liberty in Post-Napoleonic Europe.* Oxford: Oxford University Press, 2014.

Tanck de Estrada, Dorothy. *Pueblos de indios y educación en México colonial.* Mexico City: Colegio de México, 1999.

Taylor, William. *Drinking, Homicide, and Rebellion in Colonial Mexican Villages.* Redwood City, CA: Stanford University Press, 1979.

———. *Magistrates of the Sacred: Priests and Parishioners in Colonial Mexico.* Redwood City, CA: Stanford University Press, 1997.

Tone, John. *The Fatal Knot: Guerrilla War in Navarre and the Defeat of Napoleon in Spain.* Chapel Hill: University of North Carolina Press, 1995.

Torres Puga, Gabriel. "La ciudad novohispana: ensayo sobre su vida política, 1521–1800." In Rodríguez Kurí, *Historia política de la Ciudad de México,* 67–158.

Trujillo Bolio, Mario. *El péndulo marítimo-mercantil en el Atlántico novohispano, 1798–1825: comercio libre, circuitos de intercambio, exportación e importación.* Mexico City: CIESAS, 2009.

Tutino, John. "The Americas in the Rise of Industrial Capitalism." In *New Countries,* 17–70.

———. "Capitalist Foundations: New Spain, Mexico, and the United States." In *Mexico and Mexicans in the Making of the United* States, 36–82.

———. "Creole Mexico: Spanish Elites, Haciendas, and Indian Towns, 1750–1810." PhD diss., University of Texas at Austin, 1976.

———. "De Hidalgo a Apatzingán: insurgencia popular y proyectos políticos en la Nueva España, 1811–1814." In *La insurgencia mexicana y la Constitución de Apatzingán*, edited by Ana Carolina Ibarra, Marco Antonio Landavazzo, Juan Ortiz Escamilla, José Antonio Serrano, and Marta Terán, 49–78. Mexico City: Universidad Nacional Autónoma de México, 2014.

———. *From Insurrection to Revolution in Mexico: Social Bases of Agrarian Violence, 1750–1940*. Princeton, NJ: Princeton University Press, 1986.

———. "Hacienda Social Relations in Mexico: The Chalco Region in the Era of Independence." *Hispanic American Historical Review* 55:3 (1975), 496–528.

———. *Making a New World: Founding Capitalism in the Bajío and Spanish North America*. Durham, NC: Duke University Press, 2011.

———. *The Mexican Heartland: How Communities Shaped Capitalism, a Nation, and World History, 1500–2000*. Princeton, NJ: Princeton University Press, 2018.

———, ed. *Mexico and Mexicans in the Making of the United States*. Austin: University of Texas Press, 2012.

———, ed. *New Countries: Capitalism, Revolutions, and Nations in the Americas, 1750–1870*. Durham, NC: Duke University Press, 2016.

———. "Power, Class, and Family: Women and Men in the Mexico City Elite, 1750–1810." *The Americas* 39:3 (1983), 359–81.

———. "Querétaro y los orígenes de la nación mexicana: las políticas étnicas de soberanía, contrainsurgencia e independencia, 1808–1821." In *México a la luz de sus revoluciones*, 2 vols., 17–64. Edited by Laura Rojas y Susan Deeds. Mexico City: Colegio de México, 2014.

———. "The Revolution in Mexican Independence: Insurgency and the Renegotiation of Property, Production, and Patriarchy, 1800–1850." *Hispanic American Historical Review* 78:3 (1998), 367–418.

———. "Soberanía quebrada, insurgencia popular y la independencia de México: la guerra de independencias, 1808–1821." *Historia Mexicana* 59:1 (2009), 11–59.

Valle Pavón, Guillermina de. *Donativos, préstamos y privilegios: los mercaderes y mineros de la Ciudad de México durante la guerra anglo-española de 1779–1783*. Mexico City: Instituto Mora, 2016.

———. *Finanzas piadosas y redes de negocios: los mercaderes de la Ciudad de México ante la crisis de Nueva España, 1804–1808*. Mexico City: Instituto Mora, 2012.

Van Young, Eric. "Islands in the Storm: Quiet Cities and Violent Countrysides in the Mexican Independence Era." *Past and Present* 118 (1988), 120–56.

———. *The Other Rebellion: Popular Violence, Ideology, and the Mexican Struggle for Independence, 1810–1821*. Redwood City, CA: Stanford University Press, 2001.

Velázquez Gutiérrez, María Elisa. *Las mujeres de origen africana en la capital novo-hispano.* Mexico City: Universidad National Autónoma de México, 2006.

Vinson, Ben. *Bearing Arms for His Majesty: The Free Colored Militia in Colonial Mexico.* Redwood City, CA: Stanford University Press, 2001.

Viqueira Albán, Juan Pedro. *Relajados o reprimidos? Diversiones públicas y vida social en la Ciudad de México durante el siglo de las luces.* Mexico City: Fondo de Cultura Económica, 1988.

Voekel, Pamela. *Alone Before God: The Religious Origins of Modernity in Mexico.* Durham, NC: Duke University Press, 2002.

Walker, Charles. *The Tupac Amaru Rebellion.* Cambridge, MA: Harvard University Press, 2014.

Webb, Stephen. *1676: The End of American Independence.* New York: Knopf, 1984.

Wobeser, Gisela von. *Dominación colonial: la consolidación de vales reales, 1804–1812.* Mexico City: Universidad Nacional Autónoma de México, 2003.

Yuste López, Carmen. *Emporios transpacíficos: comerciantes mexicanos en Manila, 1710–1815.* Mexico City: Universidad Nacional Autónoma de México, 2007.

Zárate Miramontes, Oscar. "Un gobierno precario: relaciones de poder e incertidumbre dela legitimidad política en la Nueva España, 1808–1809." Licenciatura thesis, Universidad Nacional Autónoma de México, 2010.

Index

Page numbers in italic text indicate illustrations.